THE LIFE OF HINDUISM

THE LIFE OF RELIGION

Mark Juergensmeyer, editor; Richard Carp, photo editor

1. *The Life of Buddhism,*
   edited by Frank E. Reynolds
   and Jason A. Carbine
2. *The Life of Judaism,*
   edited by Harvey E. Goldberg
3. *The Life of Hinduism,*
   edited by John Stratton Hawley
   and Vasudha Narayanan

THE LIFE OF HINDUISM

EDITED BY

John Stratton Hawley
and Vasudha Narayanan

University of California Press

Berkeley Los Angeles London

University of California Press, one of the most distinguished university presses in the United States, enriches lives around the world by advancing scholarship in the humanities, social sciences, and natural sciences. Its activities are supported by the UC Press Foundation and by philanthropic contributions from individuals and institutions. For more information, visit www.ucpress.edu.

University of California Press
Berkeley and Los Angeles, California

University of California Press, Ltd.
London, England

Library of Congress Cataloging-in-Publication Data

The life of Hinduism / edited by John Stratton Hawley and Vasudha Narayanan.
p. cm. — (The life of religion)
Includes bibliographical references and index.
ISBN-13: 978-0-520-24913-4 (cloth : alk. paper)
ISBN-10: 0-520-24913-5 (cloth : alk. paper)
ISBN-13: 978-0-520-24914-1 (pbk. : alk. paper)
ISBN-10: 0-520-24914-3 (pbk. : alk. paper)
1. Religious life—Hinduism. 2. Hinduism—Customs and practices. 3. Hinduism—Social aspects. I. Hawley, John Stratton, 1941– II. Narayanan, Vasudha.

BL1226.13.L55 2007
294.5—dc22 2006024692

Manufactured in the United States of America

16 15 14 13 12 11 10 09 08 07
10 9 8 7 6 5 4 3 2 1

This book is printed on New Leaf EcoBook 50, a 100% recycled fiber of which 50% is de-inked post-consumer waste, processed chlorine-free. EcoBook 50 is acid-free and meets the minimum requirements of ANSI/ASTM D5634-01 (*Permanence of Paper*).

CONTENTS

ILLUSTRATIONS

The following images may be viewed at the web site http://www.clas.ufl.edu/users/vasu/loh. We are grateful to Bradley Ackroyd, doctoral student at the University of Florida, for its design.

A NOTE ON TRANSLITERATION

The essays assembled in this volume were written for a variety of purposes and audiences, and they adopt a variety of schemes for transliterating Indic words. We have chosen to respect that diversity; no single system of transliteration is correct for every use. Certain terms are so important, however, that they recur often, and sometimes with different spellings. In the list that follows, we provide a partial list of such terms, hoping it will help readers make connections between one chapter and the next.

acarya, ācārya, acharya

avatar, avatār, avatāra

Banaras, Banāras, Benares, Varanasi

brahmacari, brahmacārī, brahmachari; feminine: brahmacarini, brahmacharini

brahman, Brahman, Brahmin (caste or status); Brahman (ultimate reality)

Braj, Vraja

Bhagavad Gita, Bhagavath Geetha

Brindavan, Vrindaban, Vrindāban, Vrndavan, Vṛndāvana

darśan, darśana, darshan

daśahrā, Dassehra, Dussehra

deepa, dīpa, diya

dharm, dharma

Deepavali, Divali, Divālī

Ganapati, Gaṇeśa, Ganesh, Ganesha

Gobardhan, Govardhan

Hara hara Mahadev, hara hara mahādeva

Jamuna, Jamunā, Jumnā, Yamuna

jyot, jyoti

Krishna, Kṛṣṇa

kumkum, kuṅkum

Lakshmi, Lakshmiji, Lakṣmī

Maharajji, Maharaj-ji

Mathura, Mathurā

prasad, prasāda, prashad

Ram, Rām, Rama, Rāma

Ramayan, Ramayana, Rāmāyaṇa

Rāmcaritmānas, Ramcharitmanas

Ramlila, rāmlīlā

rāsa; raas leela, rāsa līlā, rās līlā, ras lila

sadguru, satguru, Satguru

Śaiva, Shaiva

śākta, shakta

śakti, shakti

samskara, saṁskāra, sanskar, saṅskāra

Shudra, śūdra

Shiva, Siva, Śiva

Sri Vaisnava, Śrī Vaiṣṇava

svarup, swarup

tika, ṭīkā, teeka

Vaishnava, Vaiṣṇava

Varanasi. *See* Banaras.

Venkatesvara, Venkateswara

Vishnu, Viṣṇu

Vraja. *See* Braj.

vrata, vratam

Vrindaban, etc. *See* Brindavan.

· Introduction

JOHN STRATTON HAWLEY
and VASUDHA NARAYANAN

BANGALORE AND BEYOND

January 1, 2004, was a happy day for India's surging middle classes. For the first time in history the Sensex, which measures investments on the Bombay stock exchange, was hovering on the verge of 6,000. Reports issued on that day confirmed that the country's GNP had risen 8.4 percent in the year just past, and the news sent the stock exchange over 6,000 as soon as it opened on the second. Nowhere could the mood of optimism be felt more palpably than in Bangalore, the graceful southern city on the Deccan plateau that serves as capital of India's information technology industry.[1] Bands of young revelers roamed through the streets on New Year's Eve, people ate out, fireworks lit the sky, and there were plenty of parties throbbing with the latest mix of Bollywood hits and Western rap riffs.

Had religion been forgotten in this thrust toward a global future? Not at all. For many years Bangalore's Christian communities had marked the shift from old year to new with masses and services at midnight, and this year was no exception. Muslims observed the evening call to prayer. Yet nothing could compare with the vast crowds of people who filled the city's Hindu temples the following morning. Many sought the blessing of Hanuman, the monkey deity whose strength and unwavering devotion to Rama and Sita had earned him his own prominent place in the pantheon. They filed before his massive, twenty-two-foot granite form in Bangalore's Mahalakshmipuram neighborhood, echoing his devotion with devotion of their own (see figure 1). As they watched, a little gondola made its transit across a high metal scaffolding so that priests could deck the deity with jewels and garlands. The widespread worship of Hanuman, especially in monumental representations such as this, is one of the most striking developments in Hindu practice over the past several decades. Sure enough, Bangalore's Hanuman was carved out of a huge slab of stone only in 1976. The rock, standing erect like a sentinel on an empty hill, had long been venerated, almost as if it had been waiting for its inner identity to be revealed—as part and parcel of the new Bangalore. In similar fashion, many people think Bangalore itself is a harbinger of the India yet to be. (See figure A at the Web site http://www.clas.ufl.edu/users/vasu/loh.)

Hanuman's crowds were substantial, but they were dwarfed by those that pressed in on another temple in the neighborhood. This was the "temple on a hill," inaugurated in 1997 by ISKCON, the International Society for Kṛṣṇa Consciousness, the organization popularly known in the West as the Hare Krishna movement. ISKCON traces its lineage to the Bengali ecstatic Chaitanya (ca. 1500), whose full name, Krishna Chaitanya, means "consciousness of Krishna." ISKCON insists it is also heir to a Vedic past that stands at the horizon of humankind's historical memory. But ISKCON's own founding event transpired only much later, when a Calcutta businessman named Abhay Charan De, soon to be called Bhaktivedanta Swami Prabhupada, landed on the Lower East Side of New York City in 1965 and began to dance and sing. In those days of spiritual searching and disaffection with the Vietnam War, he quickly attracted a following; ISKCON was incorporated as a storefront mission near Tompkins Square Park within a year. Coincidentally, this was also the time when American immigration laws were revised, and substantial numbers of highly educated Indians began settling in the United States. ISKCON temples in New York and elsewhere quickly became shared East/West space: where else could the new immigrants gather to see the images and sing the songs that provide so much of the vocabulary of Hindu life?

Prabhupada thought the movement ought to be not just east-to-west but west-to-east, and in that regard the temple on "Hare Krishna Hill" in Bangalore is one of his followers' most impressive accomplishments. Its upscale patrons are definitely local—they've had to fight off denominational leaders based elsewhere in India to protect their autonomy—but their inspiration is global. It shows in their ahead-of-the-curve architecture and Web site (www.iskconbangalore.org), and in the elaborate crowd-control systems that funnel visitors toward an auspicious vision of Krishna and his beloved consort Radha deep in the sparkling marble South Indian–style temple. A maze of metal bars and covered aerial walkways guides

FIGURE 1
Hanuman receiving New Year's garlands, Mahalakshmipuram, Bangalore, January 1, 2004. Photo by John Hawley.

worshippers up toward the main sanctuary as if they were visitors to the Statue of Liberty or Walt Disney World; and a long series of displays, eateries, and gift shops awaits them on the descent, after they've seen the golden deities. These eager, well-dressed pilgrims are a collage of Bangalore today: students in the nearby science colleges, middle-class families with children, and a few representatives of the older generation. All come to orient themselves to the year ahead with vows, petitions, and thanksgivings expressed before the city's newest, most impressive gods. Hindu practice already incorporates several New Years, and many Hindus calculate the fiscal year on those days, with festivals to mark the passage. January 1 has been added only in the last decade, a New Year calibrated to the calendar of international business and global society. For Hinduism, the meaning of "tradition" is cumulative, not unchanging. (See figure B at the Web site http://www.clas.ufl.edu/users/vasu/loh.)

Other events in the first week of 2004 filled out this picture. A full-page color ad on the back page of the New Year's Day Bangalore edition of the *Economic Times*, for instance, urged readers to contribute to projects launched by the Tirumala Tirupati Devasthanams (TTD). TTD is the organization that manages India's wealthiest and most influential temple complex *(devasthanam)*, the home of Vishnu as Venkatesvara at Tirupati on "the holy mountain" *(tirumalai)* in Andhra Pradesh. Its current projects feature a hospital offering free medical care to the poor, a fund for the protection of cows ("The very existence of mankind depends on cow's milk," said the *Economic Times*), and a religious theme park to be installed on Tirupati's mountain with the purpose of educating pilgrims "through modern Imax technics." The ad explaining all this had been donated by Amarjothi Spinning Mills, Ltd., and it contained multiple images of Venkatesvara himself, displaying a vision *(darsana, darsan, darshan)* of Venkatesvara to the public at large on this auspicious day of beginnings. Halfway around the world, in the Venkatesvara temple that TTD helped establish just outside Pittsburgh, pilgrims from all over North America gathered for a similar *darshan*. Lord Venkatesvara graces both continents, and many who come to see him in Pittsburgh have relatives in or near Bangalore.

The *Economic Times* also reported that Pramukh Swami Maharaj, the leader of the BAPS Swaminarayan Sanstha, was in Bangalore to officiate at the installation of new images in the Swaminarayan temple in Rajajinagar Industrial Town.[2] Like ISKCON and Tirupati, Swaminarayan is a religious organization with a densely multinational identity. Based in Gujarat and working with a distinctly Gujarati core of devotees, it nonetheless strives to create a form of high-minded Hindu consciousness with global appeal. Bangalore is necessarily an important node in Swaminarayan's emerging network. A major feature of Swaminarayan faith is its adherence to *ahimsa,* nonviolence, and Pramukh Swami made history in September 2002 when he urged his followers not to take vengeance on Muslim militants who killed thirty-two people and injured scores more in an attack on Swaminarayan's most important monument, the sparkling new temple and religious theme park called Akshardham, just outside Ahmedabad, the capital of Gujarat. People listened: not a single Muslim life was lost.

This presented a stunning contrast to the many Muslims killed—and many more rendered homeless and indigent—in a campaign condoned and supported by the Gujarat state government earlier the same year. The party in power was the Hindu revivalist Bharatiya Janata Party (BJP), which is particularly strong in Gujarat, and the mobs marshaled by the party and its ideological confreres were avenging an attack on a train filled with Hindu nationalists that made a stop in the city of Godhra, Gujarat, on February 19. Fifty-eight people died in a fire that swept through one bogie of that train while it stood in Godhra station. Most early reports said a Muslim mob on the platform had torched the bogie as a Hindu-Muslim argument escalated out of control. The Hindu activists on the train had been returning from the fervor of a rally in Ayodhya, the city in North India that is widely regarded as the birthplace of the god-king Rama. They were trying to pressure the government to remove obstacles standing in the way of the construction of a massive temple on the spot believed to be the place where Rama was born, the very spot where carefully organized cadres of young Hindus had destroyed a sixteenth-century mosque in 1992. A great many Muslims—and a few Hindus—had been killed in rampages that followed that attack, too.

But it's far from certain that Muslims really did torch the train in Godhra in response to insults from Hindu-chauvinist pilgrims. Early investigations reported that the fire actually started at a particular seat inside the bogie—possibly ignited by a kerosene burner. Hindus claiming to have seen things with their own eyes rejected those conclusions. As for Pramukh Swami, he didn't care how that issue or any other in this long chain of violence would be adjudicated. He just said it was time to stop, and the weight of his authority was such that people paid attention. Now he was in Bangalore on a much happier mission.

The New Year also brought other news of violence—this time in the western state of Maharashtra. Like several other Indian regions that claim a language and history of their own, Maharashtra has spawned a number of chauvinist organizations committed to singing the region's glory and defending its honor. Much of this has been done in overtly Hindu terms, portraying Muslims as the enemy. But other "foreigners" also count—South Indians and Brahmins, since their roots are not specifically Maharashtrian. So it was that on the morning of January 5, 2004, a mob of young men recruited by the Sambhaji Brigade, a branch of the Maratha Seva Sangh, attacked one of India's most distinguished research facilities, the library of the Bhandarkar Oriental Research Institute in Pune. They threw bricks at the windows, beat up the guards, pulled down as many bookshelves as they could, and made the Brahmin scholars who labor there feel deeply threatened. They stole or damaged countless volumes and manuscripts and danced on the pile before they withdrew.

Why? Because the Institute had been mentioned in the acknowledgments section of a book by an American scholar named James Laine. Hard-line Maharashtrian leaders and several well-respected Maharashtrian scholars charged that Laine's book *Shivaji: Hindu King in Islamic India* said objectionable things about the person they regard as Maharashtra's exemplary ruler, the man who brought the Muslim Oppressor to his knees. This was Shivaji, a seventeenth-century Maratha leader who through cleverness and bravery managed to challenge the hegemony of Aurangzeb, the Mughal emperor who has come to exemplify intolerant Muslim power in the minds of many Hindus. Laine had repeated some irreverent gossip about Shivaji's parentage, and in reaction Oxford University Press was pressured into withdrawing the book from print. But that was not enough. Now countless precious books and documents were destroyed, and armed guards had been posted at the homes of scholars and Institute employees whom Laine had thanked in the acknowledgments. This was not specifically Hindu violence—in fact, Brahmins were among the primary targets—but it did trade on a view of Indian history that has been deeply colored by a perceived Hindu/Muslim dichotomy. In that way it related to other Hindus' efforts to police the past, especially the campaign to rewrite history textbooks that was undertaken by the Bharatiya Janata Party, which largely ruled the country from 1996 to 2004.[3]

Fortunately, violence was not the only aspect of religious life to show up in the daily paper at New Year's. On Thursday, January 1, the *Deccan Herald*, Bangalore's leading newspaper, carried several "thanksgiving" advertisements dedicated to Jesus as he appears in the Infant Jesus shrine in the suburb of Viveknagar. Although this church is quite new—the foundation was laid only in 1969, and the edifice was built several years later—it is considered by local Christians and Hindus to be a holy place. Hindus flock to this church, as they do to specific churches and basilicas all over South India, searching for divine favors and miracles. On Thursdays, the day considered to be most important at the Infant Jesus shrine, hundreds of Hindus stand in line to revere the icon of Infant Jesus and garland him. Thousands of Hindus also go regularly to the Basilica of the Holy Mother of Health at Velankanni in

Tamil Nadu, and they worship Arokia-mariamma (Mary, Our Lady of Health) in St. Mary's Basilica in Bangalore. Thursday is also a day when Bangalorean Hindus like to visit local *dargahs*—places where powerful Sufi saints are said to be entombed—seeking cures, promotions, and a host of other favors. These public acts of reverence, petition, and thanksgiving remind us that although there are relatively crisp boundaries between religious communities if an issue like marriage is on the table, these clear boundaries fade away when it comes to recognizing divine power in the "other" tradition. Hundreds of *dargahs* throughout India serve as shared ritual spaces accommodating Hindus, Christians, and Muslims, and they are joined by a host of Christian shrines and Hindu temples.

Despite the dramatic developments signaled by what we have described at ISKCON, Swaminarayan, and elsewhere, in most of Bangalore's small neighborhood temples and homes Hindu devotional life was proceeding as usual. There it seemed nothing had changed, except that now radio and television stations were broadcasting songs of the season—songs of the Hindu season. The first week of January in any year comes right in the middle of the South Indian month of Margali (Skt. *margasirsa*). This month is considered to be especially sacred to Andal and Manikkavachakar, two Tamil poet-saints who lived around the eighth century C.E. Andal, a woman who refused to get married to a human being and instead wanted to marry Vishnu, wrote two poems expressing her passion for this deity. Between mid-December and mid-January Andal is venerated in the Vishnu temples in South India and in the South Indian temples in dozens of American cities, including Pittsburgh, Malibu, and Atlanta. In Bangalore several temples sponsored oral commentaries on Andal's poetry, and the mornings started with a recitation of her songs in thousands of households, just as they did in temples located in Livermore, California; Queens, New York; and Aurora, Illinois.

In many Bangalore households, a television channel called Jaya TV is turned on at 5:30 A.M. every morning. Ordinarily the broadcast begins with *darshan* of the famous Pillaiyar (Ganesha) temple in Pillaiyarpatti, Tamil Nadu, and continues immediately with twenty minutes of the Tamil version of the "good morning" *(suprabhatam)* prayer performed at the great temple of Lord Venkatesvara in Tirupati. During the month of Margali, however, the *suprabhatam* is replaced by the *Tiruppavai*, the prayer that Andal composed to awaken Krishna—not just on Jaya TV but on at least three other television channels and many more radio stations. On the first day of Margali (December 16, 2003) Jaya TV started with a male voice reciting a traditional invocatory verse glorifying Andal. This was followed by students from the well-known Padma Seshadri High School in Chennai—young women between twelve and fifteen years of age—singing the first verse of the *Tiruppavai*. Other stations carried commentaries not just by Brahmin males but by men and women of varying castes and ages, speaking in Telugu and Tamil.

Later that morning of the first day of Margali, at a neighborhood temple of Hanuman in Bangalore's Indiranagar district, a few hundred citizens came to worship at Andal's shrine. Women left strings of flowers for her, for this was the saint who had made garlands for Krishna. In fact, Andal's real name is Kodai, which means "wreath of flowers." All month long, as at so many other South Indian Vaishnava places of worship, this temple gave rice boiled in milk *(pongal)* as a token of divine favor *(prasad)*. In many homes and temples *pongal* is truly the dish of the month, for Margali culminates in the middle of January with a big festival called just that. As observed today, Pongal is not just Vaishnava or even Hindu but a general celebration of Tamil and Telugu identity. Arguably, the focus for most South Indians this month is on the *bhojan* (food) of Pongal rather than the *bhajan* (devotional song) of Andal, but the two are closely intertwined—not just in people's minds, but in the poetry of Andal herself.

Thus the year began—with high hopes for an economic future worthy of Lakshmi, the goddess of wealth and good fortune; with rearticulations of traditional patterns of worship that persist alongside practices that trumpet a new Hindu transnationalism; and with actions that would both support and refute the oft-repeated claim that Hinduism is the most tolerant and all-embracing of the world's major religious traditions. We have launched this New Year from Bangalore, a city with a distinctly forward-looking profile; other locales would have presented a different sorting of events. But it is safe to say that throughout the Hindu world—from Kathmandu to Trinidad to London, Malibu, and Delhi—one would have found a greater consciousness of the global reach of the Hindu tradition than one might have encountered even a year before. The trend is clear.

Some of its manifestations have spread far beyond Hindu homes and temples. At the end of the first week of 2004 Deepak Chopra, the amiable M.D. whose take on mind/body spirituality has made him a best-selling author and celebrity in the United States, arrived in Kerala for an eight-day retreat called "Spontaneous Fulfillment of Desire." Many of the fifty people who joined him on this high-end venture were from California (like Indian-born Chopra) and other places in America, but others gathered from points as far-flung as Thailand, Hong Kong, Australia, and South America. With yoga as a twice-daily unifying act, everyone in the group was aware that they owed a deep debt to Hinduism. Chopra's discourses strengthened that sense by appealing to certain passages from the Vedas and the Shiva Sutras that for him epitomized the message he wanted to convey: that reality is fundamentally synchronistic, nonlocal, nondual. These passages, he said, showed his perception about synchronicity to be the wisdom of the ages—at least, the Indian ages. Certain participants stressed the idea that they were on a journey of world-discovery that eluded the practices of any particular religious tradition, yet many Hindus would insist on the point that this very stance—liberal and exploratory—imbibes a religious sensibility that has long thrived on Hindu soil.

Some aspects of Hinduism's increasingly global sense of self are far less obvious than a visit from Deepak Chopra. After all, in 2004 only about 30 percent of India's population could be said to be urban. The rest, some 700 million people, are still closely tied to the land; and the religious lives of the Hindus among them bear distinctive regional and local flavors. In the Himalayan regions of Garhwal and Kumaon, for example, the complicated, classic battles over good and evil that were fought out in the ancient epic *Mahabharata* are still ritually enacted, and there are great goat and buffalo sacrifices to the Goddess. Such sacrifices are perennial among these mountain people, but in recent years they have felt a definite pressure to desist. This pressure comes not just from a steadily increasing conviction among Hindus all over India that Hindu religion is in some fundamental way about nonviolence and vegetarianism, but also from the Indian government, which in turn is responding in part to the agendas of animal-rights groups worldwide.[4]

As with any religious tradition, of course, there are still many aspects of "the life of Hinduism" that proceed more or less the same from year to year. If cosmopolitan Delhi is a long way from the pilgrimage town of Brindavan, though less than a hundred miles distant on the map, and Brindavan in turn is well removed from the sleepy villages that surround it, then it doesn't take much imagination to see that Bali is worlds away from Guyana. Lived Hinduism presents us with a fascinating and considerable range: practices and views that are sometimes obdurately conservative, sometimes subject to rapid change, sometimes overlapping. Hinduism is globalizing fast, but the danger of its succumbing to anyone's vision of global homogeneity is still very remote.

The diversity of Hindu life is legendary, and the purpose of this volume is to present a selection of essays that will help bring that diversity into focus. But before describing our plan for the book, we must deal with two basic questions. First, we must consider precisely what we mean when we speak of such a thing as Hinduism. And second, we must ask whether there is a range of practices and sensibilities in lived Hinduism that really does make the tradition cohere, despite its much-vaunted (or much-lamented) variety.

THE TERM "HINDUISM"

The English word Hinduism was coined by British writers in the final decades of the eighteenth century and became familiar as a designator of religious ideas and practices distinctive to India through such books as Monier-Williams's much-read *Hinduism*, published in 1877.[5] Initially it was an outsiders' word, building on usages of the term Hindu that go back many centuries. Early travelers to the Indus Valley, beginning with the Greeks, spoke of its inhabitants as "Hindu" (Gr. *indoi*), and by the sixteenth century residents of India themselves had begun to employ the term to distinguish themselves from "Turks." Gradually the distinction became not primarily ethnic, geographic, or cultural, but religious.

Since the late nineteenth century, Hindus have reacted to the term Hinduism in several ways. Some have rejected it in favor of indigenous formulations. Those preferring "Veda" or "Vedic religion" want to embrace an ancient textual core and the tradition of Brahmin learning that preserved and interpreted it. Those preferring *sanatana dharma* ("eternal law" or, as Philip Lutgendorf has playfully suggested, "old-time religion")[6] emphasize a more catholic tradition of belief and practice (worship through images, dietary codes, veneration of the cow, etc.) not necessarily mediated by Brahmins. Still others, perhaps the majority, have simply accepted the term Hinduism or have adopted one of its analogues in various Indic languages, especially *hindu dharma*.

From the first decades of the twentieth century onward, textbooks on Hinduism have been written by Hindus themselves, often under the rubric of *Sanatana Dharma*. An important early example is the primer called just that—*Sanatana Dharma: An Elementary Text-book of Hindu Religion and Ethics*—first published in 1903 by the Central Hindu College in Banaras for use by boys studying there. It bears an interestingly cross-cultural stamp, not only because its language is English (interspersed with extensive quotations from Sanskrit) but because a guiding force behind its production was the Theosophist Annie Besant, a Hindu convert born in England. Such efforts at self-explanation were and are intended to set Hinduism parallel with other religious traditions. The idea of *sanatana dharma* emphasizes the importance of a general human goal—maintaining personal and universal equilibrium—while at the same time calling attention to the crucial role that Hindus assign to the performance of traditional *(sanatana)* religious practices in achieving that goal. Here tradition is understood to be inherently pluriform, since no one person can occupy all the social, occupational, and age-defined roles that are requisite to maintaining the health of life as a whole. Hence the stress laid upon universal maxims such as *ahimsa*, the desire not to harm, tends to be qualified by a recognition that people in different life-positions will need to address themselves to *ahimsa* in different ways. In some cases, perhaps reluctantly, they will need to abandon that ideal altogether.

More strikingly than any other major religious community, Hindus accept and indeed celebrate the complex, organic, multileveled, and sometimes internally inconsistent nature of their tradition and emphasize its desire to coexist peacefully with other religious traditions. (Except when they don't, as we have seen.) This expansiveness is made possible by the widely shared Hindu view that truth or reality cannot be encapsulated in any creedal formulation. As many Hindus affirm through the prayer "May good thoughts come to us from all sides" (*Rg Veda* 1.89.1), truth is of such a nature that it must be multiply sought, not dogmatically claimed.

On a Hindu view, anyone's understanding of truth—even that of a guru regarded as possessing superior authority—is fundamentally conditioned by the specifics of time, age, gender, state of consciousness, social and geographic location, and stage of attainment. People see things differently, which enhances the nature of religious truth rather than diminishing it. It also suggests that people have much to learn from one another, or at least that they should respect their differences; hence there is a strong tendency for contemporary Hindus to affirm that tolerance is the foremost religious virtue. On the other hand, even cosmopolitan Hindus living in a global environment recognize the fact that their religion has developed in the specific geographical, social, historical, and ritual climates of the Indian Subcontinent. Religious practices and ideological formulations that emphasize this fact affirm a strong connection to the Hindu "homeland." A dialectic between universalist and particularist impulses has long animated the Hindu tradition. When Hindus speak of their religious identity as *sanatana dharma*, a designation made popular late in the nineteenth century, they emphasize its continuous, seemingly eternal *(sanatana)* existence. They also underscore the fact that it describes an organic net of customs, obligations, traditions, and ideals *(dharma)*, not just a system of beliefs, as recent Christian and Western secularist thinking has led us to expect of a religion. A common way in which English-speaking Hindus distance themselves from that frame of mind is to insist that Hinduism is not a religion at all, but a way of life.

FIVE STRANDS IN THE LIFE OF HINDUISM

But if "Hinduism" is such a recent formulation, and if there is such breadth in Hindu conviction and practice, then what gives coherence to the tradition as a whole? The answer is not easy, but across the sweep of Indian religious history over the past two millennia, one can settle on at least five elements that give shape to Hindu religion: doctrine, practice, society, story, and devotion. None of these is univocal; no Hindu would claim that they correspond to the five pillars of Sunni Islam. Still, there are real commonalities that make Hinduism cohere as a powerful and distinct religious tradition. Hindus tend to relate to one another as strands in an elaborate braid (a favorite Hindu metaphor), and each strand develops out of a history of conversation, elaboration, and challenge. The last point deserves emphasis. In looking for what makes the tradition cohere, we should not only seek out clear agreements about thought and practice, but also pay attention to characteristic points of tension—matters Hindus have thought sufficiently important that they needed to be argued out.

DOCTRINE

The first of the five strands in the braid of Hinduism is doctrine, as enunciated and debated in a vast textual tradition anchored to the Veda (meaning "knowledge"), the oldest core of Hindu religious utterance, and organized through the centuries primarily by members of the scholarly Brahmin caste. Here several characteristic tensions appear. One concerns issues of polytheism, monotheism, and monism—the status of the One in relation to the Many, that is, or of supernal truth in relation to its embodied, phenomenal counterpart. Another tension concerns the disparity between the world-preserving ideal of *dharma*, proper behavior defined in relation to the gods and society, and that of *moksa*, release from an inherently flawed world. A third tension exists between one's individual destiny, as shaped by *karma* (action in this and other lives), and any person's deep bond to family and society. A fourth separates thinkers who insist on the efficacy of human action from those who emphasize the power and wonder of divine grace.

PRACTICE

A second strand in the fabric of Hinduism is practice. Many Hindus, in fact, would place this first. Despite India's enormous variety, a common grammar of ritual behavior does connect various places, strata, and periods of Hindu life, and at various points in time this grammar has also been exported—either within India itself, as tribal regions were sought to be integrated into a larger fold, or abroad, as Hindus moved overseas, and others came to embrace their religion. It is sometimes suggested that these commonalities are Vedic, emanating from the earliest known core of Indian religious practice. True, various elements of Vedic ritual do survive in modern practice, especially in life-cycle rites, and they do thereby serve a unifying function. But much more influential commonalities appear in a ritual vocabulary that is completely unknown in Vedic texts, where the worship of God is articulated through icons or images *(murti, arca)*.

Broadly, this worship is called *puja* ("praising [the deity]"). It echoes conventions of hospitality that might be performed for an honored guest, and the giving and sharing of food is central. Such food is called *prasada* (Hindi, *prasad:* "grace"), reflecting the recognition that when human beings make offerings to divine ones, the initiative is not really theirs. They are actually responding to the prevenient generosity that bore them into a world fecund with life and auspicious possibility. The divine personality installed as a home or temple image receives such food, tasting it (Hindus differ as to whether this is a real or symbolic act, gross or subtle), and offering the remnant to worshippers as leftovers. Consuming these leftovers, worshippers accept their creaturely status as beings inferior to and dependent upon the divine. An element of tension arises because the logic of *puja* and *prasada* would seem to accord all humans an equally ancillary status with respect to God, yet rules of exclusionary commensality have often been sanctified rather than challenged by *prasada*-based ritual. People regarded as low caste or entirely beyond caste by Hindus whose caste position is secure have historically been forbidden to enter certain Hindu temples out of the conviction that their presence would pollute the holy precincts. This practice can still be found today, but only rarely: it has been outlawed in India's constitution, and a number of groups are dedicated to eradicating it completely.

SOCIETY

This area of activity introduces a third aspect that has perennially served to organize Hindu life: society. When the Central Asian scholar al-Biruni traveled to India in the early eleventh century, he was struck by an apparently ancient, unusually well-stratified (if locally variant) system of social relations that has come to be called in English the caste system. When one hears the term, one thinks of the four ideal classifications *(varna)* that are enshrined in certain ancient texts—Brahmins (scholars, priests), Kshatriyas (rulers, warriors), Vaishyas (artisans), and Shudras (laborers)—and sometimes it is necessary to add a fifth, lowest classification ("Untouchables") that doesn't even make it onto the chart. There is a vast slippage between this conceptual system and the thousands of endogamous birth-groups *(jati)* that constitute Indian society "on the ground," but few would dispute the perception that Indian society has been notably plural and hierarchical both in concept and in fact. Non-Hindu groups living in India are also affected—Christians, Jains, Sikhs—and the idea of the four *varnas* has had an impact on the organization of Hindu societies outside India. Bali is a good example. This vision of layered social plurality has much to do with an understanding of truth or reality as being similarly plural and multilayered, whether one understands the direction of influence to proceed from social fact to religious doctrine or vice versa.[7] Seeking its own answer to this conundrum, a well-known Vedic hymn (*Rg Veda* 10.90) describes how in the beginning of time a primordial Person underwent a process of sacrifice that produced a four-part cosmos and its human aspect, a four-part social order. A thinker and activist like Gandhi was eager to reshape this age-old vision in a way that would work for contemporary sensibilities. In this he joined a long lineage of earlier reformers. Many Hindus have thought Gandhi's effort was noble and creative; others, that it was futile and misguided. But all acknowledge the weight of India's social past.

As in the realms of doctrine and religious practice, so too in this social domain we may see a characteristic tension or dialectic. Here the issue is the relation between the seemingly humble and evenhanded perspectival view of truth/reality about which we have spoken and an array of social formations that enshrine privilege and prejudice. Many Hindus espouse the former (as tolerance) and disown the latter (as caste), even if they acknowledge that caste discrimination is all too prevalent in Indian society. Responding to such oppression, groups despised by caste Hindus have sometimes thrown the challenge back, saying, "We are not Hindus!" Yet their own communities may enact similar inequalities, and their religious practices and beliefs often continue to tie them to the greater Hindu fold. To break this chain, B. R. Ambedkar, the principal framer of India's constitution and a man of extremely low-caste birth, ended up urging his caste-fellows to abandon Hinduism altogether and become Buddhists.

STORY AND PERFORMANCE

A fourth dimension drawing Hindus into a single religious community is narrative. For at least two millennia, people in almost all corners of India—and now well beyond—have responded to certain prominent stories of divine play and divine/human interaction. These concern major figures in the Hindu pantheon: Krishna and his beloved Radha, Rama and his wife Sita and brother Lakshmana, Shiva and his consort Parvati, and the great goddess Durga or Devi as a slayer of the buffalo demon Mahisa. Such narratives focus in different degrees on *dharmic* exemplitude, genealogies of human experience, forms of love, and the struggle between order and chaos or duty and play. In generating, performing, and listening to these stories, Hindus have often experienced themselves as members of a single imagined family.

Yet simultaneously, once again, these narratives serve as an arena for articulating tensions. Women performers sometimes tell the *Ramayana* as the story of Sita's travails at the hands of Rama rather than as a testament of Rama's righteous victories. Low-caste musicians of North India present religious epics enacting their own experience of the world rather than performing their way into the upper-caste milieu of the *Mahabharata,* which these epics nonetheless echo. And an influential South Indian reformer of the early twentieth century went so far as to extol the virtues of Rama's enemy, the "demon" Ravana, as a way of rejecting the pan-Indian Brahmin hegemony he saw embedded in the story as it has usually been told. In relation to broadly known pan-Hindu, male-centered, upper-caste narrative traditions, these variants provide both resonance and challenge.

BHAKTI

Finally, there is a fifth strand that contributes to the complex unity of Hindu experience through time: *bhakti* (intense sharing, devoted adoration), a broad tradition of loving God that is especially associated with the lives and words of vernacular poet-saints throughout India. Devotional poems attributed to these inspired figures, who represent both sexes and all social classes, have elaborated a store of images and moods to which access can be had in a score of languages. Individual poems are sometimes strikingly similar from one language or century to another, without there being any trace of mediation through the pan-Indian, upper-caste language of Sanskrit. Often individual motifs in the lives of *bhakti* poet-saints also bear strong family resemblances. Because vernacular *bhakti* verse first appeared in Tamil, in sixth-century South India, *bhakti* is sometimes hypostasized as a muse or goddess who spent her youth there, aging and revivifying as she moved northward into other regions and languages. With its central affirmation of religious enthusiasm as being more fundamental than rigidities of practice or doctrine, *bhakti* provides a common challenge to other aspects of Hindu life. At the same time it contributes to a common Hindu heritage—sometimes also a common heritage of protest. Yet certain expressions of *bhakti* are far more confrontational than others in their criticism of caste, image worship, and the performance of vows, pilgrimages, and acts of self-mortification.

The range of *bhakti* is great, and, as with each of the other strands in the great Hindu braid, there is contestation along the way. Tulsidas, author of the most widely recited version of the *Ramayana* in Hindi-speaking India, is sometimes praised for articulating a version of *bhakti* that is accepting of hierarchical differences along lines of caste and gender. Other voices, following the lead of iconoclastic *bhakti* figures such as Kabir, reject such a view as entirely antithetical to the true meaning of *bhakti*. And the remarkable thing is that Tulsidas and Kabir are often conceptualized as belonging to the same broad *bhakti* family, even so.

OVERVIEW

The five strands we have just described intertwine to constitute Hindu *dharma* in its many facets, and it's good to have the whole cloth in mind as we begin. Yet our purpose in this volume is to unravel the fabric a bit and look at just one strand: practice. There is no need to feel diminished by this act of selection. The practice of lived Hinduism turns out to be a huge subject, one that deserves to be approached from a wide range of perspectives: different geographical regions, different social locations, different ages, genders, and times. The essays that appear in this volume have been drawn together to bring those many perspectives to life. Life continues to be lived, and inevitably changes as it does. These essays reflect that fact. The earliest of them was written almost half a century ago, and one short story predates even that, whereas the most recent are published here for the first time. We think this witness to the passage of time in reporting "the life of Hinduism" is a good thing, but we caution readers to take it into account.

We begin with the act of worship itself—the sort of action that constitutes the core of Hindu ritual life (part 1). Stephen Huyler introduces the general vocabulary of Hindu worship by following an observant Brahmin out the door as he begins his day as a computer repairman somewhere in Tamil Nadu. Huyler uses the occasion to speak about vows *(vrata)*, acts of praise and service to the gods *(puja)*, offerings of fire and light *(arati)*, and the food that is exchanged between human beings and divinities *(prasada)*. Diana Eck takes a closer look at the aspect of Hindu practice that has always been most difficult for Muslims, Christians, and Jews to fathom: What does it mean to worship an image—indeed, many images? And should we think of worshipping an image or worshipping *through* an image? Finally, Shrivatsa Goswami and Margaret Case report a special ritual event, an act of worship that was transformed by the sudden and evidently active presence of one of the beings whom worshippers were just then addressing. This remarkable visitor was a bee—a bee who figures in stories of Krishna as one of his most important messengers. To many observers his appearance at this ritual juncture was a miracle, but in another way it was perfectly in keeping with the deep meaning of all ritual events. It was an act of transformation, a time when life came to life.

In part 2 we focus on the sorts of rituals that hallow and structure transformations that occur in any individual life. We select one of the most important for our initial attention: marriage. Then in place of an obvious second—death, which certainly commands a series of rituals all its own[8]—we turn to a description of self-inflicted "death," the death that brings release from worldly involvements. Like religious people everywhere, Hindus use rituals as ways to draw out the significance of biologically given events, thereby transmuting them into something beyond what nature commands. The ceremonies we introduce in this section of the volume come from the middle and north of India, and no one would claim that they are invariant from region to region. Even what is written in Brahminical textbooks varies from place to place, and practice introduces many more variations. But there are common threads, one being that the life cycles of girls and women are regarded differently from those of boys and men, even when, as in marriage, they obviously converge.

If the reader comes away with the impression that the persons involved are actually *constructed* by these events, that would be directly in line with the way these life-cycle ceremonies are often described as a class. They are called *samskaras (= sanskars)*—events in which a person is "put together, perfected." These *samskaras* are prescribed in Sanskrit texts, but less clearly for girls than boys. Puberty rites for girls tend to be transmitted orally from women to women, not written in any book. To show us how such traditions work, Doranne Jacobson takes us to a village in Chattisgarh, a state in Central India, where we meet an upper-caste Thakur girl called Munni. Jacobson follows Munni from menstruation through marriage, "the most important event in her life," and she uses that occasion as a chance also to cast a comparative glance at a range of other locations in North India.

One of these is Banaras, or, as it is formally called nowadays, Varanasi, the Hindu city that is famous for death. For millennia Hindus have believed that to die in Banaras, city of Shiva and the Ganges, is to secure for oneself the best chance of a favorable rebirth—or, better yet, release from the cycle of birth and death altogether. But one need not wait for death. Death can also be induced—a death to self that makes a man a renouncer, a *sannyasi*. (Women also adopt this role, but rarely.) This sort of death ritual is chronicled by Agehananda Bharati, an Austrian who was born Roman Catholic in Vienna, became attracted to Hinduism in his early teens, for years lived as a teaching *sannyasi* in India, and concluded his life as a university professor in the United States. Bharati describes the radical reconstruction of personhood that made it possible for him to become a *sannyasi:* ritual death on a full-moon midnight in Banaras's main cremation ground. It was at that point that his initiating guru, who bore the lineage-title Bharati, gave him the name Agehananda, "the joy of being homeless." Brahminical texts position this act of renunciation as the beginning of the fourth and final stage of life, suggesting that one has to have lived through the rest and performed all the duties pertaining thereunto before one has a life truly worth renouncing. Bharati's path to renunciation was far more direct—he came to it as a young man—and although other aspects of his story are most unusual, this feature is actually far more common than the fourth-stage pattern the texts enshrine. Here too, lived Hinduism tends not to be Hinduism by the book.

If life is a cycle, cremation's aim of transforming death to life gives it a hopeful spin, preparing the way for life to come. A *sannyasi*'s cremation marks a different kind of hope: release from the painful, prisonlike round of birth after birth after birth. Yet the cycling of an individual life is only one of several cycles marked out in Hindu ritual time; in part 3 we move on to consider others. The two essays in this section of the volume focus on ritual events that structure the calendar year as it is experienced in North India, and each of them participates not just in a solar cycle but a lunar one. Divali, the subject of Om Lata Bahadur's essay, occurs at the new moon, and Holi, the spring festival described by McKim Marriott as "the feast of love," comes when the moon is full. Divali is an autumn festival, and it has come to be the single most prominent annual event in the lives of many Indians resident in the diasporic West. If one Hindu festival deserves to be integrated into the public calendar of religious festivals observed in Euro-American countries, they feel, it should be Divali.

Though positioned on the other side of the solar calendar, Holi matches Divali in a number of interesting ways. Both are harvest festivals with elements that relate to the renewal of time, and both trace a dramatic progression from chaos to order. With Divali the chaos is carefully ritualized. Worshippers light lamps to guide Lakshmi, the goddess of auspiciousness, through the darkness to their homes and businesses, and play further with the motif of uncertain fortune by gambling on her behalf. Ritually, she is required to win. At Holi, by contrast, all hell breaks loose. McKim Marriott describes what it feels like to reenact the dissolution of order in this way—or at least, he does the best he can. It's hard to coax memory back from a fog of marijuana. On both occasions, fall and spring, order returns resplendent. Lakshmi does indeed arrive on the night of Divali, and the day following celebrates the reestablishment of temporal and spatial order in relation to unshakable Mount Govardhan, an enduring form of Krishna. As for Holi, the clamor of fire-walking and burning the demoness Holika deep in the night and the dousing of passersby with brightly colored water and a lot else the following morning is followed by a complete reversal of mood at noon. People don their whitest clothes and reconstitute society by visiting one another with a sense of peace and decorum that is unrivaled at any other time of year. What was upside down is right side up again, the insecurities grounded, the injustices of life revenged for another year.

It is interesting to see that Om Lata Bahadur concludes her essay on Divali with a recipe, a practice she adopts for every chapter of her *Book of Hindu Festivals and Ceremonies*. This one is for *mandhi*, a fried sweet especially associated with Divali. While Bahadur's habit of providing recipes is especially driven by her desire to write a book that will be useful to women set adrift from traditions their mothers and grandmothers knew by oral transmission, food is hardly just a woman's corner in the house of Hinduism—and hardly a corner at all. "Food is Brahman," as A. K. Ramunujan once underscored in a well-known essay, and Brahman is ultimate reality.[9] Food is the cycling of that reality through all beings, including the gods themselves. No wonder so many Hindu rituals are unabashedly about food, as indicated by the foregrounding of *prasada* in the very first essay in this volume. Food is even important in its absence, as one can see in the widespread Hindu practice of undertaking self-denying vows *(vrata)*.[10] Here the gender element surfaces again, for vows are often a women's activity and often adopted for the benefit of men. Yet as Huyler's opening essay reminds us, men too can saddle themselves with vows, as in the case of his Tamil computer mechanic. Intriguingly, however, this man's vow was dedicated to a female divinity.

In part 4 we move from ritual to performance, but the line between the two is thin. We see this immediately in Linda Hess's portrayal of the *ramlilas* of Banaras, where the Brahmin boys who take the leading roles are not considered actors but *svarups*, "intrinsic forms," of the divine figure they represent—Sita and Rama and Rama's three brothers.[11] These boys bear the aura of divinity as long as the play continues, and are surrounded by many other figures, including a host of monkeys led by Hanuman. The *ramlilas* of Banaras, patronized by the Maharaja and performed on his extensive palace grounds at Ramnagar, just across the Ganges, are famous all over India. People come from far and wide to see them. Of course, Hess is interested in the dramatic particulars of what transpires "on stage"—a stage that ambles through fields and groves that become, in the course of a month, the *Ramayana*'s primal landscape of exile, battle, and homecoming. But she is even more interested in what happens to the pilgrims, the vow-fulfillers *(nemis)*, the regulars who follow the *svarups* wherever they go. This, then, is Hess's "Ramlila: The Audience Experience," and like so many other experiences recounted in this volume, it is a chronicle of collective self-transformation.

In the essay that follows Philip Lutgendorf shows us what happened when the *Ramayana* moved into the medium of television. For eighteen months in 1987 and 1988, the writer-producer Ramanand Sagar succeeded in gluing the eyes of the entire nation to the screen on Sunday mornings. Lutgendorf plays close attention to the changes that occurred when Tulsidas's sixteenth-century Hindi *Ramayana* made its transit from stage (as in Banaras) to screen, but he also comments on the surprising continuities from medium to medium. Sometimes the new medium was unable to solicit audience participation in the same way the *svarups* do as they move around the *ramlila* grounds at Ramnagar, but television also made it possible to breathe new life into certain beloved moments in Tulsidas's epic, particularly those that required close-up intimacy to be savored. To the surprise of many, the TV *Ramayana* succeeded in generating its own brand of ritual etiquette. Television sets were often garlanded in preparation for the weekly episode, and the producers paced the performance to allow for the long moments of *darshan* that worshippers would have expected in other settings. Since 1988 television has become a major force in the daily life of countless Hindus living in India. The early morning hours are packed with discourses, meditation, and religious singing: some of Hinduism's best-known preachers—Murari Bapu, Asaran Bapu, Kripalu, Jai Guru Dev—address the public there on a daily basis. As for Ramanand Sagar's *Ramayana,* it's gone on to a happy afterlife in video shops around the globe.

The final essay in part 4 deals with medium and performance of quite a different kind: religious possession. As this term and its correlates in Indian languages imply, there is a certain way in which we are approaching this important aspect of lived Hinduism backwards by grouping it with other examples of performance. Here, after all, there is apparently no script. Kathleen Erndl, in introducing possession as she has encountered it in the Punjab, says this quite explicitly. Preferring to see actuality here rather than acting, she remarks that it "presents the greatest challenge to the Western worldview . . . to meet the Goddess face-to-face." Yet like others who have reported on the reality of possession in various Hindu settings, only some of which occur as part of larger staged events we would naturally call dramas, Erndl acknowledges that the Punjabi women possessed by Durga do respond to dramatic protocols. Their performances in the course of all-night vigils called *jagratas* are not as unscripted as they might seem. Still, in understanding this whole process it makes a big difference to be aware, as Erndl says, that "Hinduism does not draw a clear dividing line between divine and human; gods can become humans, and humans can become gods."

This observation provides the perfect segue to the next section of this volume, which concerns gurus—beings who straddle the line between the human and the divine, or obliterate it altogether. Part 5 begins with Lisa Hallstrom's portrait of Anandamayi Ma ("Joy-filled Mother"), one of the most widely revered gurus in recent Indian memory. Although she died in 1982, Anandamayi Ma's devotees still experience her as alive today. When she was present in her earthly body, they resisted the notion that she was either a woman or a saint; she was God. The nature and force of this sense of divinity, however, is closely connected to human motherhood: its irresistible power exceeds its moral attributes, and nothing is more powerful than the sense of sitting in its—her—lap. While she was alive, Anandamayi Ma counted among her devotees some of India's most powerful people, including Prime Minister Indira Gandhi. Now that people can no longer experience "live" the electric power of her *darshan,* Anandamayi Ma's following has understandably waned. But another "joy-filled mother"—Amritanandamayi Ma of Kerala, or, for short, Ammachi—seems to have come forward to take her place, though without any claim to spiritual succession. Succession is not what matters here, but the immediate experience of being accepted. Yet if living in the lap of the Mother was the defining experience for many of Anandamayi Ma's devotees, then the ample, unquestioning hug that Amritanandamayi Ma tirelessly offers seems to follow in close succession.

Succession is much more formalized in the Radhasoami tradition of North India, where the lineage itself is understood to bear the charisma of guruship. On this account, lack of agreement about who should succeed to the throne when any given guru passes away has led to a number of schisms since Radhasoami was established in the mid-nineteenth century. Sudhir Kakar takes us to the compound of the community that has emerged from these struggles as the most populous and globally influential Radhasoami lineage—the stately *dera* at Beas in the Punjab. He describes what it was like to be there in the presence of Maharaj Charan Singh, who served as guru for the remarkably long period extending from 1951 to 1990. Kakar tells how he felt the boundaries of his own personality melt away as he sat among the thousands who waited for Charan Singh to give *darshan,* and reflects on the connections between that and what an infant experiences in communion with its mother. The guru has the power, especially through the magic of *darshan* but also through his entire presence, to reactivate this basic stratum in human personality, eliciting the sense of trust and well-being that is essential for personal and spiritual health. Kakar does not hesitate to call it "psychological regression" (Radhasoami adherents would doubtless prefer "progression"), but when Kakar uses this term he does not mean to imply that this shared psychological space is substandard or in any limiting sense infantile. After all, it was Freud who spoke of regression in the service of the ego.

Actually it is not the charisma of *darshan* that bothers Kakar, but some of what Charan Singh says as he gives it. When Charan Singh urges spiritual seekers to accept their social station, whatever it might be, and acquiesce in "the iron law of karma," Kakar parts company. Yet it is important to acknowledge that although the Beas *dera* over which Charan Singh presided may fall short of egalitarian perfection, as most if not all religious communities do, it nonetheless remains one of India's least caste-conscious religious environments.

That brings us to an aspect of "lived Hinduism" that some Hindus think ought to be excluded from any treatment of the subject (part 6). At a conference on local expressions of Hinduism held in New York in 2003, for example, certain participants were adamant that "sociology" of this sort (as they called it) has no proper place in the representation of religion—and Hinduism has nothing to do with caste.[12] Undoubtedly they are right that caste has long been used as a whipping boy by Western, Christian critics of Hindu India, and of late there has been some important work confirming that common notions of caste both in India and abroad owe a great deal to the ways British administrators managed the concept in the course of the late nineteenth and early twentieth centuries.[13] But Hinduism without caste? That is something many Hindus themselves would reject—some merely to acknowledge the reality of the connection, others because they feel caste points not just to actualities but to ideals. Here Gandhi's view is important to remember. He saw caste as signifying a religiously based society whose parts cohere in complementary ways and articulate a sense of shared need, by contrast to individual-focused, contract-arranged Western notions of what constitutes a healthy society.

Not all of this came out at the New York conference, but a good bit did. One set of participants insisted that caste was a figment of the Western imagination, or at least something the British grafted onto Indian society. But some of the people they were trying to persuade represented religious worldviews that had been deeply shaped by the reality of social oppression, and by caste in particular. These conference participants, like millions of other Indians, have long been called Untouchables. Even though many of them have now lived in the United States for decades, and some of the younger ones were born there, they all report that they have experienced the reality of caste. No one was about to tell them somebody made it up. In partial consequence of that fact, these particular New Yorkers have found it makes more sense to think of their religious group as aligned with Sikhism rather than Hinduism.

The group of which we are speaking is the Shri Guru Ravidas Sabha of Woodside, Queens, and the guru they venerate in their title is one of the most important religious voices to have emerged from the "bottom" of Indian caste society. He is a sixteenth-century *bhakti* poet-saint whose memory is alive across North India and beyond. In the first of two essays devoted to caste, John Hawley describes the religious institutions that Ravidasis have established in their guru's name during the past several decades in Banaras, the city where he lived. These are well connected to the international network in which the Ravidas Sabha in Queens participates, but it is notable that the bow to Sikhism is far less deep in Banaras than abroad. The Ravidas temples of Banaras serve in a much more direct way as a comment on Hindu life there—and form an important part of it in the eyes of many. For centuries certain *bhakti* hagiographies have tried to show how Ravidas belonged to the Hindu domain, though others have rejected the notion. Obviously, the debate continues today.

The second essay on caste contrasts with the Ravidas essay in every way. It is South Indian rather than North, Brahmin rather than Untouchable, fiction rather than ethnography, female rather than male. People normally think of being Brahmin as a privileged state, and doubtless it is in many respects. But in her short story "Revenge Itself," Lalitambika Antarjanam (1901–1987) fictionalizes a celebrated nineteenth-century event that vividly dramatized the costs of being a Nambudiri Brahmin woman. The Nambudiris of Kerala, at least in their own perception, occupy the very highest rungs of the ladder of caste. Until the early twentieth century, when Antarjanam wrote, Nambudiris maintained their eminence in large part through the control of women. Marriage was strictly confined to the Nambudiri fold, and a Nambudiri woman's sexuality was closely watched. "Revenge Itself" is doubtless a comment—caustic, tragic, ironic—on the contrast between the seclusion of these Brahmin women and the much more open lives of the powerful women who belonged to Kerala's other major high-caste group, the matrilineal Nayars. But it also comments on the consequences of the very widely shared Hindu idea that a woman's religion is fundamentally different from a man's. The nub of it is this: in many communities a woman's most important deity is her husband. This has led some observers to urge that a story like "Revenge Itself" actually concerns two castes: Brahmins and women. Readers will want to think about the extent to which religion figures in the construction of either—or is it just "sociology"?

In the last two sections of this volume, we look toward Hinduism's future. As we do so, two questions face us inescapably—questions that first emerged as we stood in Bangalore and watched the New Year dawn. First, how will Hinduism change, both in India and abroad, as it responds to its recent rapid spread around the globe? Second, how do Hindus live with people representing other religious communities?

We begin with issues that arise in connection with Hinduism's recent diasporization. Early in this introduction we had a taste of how this global fact exerts a powerful influence on Hindu life in modern India, but we have yet to explore "the life of Hinduism" abroad. This we do in the two essays that comprise part 7. In her essay on the impressive temple to Vishnu as Ventakesvara (Lord of the Venkata Hill) in Pittsburgh, Vasudha Narayanan describes what it took to transplant this major deity from the hills of Andhra Pradesh to Penn Hills, Pennsylvania. She concludes with some observations about the cardinal features of Hinduism as understood not just in Pittsburgh but in the American Hindu diaspora at large. (The second of these, by the way, is the conviction that Hinduism is a tolerant religion.) In the essay that follows, Sitansu Chakravarti, a professor of philosophy living in Toronto, settles on a somewhat different rubric for laying out "some basic features of Hinduism." These tenets of faith figure prominently in his primer *Hinduism: A Way of Life*, a book aimed specifically at Hindus living in the diaspora and prompted by the exigencies of his own diasporic experience. But his book is printed in Delhi and has sold briskly there as well.

Most of the Hindus described by Narayanan and addressed by Chakravarti have migrated to the United States and Canada directly from India, but some have a longer diasporic history. A good example is provided by Hindus who in the 1980s and 1990s immigrated to Queens, a borough of New York City, from Guyana on the northeastern shore of South America. By and large, twice-migrant Caribbean Hindu communities in Europe and North America have remained quite separate from their once-migrant Indian Hindu neighbors, but a series of recent experiences, including the younger generation's education at the same universities, have brought them increasingly together. This has brought to the surface a series of problems of "internal" adjustment, as Hindus from one part of the world meet Hindus from others. In Queens, for instance, a Guyanese religious leader was invited to manage a high-profile temple whose founders and constituents came primarily from Gujarat and North India. The results were challenging, and, for some old-time supporters of the temple, uncomfortable.[14]

These diasporic growing pains—and graftings—can sometimes be hard, and they are complicated by a further set of issues that arise when Hindus relate to people who stand outside the Hindu tradition altogether. In the volume's concluding section—part 8—we see how these issues of identity are shaped by two major questions: (1) Should Hinduism be militant or tolerant? (2) Should it be studied and represented by Hindus alone, or is there also room for outsiders?

In regard to the question of militancy versus tolerance, we turn again to contributions by the editors of this volume. In the first of these, John Hawley reports on a trip he made to Ayodhya in early 1993, a month after Hindu militants destroyed the mosque that had been built there by a lieutenant of the Mughal emperor Babar in 1528. A symbol of Muslim hegemony in India's past—and perhaps of any foreign hegemony over Hindu religion—the Babri Mosque had emerged in the 1980s as a central feature of the rhetoric of *hindutva* ("Hindu-ness") that was spread by India's principal right-wing organizations. One of these is the Vishwa Hindu Parishad (VHP: "World Hindu Council"), which has had a particularly strong impact on diasporic Hinduism through its educational activities and its efforts to organize Hindu students worldwide. Another is the Bharatiya Janata Party (BJP: "Indian People's Party"), which until the elections of spring 2004 had led India's ruling political coalition with one short break since 1996. The BJP has refrained from moving ahead too fast—or in open defiance of the judiciary—toward constructing the massive temple it proposed be built to mark Rama's birthplace; clearing its way was the ostensible purpose of destroying Babar's mosque. On the whole, the need to build a ruling coalition took precedence over the need to build Rama's temple. Yet as events in Gujarat and Maharashtra have shown, anti-Muslim Hindu militancy backed by the BJP and its associate organizations is far from dead.

But neither is Hindu tolerance or the long tradition of amity and shared worship that has characterized relations between Hindus and Muslims living in India.[15] Vasudha Narayanan introduces this subject with a brief essay on the shrine *(dargah)* of Shahul Hamid in Nagore, Tamil Nadu. Shahul Hamid is remembered as the descendant of a noted Sufi *pir*, but his shrine was built with help from Hindu kings, and more than half of the people who worship there today are Hindus. A law enacted by the Tamil Nadu state legislature in 2002 forbids religious conversion, but this shrine makes us ask what conversion as a monolithic idea might mean—and perhaps why it would be necessary. For that very reason, perhaps, *hindutva* leaders have recently taken aim at just this sort of institution.[16]

Another kind of targetting has also become prominent recently—in relation not to the practice of Hinduism, but to its study. Here the critics tend to be Hindus living in the Western diaspora, and they criticize non-Hindu academics and media persons who discuss, analyze, and teach Hinduism. An example of this sort of challenge is provided by Shrinivas Tilak, who calls on the Hindu community to join in the task of "taking back Hindu studies." The publication of his article on January 6, 2004, adds yet another item to the list of inaugural events with which we began. It appeared in a medium that has become increasingly important to the conduct of global Hindu life—the Internet—and the place of its publication, sulekha.com, guaranteed that it would instantly come to the attention of Hindus living in countries all over the world. Yet although its reach is global, sulekha.com especially engages a North American readership, and the issue raised by Shrinivas Tilak has newly crystallized in that part of the world. Have foreigners distorted the meaning of Hinduism? What about Hindu scholars who work with foreigners and have been trained in non-Hindu institutions—a group Rajiv Malhotra of the Infinity Foundation has called "sepoys," "neocolonizers," and "honorary whites"?[17] Should either set of scholars be allowed to continue? What can Hindus do to reverse the tide?

It doesn't take much to see that this set of questions is a direct challenge to the validity of some essays that appear in this volume, since their authors have been criticized as being "foreigners" or "sepoys." But the book's final essay views this landscape in a very different way. Written collaboratively by Kala Acharya, Laurie L. Patton, and Chakravarthi Ram-Prasad, this essay focuses on a process of "interlogues," as its title says—the constructive engagement of people who are and are not Hindu as they attempt to understand what Hinduism is and has been. These three writers pick up on Shrinivas Tilak's suggestion that this subject calls for what Mahatma Gandhi called *satyagraha*—an open-ended struggle to grasp the truth—but they argue that *satyagraha* leads in a direction quite a different from what Shrinivas Tilak envisages. *Satyagraha* soon reveals that the categories "Hindu" and "non-Hindu" are far from being the binary, opposite entities Tilak seems to believe them to be.

Acharya, Patton, and Ram-Prasad go on to explore the many ways that processes of mutual engagement play themselves out in today's religiously plural world, and they are not afraid to face the real challenges that such pluralism poses. In doing so, they look back toward some of Hinduism's most ancient texts and find there not monoliths or models of internal consistency, but a style of thinking that values the ability to understand and speak from more than one perspective on any given issue. Here Hinduism emerges as something intrinsically complex and dialogical—inter-logical—so it makes sense that the authors themselves emerge from very different locations: a Hindu living in India (Acharya), a Hindu born in India but living in the diaspora (Ram-Prasad), and a non-Hindu whose life and thought have been deeply affected by what Hinduism has to teach (Patton).

We offer this volume to readers in just that spirit. You come from everywhere, and we have no way of knowing where you are going. We hope that as you think about the life of Hinduism, the essays assembled here will serve as guideposts along the way—even if they sometimes seem to point in wildly different directions.

NOTES

1. James Heitzman, *Network City: Planning the Information Society in Bangalore* (Delhi: Oxford University Press, 2004).

2. The letters BAPS stand for the following words, in their standard Swaminarayan transliteration: Bochasanwasi Akshar Purushottam Sanstha. The first of these indicates that this branch of the Swaminarayan religion is closely associated with the town of Bochasan, Gujarat, where a major temple was erected in the first decade of the twentieth century. It was the first of many impressive edifices constructed by the Akshar Purushottam Sanstha branch of Swaminarayan—the "organization [dedicated to] the immutable highest person." That person is the Deity, but the Deity is visible in a full earthly manifestation as Sahajanand Swami, the founder of the Swaminarayan religious community. Akshar, "the immutable," is his eternally coexistent abode, and this role too can be glimpsed in earthly form—as Sahajanand's pradigmatic devotees, the leaders of the ascetic lineage that established itself in Bochasan in 1906. Pramukh Swami is the current representative of that lineage.

3. The Laine/Bhandarkar controversy is a complex one. Readers interested in further detail are referred particularly to Christian Lee Novetzke, "The Laine Controversy and the Study of Hinduism," *International Journal of Hindu Studies* 8:1–3 (2005), 183–201.

4. For further information on the *mela* at Bunkal ki Devi, see D. R. Purohit, "Fairs and Festivals: Place, Occasion, and Events," in *Garhwal Himalaya: Nature, Culture, and Society*, ed. O. P. Kandari and O. P. Gusain (Srinagar, Garhwal: Transmedia, 2001), 370; cf. Stephen Alter, *Sacred Waters: A Pilgrimage to the Many Sources of the Ganga* (New Delhi: Penguin, 2001), 255–57. At the other end of India a ban against animal sacrifice was enacted by the Tamil Nadu state legislature in 2003 but was repealed early in 2004. Some observers wonder whether the repeal may have been motivated by the ruling party's fear of alienating members of the populous lower echelons of society as the April 2004 elections approached, since these are largely the people who practice animal sacrifice (Rupa Viswanath and Nate Roberts, private conversations, Chennai, March 12–13, 2004). Repeals can have other causes, too. In the year that a ban was enacted on the sacrifice of chickens to the local goddess of Kaup, a town located on India's main west-coast highway in Karnataka, an alarming increase in road accidents was reported. Rather than continuing to court the goddess's anger, the sacrifices were resumed.

5. The general design and some of the specific wording for this and the following section were first worked out in John Hawley's entry "Hinduism" in the *Encyclopedia of World Religions* (Springfield, MA: Encyclopedia Britannica and Merriam-Webster, 1999), 434–36. Earlier usages of the term Hinduism can be traced back as far as the correspondence of Charles Grant in 1787. See Henry Morris, *The Life of Charles Grant* (London: J. Murray, 1904), 105, 110, as cited by Geoffrey A. Oddie, "Constructing 'Hin-

duism': The Impact of the Protestant Missionary Movement on Hindu Self-Understanding," in *Christians and Missionaries in India: Cross-Cultural Communication since 1500, with Special Reference to Caste, Conversion, and Colonialism,* ed. Robert Frykenberg (Grand Rapids: Eerdmans, 2003), 156. For a general overview of the subject, see David N. Lorenzen, "Who Invented Hinduism?" *Comparative Studies in Society and History* 41:1 (1999): 630–59.

6. Philip Lutgendorf, *The Life of a Text: Performing the Ramcaritmanas of Tulsidas* (Berkeley: University of California Press, 1991), 363.

7. Cf. A. K. Ramanujan, "Is There a Hindu Way of Thinking?" in *India through Hindu Categories,* ed. McKim Marriott (New Delhi: Sage Publications, 1990), 41–58.

8. Interested readers are particularly referred to the fascinating analysis provided by Jonathan Parry, "The Last Sacrifice," in *Death in Banaras* (Cambridge: Cambridge University Press, 1994), 151–66.

9. A. K. Ramanujan, "Food for Thought," in *The Eternal Food: Gastronomic Ideas and Experiences of Hindus and Buddhists,* ed. R. S. Khare (Albany: State University of New York Press, 1992), 223–37.

10. For a short exposition on this topic see Mary McGee, "Desired Fruits: Motive and Intention in the Votive Rites of Hindu Women," in *Roles and Rituals for Hindu Women,* ed. Julia Leslie (New Brunswick: Rutgers University Press, 1991), 71–88.

11. This also happens when Krishna's life is portrayed, and in many similar settings. See J. S. Hawley, "Pilgrims' Progress through Krishna's Playground," *Asia,* Sept.–Oct. 1980, 12–19, 45.

12. Rajiv Malhotra, whose position as president of the Infinity Foundation connected him with a number of conference participants, emphasized this point in "Problematizing God's Interventions in History," www.sulekha.com (accessed March 21, 2003). The draft title of this same article was "Indic Challenges to the Discipline of Science and Religion." A brief description of the conference, held at Barnard College, Columbia University, on May 3, 2003, can be found at www.barnard.edu/religion/hinduismhere.

13. E.g., Nicholas Dirks, *Castes of Mind* (Princeton: Princeton University Press, 2001).

14. See J. S. Hawley, "Global Hinduism in Gotham," in *Asian-American Religion,* ed. Tony Carnes and Fenggang Yang (New York: New York University Press, 2004), 112–37.

15. Generally on this topic, but from the Islamic side, see Imtiaz Ahmad and Helmut Reifeld, eds., *Lived Islam in South Asia: Adaptation, Accommodation, and Conflict* (Delhi: Social Science Press, 2004).

16. Yoginder Sikand, "Sri Guru Dattatreya Baba Budhan Dargah," in *Sacred Spaces: Exploring Traditions of Shared Faith in India* (New Delhi: Penguin Books, 2003), 53–68. Sikand takes his readers to a *dargah* in the hills of Karnataka where the founding *pir,* a Sufi saint, is commonly understood to have been an incarnation of the Hindu god

Dattatreya. Hindus and Muslims visit this shrine in common and have done so for generations, but the VHP is determined to tidy the borders and "liberate" the shrine for Dattatreya. There is plenty of resistance—not just from Muslims, but from Hindus as well.

17. Sepoys: Rajiv Malhotra, "Problematizing God's Interventions in History," www.sulekha.com, 23 (accessed March 21, 2003); "neocolonial brown (mem)sahibs . . . who often guard the India and/or Hindu bashing fortresses at many American university departments": "The Axis of Neocolonialism," www.sulekha.com, 15 (accessed July 10, 2002); " 'honorary white' Indian thinkers": "The Position of Hinduism in America's Higher Education," www.infinityfoundation.com, 1 (downloaded December 4, 2000).

PART I · WORSHIP

1 · The Experience

Approaching God

STEPHEN P. HUYLER

Having just shaved and bathed, Ramachandran wraps the three meters of his clean, freshly starched white cotton *dhoti* around his waist. He places a matching shawl over his shoulders, leaving his chest bare. He then steps into his rubber sandals and slips out the door of his home. Just in front of him, on the ground before the door, his younger sister has almost finished painting an elaborate *kolam*, a sacred design made with bleached rice flour (see figure 2). It is an activity that either she or his mother or his aunt performs every day of the year. As he walks carefully around it he admires the beautiful lotus she is creating. All around him the town is coming to life. He weaves among countless other kolams as he moves down the street, waving to his neighbor, an old man intent on milking his cow. Ramachandran is on his way to the temple.

Today is Tuesday, dedicated in southern India to the Goddess Mariamman, the embodiment of Shakti, the feminine power that conquers evil and heals disorder. When Ramachandran was sixteen he vowed that for the rest of his life he would fast every Tuesday. Now, ten years have passed, and he still maintains his vow. After his bath before sunrise, he drank a cup of tea and ate some rice cakes. For the rest of the day he will have only liquids, keeping his mind and body ritually pure in order to be a proper vessel for the Goddess's guidance. Although Ramachandran worships

This essay was previously published as "Approaching God," in *Meeting God* (New Haven: Yale University Press, 1999), 46–63.

FIGURE 2
Adorning a *kolam* diagram, Madurai, Tamil Nadu. Photo by Stephen Huyler.

Mariamman every day in his household shrine, on Tuesdays he chooses to go to the temple. Usually he goes alone, although sometimes he is accompanied by other family members.

Near the temple the streets grow more crowded (see figure 3). From the stalls on each side hawkers call out their wares. Many sell the offerings that devotees take to the temple; others sell objects that are used in household shrines. Ramachandran purchases a coconut and a packet of white camphor from the vendors that he frequents every week. He puts these into the small wicker basket that he carries, which already contains some bananas and the bright red hibiscuses that he picked from the garden behind his home.

He approaches the temple gate, then leaves his sandals at the door and steps inside. Already he can hear the clanging of bells from the sanctum. Repeating the name of his Goddess—"Mariamman, Mariamman, Mariamman"—he joins the many other devotees who circle the central temple in a clockwise direction. Returning to the entrance, he pushes through the crowd to enter the temple itself. Inside it is dark and cool, filled with the thick, sweet smell of incense. Ramachandran joins the line of other male worshippers to the left of the inner sanctum. The women, wearing their brightest saris and flowers in their hair, line up opposite him.

FIGURE 3
On the way to temple, Srirangam, Tamil Nadu. Photo by Stephen Huyler.

Children are on both sides. He reaches up to ring a bell suspended from the stone ceiling. Its strong tone clears his brain of extraneous thought and allows him to focus on the deity. By craning his neck he can just get a glimpse of the blackened stone image of the Goddess. She is dressed in a brilliant red sari, her neck covered with jewels and garlands of flowers, her head crowned with a diadem. The priest comes down the line of devotees, collecting their offerings, and returns to the sanctum. A curtain is drawn across the shrine for a few minutes of eager anticipation. Then, amid the clamor of bells, it is opened. The image of Mariamman is radiantly beautiful to him, newly adorned with fresh flowers, including two of Ramachandran's hibiscuses. The priest waves a brass lamp lit with seven flames in a circular motion in front of the Goddess. Looking into the shrine, Ramachandran locks his eyes with those of the image: he has *darshan* with the Goddess. At that moment he is filled with a feeling of well-being, of centeredness and belonging. His world is in balance.

The priest then brings out a tray of lighted camphor. All the worshippers place their hands quickly into the cool flame before touching them to their closed eyelids, symbolically opening their souls to communion with the Divine. On the same tray are little mounds of white sacred ash and red vermilion powder. With the fourth finger of his right hand, Ramachandran puts a dot of each in the center of his forehead between his eyebrows, the ash symbolizing purification through worship and the red symbolizing Shakti, the power of the Goddess. Then each person's basket of offerings is returned, some of its contents remaining as a donation to the temple, the rest blessed by the Goddess to be shared by the devotees. Ramachandran will take this *prashad* back to his family, so that they may partake in Mariamman's blessing.

The purpose of his weekly temple visit is over, and Ramachandran must return home quickly. Once there he changes out of his dhoti and shawl and puts on the black pants and white buttoned shirt of his work attire. After drinking only a glass of water he mounts his bicycle to ride to the shop where all day he repairs the computers that are so essential to maintaining business in contemporary India. As he solders the memory boards of broken mainframe hardware, he is content in the memory of his link with his Goddess and with the rituals that bring balance to his life.

Like Ramachandran, many Hindus observe a weekly fast, the choice of day depending on the deity to whom they have vowed. Whether fasting or not, worshipping at home or in the temple, all Hindus begin their day by bathing. It is considered essential to approach a deity in as clean a manner as possible, both in body and in dress. Even the destitute will wash in a local reservoir or under a hand pump before approaching their household or community shrine. And those who live in the desert or in drought conditions will sprinkle a few drops of precious water on their faces, hands, and feet before beginning their *pujas.* Those who can afford it always put on fresh clothes in order to pray, the men either in simple traditional dress or contemporary pants and shirts, the women, depending on the region, in their cleanest saris or sets of tunic and pajamas, or blouses, skirts, and veils. Footwear is always taken off before entering a shrine—one symbolically removes the dirt of the outside world and enters the sacred space clean in body and in spirit.

Once the image of a deity has been consecrated, Hindus believe it to be the deity incarnate, no matter what its form. It may be an unaltered element of nature, such as a rock or tree or body of water; or it could be a stone- or wood-carving, a casting in brass or bronze, a painting, even a mass-produced print. The rituals of consecration for temple images are elaborate and closely proscribed through ancient texts and canons. The installation of images in the household shrine may be less complex, depending on the traditions of the caste, family, and community; but once the images are consecrated they are viewed as deities themselves and accorded profound respect. Images in temples and shrines are given the same treatment that would be shown to royalty or to a very honored guest. In a temple, this preferential treatment, called *upacharas,* is carried out by the chief priest and, possibly, his assistants; in the home it is most often the responsibility of the senior female, the matriarch.

The first thing every morning, the image is gently awakened. Then it is bathed in holy water that comes from the Ganga (the Ganges River, which is also viewed as a Goddess) or from another sacred body of water. (There are many sacred rivers, streams, and springs in India.) Whatever its source, any water used in a shrine is considered mystically transformed into Ganga. After the image's initial bath it is anointed with substances believed to enhance its purity. (Prints or paintings, for obvious reasons, cannot receive daily applications of liquids. They are instead cleaned carefully and may be adorned with sacred powders or garlands of flowers.) Sculptures are first anointed with one substance, then rinsed with holy water; a second substance is applied, and again the sculpture is washed with water before the third application, and so on. These materials vary according to local traditions but often include honey, milk, yogurt, sandalwood paste or turmeric, coconut water, a mixture of five fruits *(panchamrita),* and sacred ash *(vibhuti).* Once cleaned and anointed, the image is dressed in garments befitting its gender and station: a dhoti and shawl, or a sari or skirt and veil. It will then be adorned with jewelry (bangles, necklaces, nose rings, and a crown), depending on the "wealth" that it has acquired over the years as gifts from devotees. Finally it will be garlanded with flowers. This bathing and anointing ceremony is usually conducted in private. Public viewing is considered indiscreet and invasive to the deity. The image may be seen by others only when it is properly dressed and adorned. Few Westerners recognize that the manner in which Hindu sculptures are most often exhibited in museums, galleries, and private collections both inside and outside India is considered disrespectful by many Hindus. The images may be beautiful in elemental form and design, but without their ritual apparel and adornment their display is thought inappropriate.

Hindus chant prayers and songs of praise to the deity during all the ceremonies of preparation, as well as during the puja itself. Many of these prayers *(shlokas)* are derived from the Vedas and have been recited in this precise form for many thousands of years. Others were collected or written by sages and saints in the past two millennia. It is considered essential that shlokas be repeated precisely and with proper reverence. Hindus believe that the very name of a God or Goddess has magical properties, as do many other sacred words and verses. The cadence, quality, pitch, and vibration of a voice may pierce through the illusion of the material world and speak directly to God. In fact, many texts state that the Absolute, Brahman, is pure sound. Most classical Indian music is considered sacred, and fine musicians are treated as divinely inspired and are sometimes even regarded as saints, for through the magic of their voices and instruments they enable the listener to experience darshan. The tonal purity of bells ringing during a puja shatters the devotee's mundane train of thought and makes him or her directly receptive to the miracle of divine presence.

DIVINE GIFTS

Hinduism revolves around the concept of reciprocity: a devotee's life is enhanced by the gifts he or she bestows. Both religion and hereditary society are based on this principle. In a belief system that separates the unknowable Brahman into individually personified Gods and Goddesses, this exchange is essential. Most Hindu pujas involve expressions of thankfulness through the symbolic offering of gifts to the deity, usually in the form of food and flowers. The type of offering depends on the financial ability of the devotee as well as the climate, season, and local tradition. Those living in wet, tropical areas might offer rice, bananas, and fresh fruits, while those in drier environments may give breads or sweets made of wheat or millet, or simple pellets of sugar. People in northern India prefer to give garlands of marigolds and roses, while in the south devotees offer more exotic flowers, such as jasmine, tuberose, and hibiscus. Lotuses are highly valued as sacred gifts everywhere in India. Flowers are used to adorn the image of the deity, and food is placed in close proximity to it. During the puja rituals the deity is believed to symbolically consume the food. In doing so, his or her sacred energy seeps into the flowers and the remaining food, transforming them with vibrant divine power.

Many of the items donated to shrines are purchased in markets just outside or even within the temple compound. Florists sell individual blooms and garlands of flowers strung together by hand, and fruit sellers provide coconuts, bananas, and other produce. Confectioners display varieties of sweets and cakes, all to be given to the Gods. Other vendors peddle incense and camphor. Many cater primarily to the needs of household shrines, stocking their stalls with framed and unframed prints of painted portraits of the principal deities being worshipped inside the temple, as well as those of many other Gods and Goddesses that might be of interest to devotees. Brass shops not only carry lamps, incense burners, trays, and water vessels, but also metal sculptures of popular Gods and Goddesses; other vendors sell the brocaded and embroidered costumes and miniature jewelry for these household images.

Certain occasions may require significant gifts to the Gods. The annual festival of one's patron deity may be an auspicious time to give something extra to the temple or shrine. Rituals that herald important life-changing events, such as birth, coming of age, or marriage, often involve the donation of presents to the family's temple. When a devotee prays for a specific boon from a deity—for example, the healing of a disease, success in a new project, or a raise in income—she or he promises to give a gift to the God or Goddess if the wish is granted. The quality and value of the gift depends on the financial capabilities of the donor. A common offering is a new garment for the image, often a cotton or silk sari or dhoti. Women may offer their own jewelry: glass, silver, or gold bangles or gold or silver bracelets, anklets, earrings, necklaces, or rings. Wealthy individuals might commission fine jewelry, such as a crown or diadem, or perhaps even silver or gold coverings for a part of the body of the image. Terra-cotta sculptures are given by the poor to community shrines, although rarely to large temples. Typically these sculptures, ordered from local potters, represent those animals (horses, cows, or elephants) that tradition states are of particular interest to the deity. Many believe that the sculptures are transformed into their real counterparts in the spirit world for the deity's own use.

Once the deity is suitably prepared for worship, the puja begins. Fire is an essential part of all Hindu rituals. Lamps *(deepas)* are lighted during a puja and waved clockwise in front of the image with the right hand, first around its head, then around its central portion, and finally around its feet. The left hand of the priest or person conducting the puja usually holds a small bell that is rung continuously while the lamp is being waved. Fire was worshipped in ancient India as the God Agni, and today fire is a primary symbol of divine energy. In lighting the flame in front of the image the devotee acknowledges the sacred supremacy of the God or Goddess. Various vegetable oils may be used in deepas, but the most auspicious fuel is *ghee,* or clarified butter. Most lamps are brass, and many are sculpted with sacred symbols relevant to the deity being worshipped. Camphor, known locally as *karpura,* is processed from the pitch of the camphor tree. When lighted, it has the unique property of creating a bright, cool flame that leaves no residue or ash. It is usually placed in a flat tray known as an *arati.* After being waved in front of the image, the arati is customarily brought close to the devotees so that they may put their hands into the fire and then touch their eyelids or the tops of their heads with their fingertips, an action with great symbolic value. The fragrant flame represents the brilliant presence of the deity. Contact with the fire is believed to purify and elevate the devotee's soul, allowing it to merge with the magnificence of the Divine; at the same time, the energy of the absolute unknowable deity is transformed and channeled into palpable connection with the devotee. The arati puja and the darshan (the moment of visually recognizing and being recognized by God) are the most important acts in Hindu worship. (See figure C at the Web site http://www.clas.ufl.edu/users/vasu/loh.)

The arati is usually directly followed by the dispersion of water to the worshipper. A small brass container of holy water blessed by the deity is brought out of the sanctum. A spoonful is poured into the cupped right hand of the devotee, who drinks it and then rubs the remaining drops through his or her hair, thereby melding both the inside and the outside of the body with the essence of the Divine. It is again an acknowledgment of the complement of opposites, the two primary elements: fire (masculine) and water (feminine), like the early morning prayers to the river and the rising sun.

According to ancient Indian philosophy, the human body is divided into seven vortices of energy, called *chakras,* beginning at the base of the spine and ending at the top of the head. The sixth chakra, also known as the third eye, is centered in the forehead directly between the eyebrows and is believed to be the channel through which humankind opens spiritually to the Divine. At the end of each puja ceremony the devotee marks this chakra with sacred powder, usually either *kumkum* (vermilion) or vibhuti, or with a paste made of clay or sandalwood as a symbol and reminder of the darshan. The mark, or *tilak,* is a public proclamation of one's devotion and may identify a specific spiritual affiliation. Most common is a simple dot of bright vermilion that symbolizes the Shakti of the deity. Worshippers of Vishnu use white clay to apply two vertical lines joined at the base and intersected by a bright red streak. The white lines represent the footprint of their God, while the red refers to his consort, Lakshmi. Devotees of Shiva customarily draw three horizontal lines across their brows with vibhuti, symbolizing the three levels of existence and the three functions of their Lord as Creator, Preserver, and Destroyer of all existence. A married woman in some parts of India may be identified by the vermilion used in her tilak and in the part of her hair. Contrary to popular belief outside of India, the *bindi,* or beauty mark, that modern Indian women and girls put on their foreheads has no other contemporary significance, although it evolved from these symbolic tilaks. It does not refer to caste, community, or marital status.

After the symbolic purification with fire, the drinking of holy water, and the marking of the third eye, the final act in most pujas is the return to the devotee of some of the flowers and the newly blessed food, called *prashad.* In the household, all the prashad will be consumed by family members. Some of the food remains in the temple as payment to the priests who facilitate the rituals, while the remaining prashad is taken home and eaten. Hindus believe that the ingestion of prashad fills them with the divine energy of the deity to whom they have prayed, in the same way that Christians believe that by partaking of the bread and wine in Holy Communion they accept the spirit of Christ into their bodies. While pujas may be made either before or after meals, depending on family tradition, all food that is cooked in the home must first be symbolically offered to the Gods before it is eaten. In the strictly traditional home the cook will not ever even taste the food while it is being prepared, as that would alter the purity of the offering. Consequently, all food cooked in these homes becomes prashad. The kitchen is therefore considered a sacred space that should not be violated by uncleanness or by impure actions, words, or thoughts.

2 · The Deity

The Deity

The Image of God

DIANA L. ECK

The vivid variety of Hindu deities is visible everywhere in India. Rural India is filled with countless wayside shrines. In every town of some size there are many temples, and every major temple will contain its own panoply of shrines and images. One can see the silver mask of the goddess Durgā or the stone shaft of the Śiva *liṅga* or the four-armed form of the god Viṣṇu. Over the doorway of a temple or a home sits the plump, orange elephant-headed Gaṇeśa or the benign and auspicious Lakṣmī. Moreover, it is not only in temples and homes that one sees the images of the deities (see figure 4). Small icons are mounted at the front of taxis and buses. They decorate the walls of tea stalls, sweet shops, tailors, and movie theaters. They are painted on public buildings and homes by local folk artists. They are carried through the streets in great festival processions.

It is visibly apparent to anyone who visits India or who sees something of India through the medium of film that this is a culture in which the mythic imagination has been very generative. The images and myths of the Hindu imagination constitute a basic cultural vocabulary and a common idiom of discourse. Since India has "written" prolifically in its images, learning to read its mythology and iconography is a primary task for the student of Hinduism. In learning about Hinduism, it might be argued that perhaps it makes more sense to begin with Gaṇeśa, the

This essay was previously published as "The Image of God," in *Darsan: Seeing the Divine in India*, 3d ed. (New York: Columbia University Press, 1998), 16–31.

FIGURE 4
"One Soul, Two Bodies." Poster illustration by Yogendra Rastogi, purchased in Brindavan, August 2005.

elephant-headed god who sits at the thresholds of space and time and who blesses all beginnings, and then proceed through the deities of the Hindu pantheon, rather than to begin with the Indus Valley civilization and proceed through the ages of Hindu history. Certainly for a student who wishes to visit India, the development of a basic iconographic vocabulary is essential, for deities such as the monkey Hanumān or the fierce Kālī confront one at every turn.

When the first European traders and travelers visited India, they were astonished at the multitude of images of the various deities they saw there. They called them "idols" and described them with combined fascination and repugnance. For example, Ralph Fitch, who traveled as a merchant through North India in the 1500s writes of the images of deities in Banāras: "Their chiefe idols bee blacke and evill favoured, their mouths monstrous, their eares gilded and full of jewels, their teeth and eyes of gold, silver and glasse, some having one thing in their hands and some another."[1]

Fitch had no interpretive categories, save those of a very general Western Christian background, with which to make sense of what he saw. Three hundred years did little to aid interpretation. When M. A. Sherring lived in Banāras in the mid-1800s he could still write, after studying the city for a long time, of "the worship of uncouth idols, of monsters, of the linga and other indecent figures, and of a multitude of grotesque, ill-shapen, and hideous objects."[2] When Mark Twain traveled through India in the last decade of the nineteenth century, he brought a certain imaginative humor to the array of "idols" in Banāras, but he remained without what Rudolf Arnheim would call "manageable models" for placing the visible data of India in a recognizable context. Of the "idols" he wrote, "And what a swarm of them there is! The town is a vast museum of idols—and all of them crude, misshapen, and ugly. They flock through one's dreams at night, a wild mob of nightmares."[3]

Without some interpretation, some visual hermeneutic, icons and images can be alienating rather than enlightening. Instead of being keys to understanding, they can kindle xenophobia and pose barriers to understanding by appearing as a "wild mob of nightmares," utterly foreign to and unassimilable by our minds. To understand India, we need to raise our eyes from the book to the image, but we also need some means of interpreting and comprehending the images we see.

The bafflement of many who first behold the array of Hindu images springs from the deep-rooted Western antagonism to imaging the divine at all. The Hebraic hostility to "graven images" expressed in the Commandments is echoed repeatedly in the Hebrew Bible: "You shall not make for yourself a graven image, or any likeness of anything that is in heaven above, or that is in the earth beneath, or that is in the water under the earth."

The Hebraic resistance to imaging the divine has combined with a certain distrust of the senses in the Greek tradition as well. While the Greeks were famous for their anthropomorphic images of the gods, the prevalent suspicion in the philosophies of classical Greece was that "what the eyes reported was not true."[4] Like those of dim vision in Plato's cave, it was thought that people generally accept the mere shadows of reality as "true." Nevertheless, if dim vision described human perception of the ordinary world, the Greeks continued to use the notion of true vision to describe wisdom, that which is seen directly in the full light of day rather than obliquely in the shadowy light of the cave. Arnheim writes, "The Greeks learned to distrust the senses, but they never forgot that direct vision is the first and final source of wisdom. They refined the techniques of reasoning, but they also believed that, in the words of Aristotle, 'the soul never thinks without an image.' "[5]

On the whole, it would be fair to say that the Western traditions, especially the religious traditions of the "Book"—Judaism, Christianity, and Islam—have trusted the Word more than the Image as a mediator of the divine truth. The Qur'ān and the Hebrew Bible are filled with injunctions to "proclaim" and to "hear" the word. The ears were somehow more trustworthy than the eyes. In the Christian tradition this suspicion of the eyes and the image has been a particularly Protestant position.

And yet the visible image has not been without some force in the religious thinking of the West. The verbal icon of God as "Father" or "King" has had considerable power in shaping the Judeo-Christian religious imagination. The Orthodox Christian traditions, after much debate in the eighth and ninth centuries, granted an important place to the honoring of icons as those "windows" through which one might look toward God. They were careful, however, to say that the icon should not be "realistic" and should be only two-dimensional. In the Catholic tradition as well, the art and iconography, especially of Mary and the saints, has had a long and rich history. And all three traditions of the "Book" have developed the art of embellishing the word into a virtual icon in the elaboration of calligraphic and decorative arts. Finally, it should be said that there is a great diversity within each of these traditions. The Mexican villager who comes on his knees to the Virgin of Guadalupe, leaves a bundle of beans, and lights a candle would no doubt feel more at home in a Hindu temple than in a stark, white New England Protestant church. Similarly, the Moroccan Muslim woman who visits the shrines of Muslim saints would find India less foreign than did the eleventh-century Muslim scholar Alberuni, who wrote that "the Hindus entirely differ from us in every respect."[6]

Worshipping as God those "things" that are not God has been despised in the Western traditions as "idolatry," a mere bowing down to "sticks and stones." The difficulty with such a view of idolatry, however, is that anyone who bows down to such things clearly does not understand them to be sticks and stones. No people would identify themselves as "idolaters," by faith. Thus idolatry can be only an outsider's term for the symbols and visual images of some other culture. Theodore Roszak, writing in *Where the Wasteland Ends,* locates the "sin of idolatry" precisely where it belongs: in the eye of the beholder.[7]

In beginning to understand the consciousness of the Hindu worshipper who bows to "sticks and stones," an anecdote of the Indian novelist U. R. Anantha Murthy is provocative. He tells of an artist friend who was studying folk art in rural North India. Looking into one hut, he saw a stone daubed with red *kunkum* powder, and he asked the villager if he might bring the stone outside to photograph it. The villager agreed, and after the artist had photographed the stone he realized that he might have polluted this sacred object by moving it outside. Horrified, he apologized to the villager, who replied, "It doesn't matter. I will have to bring another stone and anoint *kunkum* on it." Anantha Murthy comments, "Any piece of stone on which he put *kunkum* became God for the peasant. What mattered was his faith, not the stone."[8] We might add that, of course, the stone matters too. If it did not, the peasant would not bother with a stone at all.

Unlike the zealous Protestant missionaries of a century ago, we are not much given to the use of the term "idolatry" to condemn what "other people" do. Yet those who misunderstood have still left us with the task of understanding, and they have raised an important and subtle issue in the comparative study of religion: What is the nature of the divine image? Is it considered to be intrinsically sacred? Is it a symbol of the sacred? A mediator of the sacred? How are images made, consecrated, and used, and what does this tell us about the way they are understood? But still another question remains to be addressed before we take up these topics. That is the question of the multitude of images. Why are there so many gods?

THE POLYTHEISTIC IMAGINATION

It is not only the image-making capacity of the Hindu imagination that confronts the Western student of Hinduism, but the bold Hindu polytheistic consciousness. Here too, in attempting to understand another culture, we discover one of the great myths of our own: the myth of monotheism. Myths are those "stories" we presuppose about the nature of the world and its structures of meaning. Usually we take our own myths so much for granted that it is striking to recognize them as "myths" that have shaped not only our religious viewpoint, but our ways of knowing. Even

Westerners who consider themselves to be secular participate in the myth of monotheism: that in matters of ultimate importance, there is only One—one God, one Book, one Son, one Church, one Seal of the Prophets, one Nation under God. The psychologist James Hillman speaks of a "monotheism of consciousness" that has shaped our very habits of thinking, so that the autonomous, univocal, and independent personality is considered healthy; single-minded decision-making is considered a strength; and the concept of the independent ego as "number one" is considered normal.[9]

In entering into the Hindu world, one confronts a way of thinking that one might call "radically polytheistic," and if there is any "great divide" between the traditions of India and those of the West, it is in just this fact. Some may object that India has also affirmed Oneness as resolutely and profoundly as any culture on earth, and indeed it has. The point here, however, is that India's affirmation of Oneness is made in a context that affirms with equal vehemence the multitude of ways in which human beings have seen that Oneness and expressed their vision. Indian monotheism or monism cannot, therefore, be aptly compared with the monotheism of the West. The statement that "God is One" does not mean the same thing in India and the West.

At virtually every level of life and thought, India is polycentric and pluralistic. India, with what E. M. Forster called "her hundred mouths,"[10] has been the very exemplar of cultural multiplicity. There is geographical and racial diversity from the Pathans of the Punjab to the Dravidians of Tamilnād. There are fourteen major language groups. There is the elaborate social diversity of the caste system. There is the religious diversity of major religious traditions: the Hindus, Muslims, Sikhs, Christians, Buddhists, Jains, and Parsis. (As Mark Twain quipped in his diaries from India, "In religion, all other countries are paupers. India is the only millionaire.")[11] And even within what is loosely called "Hinduism" there are many sectarian strands: Vaiṣṇavas, Śaivas, Śāktas, Smārtas, and others. Note that the very term Hinduism refers only to the "ism" of the land that early Muslims called "Hind," literally, the land beyond the Indus. Hinduism is no more, no less than the "ism" of India.

The diversity of India has been so great that it has sometimes been difficult for Westerners to recognize in India any underlying unity. As the British civil servant John Strachey put it, speaking to an audience at Cambridge University in 1859, "There is no such country, and this is the first and most essential fact about India that can be learned."[12] Seeking recognizable signs of unity—common language, unifying religion, shared historical tradition—he did not see them in India.

In part, the unity of India, which Strachey and many others like him could not see, is in its cultural genius for embracing diversity, so that diversity unites, rather than divides. For example, there are the six philosophical traditions recognized as "orthodox." But they are not called "systems" in the sense in which we use that term. Rather, they are *darśanas.* Here the term means not the "seeing" of the deity, but the "seeing" of truth. There are many such *darśanas,* many "points of view" or "perspectives" on the truth. And although each has its own starting point, its own theory of causation, its own accepted enumeration of the means by which one can arrive at valid knowledge, these "ways of seeing" share a common goal—liberation—and they share the understanding that all their rivals are also "orthodox." Philosophical discourse, therefore, takes the form of an ongoing dialogue, in which the views of others are explained so that one can counter them with one's own view. Any "point of view" implicitly assumes that another point of view is possible.

Moving from the philosophical to the social sphere, there is the well-known diversity of interlocking and interdependent caste groups. On a smaller scale, there is the polycentric system of family authority; which is integral to the extended, joint family. Here not only the father and mother, but grandparents, aunts, and uncles serve as different loci of family authority and fulfill different needs.

Not unrelated to this complex polycentrism of the social structure is the polycentric imaging of the pantheon of gods and goddesses. Just as the social and institutional structures of the West have tended historically to mirror the patriarchal monotheism of the religious imagination, so have the social structure and family structure of India displayed the same tendency toward diversification that is visible in the complex polytheistic imagination. At times, the ordering of the diverse parts of the whole seems best described as hierarchical;[13] yet it is also true that the parts of the whole are knotted together in interrelations that seem more like a web than a ladder. The unity of India, both socially and religiously, is that of a complex whole. In a complex whole, the presupposition upon which oneness is based is not unity or sameness, but interrelatedness and diversity.

The German Indologist Betty Heimann uses the image of a crystal to describe this multiplex whole:

> Whatever Man sees, has seen or will see, is just one facet only of a crystal. Each of these facets from its due angle provides a correct viewpoint, but none of them alone gives a true all-comprehensive picture. Each serves in its proper place to grasp the Whole, and all of them combined come nearer to its full grasp. How-

ever, even the sum of them all does not exhaust all hidden possibilities of approach.[14]

The diversity of deities is part of the earliest Vedic history of the Hindu tradition. In the Ṛg Veda, the various gods are elaborately praised, and in their individual hymns, each is praised as Supreme. Indra may in one hymn be called the "Sole Sovereign of Men and of Gods," and in the next hymn Varuṇa may be praised as the "Supreme Lord, Ruling the Spheres." Max Müller, who was the first great Western interpreter of the Vedas, searched for an adequate term to describe the religious spirit of this literature. It is not monotheism, although there certainly is a vision of divine supremacy as grand as the monotheistic vision. It is not really polytheism, at least if one understands this as the worship of many gods, each with partial authority and a limited sphere of influence. He saw that these Western terms did not quite fit the Hindu situation. To describe the deities of Hinduism, Müller coined the word *kathenotheism*—the worship of one god at a time. Each is exalted in turn. Each is praised as creator, source, and sustainer of the universe when one stands in the presence of that deity. There are many gods, but their multiplicity does not diminish the significance or power of any of them. Each of the great gods may serve as a lens through which the whole of reality is clearly seen.

The spirit that Müller saw in the Vedic hymns continues to be of great significance in many aspects of Indian religious life. To celebrate one deity, one sacred place, one temple, does not mean there is no room for the celebration of another. Each has its hour. One learns, for example, that there are three gods in the tradition today: Viṣṇu, Śiva, and the Devī. But it is clear from their hymns and rites that these deities are not regarded as having partial powers. Each is seen, by those who are devotees, as Supreme in every sense. Each is alone seen to be the creator, sustainer, and final resting place of all. Each has assembled the minor deities and autochthonous divinities of India into its own entourage. The frustration of students encountering the Hindu array of deities for the first time is, in part, the frustration of trying to get it all straight and to place the various deities and their spouses, children, and manifestations in a fixed pattern in relation to one another. But the pattern of these imaged deities is like the pattern of the kaleidoscope: one twist of the wrist and the relational pattern of the pieces changes.

In the Bṛhadāraṇyaka Upaniṣad, a seeker named Vidagdha Śākalya approaches the sage Yājñavalkya with the question "How many gods are there, Yājñavalkya?"[15]

"Three thousand three hundred and six," he replied.
"Yes," said he, "but just how many gods are there, Yājñavalkya?"
"Thirty-three."
"Yes," said he, "but just how many gods are there, Yājñavalkya?"
"Six."
"Yes," said he, "but just how many gods are there, Yājñavalkya?"
"Three."
"Yes," said he, "but just how many gods are there, Yājñavalkya?"
"Two."
"Yes," said he, "but just how many gods are there, Yājñavalkya?"
"One and a half."
"Yes," said he, "but just how many gods are there, Yājñavalkya?"
"One."

Yājñavalkya continues by explaining the esoteric knowledge of the different enumerations of the gods. But the point he makes is hardly esoteric. It is not the secret knowledge of the forest sages but is part of the shared presuppositions of the culture. In any Hindu temple there will be, in addition to the central sanctum, a dozen surrounding shrines to other deities: Gaṇeśa, Hanumān, Durgā, Gaurī, and so on. Were one to ask any worshipper Vidagdha Śākalya's question, "How many gods are there?" one would hear Yājñavalkya's response from even the most uneducated. "Sister, there are many gods. There is Śiva here, and there is Viṣṇu, Ganeśa, Hanumān, Gangā, Durgā, and the others. But of course, there is really only one. These many are differences of name and form."

"Name and form"—*nāma rūpa*—is a common phrase, used often to describe the visible, changing world of *saṁsāra* and the multiple world of the gods. There is one reality, but the names and forms by which it is known are different. It is like clay, which is one, but which takes on various names and forms as one sees it in bricks, earthen vessels, pots, and dishes. While some philosophers would contend that the perception of the one is a higher and clearer vision of the truth than the perception of the many, Hindu thought is most distinctive for its refusal to make the one and the many into opposites. For most, the manyness of the divine is not superseded by oneness. Rather, the two are held simultaneously and are inextricably related. As one of the great praises of the Devī puts it, "Nameless and Formless Thou art, O Thou Unknowable. All forms of the universe are Thine: thus Thou art known."[16]

The very images of the gods portray in visual form the multiplicity and the oneness of the divine, and they display the tensions and the seeming contradictions that are resolved in a single mythic image. Many of the deities are made with multiple arms, each hand bearing an emblem or a weapon, or posed in a gesture, called a *mudrā*. The emblems and *mudrās* indicate the various powers that belong to the deity. Ganeśa's lotus is an auspicious sign, while his hatchet assures that in his role as guardian of the threshold he is armed to prevent the passage of miscreants. The Devī Durgā has eight arms, and in her many hands she holds the weapons and emblems of all the gods, who turned their weapons over to her to kill the demon of chaos. Multiple faces and eyes are common. The creator Brahmā, for example, has four faces, looking in each of the four directions. Śiva and Viṣṇu are depicted together in one body, each half with the emblems appropriate to its respective deity. Similarly, Śiva is sometimes depicted in the Ardhanārīśvara, "Half-Woman God" form, which is half Śiva and half Śakti. The androgynous image is split down the middle: one-breasted, clothed half in male garments and half in female. In a similar way, Rādhā and Kṛṣṇa are sometimes shown as entwined together in such a fashion that while one could delineate two separate figures, they appear to the eye as inseparably one.

The variety of names and forms in which the divine has been perceived and worshipped in the Hindu tradition is virtually limitless. If one takes some of the persistent themes of Hindu creation myths as a starting point, the world is not only the embodiment of the divine, but the very body of the divine. The primal person, Puruṣa, was divided up in the original sacrifice to become the various parts of the cosmos (Ṛg Veda 10.90). Or, in another instance, the original germ or egg from which the whole of creation evolved was a unitary whole, containing in a condensed form within it the whole of the potential and life of the universe (Ṛg Veda 10.121; Chāndogya Upaniṣad 3.19; Aitareya Upaniṣad 1.1). If all names and forms evolved from the original seed of the universe, then all have the potential for revealing the nature of the whole. While far-sighted visionaries may describe the one Brahman by the negative statement "Not this . . . Not this . . . ," still from the standpoint of this world, one can as well describe Brahman with the infinite affirmation "It is this. . . . It is this. . . . " The two approaches are inseparable. As Betty Heimann put it, "whenever the uninitiated outsider is surprised, embarrassed, or repulsed by the exuberant paraphernalia of materialistic display in Hindu cult, he must keep in mind that, side by side with these, stands the utmost abstraction in religious feeling and thought, the search for the *Neti-Neti*

Brahman; the 'not this, not that,' which denies itself to all representations, higher or lower."[17]

NOTES

1. William Foster, ed., *Early Travels in India, 1583–1619* (London: Oxford University Press, 1921), 23.

2. M. A. Sherring, *The Sacred City of the Hindus* (London: Trubner & Co., 1868), 37.

3. Mark Twain, *Following the Equator* (Hartford: The American Publishing Company, 1898), 504.

4. Rudolf Arnheim, *Visual Thinking* (Berkeley: University of California Press, 1969), 5.

5. Ibid., 12.

6. Edward C. Sachau, ed., *Alberuni's India* (Delhi: S. Chand & Co., 1964), 17

7. Theodore Roszak, *Where the Wasteland Ends* (Garden City, NY: Doubleday & Co., 1972), chap. 4, "The Sin of Idolatry."

8. U. R. Anantha Murthy, "Search for an Identity: A Viewpoint of a Kannada Writer," in *Identity and Adulthood*, ed. Sudhir Kakar (Delhi: Oxford University Press, 1979), 109–10.

9. James Hillman, *Re-Visioning Psychology* (New York: Harper & Row, 1975), xiv–xv, 158–59.

10. E. M. Forster, *A Passage to India* (1924; repr., Harmondsworth, England: Penguin Books Ltd., 1974), 135.

11. Twain, *Following the Equator*, 397.

12. Francis G. Hutchins, *The Illusion of Permanence* (Princeton: Princeton University Press, 1967), 142.

13. The hierarchical model is the one adopted by Louis Dumont in *Homo Hierarchicus* (Chicago: University of Chicago Press, 1970).

14. Betty Heimann, *Facets of Indian Thought* (London: George Allen & Unwin, 1964), 21–22.

15. Bṛhadāraṇyaka Upaniṣad 3.9.1, quoted here from Robert E. Hume, *The Thirteen Principal Upanishads*, 2d rev. ed. (1921; London: Oxford University Press, 1931).

16. From the "Nārāyaṇīstuti" in the *Devī Māhātmya* of the *Mārkaṇḍeya Purāṇa*, quoted in Stella Kramrisch, *The Hindu Temple* (Calcutta: University of Calcutta, 1946), 298.

17. Heimann, *Facets of Indian Thought*, 33.

3 · The Miraculous

The Birth of a Shrine

SHRIVATSA GOSWAMI
and MARGARET H. CASE

Some seventy-five miles south of Delhi, as the Yamuna River flows south from the foothills of the Himalayas and just before it passes the ancient and holy city of Mathura, it makes a loop to the east. This loop encircles the temple town of Vrindaban, where residents and pilgrims alike believe the god Krishna lived and played as a boy.

On the north side of Vrindaban, there is a stretch of the riverbank that is particularly rich with stories about Krishna. Here, in November 1992, a gathering of his devotees witnessed his appearance in the form of a *bhramara*—a large insect resembling a bumblebee—on three separate evenings. The event was unanticipated, and yet painstakingly prepared for. It occurred at a conjunction of time and space in the spiral of remembered history; and it appeared as an opening to a different dimension made possible by the attentive efforts of the devotees.

There were many layers to the event, which contributed to the richness of its meaning: the feelings evoked by remembering the life of Krishna, said to have lived here some 5,000 years ago, and to be living here still; the places associated with the sixteenth-century saint Sri Caitanya Mahaprabhu; the buildings erected here in the early eighteenth century by the chief lieutenant of the last great Mughal emperor; and the preparations made by the present generation to express their devotion to Krishna.

This essay was previously published as "The Birth of a Shrine," *Parabola*, Summer 1993, 31–36.

This god, with skin the color of blue-gray storm clouds, had spent his childhood and adolescence in Vrindaban, on the pastoral shores of the Yamuna River. There he faced and defeated demons, played pranks on the women of the countryside, and, when he was older, enjoyed all the moods of love with the beautiful Radha. One of his most famous pranks was to tease a group of cowherd women who had left their clothes on the bank of the Yamuna when they bathed. While they were in the water, Krishna stole their clothes and hung them in the branches of a *kadamba* tree on the riverbank. The young women pleaded with Krishna to give them back their clothes, but he refused to do so until they came out of the river and faced him in their nakedness. Once they had dropped their veils before the divine presence, it is said, Krishna promised them that for the first time they could join him in the great circle dance of union.

In time Krishna had to leave the scenes of his happy youth and assume his rightful place in the royal house of Mathura. He left behind Radha and her friends, who were inconsolable. One day as the women were sitting on the banks of the Yamuna, at the spot where Krishna had come ashore for his nocturnal trysts with Radha, Krishna's trusted friend Uddhava arrived from Mathura to comfort them. He told them that Krishna, the fundamental essence of everything in the world, could in no way be separated from them, so why should they grieve?

In reply, the women spoke eloquently of their love for Krishna, of their delight in caring for him, serving him, and embracing him. So great was their feeling that Uddhava was convinced that devotion like theirs was a more direct path to realization of Krishna than all the knowledge and ritual practice he had assiduously cultivated. Overcome, he was about to prostrate himself before them and touch Radha's feet in devotion. Just then, a bhramara landed on the ground near Radha's feet. But Radha pulled back, saying, "Go away! You are just like the fraud and cheat who has left us—you are dark, like him, and draped in yellow. You are fickle, like him, and flirt with one flower after another. Your moustaches, like his clothes, are yellow with the pollen of garlands pressed to the breasts of the women at the court of Mathura. Go away!" Some say that the bhramara was the embodiment of Uddhava's newfound devotion, others that it was Krishna himself, who could not bear the separation from his beloved Radha.

The places where these events occurred are known to the followers of Krishna. The kadamba tree, the landings where Radha and Krishna met for their nightly trysts, and the riverbank where Uddhava came to comfort Radha and the cowherd women are all within a few hundred feet of each other. In 1515 C.E., when the area around what is today Vrindaban was still an uninhabited forest, the Bengali saint

Caitanya came here to identify the sites. He used to sit in meditation near the same long-lived kadamba tree under which the cowherd women had emerged without their clothes, and pray that he, too, would lose the veils before his eyes. In a state of ecstasy, he became aware of the location of many of the sacred sites, and other holy men associated with him identified additional ones. When Caitanya left Vrindaban, he charged his most able followers, the Six Goswamis, to establish Vrindaban as a pilgrimage center where reenactments of the pastimes of Radha, Krishna, and their companions could be enjoyed by devotees.

About two hundred years later, Raja Sawai Jai Singh of Amber, the most powerful minister of the Mughal emperor Aurangzeb and a devout worshipper of Radha and Krishna, established a retreat for himself in Vrindaban. The two-and-a-half-acre site he chose was a stretch of riverbank just downstream from the kadamba tree, which included Radha's and Krishna's landing places and the place where Caitanya used to sit. There he constructed a house for himself; a pavilion on the riverfront, marking the place where Caitanya had sat; behind it, a shrine to Caitanya and two of his close companions; *ghats*, or steps leading down to the river at Krishna's and Radha's landing places; and a temple for his personal deity. Jai Singh also built a large platform next to his house, for the performance of *rasa lilas*, musical dance dramas depicting the pastimes of Krishna and his companions.

This compound came to be known as Jaisingh Ghera, and today the kadamba tree and all the buildings are still standing. It was here that Jai Singh drew up the plans for the pink city of Jaipur. After his death, Jaisingh Ghera remained in the hands of the rajas of Amber and Jaipur, and after Independence it passed under the control of the state government of Rajasthan.

In 1962 Jaisingh Ghera was purchased by the foremost leader of the Caitanyite branch of Krishna worship, Parampujya Jagadguru Sri Purushottam Goswami ji Maharaj, known to his followers as Maharaj-ji. He is a direct descendant of one of the followers of the Six Goswamis. An energetic leader, he, his family, and followers have established a thriving spiritual and cultural center at Jaisingh Ghera. The center patronizes music and the arts, as well as scholarship on Vrindaban and on the spiritual traditions of those who worship Krishna, and supports the rasa lilas with their associated arts. A building to house these activities was built, encompassing Jai Singh's residence, as well as a performance hall on the site of the old rasa lila platform.

Part of the property along the river had been leased to a small school by the Rajasthani government, and for thirty years this area could not be used by the Goswamis. In the late summer of 1992, the school was vacated, and Jaisingh Ghera was once again nearly complete, lacking only the temple in the center of the compound. This remained in the hands of the Rajasthan government, which is not permitted to sell temples.

At this time, Maharaj-ji decided to organize an *astayama lila*—the eternal lila—eight successive daily performances depicting twenty-four hours in the life of Radha and Krishna, three hours at a time. Throughout the summer both the site and the event were prepared. Work was begun to excavate the ghats and restore the existing structures. Meanwhile Maharaj-ji wrote scripts and devotional songs for the lila, based on the sixteenth-century Sanskrit text of the *Govinda-lilamrtam,* which in twenty-three chapters describes the divine day in detail. Maharaj-ji's family and followers created sumptuous costumes in brilliantly colored silks and gold cloth, stage hangings of rich velvets, settings of forest groves and bowers, thrones of red, peacock blue, and gold fabrics, and lighting to highlight the dramas being enacted on the stage. In September, rehearsals began for the troupe of boys and men who play all the parts.

His devotees believe that Krishna still lives in Vrindaban and the land around it, and that he and Radha play there still. Before the lila could begin, it was necessary to invoke these eternal performers, to bring the space and the time to life. Beginning on the morning of October 31, for twenty-four hours, a relay team of *sadhus* recited the *mahatnanlra:* "Hare Krishna, Hare Krishna, Krishna, Krishna, Hare, Hare, Hare Rama, Hare Rama, Rama, Rama, Hare, Hare," marking out time and space with the name of the divinity. (Hare is the vocative of Hara, which means "one who steals the heart" of Krishna—that is to say, Radha. "Hare Krishna" thus means "Radha Krishna." Rama comes from the Sanskrit too, meaning "to dally, go around with, keep company with" Radha, so "Hare Rama" again invokes the names of Radha and Krishna.)

In addition, the 350 chapters of the *Bhagavata Parana*—the basic sacred text for devotees of Krishna—were read in one day by fourteen scholars, each one reading 25 chapters. The sound of the chanting transformed time and place. Within this setting, Maharaj-ji performed *puja* (worship) at Krishna's ghat, which was also the place where the bhramara had appeared to Uddhava and Radha. Then he led the way to Radha's ghat, a place of particularly intense feeling for Maharaj-ji, since he had twice had a vision of Radha there. There he performed puja a second time. That evening, Krishna was evoked again in the performance hall by the great dancer Birju Maharaj, whose choreography for the occasion was based on the text of the *Govindalilamrtam.*

The next day was devoted to intense preparation, particularly blessings by various groups of the brahmins of Vrindaban. During the morning and afternoon, five groups of thirty one brahmins came to be honored by Maharaj-ji: ritual priests, scholars of the *Bhagavata Parana,* secular scholars and teachers, pilgrim guides, and the men and boys who would be performing the rasa lila. Each spoke briefly about the place and its significance.

These ceremonies all took place under a large tent that covered the site of Radha's and Krishna's trysts, right behind Krishna's ghat. On the rear wall of the tent was a large painted hanging that had been created especially for the occasion. It depicted Radha and her companions under a tree, looking at a large bhramara at Radha's feet (see figure 5).

After all the brahmins had spoken, Maharaj-ji asked one of his followers to speak. Just as she finished her invocation, a large black insect, about two inches long and looking very much like the bhramara in the painting, flew into the tent from the direction of the river and landed on the ground in front of her. Astounded, those devotees who were close enough to see rose to their feet, exclaiming, "Jai ho!" and "Jai Sri Radhe!" The visitor danced on the ground and flew up to dance in the air, alighting two or three more times. After less than a minute, it flew off again in the direction from which it had first come. Maharaj-ji spoke, saying that the divine spirit can take any form, and for those who could see with devotion and love, it was Krishna's presence that had become visible. He declared that a beautiful bower should be created to commemorate this manifestation.

Among the devotees who had gathered in Jaisingh Ghera for the astayama lila, the general reaction that evening and the next day was happiness (but not complete acceptance) that a real miracle had occurred. A wonderful, unusual event, yes—the appearance of this bhramara with such perfect timing—but to fully absorb and accept that this was a manifestation of divinity was difficult. Trying to help his followers absorb what had happened, Maharaj-ji told the devotees that four factors contributed to this miracle: first, this was the site of the original bhramara's appearance; second, the deity was summoned by the devotion of the people gathered there; third, this was the site of the eternal astayama lila; and fourth, the day of the bhramara's appearance had been spent in concentrated spiritual activity by the 155 brahmins, which had compelled it to appear.

At 3:36 A.M. on November 2, the astayama lila began in the great hall, watched by a packed house of about fifteen hundred enthusiastic devotees of Krishna. At 6:00 A.M. on November 3, the second lila began. Since this was a day in the lunar ritual calendar that is considered to be a time when any action taken would not decay, Maharaj-ji decided to consecrate the site of the bower that evening. An octagonal

FIGURE 5
Radha looking at the *bhramara* bee, with other cowherd women in attendance. Painting on cloth by Bihari Lal Chaturvedi, Brindavan. Photo by Robyn Beeche.

platform was prepared from the sand of the Yamuna River and decorated with small statues of Radha's companions, as well as flowers, banana-wood carvings, and auspicious patterns drawn with colored powders. In the center was an eight-petaled lotus made of banana wood. To dedicate a shrine to a deity, an image is needed, so a photograph of the bhramara taken at its first appearance was placed in a silver frame and kept to one side until needed by the priest. During the first part of the ritual, all went as planned. But then, just at the moment when the priest asked for the photograph of the bhramara to be placed on the platform, the bhramara itself was sighted. It flew in again from the north and landed on the ground next to the octagonal platform, opposite the priests. A devotee picked it up carefully on a leaf and placed it on the platform, where it walked directly to the central lotus and installed itself underneath the flower. There it stayed quietly throughout the rest of the ceremony.

Pandemonium broke out. This time everyone saw the bhramara and began shouting and pushing to come closer. Transforming the bedlam into celebration, Maharaj-ji led the chanting devotees in several circumambulations of the platform. Throughout all this, a brahmin sat quietly a few yards from the platform, continuing to read the chapters of the *Bhagavata Purana*. After things had quieted down, the consecration ceremony continued, and throughout that evening and the next day there grew among the devotees an appreciation of the significance of the bhramara's perfectly timed appearance and precisely appropriate behavior. Maharaj-ji announced that he was now determined to restore the riverfront to its original glory, as described in the *Govindalilamrtam* and planned and built by Raja Jai Singh. He also vowed never again to go outside the boundaries of Vrindaban, and that the reading of the *Bhagavata Purana* would continue for perpetuity.

The bhramara made a third appearance two nights later. This was the night in the ritual calendar when the gods are awakened from a four-month sleep, and the auspicious season begins for marriages and other rituals. Evening pujas were held in the temple and the Goswami household, and for the first time since its consecration the new shrine was used as a ritual site. This time there was no image on the platform—the site itself was the sacred object of worship. Puja was performed: oblations of milk, honey, yogurt, *ghee,* and sugar were poured into the sand of the platform during the chanting of mantras. Then as devotional songs were being sung, the bhramara flew in. This time it stayed behind the small gathering, landing on the rug and rising repeatedly to dance and swoop in the air, with every appearance of pure happiness. There was little commotion this time—the miracle had been accepted, the manifestation of divinity was acknowledged.

A sacred space is a place where two worlds intersect. At Jaisingh Ghera, time measured in centuries (Krishna's boyhood, Caitanya's ecstatic discoveries, Jai Singh's building) came together under Maharaj-ji's direction with time measured in hours and minutes (depictions of the daily activities of Krishna, regular recitation of sacred text, and the offerings of music and song that defined and filled the space). In the moment when these two came together, the concentrated devotion of a holy man and those who looked to him for teaching had evoked the manifestation of divinity. Time and space had danced together like the flight of the bhramara. What had been and what eternally is came together to create a new beginning.

PART II • THE LIFE CYCLE

4 · Marriage

Women in India

DORANNE JACOBSON

Munni had heard older girls whispering about *mahinā*, something that happened to a woman every month. She had an idea what it was, but still she was not prepared for its happening to her. One day she found a spot on her clothes. She knew it was something embarrassing and tried to hide it, but her cousin's wife noticed it and took her aside. Bhabhi explained to Munni what *mahinā* was and told her how to deal with it. She told her to use cotton batting or even fine ash wrapped in bits of old saris and other rags for padding and to dispose of the pads very carefully. "Put them under a stone or a thick bush when you go out to eliminate. That way no one can get hold of them and do magic on them, and they won't cause trouble to anyone else." Bhabhi told Munni a trick to ensure that her period every month would be a short one. "Secretly put three dots of blood on the cowshed wall, then draw a line through one of the dots. That way your period will only be 2 1/2 days long." Bhabhi also told Munni never to touch a man or even a woman during her period. She should sit apart from others and not go to religious or social events, because a menstruating woman is considered "dirty" until she takes a full bath five days after the start of her period. After her bath, she can again enter the kitchen, draw water, and resume normal interaction with others. Muslim women do not follow all these restrictions, but they refrain from praying or touching the holy Koran.

This essay was previously published as "Marriage," in *Women in India: Two Perspectives*, ed. Doranne Jacobson and Susan S. Wadley (Columbia, MO: South Asia Books, 1977), 40–56.

Munni never discussed menstruation with her mother, and no men of the family learned of the event. But Munni's *bhābhī* quietly told Rambai, Munni's mother, "Your little girl has begun to bathe."

When she was young, Munni and her friends sometimes played "wedding." A small child posed as the bride and was draped in a white sari. Laughing children carried the "bride" to meet her "groom," a baby brother being cared for by one of the girls. But as Munni and her friends approached puberty, playing wedding was no longer fun. Their own weddings were not too far off, and the game became embarrassing.

It was very embarrassing to be married. First of all, even if a girl should want to be married, it would be shameless for her to admit it; her parents must arrange her marriage. Only a very brazen girl would ever ask questions about what it was like to have a husband. And a wife must never say her husband's name. Even to mention the name of his village is embarrassing. Sometimes girlhood friends whispered to each other about their husbands, but to discuss marriage with an older person would be shameless. Munni had heard older girls talking about sex, but she could never ask anyone about it. It is most embarrassing when a girl's husband comes to visit in her parents' village, where she does not veil her face. She must veil in front of her husband, but she should never cover her face in front of her parents. The only thing to do is run and hide. Munni knew a girl should never talk to her husband in front of anyone; it would be mortifying. Still, marriage would be very exciting, and Munni anticipated it with a mixture of eagerness and dread.

Unknown to Munni, her parents had already begun making inquires about her marriage several years before she reached puberty, and they had hoped to have the wedding before the girl "began bathing." A generation ago, parents who had an unmarried pubescent girl in the house would have been severely criticized, but today villagers are more tolerant of marriages after puberty. Still, the average age of marriage for village girls in the Bhopal area is about eleven, and brides of seven or eight are not unknown in Central India. In 1955 the government of India enacted a law providing legal penalties for those responsible for the marriage of a girl younger than fifteen or a boy younger than eighteen, but this law is widely ignored.[1] Most villagers are ignorant of its existence, and since village marriages are not registered with any government authority, "child marriage" occurs with great regularity throughout the northern half of India. In Senapur village, near Varanasi, high-caste weddings usually unite couples older than the legal age, but low-caste children often marry before twelve. Despite early marriage, most village marriages are not consummated until after a second ceremony, the *gaunā*, which usually occurs after the bride has reached puberty or is fifteen or sixteen. City brides are usually older than seventeen, and college girls typically marry after graduation. In general, the age of marriage is rising throughout India.

Munni, like most Indian girls, considered marriage to be something that would happen to her without her having to do anything to make it happen. She never for a moment worried about the possibility of becoming an old maid—even the ugliest and most deformed girls were always married, if not to the most desirable husbands. One old woman in Nimkhera, Langribai, had been stricken with a crippling paralysis when she was about nine. Though she could only creep about in a crouching position, she was wed to an older man blind in one eye. Now widowed, she is the mother of four grown children and still runs her own household. Only once did Munni hear of an unmarried girl past fifteen—an idiot girl in a distant village. Somehow, every girl's parents found her a husband.

Munni would have been startled to learn that in cities not too far from her village there are scores of spinsters. Among educated urban classes, there are nurses, teachers, social workers, and other women who for a variety of reasons have never wed. These women must walk a difficult path, for unmarried women attract attention even in cities. Forbidden by ultra-Victorian mores still in vogue in urban Indian to date men or to receive gentlemen callers who are not close relatives, the career woman must constantly guard her reputation and check her desires for pleasure. The network of communication in India is so efficient that a minor transgression would bring immediate disgrace to a woman and her family. In some coed colleges, teachers are quick to note a budding romance and report it to the girl's parents.

In rural India, too, chastity for the single girl and fidelity for the wife are considered ideal, but quietly committed sins are far from uncommon. In fact, old Mograwali sometimes whispered to Rambai's mother-in-law that they were about the only women in the village who were unsullied. This was an exaggeration, but it was true that barely a dozen of Nimkhera's 160 postpubescent females had never been the subject of innuendo or gossip. In fact, any grown girl or woman seen alone with an unrelated male is likely to be quietly criticized, but a public scandal rarely results unless a woman is extremely promiscuous or an illicit pregnancy occurs. In some areas, a woman is likened to an earthen pot that, once polluted, can never be cleansed, and a man is compared to a metal pot that is easily purified with water. Thus a promiscuous girl may find her reputation irreparably damaged, while an errant boy is forgiven. In North India, if a girl who goes to her husband pregnant is rejected by his family, she may even be killed by her own shamed father. High-ranking Muslims insist that a bride be a virgin, and the marital bedsheet may be inspected by the husband's female kin. Birjis Jahan, a Pathan Muslim, told me that a sullied bride would be returned to her family in disgrace, but she had never heard of such an incident. Hindus need pass no such test, and a village bride suspected of being nonvirgin is almost always accepted by her husband.

An unarranged "love marriage" is considered by most Indians to be a daring and perhaps ill-fated alternative to an ordinary arranged marriage. Many urban youths who have studied and dated abroad return home to wed mates selected for them by their parents. Even a tribal girl who has lovers before marriage usually expects to marry a boy chosen by her parents. Intercaste marriages (seldom arranged) occur now with increasing frequency, particularly in cities, but they are still disapproved by the vast majority of Indians. Only in the most Westernized circles, among less than 1 percent of the population, do young couples date and freely choose their own mates. (See figure D at the Web site http://www.clas.ufl.edu/users/vasu/loh.)

In Nimkhera, one Pathan Muslim couple told me proudly of their arranged "love marriage." Muslims are often encouraged to marry cousins (although North and Central Indian Hindus forbid it), and young cousins who are potential mates normally know each other well. Seventeen-year-old Latif Khan and his sixteen-year-old cousin Birjis Jahan had a crush on each other and were secretly heartbroken when Birjis Jahan's parents engaged her to an older man. "Birjis Jahan's mother offered me some of the sweets Birjis's fiance had sent to her," Latif Khan remembered, "but I couldn't take any. I said I was sick and left quickly. I felt terrible." Each hesitantly confessed their true feelings to a relative, and their parents had a conference. Soon Latif and Birjis Jahan were happily wed, and even now, as the parents of twelve children, they say their love for each other is the most important thing in their lives.

By contrast, virtually all village Hindus are married to someone they have never met before or have perhaps only glimpsed. Although a Hindu girl should marry within her own caste, her groom cannot be someone to whom she is known to be related by blood. Most Hindus belong to a named patrilineal clan *(gotra);* normally a girl cannot be matched with a youth of her own or her mother's clan. In some areas, members of other clans are also ineligible, as are members of lineages from which men of her own kin group have taken brides. From Rajasthan to Bihar, over much of northern India, a girl should not marry a boy of her own village. In the Delhi area, a boy of a neighboring village or even one in which the girl's own clan or another clan of her village is well represented must be avoided.[2] In Central India, although village exogamy is preferred, some marriages unite unrelated village "brothers" and "sisters."

Hindu men ask about available mates for their children among their in-laws and relatives in other villages, and they discuss the virtues of each candidate with their womenfolk. Munni's father and uncles spoke with many relatives and caste fellows and heard of several prospects. One youth seemed acceptable on all counts, but then Rambai learned from a cousin that his mother had been widowed before she married the boy's father. Although widow remarriage is acceptable among members of Munni's caste, children of remarried widows are considered to have a very slightly tainted ancestry. Munni's parents looked further and finally decided that the best candidate was a seventeen-year-old youth named Amar Singh, from Khetpur, a village twenty miles away. He was the eldest son of a well-to-do farmer hitherto unrelated to their family. Munni's father's brother was able to visit Khetpur on the pretext of talking to someone there about buying a bullock, and he made inquiries and even saw the youth. Amar Singh had no obvious disabilities, had attended school through the fifth grade, and his family had a good reputation. Thus, after all in the family agreed, they asked the Nimkhera barber to visit Khetpur and gently hint at a proposal to Amar Singh's family. His relatives sent their barber to similarly glimpse Munni as she carried water from the well and to learn what he could about her and her family. Before too long, the fathers of the two youngsters met and agreed that their children would be married. A Brahman examined the horoscopes and saw no obstacle to the match. Each man gave the other five rupees as a gift for his child. Later, larger gifts were exchanged in a formal engagement ceremony.

In Bengal, a prospective bride may have to pass a rigorous inspection by her prospective father-in-law. At one such public examination, a village girl was tested in knowledge of reading, writing, sewing and knitting, manner of laughing, and appearance of her teeth, hair, and legs from ankle to knee.

> Rishikumar . . . asked the girl to drop the skirt and walk a bit.
>
> The bride began to walk slowly.
>
> "Quick! more quick!" and silently the girl obeyed the order.
>
> "Now you see there is a brass jar underneath that pumpkin creeper in the yard. Go and fetch that pot on your waist, and then come here and sit down on your seat."
>
> The girl did as she was directed. As she was coming with the pot on her waist, Rishikumar watched her gait with a fixed gaze to find out whether the fingers and soles of the feet were having their full press on the earth. Because, if it is not so, the girl does not possess good signs and therefore would be rejected.[3]

The man read her palm, quizzed her on her knowledge of worship, demanded her horoscope, and asked that she prepare and serve tea. Even after he had found her acceptable and a dowry had been agreed upon, her bridegroom, eager to be modern, insisted upon seeing her—and could thus himself be seen by the girl and her people.

In cities, prospective marriage partners may exchange photographs, and the youth and his parents may be invited to tea, which the girl quietly serves to the guests. Each group assesses the other's candidate quickly under these awkward circumstances. Frequently, a girl is rejected for having too dark a complexion, since fair skin is a highly prized virtue in both village and town.

For city dwellers, matrimonial advertisements in newspapers often provide leads to eligible spouses. These advertisements typically stress beauty and education in a prospective bride and education and earning capacity in a groom. Regional and caste affiliations are usually mentioned.

> REQUIRED FOR OUR DAUGHTER suitable match. She is highly educated, fair, lovely, intelligent, conversant with social graces, home management, belongs to respected Punjabi family of established social standing. Boy should be tall, well educated, definitely above average, around thirty years of age or below, established in own business or managerial cadre. Contact Box 44946, The Times of India.

> MATRIMONIAL CORRESPONDENCE INVITED from young, beautiful, educated, cultured, smart Gujarati girls for good looking, fair complexioned, graduate bachelor, well settled, Gujarati Vaishnav Vanik youth of 27 years, earning monthly Rs. 3000/-. Girl main consideration [i.e., large dowry not important]. Advertisement for wider choice only. Please apply Box 45380, The Times of India.

Discussions of dowry are important in marriage negotiations in conservative Hindu circles in many parts of North India. The parents of a highly educated boy may demand a large dowry, while a well-educated girl's parents may not have to offer as large a dowry as the parents of a relatively unschooled girl. In Central India, dowries are not important, although expensive gifts are presented to a groom.[4] In a few groups, the groom's family pays a bride-price to the girl's kinsmen. Almost all weddings involve expensive feasts, and the number of guests to be fed is sometimes negotiated.

As her wedding approached, Munni heard her relatives discussing the preparations. She pretended not to hear but was secretly excited and frightened. No one spoke directly to her of the wedding, but nothing was deliberately kept from her.

For Munni as for other villagers, her wedding was the most important event in her life. For days she was the center of attention, although her own role was merely to accept passively what happened to her. She was rubbed with purifying turmeric, dressed in fine clothes, and taken in procession to worship the Mother Goddess. Her relatives came from far and near, and the house was full of laughter and good food. Then excited messengers brought news of the arrival of her groom's all-male entourage from Khetpur, and fireworks heralding their advent lit the night sky. Munni was covered with a white sari, so that only her hands and feet protruded, and amid a wild din of drumming, singing, and the blaring of a brass band, she was taken out to throw a handful of dust at her groom.

The next day was a rush of events, the most exciting of which was the ceremony in which she was presented with an array of silver jewelry and silken clothing by her father-in-law and his kinsmen. Under her layers of drapery, the bride could neither see nor be seen but could hear the music and talking all around her. Many of the songs, sung by the Nimkhera women and female guests, hilariously insulted the groom and his relatives. Later, at night, in the darkest recesses of the house, her mother and *bhābhī* dressed Munni in her new finery. These valuable and glistening ornaments were hers, a wonderful treasure. Bright rings were put on her toes, a mark of her impending married state. Munni's little sister watched every ritual with wide eyes, realizing that one day she too would be a bride.

The wedding ceremony itself was conducted quietly at the astrological auspicious hour of 4 A.M. by a Brahman priest, before whom the couple sat. Amar Singh looked handsome in his turban and red wedding smock, but Munni was only a huddled white lump beside him. The priest chanted and offered sacrifices to the divine, and then, in a moving ritual, Rambai and Tej Singh symbolically gave Munni away to Amar Singh. As women sang softly, the garments of the couple were tied together, and the bridal pair were guided around a small sacrificial fire seven times. With these acts, Munni and Amar Singh were wed, and Munni officially became a *bahū,* a daughter-in-law and member of her husband's lineage.

As a *bahū,* she became a symbol of fertility, of promise for the continuation of her husband's family line. She also became an auspicious *suhāgin,* a woman with a living husband. The word *suhāgin* emphasizes the concept that neither man nor woman is complete as an individual but only in their union. Traditionally, no woman except a prostitute remains unmarried, and villagers believe that men who die single become ghosts who haunt the descendants of their more fortunate brothers. For some devout individuals, asceticism may be a stage of life, but except for a few holy men, all people are expected to marry.

The next day was another round of feasting, fun fests, ceremonies, and gift giving. As a send-off for the groom's party, Munni's kinswomen playfully dashed red dye into their faces. The relatives departed, the house was quiet. Only tattered colored paper decorations and her new jewelry served to remind Munni of her change in status. Life continued as before.

But Munni and Amar Singh, though strangers to each other, were now links between two kin groups, and their male relatives began to meet each other and become friendly. Munni's relatives were always properly deferential to Amar Singh's, as befitted the kinsmen of a bride in relationship to those of her groom. It would have been improper, too, for Munni's mother to meet Amar Singh or his mother or to speak to any of his male relatives. Having given a bride to Amar Singh's family, it now would be shameful for Munni's family ever to accept their gifts or hospitality.

Among Thakurs in North India, a girl is given in marriage to a boy who belongs to a group of higher rank than her own. Thus the bride's kinsmen are not merely deferential but are considered actually inferior to the groom's kin. This lower status of the bride's family adds to the relatively low status all North Indian brides have in their new homes. Among most Muslims, however, the kin of both bride and groom consider themselves equals, particularly since they often are close blood relatives (for example, the children of two siblings may marry).

The Muslim wedding consists of a series of rituals, gift exchanges, and feasts. The couple are legally united in a simple ceremony during which both bride and groom indicate their assent to the marriage by signing a formal wedding contract in the presence of witnesses. The groom and his family pledge to the bride a sum of money, known as *mehr,* to be paid to her upon her demand. (Most wives do not claim their *mehr* unless their husbands divorce them.) During the wedding the bride and groom sit in separate rooms and do not see each other. Latif Khan's mother was married by mail to her first cousin, living hundreds of miles away, and did not see her husband for over a year.

Munni expected to spend the rest of her married life as Amar Singh's wife, but she could remarry if he died. In her caste, as among most high-ranking groups, divorce is always a possibility, but it involves shame. For a Brahman girl, her first marriage would definitely have been her last until recently. Although most Brahman widows are expected to remain celibate for life, some Brahman groups now allow young widows to remarry without suffering ostracism. Among high-ranking Muslims, divorce is relatively rare, but it does occur, and remarriage is usually easy. In educated urban Hindu circles, divorce is almost unthinkable; but among tribals and low-status Hindus and Muslims, it is not uncommon, and scandalous elopements occasionally take place. In any case, a second marriage for a woman never involves the elaborate ceremonies of the first wedding but may simply entail setting up house with a new man.

During past centuries, very high castes prohibited widow remarriage, and a widow was sometimes expected to immolate herself on her husband's funeral pyre. This practice, known as *satī*, occurred in only a very small percentage of families and was legally abolished over a century ago. Rajputs remember with pride the *jauhar*, the rite in which the widows of warriors slain in battle died in a communal funeral pyre. Today, reports of *satīs* appear in North Indian newspapers once or twice a year.

In the past, a widow was sometimes treated harshly, since the death of her husband was thought to be punishment for her misdeeds in a previous life. However, widows of lower-ranking castes have always been allowed to remarry. Under Indian law today, any woman may divorce her husband for certain causes, and any widow can remarry, but considerations of property and social acceptability rather than legality usually determine whether or not a woman seeks a divorce or remarriage. Among Hindu villagers, a widow who remarries customarily loses her rights in her husband's land. If she has young sons, a widow usually remains unmarried in order to protect her children's right to their patrimony.

In North and Central India, monogamy is generally practiced. Hindus may legally have only one wife, but Muslims are allowed four wives under both Indian and Muslim law. Village Hindus, whose marriages are seldom registered with legal authorities, occasionally take two or three wives, and the women of some Himalayan groups have several husbands.[5] Wealthy Muslim men occasionally avail themselves of their legal limit, but most cannot afford to do so. When Yusuf Miya, a Bhopal man, wanted to marry a second time, his wife spoke of suicide, and the matter was dropped. Some women, particularly those who have borne no children, do not openly object to having a co-wife. In Nimkhera, one untouchable sweeper man has four wives, all of whom contribute to his support.

Munni spent three more years in the bosom of her family, happily taking part in household and agricultural work and enjoying the frequent festivals observed in the village. Not long after her wedding, she went with her brothers and father to a fair in the district market center, where they watched the Ram Lila, a religious drama, and bought trinkets in the bazaar.

The next winter, her grandfather was stricken by pneumonia and died. This tragic event deprived the family of its patriarch and Hirabai of her husband. As she wept beside her husband's bier, her glass bangles were broken, never to be replaced. After the cremation, relatives arrived to pay their condolences and to take part in ritual gift exchanges and a large death feast. Munni joined the visiting women in weeping and singing sad songs.

The following year she went with her parents, uncle, and a large group of villagers by train on a pilgrimage to Varanasi and Allahabad, where they bathed in the sacred river Ganges. Her father's older brother carried with him a small packet of his father's charred bones, which he threw into the river. The trip was exciting and eye-opening. Although it was expensive, the journey allowed the pilgrims to carry out important religious and family obligations and was therefore considered more a necessity than a luxury.

Munni knew that her idyll among her natal kin would not last much longer. Many of her friends had already been sent to their husbands' homes, and Munni too would soon go. Her *gaunā* (consummation ceremony) was set for March. The night before her *gaunā*, Munni's *bhābhī* took her aside and told her about sex and what to expect from her husband. Munni had heard some stories from her friends but was shocked to hear the details. (Parents and children never discuss sex.) Her mother reminded her that she was going among critical strangers and that she should do whatever work was asked of her without complaint.

Beating drums and blaring trumpets soon announced the arrival of Amar Singh and a group of his male kinsmen. Munni sat passively as her mother and the barber woman dressed her in finery and ornamented her with silver. She was truly agitated: now she would meet her husband and her in-laws and see Khetpur, the village in which she would spend her adulthood. Her life would be forever changed.

Her departure from her parents, grandmother, brothers, sisters, uncles, aunts, and cousins was heartrending. Clinging to each in turn, she sobbed piteously and pleaded not to be sent away. They, too, cried as they put her in a small, covered palanquin and saw her borne away by her in-laws. With her went baskets of food and clothes and a little cousin to act as intermediary.

Heavily veiled, she was transferred to a bus and sat miserable and silent for the entire journey. At Khetpur she was put into a palanquin again and carried to her new home. Women's voices all around were talking about her, referring to her as *dulhan* (bride), *bahū* (daughter-in-law), and *nīmkherāvālī* (the woman from Nimkhera). Here in her husband's home she would never be known as Munni. There were some "games" she had to play with her husband before a group of village women who had gathered to sing and welcome her. Almost overcome with shyness and apprehension, she was made to sit near her husband and compete with him in finding some silver rings in a platter of turmeric water. Whichever partner won this game was said to be likely to dominate in the marriage. It is rare for a veiled and shy bride to win, and Munni, too, lost the competition. Then the couple were taken inside the house and told to feed each other some rice pudding. Embarrassed and awkward attempts ended when Amar Singh ran out of the house. Finally, Munni's mother-in-law escorted her to a decorated cot, left, and locked her in the room. Clutching her veil, Munni apprehensively awaited her husband. He came in quietly, after the house was silent, and put out the lamp.

Modesty required that she try to fend him off and succumb only after great protestation (even an experienced girl must feign modesty), but Munni was sixteen at her *gaunā* ceremony, and her introduction to her husband was not traumatic. Some younger girls have been genuinely terrified of their husbands, and their *gaunā* nights have involved virtual rape. One Brahman girl, Kamladevi, who met her husband when she was just thirteen, described her *gaunā* as follows:

> I had my *gaunā* when I was still little; I hadn't started bathing yet. My *bhābhī* told me about sex and what to expect; I was really frightened. I came to Nimkhera and stayed for three days. The first night I slept with Amma [her husband's grandmother]. The second night Jiji [her husband's cousin's wife] took me into the house and told me to sleep there. She said she'd be coming in shortly. She spread the blankets on the bed, and then she went out and locked the door from outside. I was really scared; I cowered near the door. I didn't know it, but he [her husband] had gone in before and hidden in the dark near the hearth. He came out then and grabbed hold of me. I let him do whatever he wanted to do; I just clenched my sari between my teeth so I wouldn't cry out. But I cried a lot anyway, and there was lots of blood. In the morning I changed my sari before I came out of the room, and bundled the dirty sari up and hid it from everyone. I had a fever; and I was so sick that some people criticized him for sleeping with such a young and weak girl. My brother came to get me on the third day and took me home.

Munni stayed in her husband's home for a week before her father and a group of male relatives came to fetch her. During the week she became acquainted with her husband and was viewed by all his female relatives and friends. Each woman paid her a small sum for the privilege of looking under her veil at her shy face with downcast eyes. All commented on her complexion (they said she was fair) and on the clothing she had brought. She spoke almost nothing to anyone but her own little cousin and Amar Singh's little sister, to whom she was *bhābhī*. Several songfests were held by the women, most of whom had themselves been brought to Khetpur as brides.

At home again, Munni unveiled, relaxed, and enjoyed her normal life for several months until her husband's father came to escort her to Khetpur again. On her second visit, she was no longer a guest but was treated more like a member of the household. She began cooking, sweeping, and grinding. Her mother-in-law was polite, and Munni docilely performed the tasks expected of her. After three weeks she again went home for several months. Munni is now a young woman of about twenty-one, the mother of a baby daughter. She continues to spend a few months of each year in her parents' home.

Not all girls have a *gaunā* ceremony. Most Muslim girls and educated urban girls marry after puberty and go immediately to their husbands' homes. Nor do all girls have such an easy transition between their natal and conjugal homes as did Munni. In much of North India, a girl is sent on her *gaunā* and remains in her husband's home for a year or more, sometimes until she has produced a child, before she is allowed to visit her parents. Such an abrupt transition is difficult for a young girl. In Senapur, among a sample of sixteen Thakur women, five had remained with their in-laws between seven and eleven years on the first or second visits there. Four had never returned to their parents' villages, because their parents had died.[6]

In Central India, older wives go home at least once or twice a year for visits and festival observances, but in parts of North India several years may elapse between visits. This is partly because of the expectation that the parents of a visiting daughter will send expensive gifts to her in-laws when she returns to them—so that few parents can afford frequent visits from their daughters. In Central India, however, a visiting daughter receives relatively modest gifts and may provide vital services in her natal home (for example, helping with the harvest or doing housework for a sick mother). Consequently, whereas a North Indian bride is clearly shifted from one household to another at her *gaunā*, the Central Indian bride may become an important participant in the activities of two households. However, the young mother may feel herself to be and may be considered to be an outsider in her marital home for some time.

Given the fact that a wife is expected to live with her husband's family, usually in a village other than that of her birth, teenage marriage makes sense. A young girl easily falls under the tutelage of her mother-in-law and can be socialized to life in her husband's family. The new bride, although the center of attention for a while, has the lowest status of any adult in her new residence. Young and alone among strangers, effaced by her veil, the bride can be happy in her new surroundings only by adjusting her behavior to satisfy her in-laws. If she quarrels with her mother-in-law, her husband cannot take her side without shaming himself before his elders. Thus she quickly learns the behavior appropriate to her role as a young *bahū* in a strange household.

Virtually every new bride longs to return to the security of her natal home. Even though she may be secretly thrilled by her relationship with her husband, a bride rarely enjoys being sequestered and ruled by her mother-in-law. Songs stress the unhappiness of the young wife in her new residence, and young girls eagerly seize any opportunity to return home. Sometimes a young wife is so unhappy she commits suicide, typically by jumping in a well. Few girls can go home when they wish; a young wife must be formally called for, with the permission of her in-laws, and escorted by a responsible male from her natal household.

For the village bride, marriage does not mark attainment of independent adulthood but signals the acquisition of a new set of relatives to whom she is subordinate. Her actions had previously been guided by sometimes indulgent parents; with marriage and *gaunā,* they fall under the control of adults who are far less likely to consider her wishes. She herself can attain a position of authority only by growing older, becoming the mother of children, and outliving her mother-in-law. Until she is at least middle-aged, a woman is usually subordinate to and protected by others.

NOTES

1. Country-wide legislation has set the minimum legal marriage age for girls at eighteen and for boys at twenty-one. The average age at which village girls in the Bhopal area marry is gradually rising, and many brides are now in their late teens.

2. Oscar Lewis, *Village Life in Northern India* (New York: Vintage Books, 1965), 160–61.

3. Tara Krishna Basu, *The Bengal Peasant from Time to Time* (Bombay: Asia Publishing House, 1962), 100.

4. Among some high-status groups of Central India, dowries are currently increasing in size and importance. Such a trend has been noted in many parts of the country.

5. D. N. Majumdar, *Himalayan Polyandry* (Bombay: Asia Publishing House, 1960), 124–32; Gerald D. Berreman, *Hindus of the Himalayas* (Bombay: Oxford University Press, 1963), 171–73.

6. Mildred Stroop Luschinsky, "The Life of Women in a Village of North India" (PhD diss., Cornell University, 1962), 350–51.

5 · Death beyond Death

The Ochre Robe

AGEHANANDA BHARATI

yadahareva virajet, tadahareva pravrajet

On the day on which he renounces,
on that very day let him sally forth.

Jābāla Upaniṣad 4

The Panjab Mail is one of the three fastest trains in India. It took me to Banaras Cantonment in seven hours. I was now entirely on my own, for I did not know anyone here, except the monks of the Ramakrishna Monastery, and I would hardly seek their company. A monk is supposed to be on his own, and I felt strong and free. I thought of Ramakrishna's advice: find a place to stay, in a new city, then put your bundle there, and, with that burden off your mind, go sightseeing. His counsel had been meant metaphorically: first place your mind in the divine resting-place, then only go and enjoy whatever this world has to offer. But the amazing thing about the Indian teachers' advice is that it usually works both ways—and I took it literally. I deposited my bundle at a rest house near Assi Ghat and went to the Ghat of the Ten Horse Sacrifices for my bath. I hesitated for a moment, pondering if I should buy some sort of container for the water, to offer it to Lord Viśvanāth. A tallish man of about fifty approached me and said, "Here is your *kamandalu,* Maharaj." I took the earthen water-pot and was fascinated by its exquisite shape. When I looked up inquiringly and to thank him, he had turned and was walking away.

I had *darśan* of Lord Viśvanāth, and then I walked back to the ghat. I knew what I was looking for: a *sannyāsī* to give me *sannyāsa*—a renunciant to give me renunciatory initiation. It was as simple as this. There were some *sādhūs* (ascetics) sitting

This essay was previously published as "Pilgrimage," in *The Ochre Robe* (London: George Allen & Unwin, 1961), 144–56.

near the Chausatthi Temple wearing the robes of Daśanāmī monks. I approached them and saluted, and they beckoned me to sit down. I told them my story. They were silent when I had finished. Then the oldest among them, a stern-looking man in his late fifties, said in an unexpectedly gentle tone, "Your effort is laudable, Brother. I have not seen anything similar in all my life. You could probably earn five hundred rupees or more and have a nice family in Germany and drive in a car. And yet you want to be a *sādhū*. But you cannot have *sannyāsa;* I believe you know that only the twice-born can enter this state?" I told Swami Sumedhānanda—that was his name—that I was well aware of the stricture, yet Vivekānanda had been a *śūdra* (the lowest of the four caste groups). "That is true, Brother," Sumedhānanda continued. "But you see, it is easier with a person who has had some sort of *saṁskāras;* and where will one draw a limit? But you are from across the ocean. I don't think any *daśanāmī* would give you *sannyāsa*. And if he did, most of us would not regard you as a *sannyāsī*." That was it. I bowed and walked away.

The next two days were days of acute suspense and dismay. I must have contacted over a hundred monks and abbots in three dozen monastic establishments. I got three types of answer: the first, given by most of the orthodox Brahmanical orders, was that I was not entitled to *sannyāsa* because of my wrong birth. There could be no question of acceptance into their order. The second answer was the sectarian one: "We will gladly accept you as our own, wherever you may come from, but you must realize—and promise you will try to realize—that Viṣṇu is the only Lord of the Universe; that Guru Kabīr taught the quintessence of the Veda and that it is upon him that you will look forthwith as your own guru; that onion and garlic are the main culprits obstructing the path to perfection." Of this type, I had had a thorough experience in the two years I had just concluded at the Mayavati Ashram of the Ramakrishna Mission. The third type of answer was procrastination: "Live with us for a while, see how we think and meditate and serve, and if we find that you fit into our way of life, and if you feel you can endure it, we shall make you one of ours in due course."

I would not have any of it, I would not be a lay hanger-on: I must be in it and of it. One way was open, and I was about to decide to take it. At Hardvar and Hrishikesh formal *sannyāsa* is easy to have; one can have it for a very modest sacrificial fee or for rendering services to the monk who initiates you. Many of the hundreds of thousands of folks wearing the ochre robe in India took their *sannyāsa* this way, I presume, if they took it at all. For there is the possibility to be what is called a *svatantrasādhū*, an independent ascetic: one dons the ochre robe, takes a monastic name, and sets out as a monk, or settles somewhere. Nobody asks a monk what he was before he became a monk—except perhaps city folks and college students. I could be a *svatantra* monk and might even be the better for it, with no affiliations of any sort, and no need to vindicate my thoughts and actions to any formal superior. Among the *svatantra* monks, there are hundreds of excellent, learned people. There are also thousands of rogues, but then there are also thousands of rogues among ordained and established monks. There is no uniform control in the Hindu monastic realm; this may change—there is talk of some sort of identification paper for a person donning the robe—but so far nothing of the kind has gained ground, and the orthodox orders vehemently oppose any such movement as infringing upon their basic freedom.

As I went to my rest house late at night to retire, I saw a small crowd of devotees sitting on the steps of the Harischandra Ghat listening to a man with a pleasant, high, and even voice. He spoke in chaste Hindi, and the people around him were listening in rapt attention. I drew closer and saw a feeble, friendly old man in the ochre of *daśanāmīs*. He was discussing *māyā*. It is *māyā* that cannot be described; the Supreme is defined and described—it is being, consciousness, and bliss. We should rest on what we know, and not on what we do not know. He chanted some passages in support; his voice was thin but not shaky; and there was a lilt in it, as there was a very slight smile on his face. It was a moonlit night, and I could see his face quite well. When the men around him dispersed after the discourse, I remained where I was. He had noticed me earlier and now he said, "So you have come to join the fold." He did not mean this in any esoteric sense; nor was it a statement of clairvoyance. He saw me in the novice's clothes, he saw I was not from Banaras, and he saw me listening to his discourse. He was old and experienced, and he must have seen many who wanted to "join the fold." I told him my problems and recounted in detail my experiences of the last two days, for he seemed to be interested. At the end of my narrative, I added, "Of course I know by now that you will not make me a *sannyāsī;* that is why I am off to Hardvar to take it from any monk who will offer it to me, regardless of his own standing and his knowledge."

The old monk held up his hand, gesturing me to silence. I fell quiet immediately, for I saw he was thinking hard. This was a strange experience and a novel one to me—novel as a Hindu monk's reaction to a problem. There was nothing sanctimonious in his face, nothing of the "I know of course" mien so common on the faces of the *sannyāsīs* who are asked a question. This was the face of a scholar pondering a difficult problem, or of a defense counsel in court. He was fingering his rosary; I do not know how long we sat in silence. After a long time he said, "I shall give you a trial, *brahmacārī* [student, the first of the four stages of life]. If it proves a failure, it is still a worthwhile risk. There is a passage in the scriptures which can be so interpreted as to entitle a man like you to *sannyāsa*, 'Whenever he renounces, he should set out.' This injunction does not necessarily refer to a Brahmin. I shall initiate you on the basis of this passage."

I was struck with awe and supreme delight. Monks at Mayavati had quoted the same passage—it is from a somewhat apocryphal Upanisad—but in a totally different context. They regarded it as a weapon against the challenge frequently put forward by the more orthodox; that one has to go through three *āśramas* (stages of life) before one can enter *sannyāsa*, the fourth and final stage.

I felt very humble and grateful. I did not ask any questions and sat with folded hands; there was nobody around now except a few boatmen at some distance, smoking their *bīḍīs*. "I shall give you *sannyāsa* on the day of the new moon, so you will have to wait for a week. Meet me tomorrow for *bhikṣā* [food donated to ascetics] and bring some *dakṣiṇā* [offering to a guru or priest]. My name is Viśvānanda Bhāratī—you have only to ask for the Swamiji from Madras at the Hanuman Ghat."

I obtained half a dozen fresh plantains, a coconut, and some oranges. I performed my meditation, attended the formal worship at the Viśvanāth Temple, and kept a full fast the next morning. As I crossed into the Ghat, a young, sturdy-looking man approached me— "Was I coming to see the *sādhū* from Madras?" Indeed I was. The man was the son of the Swami's host, an old Banarsi family, originally from western India but settled for over three hundred years in the Holy City. Swami Viśvānanda hailed from South India. In each generation of his family there had been a monk, and Viśvānanda himself took orders as a boy of eighteen, a week before he was to have married. He studied at one of the head monasteries of the Daśanāmī Order and meditated at Gangotri in the Himalayas for seven years. He had taken his bath at four Kumbha Melas and had traveled the length and breadth of India several times. He was equally conversant with Sanskrit, Hindi, Canarese, and his own mother tongue Tamil, in which language, as well as in Sanskrit, he had composed some exquisite religious treatises and hymns. Moreover, he could read English, though he would not speak it. But when I entered his room at Hanuman Ghat and prostrated myself before him, he put aside a copy of the English *Amrita Bazar Patrika*, Allahabad edition, and took off his rimless spectacles. He beckoned me to sit before him, offered me betel, which I thought rather strange on that occasion, and said, "Don't you think Bengal will go Communist in the elections?" I said I did not think so, and, on his request, with some hesitation, I told him why I thought it improbable. He nodded, then asked abruptly, "Have you brought your *dakṣiṇā?*" I pointed to a piece of cloth in which I had the fruit. "I shall instruct you now until the sun sets; then you can lie down here and rest for a few hours; at midnight I shall take you to the Maṇikarṇikā and will make you a *sannyāsī* there."

It was about 1 P.M. when he began, and it was 7:30 when he finished talking to me. He spoke about *sannyāsa,* but in a rather different manner from what I had expected, for he did not say what a *sannyāsī* should or should not do, nor what he or other *sannyāsīs* are doing, but what *I* could and should do. That was very different, in many ways, from the cut-and-dried notions Hindus entertain about *sannyāsīs.* I hardly remember any specific thing he said; but in the years to come, whenever I heard something I thought important, or whenever I felt that I was striking at a new idea, it occurred to me that it had somehow been contained in my teacher's instructions before he gave me *sannyāsa.* He told me that sex was the one great obsession of the monk's mind—in various shapes and under the pressure of control: internal control on account of his vows, external control on account of society. Now, I had been worried by sexual thoughts during my Mayavati days, yet I had not really suffered. And as though the Swami had anticipated my thoughts, he said, "It is not now, when you are a young and active monk, Brahmacārī Rāmachandra, that your mind will be much troubled by sex. The real trouble begins well after forty-five. Between then and sixty you will have a hard time, for then your body revolts, your mind panics; they want to enter into their rights ere the gates close. Chastity will come relatively easily to you for the next ten years, with no more than a little care. At your age it is hard, no doubt, and it is a very great sacrifice; but it is not at all impossible. And if you do fall, occasionally, let that not worry your mind either. Perform your prescribed penance and start all over again; that is the only way. I have not seen a monk who did not fall. In fact he must fall to rise. Only the ignorant draw a dividing line between rise and fall. And the lawyers. But we are *sādhūs,* not lawyers."

What did he advise me to do after the ceremony? "That's up to you," he said. "You may stay and have your *bhikṣā* here in Banaras for a while. Viśvānath's temple is always accessible. Or you may make a pilgrimage, as our generation of *sādhūs* used to do." I told him that I would rather like to wander and live on alms as the *sādhūs* had done from time immemorial, but was it right for me to live on alms and feed on the poor when I was not needy or indigent? Was it in accordance with the times, and with the things this newly independent country needed, that men who could actively contribute should go a-begging? "This is all nonsense," he said with an almost contemptuous gesture. "As you wander through the villages, you don't just stand there and eat. You sit under a tree or at the temple and teach. For that you get some rice or *roṭī* and *dāl.* You could teach in a college, but your teaching in the villages gives the people there a chance to learn what they would not otherwise hear for a long time yet. And if some *sādhū* teaches the children the three Rs and the adults how to make their lives a little happier and wider, is that not worth some food? Would a schoolteacher, who knows so much less and has so much less inspiration, and hardly any enthusiasm, teach in village after village for no more than some rice and *dāl?* No, Brahmacārī Rāmachandra, don't be perturbed by secularism; our work is more secular than that of paid teachers. Even if it were not, even if we did just sit and meditate, we should do no wrong—and if people don't feed us, well, we shall not survive as an order, nor perhaps as individuals. A day may well come when there will be no ochre robes in this land. There are many great people in this country who would welcome such a day. But what does that bother us? Each one must go his way. You cannot prescribe interests, and you cannot forbid interests. If you do, you are a tyrant."

The Swami taught me the etiquette of the mendicant: the poise he must develop in his dealings with other monks and with the laity, the kind of virtues he must build up to make a success of renunciation—patience, forbearance, and a sense of humor in the face of physical hardship. The instructions were numerous. At one point I felt I should take a few notes, but Viśvānanda waved the idea away: "Don't write these things down; that wouldn't help you. They will come back to your mind as you need them. You don't need all these instructions at once; you need them for particular situations. Why, at times you will have to put up a show of anger, though calmness is a permanent discipline for the monk. There are no hard-and-fast rules that apply to all situations, and there are none for critical hours: then your own wisdom must decide."

It must have been around six in the evening, and Swami Viśvānanda was about to dismiss me, but as I got ready to retire, he said in a somewhat casual tone, "There is one thing which you will do well to remember. I shall take you as a full *sannyāsī* after midnight tonight; others, similarly inclined, will too. But there will be very many who will not take your *sannyāsa* seriously. There will be the orthodox, whom your learning and your renunciation will not impress in the least. You are not entitled to *sannyāsa;* you are no Brahmin by birth. You have known this story for some time, and you have spent the last two days experiencing it in your own body. Maybe you will grow in spiritual stature to such an extent that some who will not accept you now will accept you later. But very many will never accept you, even if you were the ādiguru incarnate. Do not mind this too much, even when it hurts. Set up a criterion for yourself: the minimum criterion of the Scripture. What is the minimum criterion? 'Having renounced the desire for wealth, for sons, the fear of social opprobrium and the love of social approval, they sally forth, begging their food.' This is the minimum criterion. So long as you feel you satisfy this criterion, you are a *sannyāsī*. If you do not, you are not a *sannyāsī* even if you are born of a Nambudiri father and a Nambudiri mother. Now go and lie down, and be ready before midnight. Try to sleep—for the *brahmacārī* will die tonight—it is your last sleep . . . as a *brahmacārī*," he added with a smile.

I woke up at a quarter before midnight. I took a quick bath downstairs and put on a clean *laṅgoṭhī* (loincloth), the last white *laṅgoṭhī* I should wear. I had already dyed a set of robes with the *gerrua* color that I had bought weeks earlier at the bazaar in Loha Ghat. I hesitated to take the dyed cloth along and called a servant, asking him to find out from the Swamiji whether he wanted me to take the dyed cloth with me to the ghat. But the Swami had already left an hour earlier. I told the servant to take the cloth and to follow me at a distance.

It was a fifteen-minute fast walk to the Maṇikarṇikā Ghat, through the meandering alleys of Banaras (see figure 6). I hastened my steps. The air was bright and incense laden; people looked at me more than usual, as though they sensed that I was on an important errand. There loomed the four dark silhouettes of the temples near the ghat. I stopped for a moment at the Maṇikuṇḍa, the deep well—allegedly unconnected with the Ganges from which it is separated by no more than fifteen yards—into which Śiva's earring fell when he was carrying the dead Satī on his shoulders. From time immemorial, this has been the most important cremation ground in India. Pious Hindus consider it great spiritual merit to die near this ghat and to have their bodies cremated there. Day and night, the pyres burn. One can see them from a great distance, even from the train coming in over the bridge, from Moghul Serai, when one travels at night. Corpses seem to burn brighter on this ghat. I never saw funeral pyres from so great a distance as I did here, for the bridge is at least two miles east of the ghat.

I did not quite know where to find the *ācārya*, the senior *sādhū;* there were several monks about and several *brahmacārīs*. I found out that about half a dozen novices were to take *sannyāsa* here tonight. Swami Jagadīśvarānanda, a famous monk from Hardvar, was to confer *sannyāsa* on four young men, a monk told me. "Do you know if Viśvānandaji will give *sannyāsa* to anyone?" I questioned him. "The Madrasi Sādhū? Yes, I heard he is giving *sannyāsa* to a *mlecchā* [foreigner]! What do you think of that?" "Is it quite impossible?" It was too dark for him to see my color. "How do I know?" the monk answered with a shrug. "It is certainly not customary. But the Madrasi Sādhū is a learned man. He must know what he is doing."

A tall swami, obviously a Northerner from his looks and his intonation, approached

FIGURE 6
Maṇikarṇikā Ghat, Banaras, where Agehananda Bharati received his midnight initiation, becoming a *sannyāsī*. Photo by John Hawley.

me, saying, "Hurry, Brahmacārī Rāmachandra, the *ācārya* is waiting for you." But when I came within sight of Swami Viśvānanda, he was reclining in a niche in the Durgā Temple and said calmly, "Oh, you have come fast. There is still half an hour. Go and worship the Devī. You have been wanting to; this is the time." Until that moment I had not known that I wanted to worship Her. I went to Her shrine on top of the Maṇikarṇikā, and I worshipped Her. As I rose to leave, Viśvānanda was standing at the temple entrance. "Follow me now," he said. He walked swiftly toward the cremation ground, and I followed him. The pyres are about five yards from the road that winds its way through the ghat; the stakes are set on a platform that cannot be seen from the road, though it is visible from the river. We ascended the platform. There were three burning pyres: one of them almost extinct, two burning violently with a bright flame and vehement crackling sounds. This is the stage at which even the *dāhasarīs* (the Dom-caste "burners," who officiate) no longer distinguish whether the fires are produced by the firewood or the bones of the corpse. Two dead bodies were being made ready for the cremation, one that of a young woman with her stillborn child tied to her under the same red cloth, the other that of a middle-aged man. The heat was intense, but I was only mentally aware of it—it did not seem to cause perspiration. The stench was powerful, but somehow my mind grouped it with the other external paraphernalia of the consecration.

The moment Swami Viśvānanda appeared the *dāhasarīs* bowed low with folded palms and withdrew from the platform. It appeared as though they had been told there was going to be a *sannyāsa* ceremony that night. There must be many throughout the year, although the time-honored custom of bestowing *sannyāsa* on an actual cremation ground is fast falling into disuse, as is the taking of *sannyāsa* in general. I had asked the Swami earlier whether the injunctions of the relevant texts were incumbent on every candidate. "They are, and they are not," he had said. "Some take them literally; some interpret them. Some give *sannyāsa* to *brahmacārīs* on real cremation grounds. I always do, especially when we are so fortunate as to have the Maṇikarṇikā at our doorstep. Some wander through the whole land begging their food, practicing the text 'they set out, begging their food' literally; others declare a well-built house, a fine mansion, or a temple to be the cremation ground, and beg their food in town for the rest of their lives—no one blames them. Why should they not?" Then, after a while, he had added, "You will have to make the choice yourself, Brahmacārī Rāmachandra. If you want me to give you *sannyāsa* in this house, I shall, because I have decided that you should have it. And if thereafter you want to take your *bhikṣā* here at Viśvānath's Darbar, then that will be your great pilgrimage. It is for you to decide." I made my decision then and there. I would have *sannyāsa* on the cremation ground proper, and I would beg my food on the roads, as had the mendicants of yore.

A *maṇḍala* had been drawn near the center of the platform in red and white and of the prescribed form. I sat down, and now I noticed that I was sitting in the geometrical center of an almost equilateral triangle formed by three pyres. Swami Viśvānanda sat in front of me and did *ācamana* (a ritual act of sipping water) with his left hand: the left hand rules over rituals connected with *sannyāsa,* whereas the right hand functions on all other occasions. He lit another fire from sandalwood, placing it between himself and the *maṇḍala* wherein I was sitting. He handed me two handfuls of sesamum seed and kept about the same amount. The chant began: *tilāñjuhomi sarasāṃ sapiṣṭān gandhāra mama citte ramantu svāhā* . . . (I offer this oblation of sesamum, with its juice, with its ground particles, the well-scented ones. May they delight my mind, *svāhā*. The bulls, wealth, gold, food and drink—to the Goddess of Wealth may they go. May these sesamum seeds, the black ones and the white ones, liberate me from all blemishes. May I be free from debts to the gods, manes, parents, the world. . . . May the five winds in me be purified, so I be light, free from blemish, having renounced. . . . I am now beyond life and death, hunger and grief, satisfaction and dissatisfaction.) With twenty-three *svāhās,* the sesamum and the rest of the oblational ingredients were thrown into the *virajā-homa,* the fire of final renunciation. Lastly the *ācārya* cut off the *śikhā* (topknot) from my head—the well-trained, well-oiled, stately *śikhā*—and threw it into the fire as the last gift.

The Swami asked me to stand up. I followed him to another, much smaller platform that I had not seen before. Here was a small pyre of wood, not yet alight. I was asked to lie on it. The Swami approached with a firebrand and some live charcoal. He touched my body in seven places. Symbolically, the pyre was set on fire. Symbolically, I was now being cremated. As I stood up, I made my own obsequial rite, with the *mantras* that are chanted by the living for the dead. I was now dead, though the body lived. It signifies: when the *sannyāsī* says "I," he does not mean his body, not his senses, not his mind, not his intellect. "I" means the cosmic spirit, the Brahman, and it is with This that he henceforth identifies himself. This is the only important difference between the monk and the layman. The layman too is Brahman, and so is all that lives. The monk is Brahman too, but the monk is aware of it, the *sannyāsī* is aware of nothing else. Or at least, he should be aware of nothing else. I now threw off my white novice's robe and all the other items of the neophyte wardrobe—they are not many—and walked down the few steps into the Ganges, with the four directions as my garments.

The municipality of Banaras is a puritan municipality, like all the municipalities in India. Even corpses would not be tolerated in the nude. However, it appears that for *sannyāsa* consecrations some special arrangement is made lest offense be given to the occasional late bathers and to municipal orders: people are just asked to move away whenever novices step into their last bath.

As I emerged from Gaṇgā's womb, Swami Viśvānanda, who had followed me, gave me the ochre robe, which I donned immediately. "Victory to you, HOMELESS BLISS, Victory, Master Agehānanda Bhāratī, be thou a light to the three worlds"—he spoke loudly and distinctly. This then was the name he had chosen for me, and he must have known why. Bliss through homelessness, bliss that is homelessness, bliss when there is no home—the Sanskrit compound of the privative prefix *a* + *geha* + *ānanda* covers all of these meanings.

He then gave me the *daṇḍa* (monk's staff); I bowed to it and flung it far into the River, saying, "Keep this *daṇḍa*, Mother Gaṇgā, for I have no more leisure for rules. The Supreme Swans are not bound by any rules, the *paramahaṁsas* do not carry the rod of rules and rites. They are free."

"Come with me, Swami Agehānanda," said Swami Viśvānanda softly. "Choose whom you will honor by taking your first *bhikṣā*." Then I remembered that I had promised his host that I would take my first food from him. But when we left the ghat, there was a crowd of more than a dozen people, both men and women, with lovely food in plantain leaves. They thronged around me, touched my feet, begging me to take their food, or at least a morsel of it. "It is thought to be supremely meritorious to give a *sannyāsī* his first food," said Viśvānanda. "Have you already promised anyone that you would honor him or her?" He asked this in slow, but good English. I had not known before that he could speak English at all. I told him, in English, that I had promised his host. "Then you have to accept his offering. That settles it."

The Swami's host had a large tray of dainties ready for me and placed it at my feet. I sat down and ate, for this corpse was hungry—and very, very thirsty.

I withdrew for the few hours left of this night and slept as befits the dead. The sun was high when I woke. Viśvānanda was sitting beside me and was chewing betel. He smiled when I greeted him. "Take your bath first, Agehānanda Mahārāj, then we shall talk."

There was tea and there were *laḍḍūs* and *jalebīs* (two Indian sweets) when I came back from my bath. "What will you do now, Agehānanda?" he asked. What ought I to do, Mahārāj?" "It is for you to decide, for as I said, it is your own choice whether you take the traditional directives literally or not. You may set out on a pilgrimage to the seven holy places or you may walk through Bhārat (India) or you may stay here. I would only suggest that you spend another week here meditating. Would you avoid the cremation ground for a while?" There was not really any challenge in these words, but there was a mild implication. I said, "My mind is made up, Mahārāj. I wanted to leave this morning, to walk through Bhārat. But now as you ask me to, I shall stay on for a week and meditate." "It is very good," he nodded. "You will be a literal *sannyāsī*," he added with a faint smile.

I meditated on the roof of the Annapūrṇā Temple during the next seven days, and on the cremation grounds on the Maṇikarṇikā Ghat during the six nights in between, sitting about thirty yards from the spot where I had died. There is the outward cremation ground; it has to be transferred into one's mind—the *sannyāsī*'s mind is the hypostasized cremation ground. The physical crematorium is but a symbol for the inner one. Without the inner, the physical cremation is of no avail—without the inner cremation, it is like a horror play on the stage. As a material location, the cremation ground is a farce like all places of burial, but informed by transference into an object of meditation on the inane universal evanescence as well as into a simile for the mind wherein the desires have been burnt up, it is a thing of hallowed beauty and great purity.

After a week, I went to take leave of Swami Viśvānanda Bhāratī. I told him I was going on the great pilgrimage through India. I said I wanted to be as "literal" as he suggested, and I asked him if he would suggest an approximate route. He shrugged his shoulders with what seemed to me mild annoyance, and then said: "I have told you already that all this is up to you. What do I care? You are a *sannyāsī* like myself. You are on your own. What difference does it make where you go?"

PART III · FESTIVAL

6 · Divali

The Festival of Lights

OM LATA BAHADUR

Divali marks one of the biggest and grandest celebrations in India. Divali is also known as the Festival of Lights. On this day, Lord Ram (the incarnation of Lord Vishnu in the Treta Yug) returned to his capital Ayodhya after the exile of fourteen years thrust upon him by his stepmother Kaikeyi in jealousy, because Ram would become the king and not her own son Bharat. Thousands of years have passed, and yet so ideal is the kingdom of Ram *(ram rajya)* that it is remembered to this day.

Divali comes exactly twenty days after Dussehra on Amavas (new moon), during the dark fortnight of Kartik some time in October or November. The exact date is taken from the Hindu calendar, and since that calculation is different from the European calendar, we cannot give the exact date according to the Western system.

By Dussehra the evildoer Ravan has been eliminated—along with most of his *rakshasas* (demons)—by Lord Ram and his brother Lakshman, and their army of monkeys. Sita has been returned to her husband Ram, and they now make their way to Ayodhya in triumph and glory. Kaikeyi, meanwhile, has done enough penance for the misery caused to the family and the kingdom. Bharat had refused to sit on the throne and has kept vigil as a regent and had told Ram that if he did not return on the last day of the fourteen years' exile, he would immolate himself. Consequently, to commemorate the return of Ram, Sita, and Lakshman to Ayodhya people cele-

This essay was previously published as "Diwali," *The Book of Hindu Festivals and Ceremonies* (New Delhi: UBS Publishers' Distributors, 1994), 208–19.

brate Divali with the bursting of crackers and by lighting up their houses with earthen *diyas* or other lamps in the grandest style, year after year.

The thirteenth day of the dark fortnight—that is, two days before Divali—is known as Dhan Teras. On this day a new utensil is bought for the house. The house has to be cleaned, washed, and whitewashed. On this day the children are taken out to buy crackers, candles, earthen *diyas*, and a *hatri* (a small houselike structure made of mud, in the middle of which sits a small idol of Lakshmiji). A pair of earthen Lakshmiji and Ganeshji are a must for Divali *pujan*. (Ganeshji is to be worshipped before any other god or goddess in all *pujas*.) Lakshmiji, the goddess of wealth, is supposed to visit everyone during Divali; therefore she must also be fussed over. Earthen *katoris* (dishes) known as *kulris* and *chaugaras*, lots of *kheel* (puffed rice), toys made out of candy (known as *khand ke khilone*), *batashas* (hollow sugar-cakes), and so on are required for the *puja*. The markets are extremely well decorated and full of items that one can buy for the home.

Special foods like *papri* and *deevlas* are made at home. The day prior to Divali is known as Chhoti Divali. On that day Hanuman (Pavanputra or son of the God of Wind), the great *bhakta* (worshipper) of Lord Ram, had come flying to Ayodhya to inform the family and the kingdom that Ram, Sita, and Lakshman were coming back the following day so that arrangements to welcome them could be made (of course in a great hurry). Today, we have more time at our disposal, and so we start the celebrations much earlier. On Chhoti Divali, *mithai* (sweets) are displayed by gaily decorated and well-lit shops, and they do very brisk business. Many business houses and individuals distribute *mithai* to their associates, families, and friends. A lot of visiting is done on this day. The business community begins its new year from this day.

One word of caution—one must remain within a budget. Almost everything bought during Divali time is of little use later on, except utensils, and a few other durables, so please do the buying by your own standards and not the neighbors'! One should remember that twenty-one or fifty-one *diyas* are bought (although candles are much in use these days). This is just to keep the old tradition alive and maintain a continuity from time immemorial right up to this very day. In case one is in another country, where one cannot get *diyas*, then one just has to make do with candles. One big *diya* is definitely required for the center and can be made with *atta* dough. The *diyas* are filled with oil (ordinary mustard oil), and wicks are made from old cottonwool. Please soak the *diyas* in water for a couple of hours and dry them before use, as they will soak up the oil very fast if used absolutely new.

Now let us get to the ceremonial side of Divali, so as to make it an attractive occasion for the family. Even if no one is invited, it is a busy day in itself. The *puja* starts on Chhoti Divali itself, when the place of worship is decorated with a small *chauk* made with wet *kharia matti*. Most Indians know how to decorate the floor with colors, but the quickest one is with *kharia matti*. Flowers and leaves can be the motifs of the floor decorations; or else geometrical designs can be made. A *chauki* or a *patta* (low stool or leaf) should also be decorated and placed against the wall of the place of worship to seat the gods, namely, Ganeshji and Lakshmiji along with (idols or pictures of) Ram, Sita, Lakshman, and Hanuman. Empty *diyas* or unlit candles are decorated before the *puja*, and everyone then does the *pujan*. (See figure E at the Web site http://www.clas.ufl.edu/users/vasu/loh.)

On the main Divali day, a morning bath is essential. In South India to bathe before sunrise, after a good oil massage, is considered very auspicious. A bath in starlight, before sunrise, is accepted as a bath in the holy Ganga (since the Milky Way is considered the river's heavenly form). In North India, gambling is freely allowed during the festival; usually card games are played. The children are also given money to play and join in the fun. They are even allowed to gamble in front of their parents so that they don't do it in secret. They then understand that there is a time and place even for gambling, but it must have certain limitations. These children seldom grow up to be gamblers. Gambling goes on for about a week or two, in one house or the other, and then it stops until the next Divali.

Regarding the ceremony itself, during my grandmother's time, we always used to get the whitewashing of the house done before Divali, especially the place where the *puja* was to be performed. Usually, a more open place than the *puja* room (a covered verandah is ideal) is used for the *puja*. A Madhubani type of painting was made, depicting several episodes of Lord Ram, Sita, Lakshman, Hanuman (and even Krishna with his Gopis and *raas leelas*), and the other gods. These depictions were all confined to a square or oblong limited space. A border of flowers was used to frame the painting. The painting was made by attaching cotton wool to small sticks and taking ordinary colors mixed with water in small *katoris*. The women and children all got together and filled the colors into the forms already made by the artist of the family. This kept everyone busy for a week or two preceding Divali. The drawings of the faces of the gods, Gopis, and animals were always a side view. At the center of the painting, Lakshmiji was depicted in the Madhubani style, formed by joining a number of dots together so that a face appeared with a *chunni* (spangle) on top of it. The dots were all prearranged. Of course, one can draw Lakshmiji or glue down a picture of her, but the joining of dots to form a picture is the basic way of teaching a child to draw. Thus as the wall became the canvas and everyone was filling in the colors, producing a beautiful picture, art was encouraged and taught to the children. Such togetherness is rarely found these days.

During the actual Divali day, people still drop in with sweets and crackers and other presents, and some visit elders of the family and the community out of respect. On this day, businesspeople also give presents to those working for them. Businesspeople are very particular about doing Lakshmi *puja* in their shops or offices. There is no fasting on Divali. The daughters-in-law and girls of the house are given new saris and jewelry. A new bride gets a heavier sari than the rest. This is not obligatory in North India, but very much so in South India.

In the evening, before dark, the actual *pujan* is done. First, the place of the *puja* is decorated with candles, *diyas,* and the earthen *hatri,* which is placed in the center. The pictures of several gods and goddesses—Lakshmi, Ganesh, Ram, Sita, Lakshman, and Hanuman—are placed on the *patta*. The *kulri* and *chaugara* dishes are filled with puffed rice *(kheel)* topped with a toy made out of candy; *papris* and *deevlas* are also kept on top. Sweets and fruit are placed on the side of the *puja patta* in a *thaal* (tray). The new utensil, bought for this purpose, is filled with *kheel* and kept on the side. Of course, everyone is dressed very well, in colorful and shining clothes, so that they shimmer in the *diya* or candlelight. The married girls *(suhagins)* can wear their *chunri* with its *gota* and *kinari* if they so desire. But a *chonp* (golden *bindi* dot) is a must on the forehead for the *suhagans*. Now, everyone is ready for the *puja*, which is done first by putting the *teeka* (forehead mark) on the gods and everyone present, and then worshipping the gods with water, *aipun, roli,* and rice. Everyone takes a little rice in one hand, and the story related to Divali is narrated, which goes as follows.

There was once a king who loved his queen very, very much. One day the king summoned the best jeweler in his kingdom and asked him to make a magnificent necklace costing nine hundred thousand rupees (nine lakhs) for the queen. When it was made it was so beautiful that the queen wore it all the time and wherever she went. She looked so very beautiful with the nine-lakh necklace around her neck that everyone stared at her.

Every morning she would go to the river to bathe with her ladies-in-waiting. She would take off her jewelry and fancy clothes and put them on the riverbank. One day, she did just that and was happily playing and splashing in the river when a kite came flying over the place, and seeing a shiny object, it swooped down and took the necklace away. (Kites love to take shiny objects to their nests for their young ones to get excited about, and also to decorate their homes with glitter.) When the queen came out of the river and found, to her dismay, that her necklace was missing, she was distressed beyond measure, and no one could console her. She fretted so much that the king heard of it within a few minutes and came to find out what had happened. He was also very, very upset and announced, there and then, that whosoever found the necklace would be given anything he or she desired. A man with a *dholak* (drum) went around making the announcement all over the kingdom, and everyone came to know of the great loss suffered by the queen and that the discovery of the necklace would make the person who found it rich beyond his or her wildest dreams. So everyone did nothing but look for the beautiful necklace and talk about it at their homes and in the marketplaces. The queen could not be consoled. She gave up eating and drinking, and the king was also very unhappy and kept inquiring of his servicemen as to the progress made in the matter.

Now, there used to be a very old and poor woman who lived right outside the town, just where the forest began. She used to make her livelihood by selling wood and sticks for lighting fires, which helped her meet her meager daily needs. She had no one else to look after her, as her children were away, and she had to do her own household chores and shopping. In any case, she could not buy much, as she was very poor. As Divali was approaching, she was cleaning her hut, which was very dark and dingy because it was near the forest. In a dark corner of her hut, she saw a *patragho* (a large lizardlike animal found in the forest). She killed it and threw it on her thatched roof. At this very moment, the kite with the necklace was flying past, and its eyes fell on the dead animal. The kite thought that food was better than the glittering object that it was carrying. So it dropped the necklace on the thatched roof and made off with the dead *patragho*. The old woman heard the noise and on seeing something shiny on the roof brought it down and found, to her amazement, the most beautiful necklace that one could imagine. She knew at once that it must belong to the queen. Soon she heard about the king's announcement and the misery in the palace. So she went and asked for an audience with the king. The king was surprised, but he was a good and kind person, and so the old woman was brought before him. She asked him whether he would stand by what he had promised through his announcement. The king looked hopeful and solemnly declared that he would do as he had promised.

"I have it here," the old woman said and took the necklace out of her torn jute bag, much to the amazement of all the courtiers, who looked startled and wondered what the old woman would ask for. They, as well as the king, expected her to ask for half the kingdom, or any amount of wealth, but she did not. Do you know what she asked for? "Sire, please order everyone that on Divali day no one will light up their houses except me, and the palace shall also be dark." The king was stunned but heaved a sigh of relief at the strange request and granted it at once. He was afraid that the old woman might change her mind. This was hardly a thing to think twice about. Everyone talked at length about this odd request—in the marketplaces, in their homes, and in the palace. Wise men shook their heads perplexed, not understanding what it would fetch the old woman.

Divali was near, and soon the day dawned. People were told that not a single light should be seen, or else they would be punished with death—even the king's palace stood in total darkness as the sun went down. There was pitch darkness everywhere, and only one *diya* twinkled in the old woman's house, far away in a corner of the landscape. The old woman just did what she was used to doing all her life during Divali, and lit only one *diya*, being too poor to afford any more.

At the stroke of midnight, Lakshmiji came down from the heavens in her glittering clothes so that they would shine all the more in the beautiful lights of the houses and palaces that she would visit. She loved a lot of light and gaiety, and so she visited those houses that were bright and shining. Today she was perplexed, for she could hardly move without stumbling against a pillar or post and nearly fell at several places. She was so miserable that she scanned the horizon for some light somewhere, and then she saw the little glimmer from the old woman's hut. She made a dash for it, because by now she was completely desperate.

Inside her hut, the old woman had bolted the door and had sat down to do her *puja* with her old, broken earthen utensils. Soon she saw a very bewildered and desperate-looking tiny little man, who came running to her side in great agitation, shouting, "Let me out, let me out, old woman. I cannot stand this light, I must get out at once. I am used to darkness and dinginess and dampness. I could stay but for this light."

The old woman gave him one look and asked, "Who are you, you funny-looking tiny man?"

"I am Diladdar (Absolutely Down and Out One), companion of the very poor," replied the old man. The old woman spoke to him thus: "You cannot leave me, Diladdar. You have been my constant companion year after year, and I cannot let you go. I will not allow you to go."

"O woman, have pity on me. I will die in this illuminated house. I am one who can only live in darkness and dirt, and not in light and cleanliness. There is lovely darkness all over the town tonight. Please, please, open the door."

Outside Lakshmiji was standing at the door and pleading in her lovely soft voice, "Sweet lady, I am distressed. Please show me the light and let me in—yours is the only house in which I can feel comfortable and happy. I cannot see the other houses. I cannot even see my own feet, and I am frightened. Please, please, let me in." The old woman replied, "No, no, I will not let you in; you have never bothered about me before. Why should I take pity on you?" But Lakshmiji pleaded with her. So the old woman asked her, "If I let you in, will you promise that you will never leave and will always stay in my house? If you promise me that, I will let you in." Lakshmiji replied, "Yes, yes, I promise. I will not leave your house ever."

At the same time Diladdar was shouting himself hoarse to be let out. The old woman told him, "You promise that you will never come anywhere near my house again. Only then will I let you out." "I promise, I promise," cried Diladdar.

Quickly, the old woman opened the door, and immediately Lakshmiji entered. Seeing her, Diladdar became more frightened, and he just fled into the darkness.

Very soon, the old woman summoned back all her children, who had gone away to other towns in search of food and money, to come and live with her, and they returned, and everyone lived happily ever after.

After the story is finished, all members shower the puffed rice that they have been holding in their hands on Lakshmiji and Ganeshji, saying loudly, "Get out, Diladdar. Lakshmiji has come *(Nikal Diladdar Lakshmi aayee),*" repeating this thrice.

The lady of the house then takes one *chaugara* cup, places the *prasad* on top of it, and gives it to each member present. This can be done in two installments because fruit and sweets have also to be given as *prasad,* and it is difficult to give everything all at once. Each member then takes a little puffed rice from the *prasad* and puts it inside the *hatri,* in which a silver rupee has already been placed. The *hatri* symbolizes the home; and the silver coin, the wealth of the house being saved inside it. The gesture of putting puffed rice *(kheel)* in the *hatri* is symbolic of India's basic identity as an agricultural country, and of the members of each household bringing their share of produce into the house.

The *diyas* from the *puja* are then taken to light the *diyas* or candles already placed around the house and on top of it. These *diyas* are lit only after the *puja.* The first *diya* is placed where one throws the garbage; the belief being that there is prosperity in a house where there is a lot of garbage. *Pujan* should be started at dusk, as the *diyas* or candles are lit after the *puja.* Fireworks are brought out, and the children join in the fun and frolic with all the noise and light from the *phuljharis* ("flower pots") and other crackers. Fireworks are also distributed to the servants and their children, so that there is universal enjoyment. Then start the feast and card games, which are the "order of the night." One can carry on for as long as one likes. In some cases, sons-in-law of the house are given some money as a token, along with a peg of whisky. The nondrinkers can just take the money. Thus Divali is celebrated as one of the biggest and grandest festivals of India.

A recipe for a delicious dish prepared during Divali follows.

Mandhi

INGREDIENTS AND OTHER ITEMS

1 *karahi*
1 *thaali* or *parat*
3/4 cup water
1 cup sugar
150 gm (1 1/2 cups) *suji*
250 gm (+ 50 gm if required for dipping the *rotis*) *maida*
6 dessert spoons (tablespoons) *ghee* or cooking oil for deep frying

METHOD

Warm the water in a pot. Then remove from the heat, and mix the sugar into the water. Put this mixture aside. Sieve the *maida* and *suji* and mix. Add 6 dessert spoons of melted *ghee* or oil, and knead into the breadcrumb stage. Sieve the sugar and water through a fine sieve. Blend the sugar-and-water mixture slowly with the breadcrumb-stage dough, and knead further into a soft dough. Roll out individual flat balls as for *puri;* if they stick, use a little dry *maida*. The thickness should be 1/4" or even a little more.

Pour the *ghee* or oil for deep frying into a *karahi*, and heat until very hot; then reduce the fire to low and start frying, adjusting the fire as needed. Fry to dark brown, two *mandhis* at a time. This recipe will yield about 14 *mandhis.*

7 · Holi

The Feast of Love

McKIM MARRIOTT

The intent of this essay is to interpret Krishna and his cult as I met them in a rural village of northern India while I was conducting my first field venture as a social anthropologist. The village was Kishan Garhi,[1] located across the Jumnā from Mathurā and Vrindāban, a day's walk from the youthful Krishna's fabled land of Vraja.

As it happened, I had entered Kishan Garhi for the first time in early March, not long before what most villagers said was going to be their greatest religious celebration of the year, the festival of Holī. Preparations were already under way. I learned that the festival was to begin with a bonfire celebrating the cremation of the demoness Holikā. Holikā, supposedly fireproofed by devotion to her demon father, King Harnākas, had been burned alive in the fiery destruction plotted by her to punish her brother Prahlāda for his stubborn devotion to the true god, Rāma.[2] I observed two priests and a large crowd of women reconstructing Holikā's pyre with ritual and song: the Brahman master of the village site with a domestic chaplain consecrated the ground of the demoness's reserved plot; the women added wafers and trinkets of dried cow-dung fuel,[3] stood tall straws in a circle around the pile, and finally circumambulated the whole, winding about it protective threads of homespun cotton. Gangs of young boys were collecting other combustibles—if possible in the

This essay was previously published as "The Feast of Love," in *Krishna: Myths, Rites, and Attitudes*, ed. Milton Singer (Honolulu: East-West Center Press, 1966), 200–212, 229–31.

form of donations, otherwise by stealth—quoting what they said were village rules, that everyone must contribute something and that anything once placed on the Holī pyre could not afterward be removed. I barely forestalled the contribution of one of my new cots; other householders in my lane complained of having lost brooms, parts of doors and carts, bundles of straw thatch, and an undetermined number of fuel cakes from their drying places in the sun.

The adobe houses of the village were being repaired or whitewashed for the great day. As I was mapping the streets and houses for a preliminary survey, ladies of the village everywhere pressed invitations upon me to attend the festival. The form of their invitations was usually the oscillation of a fistful of wet cow-dung plaster in my direction, and the words "Saheb will play Holī with us?" I asked how it was to be played, but could get no coherent answer. "You must be here to see and to play!" the men insisted.

I felt somewhat apprehensive as the day approached. An educated landlord told me that Holī is the festival most favored by the castes of the fourth estate, the Śūdras. Europeans at the district town advised me to stay indoors, and certainly to keep out of all villages on the festival day. But my village friends said, "Don't worry. Probably no one will hurt you. In any case, no one is to get angry, no matter what happens. All quarrels come to an end. It is a *līlā*—a divine sport of Lord Krishna!" I had read the sacred *Bhāgavata Purāṇa*'s story about Prahlāda and had heard many of its legends of Krishna's miraculous and amorous boyhood.[4] These books seemed harmless enough. Then, too, Radcliffe-Brown had written in an authoritative anthropological text that one must observe the action of rituals in order to understand the meaning of any myth.[5] I had been instructed by my reading of Malinowski, as well as by all my anthropological preceptors and elders, that one best observes another culture by participating in it as directly as possible.[6] My duty clearly was to join in the festival as far as I might be permitted.

The celebration began auspiciously, I thought, in the middle of the night as the full moon rose. The great pile of blessed and pilfered fuel at once took flame, ignited by the village fool, for the master of the village site had failed to rouse with sufficient speed from his slumbers. "Victory to Mother Holikā!" the shout went up, wishing her the achievement of final spiritual liberation rather than any earthly conquest, it seemed. A hundred men of all twenty-four castes in the village, both Muslim and Hindu, now crowded about the fire, roasting ears of the new, still green barley crop in her embers. They marched around the fire in opposite directions and exchanged roasted grains with one another as they passed, embracing or greeting one another with "Rām Rām!"—blind in many cases to distinctions of caste. Household fires throughout the village had been extinguished, and as the assembled men returned to their homes, they carried coals from the collective fire to rekindle their domestic hearths. Many household courtyards stood open with decorated fire-pits awaiting the new year's blaze. Joyful celebrants ran from door to door, handing bits of the new crop to waking residents of all quarters or tossing a few grains over walls when doors were closed. As I entered a shadowy lane, I was struck twice from behind by what I thought might be barley, but found in fact to be ashes and sand. Apart from this perhaps deviant note, the villagers seemed to me to have expressed through their unified celebration of Holikā's demise their total dependence on each other as a moral community. Impressed with the vigor of these communal rites and inwardly warmed, I returned to my house and to bed in the courtyard.

It was a disturbing night, however. As the moon rose high, I became aware of the sound of racing feet: gangs of young people were howling "Holī!" and pursuing each other down the lanes. At intervals I felt the thud of large mud-bricks thrown over my courtyard wall. Hoping still to salvage a few hours of sleep, I retreated with cot to the security of my storeroom. I was awakened for the last time just before dawn by the crash of the old year's pots breaking against my outer door. Furious fusillades of sand poured from the sky. Pandemonium now reigned: a shouting mob of boys called on me by name from the street and demanded that I come out. I perceived through a crack, however, that anyone who emerged was being pelted with bucketfuls of mud and cow-dung water. Boys of all ages were heaving dust into the air, hurling old shoes at each other, laughing and cavorting "like Krishna's cowherd companions"—and of course cowherds they were. They had captured one older victim and were making him ride a donkey, seated backward, head to stern. Household walls were being scaled, loose doors broken open, and the inhabitants routed out to join these ceremonial proceedings. Relatively safe in a new building with strong doors and high walls, I escaped an immediate lynching.

I was not sure just what I could find in anthropological theory to assist my understanding of these events. I felt at least that I was sharing Durkheim's sense (when he studied Australian tribal rites) of confronting some of the more elementary forms of the religious life. I reflected briefly on the classic functional dictum of Radcliffe-Brown, who had written that the "rites of savages persist because they are part of the mechanism by which an orderly society maintains itself in existence, serving as they do to establish certain fundamental social values."[7] I pondered the Dionysian values that seemed here to have been expressed, and wondered what equalitarian social order, if any, might maintain itself by such values.

But I had not long to reflect, for no sooner had the mob passed by my house than

I was summoned by a messenger from a family at the other end of the village to give first aid to an injured woman. A thrown water-pot had broken over her head as she opened her door that morning. Protected by an improvised helmet, I ventured forth. As I stepped into the lane, the wife of the barber in the house opposite, a lady who had hitherto been most quiet and deferential, also stepped forth, grinning under her veil, and doused me with a pail of urine from her buffalo. Hurrying through the streets, I glimpsed dances by parties of men and boys impersonating Krishna and company as musicians, fiddling and blowing in pantomime on wooden sticks, leaping about wearing garlands of dried cow-dung and necklaces of bullock bells. Again, as I returned from attending to the lacerated scalp, there was an intermittent hail of trash and dust on my shoulders, this time evidently thrown from the rooftops by women and children in hiding behind the eaves (see figure 7).

At noontime, a state of truce descended. Now was the time to bathe, the neighbors shouted, and to put on fine, fresh clothes. The dirt was finished. Now there would be solemn oblations to the god Fire. "Every cult," Durkheim had written, "presents a double aspect, one negative, the other positive."[8] Had we then been preparing ourselves all morning by torture and purgation for other rites of purer intent? "What is it all going to be about this afternoon?" I asked my neighbor, the barber. "Holī," he said with a beatific sigh, "is the Festival of Love!"

Trusting that there would soon begin performances more in the spirit of the *Gītagovinda* or of Krishna's *rāsa* dances in the *Bhāgavata Purāṇa,* I happily bathed and changed, for my eyes were smarting with the morning's dust, and the day was growing hot. My constant benefactor, the village landlord, now sent his son to present me with a tall glass of a cool, thick green liquid. This was the festival drink, he said; he wanted me to have it at its best, as it came from his own parlor. I tasted it and found it sweet and mild. "You must drink it all!" my host declared. I inquired about the ingredients—almonds, sugar, curds of milk, anise, and "only half a cup" of another item whose name I did not recognize. I finished off the whole delicious glass, and, in discussion with my cook, soon inferred that the unknown ingredient—*bhāng*—had been four ounces of juice from the hemp leaf known in the West as hashish or marijuana.

Because of this indiscretion, I am now unable to report with much accuracy exactly what other religious ceremonies were observed in the four villages through which I floated that afternoon, towed by my careening hosts. They told me that we were going on a journey of condolence to each house whose members had been bereaved during the past year. My many photographs corroborate the visual impressions that I had of this journey: the world was a brilliant smear. The stained and

FIGURE 7
Squirting colored water at passersby as Holi approaches in Brindavan. Photo by John Hawley.

crumpled pages of my notebooks are blank, save for a few declining diagonals and undulating scrawls. Certain steamy scenes remain in memory, nevertheless. There was one great throng of villagers watching an uplifted male dancer with padded crotch writhe in solitary states of fevered passion and then onanism, then join in a remote *pas de deux* with a veiled female impersonator in a parody of pederasty, and finally in telepathic copulation—all this to a frenzied accompaniment of many drums. I know that I witnessed several hysterical battles, women rushing out of their houses in squads to attack me and other men with stout canes, while each man defended himself only by pivoting about his own staff, planted on the ground, or, like me, by running for cover. The rest was all hymn singing, every street resounding with choral song in an archaic Śākta style. The state of the clothes in which I ultimately fell asleep told me the next morning that I had been sprayed and soaked repeatedly with libations of liquid dye, red and yellow. My face in the morning was still a brilliant vermilion, and my hair was orange from repeated embraces and scourings with colored powders by the bereaved and probably by many others. I learned on inquiry what I thought I had heard before, that in Kishan Garhi a kitchen had been profaned with dog's dung by masked raiders, that two housewives had been detected in adultery with neighboring men. As an effect of the festivities in one nearby village, there had occurred an armed fight between factional groups. In a third, an adjacent village, where there had previously been protracted litigation between castes, the festival had not been observed at all. (See figure F at the Web site http://www.clas.ufl.edu/users/vasu/loh.)

"A festival of *love?*" I asked my neighbors again in the morning.

"Yes! All greet each other with affection and feeling. Lord Krishna taught us the way of love, and so we celebrate Holī in this manner."

"What about my aching shins—and your bruises? Why were the women beating us men?"

"Just as the milkmaids loved Lord Krishna, so our wives show their love for us, and for you, too, Saheb!"

Unable at once to stretch my mind so far as to include both "love" and these performances in one conception, I returned to the methodological maxim of Radcliffe-Brown: the meaning of a ritual element is to be found by observing what it shares with all the contexts of its occurrence.[9] Clearly, I would need to know much more about village religion and about the place of each feature of Holī in its other social contexts throughout the year. Then perhaps I could begin to grasp the meanings of Krishna and his festival, and to determine the nature of the values they might serve to maintain.

There were, I learned by observing throughout the following twelve months in the village, three main kinds of ritual performances—festivals, individual sacraments, and optional devotions. Among sacraments, the family-controlled rites of marriage were a major preoccupation of all villagers. In marriage, young girls were uprooted from their privileged situations in the patrilineally extended families of their birth and childhood. They were wedded always out of the village, often many miles away, to child husbands in families that were complete strangers. A tight-lipped young groom would be brought by his uncles in military procession, and after three days of receiving tribute ceremoniously, he would be carried off with his screaming, wailing little bride to a home where she would occupy the lowest status of all. Hard work for the mother-in-law, strict obedience to the husband, and a veiled, silent face to all males senior to herself in the entire village—these were the lot of the young married woman. Members of the husband's family, having the upper hand over the captive wife, could demand and receive service, gifts, hospitality, and deference from their "low" affines on all future occasions of ceremony. Briefly, sometimes, there would be little outbreaks of "Holī playing" at weddings, especially between the invading groom's men and the women of the bride's village. In these games, the men would be dared to enter the women's courtyards in the bride's village and would then be beaten with rolling pins or soaked with colored water for their boldness. Otherwise, all ceremonies of marriage stressed the strict formal dominance of men over women, of groom's people over bride's. When married women returned to their original homes each rainy season for a relaxed month of reunion with their "village sisters" and "village brothers," the whole village sang sentimental songs of the *gopīs'* never-fulfilled longing for their idyllic childhood companionship with Krishna and with each other. Sexual relations between adults of humankind were conventionally verbalized in metaphors of war, theft, and rape, while the marital connection between any particular husband and his wife could be mentioned without insult only by employing generalized circumlocutions such as "house" and "children" and so on. The idiom of Holī thus differed from that of ordinary life both in giving explicit dramatization to specific sexual relationships that otherwise would not be expressed at all and in reversing the differences of power conventionally prevailing between husbands and wives.

Aside from the Holī festival, each of the other thirteen major festivals of the year seemed to me to express and support the proper structures of patriarchy and gerontocracy in the family, of elaborately stratified relations among the castes, and of dominance by landowners in the village generally. At Divālī, ancestral spirits were to be fed and the goddess of wealth worshipped by the head of the family, acting on behalf of all members. The rites of Gobardhan Divālī, another Krishna-related festival, stressed the unity of the family's agnates through their common interest in the family herds of cattle. On the fourth day of the lunar fortnight that ends at Divālī[10]—indeed, on certain fixed dates in every month—the wives fasted for the sake of their husbands. On other dates they fasted for the sake of their children. The brother-sister relation of helpfulness, a vital one for the out-married women, had two further festivals and many fasts giving it ritual support; and the Holī bonfire itself dramatized the divine punishment of the wicked sister Holikā for her unthinkable betrayal of her brother Prahlāda. At each other festival of the year and also at wedding feasts, the separation of the lower from the higher castes and their strict order of ranking were reiterated both through the services of pollution-removal provided by the lower castes and through the "lowering" gifts and payments of food made to them in return. Since the economy of the village was steeply stratified, with one third of the families controlling nearly all the land, every kind of ritual observance, sacramental or festival, tended through ritual patronage and obeisance to give expression to the same order of economic dominance and subordination. Optional, individual ritual observances could also be understood as expressing the secular organization of power, I thought. Rival leaders would compete for the allegiance of others through ceremonies. A wealthy farmer, official, or successful litigant was expected to sponsor special ceremonies and give feasts for lesser folk "to remove the sins" he had no doubt committed in gaining his high position; he who ignored this expectation might overhear stories of the jocular harassment of misers at Holī or of their robbery on other, darker nights. Once each year, a day for simultaneous worship of all the local deities required a minimal sort of communal action by women, and smaller singing parties of women were many, but comradeship among men across the lines of kinship and caste was generally regarded with suspicion. In sum, the routine ritual and social forms of the village seemed almost perfect parallels of each other: both maintained a tightly ranked and compartmentalized order. In this order, there was little room for behavior of the kinds attributed to Krishna's roisterous personality.

"Why do you say that it was Lord Krishna who taught you how to celebrate the festival of Holī?" I inquired of the many villagers who asserted that this was so. Answers, when they could be had at all, stressed that it was he who first played Holī with the cowherd boys and with Rādhā and the other *gopīs*. But my searches in the *Bhāgavata*'s tenth book, and even in that book's recent and locally most popular adaptation, the *Ocean of Love*,[11] could discover no mention of Holī or any of the local festival's traditional activities, from the bonfire to the game of colors. "Just see how they play Holī in Mathurā district, in Lord Krishna's own village of Nandgāon, and in Rādhā's village of Barsānā!" said the landlord. There, I was assured by the barber, who had also seen them, that the women train all year long, drinking milk and eating ghee like wrestlers, and there they beat the men *en masse*, before a huge audience of visitors, to the music of two hundred drums.

"I do not really believe that Lord Krishna grew up in just that village of

Nandgāon," the landlord confided in me, "for Nanda, Krishna's foster father, must have lived on this side of the Jumnā River, near Gokula, as is written in the *Purāṇa*. But there in Nandgāon and Barsānā they keep the old customs best."

The landlord's doubts were well placed, but not extensive enough, for, as I learned from a gazetteer of the district, the connection of Krishna, Rādhā, and the cowgirls with the rising of the women at Holī in those villages of Mathurā could not have originated before the early seventeenth-century efforts of certain immigrant Bengali Gosvāmin priests. The Gosvāmīs themselves—Rūpa, Sanātana, and their associates—were missionaries of the Krishnaite devotional movement led by Caitanya in sixteenth-century Bengal,[12] and that movement in turn had depended on the elaboration of the new notion of Rādhā as Krishna's favorite by the Telugu philosopher Nimbārka, possibly in the thirteenth century, and by other, somewhat earlier sectarians of Bengal and southern India.[13] The village names Nandgāon (village of Nanda) and Barsānā (to make rain—an allusion to the "dark-as-a-cloud" epithet of Krishna) were probably seventeenth-century inventions, like the formal choreography of the battles of the sexes in those villages, that were contrived to attract pilgrims to the summer circuit of Krishna's rediscovered and refurbished holy land of Vraja.[14] Of course, privileged attacks by women upon men must have existed in village custom long before the promotional work of the Gosvāmīs—of this I was convinced by published studies of villages elsewhere, even in the farthest corners of the Hindī-speaking area, where such attacks were part of Holī, but not understood as conveying the message of Lord Krishna.[15] But once the great flow of devotees to Mathurā had begun from Bengal, Gujarat, and the South, the direction of cultural influence must have been reversed: what had been incorporated of peasant practice and local geography into the *Brahmavaivarta Purāṇa* and other new sectarian texts must have begun then to reshape peasant conceptions of peasant practice. At least the Krishnaite theology of the "love battles" in Kishan Garhi, and possibly some refinements of their rustic hydrology and stickwork, seemed to have been remodeled according to the famous and widely imitated public performances that had been visible in villages of the neighboring district for the past three centuries or so. The Mathurā pilgrimage and its literature appeared also to have worked similar effects upon two other festivals of Krishna in Kishan Garhi, in addition to Holī.[16]

To postulate the relative recency of the association of Rādhā and Krishna with the battles of canes and colors in Kishan Garhi was not to assert that the entire Holī festival could have had no connection with legends of Krishna before the seventeenth century. Reports on the mythology of Holī from many other localities described the bonfire not as the burning of Holikā, but as the cremation of another demoness, Pūtanā.[17] Pūtanā was a demoness sent by King Kaṃsa of Mathurā to kill the infant Krishna by giving him to suck of her poisonous mother's milk. The Pūtanā story could no doubt claim a respectable antiquity, occurring as it did in the *Viṣṇu Purāṇa* and the *Harivaṃśa;* it was known in Kishan Garhi, although not applied currently to the rationalization of the Holī fire, and represented an acquaintance with a Krishna senior in type to the more erotic Krishna of the *Bhāgavata Purāṇa* and the later works. Even if I peeled away all explicit references to Krishna, both older and more recent, I would still have confronted other layers of Vaiṣṇavism in the Holī references to Rāma, whose cult centered in the middle Gangetic plain and in the South. And then there was the further Vaiṣṇava figure Prahlāda, another of ancient origin. Finally, I had to consider the proximity of Kishan Garhi to Mathurā, which was more than merely generically Vaiṣṇavite in its ancient religious orientations: Mathurā was thought to have been the original source of the legends of the child Krishna and his brother Balarāma, as suggested by Greek evidence from the fourth century B.C. as well as by the Purāṇic traditions.[18] Assuming that urban cults may always have been influential in villages and that such cults often carried forward what was already present in rural religious practice,[19] I thought it probable that the ancestors of the people of Kishan Garhi might well have celebrated the pranks of some divine ancestor of the Purāṇic Krishna even before their less complete adherence to the cults of Rāma and other gods later known as avatars of Viṣṇu. If these historical evidences and interpretations were generally sound, if Krishna had indeed waxed and waned before, then what both I and the villagers had taken to be their timeless living within a primordial local myth of Krishna appeared instead to represent rather the latest in a lengthy series of revivals and reinterpretations mingling local, regional, and even some quite remote movements of religious fashion.

Beneath the level of mythological enactment or rationalization, with its many shifts of contents through time, however, I felt that one might find certain more essential, underlying connections between the moral constitution of villages like Kishan Garhi and the general social form of the Holī festival—so the functional assumption of Radcliffe-Brown had led me to hope. Superficially, in various regions and eras, the festival might concern witches or demonesses (Holikā or Holākā, Pūtanā, Ḍhoṇḍhā), Viṣṇu triumphant (as Rāma, Narasiṃha, or Krishna), Śiva as an ascetic in conflict with gods of lust (Kāma, Madana, or the nonscriptural Nathurām), or others.[20] Festival practices might also vary greatly. Were there enduring, widespread features, I wondered? From a distributional and documentary study by N. K. Bose, I learned that spring festivals featuring bonfires, a degree of sexual license, and generally saturnalian carousing had probably existed in villages of many parts of India for at least the better part of the past two thousand years.[21] Spring festivals of this one general character evidently had remained consistently associated with many of India's complex, caste-bound communities. Even if only some of such festivals had had the puckish, ambiguous Krishna as their presiding deity, and these only in recent centuries, many seemed since the beginning of our knowledge to have enshrined divinities who sanctioned, however briefly, some of the same riotous sorts of social behavior.

Now a full year had passed in my investigations, and the Festival of Love was again approaching. Again I was apprehensive for my physical person but was forewarned with social structural knowledge that might yield better understanding of the events to come. This time, without the draft of marijuana, I began to see the pandemonium of Holī falling into an extraordinarily regular social ordering. But this was an order precisely inverse to the social and ritual principles of routine life. Each riotous act at Holī implied some opposite, positive rule or fact of everyday social organization in the village.

Who were those smiling men whose shins were being most mercilessly beaten by the women? They were the wealthier Brahman and Jāṭ farmers of the village, and the beaters were those ardent local Rādhās, the "wives of the village," figuring by both the real and the fictional intercaste system of kinship. The wife of an "elder brother" was properly a man's joking mate, while the wife of a "younger brother" was properly removed from him by rules of extreme respect, but both were merged here with a man's mother-surrogates, the wives of his "father's younger brothers," in one revolutionary cabal of "wives" that cut across all lesser lines and links. The boldest beaters in this veiled battalion were often in fact the wives of the farmers' low-caste field laborers, artisans, or menials—the concubines and kitchen help of the victims. "Go and bake bread!" teased one farmer, egging his assailant on. "Do you want some seed from me?" shouted another flattered victim, smarting under the blows, but standing his ground. Six Brahman men in their fifties, pillars of village society, limped past in panting flight from the quarterstaff wielded by a massive young Bhaṇgin, sweeper of their latrines. From this carnage suffered by their village brothers, all daughters of the village stood apart, yet held themselves in readiness to attack any potential husband who might wander in from another, marriageable village to pay a holiday call.

Who was that "King of Holī" riding backward on the donkey? It was an older boy of high caste, a famous bully, put there by his organized victims (but seeming to relish the prominence of his disgrace).

Who was in that chorus singing so lustily in the potters' lane? Not just the resident caste fellows, but six washermen, a tailor, and three Brahmans, joined each year for this day only in an idealistic musical company patterned on the friendships of the gods.

Who were those transfigured "cowherds" heaping mud and dust on all the leading citizens? They were the water carrier, two young Brahman priests, and a barber's son, avid experts in the daily routines of purification.

Whose household temple was festooned with goat's bones by unknown merrymakers? It was the temple of that Brahman widow who had constantly harassed neighbors and kinsmen with actions at law.

In front of whose house was a burlesque dirge being sung by a professional ascetic of the village? It was the house of a very much alive moneylender, notorious for his punctual collections and his insufficient charities.

Who was it who had his head fondly anointed, not only with handfuls of the sublime red powders, but also with a gallon of diesel oil? It was the village landlord, and the anointer was his cousin and archrival, the police headman of Kishan Garhi.

Who was it who was made to dance in the streets, fluting like Lord Krishna, with a garland of old shoes around his neck? It was I, the visiting anthropologist, who had asked far too many questions and had always to receive respectful answers.

Here indeed were the many village kinds of love confounded—respectful regard for parents and patrons; the idealized affection for brothers, sisters, and comrades; the longing of humans for union with the divine; and the rugged lust of sexual mates—all broken suddenly out of their usual, narrow channels by a simultaneous increase of intensity. Boundless, unilateral love of every kind flooded over the usual compartmentalization and indifference among separated castes and families. Insubordinate libido inundated all established hierarchies of age, sex, caste, wealth, and power.

The social meaning of Krishna's doctrine in its rural North Indian recension is not unlike one conservative social implication of Jesus's Sermon on the Mount. The Sermon admonishes severely, but at the same time postpones the destruction of the secular social order until a distant future. Krishna does not postpone the reckoning of the mighty until an ultimate Judgment Day but schedules it regularly as a masque at the full moon of every March. And the Holī of Krishna is no mere doctrine of love; rather, it is the script for a drama that must be acted out by each devotee passionately, joyfully.

The dramatic balancing of Holī—the world destruction and world renewal, the world pollution followed by world purification—occurs not only on the abstract level of structural principles, but also in the person of each participant. Under the tutelage of Krishna, each person plays and for the moment may experience the role of his opposite: the servile wife acts the domineering husband, and vice versa; the ravisher acts the ravished; the menial acts the master; the enemy acts the friend; the strictured youths act the rulers of the republic. The observing anthropologist, inquiring and reflecting on the forces that move men in their orbits, finds himself pressed to act the witless bumpkin. Each actor playfully takes the role of others in relation to his own usual self. Each may thereby learn to play his own routine roles afresh, surely with renewed understanding, possibly with greater grace, perhaps with a reciprocating love.

NOTES

1. I studied "Kishan Garhi," a pseudonymous village in Aligarh District, Uttar Pradesh, from March 1951 to April 1952, with the assistance of an Area Research Training Fellowship grant from the Social Science Research Council. I am indebted to David E. Orlinsky for his comments on this essay.

2. In this local version of the Prahlāda story, King Harnākas will readily be recognized as Hiraṇya Kaśipu of the Purāṇas, e.g., *Viṣṇu Purāṇa* 1.17 (p. 108 in the translation by Horace Hayman Wilson [Calcutta: Punthi Pustak, 1961]). Holā or Holākā, in the oldest texts a name for the bonfire or festival and unconnected with the story of Prahlāda or other scriptural gods (see the sources cited by Pandurang Vaman Kane, *History of Dharmaśāstra* [Poona: Bhandarkar Oriental Research Institute, 1958], 5: 237–39), appears only in recent popular stories as a female and as a relative of Prahlāda. For Holī stories of the Hindi region generally, see William Crooke, *The Popular Religion and Folk-Lore of Northern India* (London: Archibald Constable & Co., 1896), 2: 313; for similar tales from Delhi State; see Oscar Lewis, with the assistance of Victor Barnouw, *Village Life in Northern India* (Urbana: University of Illinois, 1958), 232; and from the Alwar district of Rajasthan, see Hilda Wernher, *The Land and the Well* (New York: John Day Co., 1946), 199–200.

3. Some of the cow-dung objects for the Holī fire are prepared after the Gobardhan Divālī festival in autumn, with the materials of Gobardhan Bābā's (= Krishna's?) body. See McKim Marriott, "Little Communities in an Indigenous Civilization," in *Village India*, ed. McKim Marriott (Chicago: University of Chicago Press, 1955), 199–200. Other objects are prepared on the second or fifth days of the bright fortnight of the month of Phāgun, whose last day is the day of the Holī fire.

4. Books 7 and 10, as in *The Srimad-Bhagavatam of Krishna-Dwaipayana Vyasa*, trans. J. M. Sanyal (Calcutta: Oriental Publishing Co., n.d.), vols. 4 and 5.

5. Alfred Reginald Radcliffe-Brown, "Religion and Society," in *Structure and Function in Primitive Society* (London: Cohen & West, 1952), 155, 177.

6. Bronislaw Malinowski, *Argonauts of the Western Pacific* (London: Routledge, 1932), 6–8.

7. "Taboo," in Radcliffe-Brown, *Structure and Function*, 152.

8. Émile Durkheim, *The Elementary Forms of the Religious Life,* trans. Joseph Ward Swain (Glencoe, IL: Free Press, 1947), 299.

9. Alfred Reginald Radcliffe-Brown, *The Andaman Islanders* (Glencoe, IL: Free Press, 1948), 235.

10. Details of some of these festivals are given in Marriott, "Little Communities," 192–206. The social organization of Kishan Garhi is described more fully in McKim Marriott, "Social Structure and Change in a U.P. Village," in *India's Villages,* ed. M. N. Srinivas (Bombay: Asia Publishing House, 1960), 106–21.

11. Lallu Lai, *Premasāgara,* trans. Frederic Pincott (London: Westminster, Constable, 1897).

12. Frederic Salmon Growse, *Mathurá: A District Memoir,* 2d ed. (Allahabad: North-western Provinces and Oudh Government Press, 1880), 72, 93, 183–84.

13. Ibid., 178–221; John Nicol Farquhar, *An Outline of the Religious Literature of India* (London: Oxford University Press, 1920), 238–40.

14. Growse, *Mathurá,* 71–94.

15. Women beat men at or near the time of Holī among the Gonds of Mandla District, according to Verrier Elwin, *Leaves from the Jungle* (London: J. Murray, 1936), 135; in Nimar, according to Stephen Fuchs, *The Children of Hari* (New York: Praeger, 1950), 300–301; and elsewhere in Madhya Pradesh, according to Robert Vane Russell and Hira Lai, *The Tribes and Castes of the Central Provinces of India* (London: Macmillan, 1916), 2: 126, 3: 117. The usage is reported also from Alwar in Rajasthan by Wernher, *Land and Well,* 208, and from Delhi by Lewis and Barnouw, *Village Life,* 232.

16. On Krishna's birthday anniversary, biographies of his life by poets of Mathurā are read. At the Gobardhan Divālī, the circumambulation of the hill by the pilgrims is duplicated in model; see Marriott, "Little Communities," 199–200.

17. See Crooke, *Popular Religion and Folk-Lore,* 2: 313–14; and Ṛgvedi [pseud.], *Āryāncā Saṇāncā Prācīna va Arvācīna Itihāsa* (in Marathi) (Bombay, n.d.), 399.

18. Growse, *Mathurá,* 103.

19. R. Redfield and M. Singer, "The Cultural Role of Cities," *Economic Development and Cultural Change* 3 (1954): 53–74.

20. Crooke, *Popular Religion and Folk-Lore,* 2: 313–14, 319–20; Kane, *History of Dharmaśāstra,* 5: 237–40; Ṛgvedi, *Āryāncā Saṇāncā Prācīna va Arvācīna Itihāsa,* 399–400, 405.

21. Nirmal Kumar Bose, "The Spring Festival of India," in *Cultural Anthropology and Other Essays* (Calcutta, 1953), 73–102.

PART IV · PERFORMANCE

8 · An Open-Air Ramayana

Ramlila, the Audience Experience

LINDA HESS

Ramlila is a generic name for the annual dramatic representations of the ancient *Ramayana* story performed in hundreds of places throughout North India, usually in September and October.[1] These Ramlilas are generally based on the Hindi version of the epic, the *Ramcharitmanas*, composed by Tulsidas in the late sixteenth century. They go on for multiple days—from three days to more than a month. This essay focuses on a particular Ramlila, that of Ramnagar, just across the Ganga from Varanasi—the largest in scale, the most famous, and, as many participants say, the most vibrant with *bhakti*, or devotion. Its special grandeur and intensity are linked to the fact that for two centuries it has been under the patronage of the Maharajas of Varanasi, who have given it both lavish material support and formidable cultural importance. Although there are dozens of Ramlilas in different Varanasi neighborhoods, many people cross the river every day for a month to attend the Ramnagar performance. Often they say, "Once you have seen Ramnagar, you don't want to look at any other Ramlila."

For three years in the late 1970s and again in 1983, I too crossed the river every day for a month. I stayed in the midst of the Ramlila from its opening moment in the early evening to its closing *arati*, or ritual of worship—usually a matter of about five hours, but sometimes seven or eight, and, on one occasion each year, a full

This essay was published in an earlier form as "Rām Līlā: The Audience Experience," in *Bhakti in Current Research: 1979–1982*, ed. Monika Thiel-Horstmann (Berlin: Dietrich Reimer Verlag, 1983), 171–90.

twelve hours, culminating at dawn. Of course it is presumptuous to say "*the* audience experience" in this essay's title. There is no single experience, and the only thing we can be sure about is that this essay reflects *my* experience. But let me state my intentions in attending, researching, and writing, as I have done here.

First, I wanted to be fully immersed in the physical circumstances of the vast performance. Like other cultural performances, the Ramlila unfolds spatially and temporally in ways that are complex, delightful, moving, amazing, bewildering, exhausting. You can't understand what that means by reading this essay. But you can get a hint, and you can appreciate the importance of putting your body into your research. Second, while I was trained as a textual scholar and was studying the *Ramcharitmanas* of Tulsidas throughout the period of fieldwork, I wanted above all to know how the text came to life in people's minds and bodies. I wanted to see the process by which the text rose up and became performance—spatial-temporal-physical-emotional-intellectual-personal-social experience. Third, I was especially interested in religious meanings. These are the meanings highlighted by people who are devoted to the Ramlila. I tried to spend my time in the center of the action (though it will soon become apparent that the center easily disappears in an event of this magnitude). I tried to focus on the experiences, actions, and statements of people who identified vividly with the Ramlila's story and the devotional meanings attached to it.

If I had focused on "margins," I would have written differently. One gets a different sense of the audience experience if one spends time in the refreshment shops adjoining the Lila ground, or with men who picnic during the acting and come back at the end for *arati*, or with women who do not follow the peripatetic performance but find a safe spot and wait for it to come to them, meanwhile chatting and looking after their children. This essay tries to give a sense of full immersion for a full month, highlighting what dedicated participants highlight. It explores certain core concepts in the culture of *bhakti* and in Tulsidas's *Ramayana* as they are brought to life in the Ramlila.

RAMNAGAR'S DISTINCTIVENESS

Here are some of the reasons that participants give for the special power of the Ramnagar Ramlila.

1. "God dwells here for a month." Many people believe that Lord Ram, together with his three divine brothers and his goddess-wife Sita, has made a promise to reside in person in Ramnagar for a full month every year. In all

Ramlilas the boys who play the deities are consecrated and worshipped like temple images. But in Ramnagar there is an especially powerful belief that God is literally present in the *svarups*—four boys dressed in gold, with glittering makeup on their faces and tall crowns on their heads, and a fifth boy who plays Sita, similarly decked with spangles and ornaments and wrapped in a magenta sari.

2. Ramnagar has an enormous space devoted to the Ramlila, including town, villages, fields, forests, temples, and ponds, covering fifteen or twenty square miles. Each scene has its fixed setting; the places were chosen and consecrated early in the nineteenth century and are known year-round by their Ramlila names. Thus the whole area has become a microcosm of the sacred *Ramayana* geography. The effect of the drama is greatly heightened as people move through the different environments, which are well suited to the scenes played in them.
3. The Maharaja attends every night's performance. He is unquestionably in charge, and his presence lends authority, dignity, and discipline. Besides being the traditional ruler of Varanasi (in which position he continued to command great respect long after the dissolution of his princely state), the Maharaja is the representative of Shiva, ruling deity of Varanasi. Everywhere he goes, he is greeted with loud cries of salutation to Shiva: *Hara Hara Mahadev!*[2]
4. The whole story of the *Ramcharitmanas* is presented in detail, with strict adherence to the letter and spirit of Tulsi's poem. This is often contrasted with the chopped versions offered in other Ramlilas, as well as with their tendency to degenerate into mere entertainments. The spoken dialogues are close to the language of Tulsidas. The main actors are well trained and serious. In Ramnagar, people assert, everything is done by rule and tradition, and nothing ever changes.
5. Thousands of *sadhus* (wandering renunciants) attend the Ramlila, camping out in Ramnagar for the month and further sanctifying the occasion.
6. It is believed that the originators of the Ramlila, who chose the sites and composed the dialogues—especially a *sadhu* named Kashthajihvasvami—had supernatural powers, and that the Ramlila grounds were made repositories of these powers.[3]
7. The people who attend the Ramnagar Ramlila have faith, and the power of their faith has been cumulatively giving its energy to the Ramlila for many

generations. "Feeling, emotion, devotion!" It is repeatedly stressed that these make Ramnagar's Ramlila special and great.

PARTICIPATION

Much more than a conventional drama, the Ramlila is a vast participatory event. At its heart are the energy and emotion of *bhakti*—a word usually translated as "devotion," but coming from a Sanskrit root whose meanings include "sharing" and "participation." It is impossible to set down all the ways in which the audience takes part. Standard kinds of activity and particular events can be described. But on the scene unexpected things are always happening; people find individual ways to express their involvement, and the borderline between actors and audience, between the Ramlila event and the world beyond it, is always fluctuating. Here are a few examples of the more prominent forms of participation:

1. The people raise a set cheer when certain important characters speak. It begins with *Bol!* ("Speak!" or "Say it!"). Ram's cheer continues, *Raja Ramchandra ki jai!* ("Victory to King Ramchandra!"). There are similar cheers for the other *svarups* and for Hanuman. One also hears countless times the Shiva cheer, *Hara Hara Mahadev!* This is shouted with great gusto when the Maharaja comes or goes, when Shiva appears as a character in the Ramlila, or when Ram worships the image of Shiva.
2. A number of people carry the text of the *Ramcharitmanas* and read it, usually aloud, as it is sung by the Ramayanis (twelve men who sing Tulsi's poem throughout the performance).
3. People sing *kirtan* (names of God—most often *jai siyaram / sitaram*—in repetitive melodies). There are certain moments when the *kirtan* always arises: one is when the exiled gods are offered meals by sages in forest ashrams; another is just before *arati*, the brilliant illumination of the gods that climaxes each night's Lila. Before the Lila begins each day, and during regular breaks, *kirtan* is the special province of the *sadhus*, among whom there are always a few with drums and cymbals to maintain the throbbing rhythm.
4. They worship. This includes making offerings and receiving *prasad* before the performance starts or during breaks. *Prasad* (grace) is any physical item that has been blessed by contact with the deities. It can be flower garlands, sweets, fruits, sacred basil leaves. Once I saw a man give *pan* (leaf-

wrapped betel nuts with spices) to the gods to eat. The he took out more *pan* and asked Ram to touch it to his lips and give it back as *prasad*. Worship also includes touching the gods' feet whenever possible, often reaching for them while they are being carried through the crowds on the shoulders of bearers.

5. They travel. Most come from Varanasi city, which means crossing the Ganga by boat, bus, bicycle, horse cart, rickshaw, or foot. (Few come by car or motorcycle.) Once in the Ramlila, they cover impressive distances during the mobile performance, which involves as much as eight miles' walking in a single night for the faithful who go to every scene.

   One traditional practice is to go barefoot. I have heard two explanations for this: (a) Ram went barefoot during his exile, and this is a way for the devotee to identify with him; (b) you don't wear shoes in a temple, and the entire Ramlila ground, sanctified by God's presence, is like a temple. Nearly all the actors, directors, and workers go barefoot, and so did I for most of two years' attendance.

6. They act out parts in the drama. Huge crowds play "huge crowds." They function as the citizens of Ayodhya who follow Ram as he goes off into exile. They become the wedding guests when the four brothers are married. Women in the audience sing *gali*, the humorous insult songs sung by women at weddings. When Bharat does the circumambulation of Chitrakut, thousands jump up and march with him, vigorously shouting "*Sitaram*" and touching the earth as they pass the sacred well. People of Ramnagar recite poems of praise from the rooftops on coronation day, and the actors stop in their tracks to listen. This reflects Tulsidas's description of how people recited poetry on joyous occasions like Ram's birth and coronation.

   Again and again the audience and citizens of Ramnagar act out what Tulsidas narrates. They drop their work and rush to gaze at the gods as they pass through town or village. They move with processions or climb on roofs to see. They illumine triumphant fireworks from their balconies as Ram's chariot returns slowly from exile. Some climb onto the chariot to make offerings. Others decorate their homes and shops just as the citizens of Ayodhya are said to have decorated theirs.

7. People carve out special roles for themselves. One man for several decades donated the special flower garlands that are placed on the gods at the clos-

ing *arati* ceremony. Every day he and his wife and son made the garlands, at a cost in the 1970s of fifteen rupees and four hours' work. At the end of the performance the old man could be seen mounting the stage and handing the garlands to the *vyas* (director/priest). He had become part of the Ramlila. One *sadhu* dressed in a long orange outfit used to lead the *kirtan,* dancing in the midst of his chanting brethren. Everyone expected to see him doing his job: another actor who had created his own role.

A legendary figure in the years that I attended was the "150-year-old *sadhu,*" known as Mauni Baba (Silent Baba), who was as familiar a presence as Ram or the Maharaja. Participants testified that according to their grandfathers he had always been there, looking just the same. He did not speak but communicated in a lively way through sign language and action. He was playful, pious, and mysterious. He gave away money and gifts, though he seemed to possess nothing except the dry banana leaf that was his only clothing. People told many stories about him. He scampered through the crowds, kicking up water in mud puddles, sometimes sitting next to the Maharaja, sometimes waving the flames in the *arati* ceremony.[4]

"I have also become an actor," I wrote in my notebook one day. "I am the foreign lady who speaks Hindi, who came to the Ramlila every day last year, who writes and writes, who has a *Ramayana* in both Hindi and English. Children and grown-ups crowd around to watch my green pen fly during the breaks. They tell stories about me in my presence."

8. The *nemi-premis.* Most people attend the Lila on and off, but an important core group comes every day. These are the *nemis,* or regulars (from *niyam,* "rule"). They are also called *premis,* lovers of the Ramlila. For them the month is a special time set apart from the rest of the year. Many stop or curtail their regular work. They leave for Ramnagar by midafternoon and usually do not return until after ten o'clock. They have their own costumes, makeup, rituals, and fellowship. They bathe in the river or in a special pond and put on clean clothes—sort of a *nemi* uniform, typically including white *dhoti,* white shirt, and colored sash tied diagonally across the chest. They carefully apply the red and yellow *tilak* to their foreheads, using mirrors they have brought with them. Some carry bamboo staffs adorned with brass. Some take *bhang,* a form of cannabis pounded and consumed in a delicious drink that is prepared with ritual regularity in the afternoon. The pious explanation is that this helps them to forget their ordinary lives and look at God with greater concentration.

9. It is difficult to convey the intensely physical quality of participation in the Ramlila. It arises from the continual movement through different kinds of space, the exposure to the elements, and the great enveloping crowds.

Coming at the end of the monsoon season, the Lila usually has about ten days of rain. The open environments afford little or no protection for the spectators, and often the actors are caught as well. Roads and paths become flooded, then clogged with mud. Only in the most impossible circumstances is any part of a scheduled Lila postponed. Large umbrellas protect the gods, the Ramayanis with their sacred manuscripts, and the Maharaja. The rest fend for themselves. When there isn't rain, there may be intense heat. As the fall season advances, the heat may turn to chill.

But perhaps the most overwhelming physical sensation of the Lila is the constant necessity of mingling with, sometimes being crushed by, the colossal crowds pressing and tumbling forward to get their vision of God. The following descriptions, from notes written on the scene, may help to vivify this experience for the reader:

Going through the Ramlila barefoot involves both convenience and hardship. Convenience when we move through watery tracts—I don't have to worry about losing my shoes in the mud or carrying them. Hardship because sometimes the road really is rocky, and you never know when you'll step on a rusty nail, a piece of glass, a thorn. Of course all fastidiousness about whether you step in excrement (human, cow, horse, elephant, dog, goat . . .), coughed-up mucous, spat-out betel, has to be abandoned, at least in the dark hours.

Why do the stones in the road seem to be getting ever bigger, sharper, more numerous? Probably because my feet, unused to night after night of rough traveling without shoes, are getting ever more tender and painful. But this experience serves to unite me with the characters in the Lila: "The blisters on Bharat's feet glistened like dew. . . . All the people were grieved when they heard he'd come that day on foot."[5]

. . .

In tonight's Lila the sage Vishvamitra takes Ram and Lakshman on a foray to kill demons in the woods. The use of the world as a stage goes far beyond anything that might be called "verisimilitude." We move from the main street of town to narrow lanes, a troop of horsemen in front, the Maharaja with his elephants behind, the golden gods in the middle gliding along at shoulder height. Shopkeepers and laborers stop to watch the gods go by, saluting them with joined palms. The setting becomes steadily more rural. Roads change from pavement to cobblestone to dirt, houses from plaster to brick to mud, on varying levels, with glittering algae-covered ponds, fields of leafy vegetables and corn, moist greenness everywhere. People are at their doorways, in the yards, on the roofs. If Ram really did go to the forest with Vishvamitra, would it not have been through lanes like this, past houses, from town to village, while the local people stopped to watch? The sky is brilliant salmon and mauve in the luminous moments before sunset.

· · ·

(Events recorded at home after a night of tremendous storm.) I moved out on the dark country road in hard-pelting rain. Someone offered to share his umbrella. It didn't do much good, but I stayed under it to try to save my *Ramayana* and notebook. My clothes and body from feet to chest were quickly flooded. When we reached the Sutikshna ashram scene the wind was blowing horribly. It blew out the petromax lamps. Everyone just stood there, waiting to see what the higher authorities would decide. The storm raged harder and harder. Lightning flashed, wind whipped violently. Someone said, "After the wind, by God's grace the rain will stop." But it didn't stop. For an hour I stood under the man's umbrella, seeing nothing. "We are also doing *tapasya* (austerities) in the jungle," he said. Finally I went to look for the gods. On a rise was a little temple built in honor of this scene in the Ramlila, containing the stone images of Ram, Sita, Lakshman, and the sage Sutikshna. In the tiny shrine the principal actors had taken shelter: Ram, Sita, Lakshman, and Sutikshna crowded in next to their own images. On the porch a few other actors and workers huddled. Finally word came that the Lila would stop and *arati* would be done here. But they couldn't find the fireworks man. Then they found him but couldn't find the garland man. At last they went on without the garlands. I stood on the rise behind the gods, looking at the people below. Sita's silk sari was wet. There were about 800 people bathed in the light of *arati*, especially jubilant in their smiles and aggressive in their shouts. "God gives us tests," a lady said next day. "Last night he tested us. The real devotees stayed, the others ran away."

· · ·

Today we the audience, along with Ram, Sita, and Lakshman, experience the exile to the forest. We walk from Ayodhya on the main street of town, through villages and fields, along narrow trails, over rocks, around lakes, and across tracts of mud. Ram's recent warning to Sita echoes in our ears: "The forest is rough, frightful, with prickly grass, thorns, stones. . . . Your lotuslike feet are delicate and lovely, while the paths are often impenetrable."[6]

As darkness thickens we slip and stumble. Finally we arrive at some unidentifiable spot in the Ramnagar forest. We squat on the comfortless ground, packed tightly together. Dense clouds of insects swarm around the hanging lanterns, dropping on everyone nearby. Ram and his party are being entertained at a forest hermitage. As food is offered to them, a plaintive voice rises out of the low hum of the crowd, crying, *"Sitaram sitaram sitaram jai sitaram."* Hundreds of voices answer, and the singing continues throughout the silent eating scene.

. . .

(After a long evening of trudging in the rain.) The place of *arati* was a great mess. Right in front of the platform was a gutter filled with water. As people crowded in, we had to sit down in the muck. Since I can't squat comfortably on my heels, I just sat, feeling the mud ooze up through my clothes and all over my skin. At least I was directly in front of the *svarups* for *arati*. What I didn't reckon for was that the great flare would be held just above me. When a piece of burning fireworks fell on my head, I jumped away and brushed it off, the smell of sizzling hair in my nose.

The faithful have to endure such tribulations in the Ramlila. Tonight there was a great feeling of pilgrimage, of undergoing sacrifices, with nothing between your body and the harsh elements. If you are a devotee you have to keep going through the dark, the mud, the rain. When the time comes to sit down in the mud for *arati*, you sit down in the mud; and if you have to smell your own hair burn, you're willing to do that too.

. . .

(The second-to-last Lila—Ram's coronation, initiating the golden age of Ram Rajya, his perfect reign—is an all-night affair. After the regular performance ends there are several hours of *darshan*, when the five deities are on display and huge numbers of devotees crowd in to touch their feet and make offerings. The great night culminates in *arati* at dawn, an event that draws the largest crowds of the whole Ramlila—people often claim over 100,000.)

10 P.M. The moment the performance ends there is a mad rush for the stage. Police holds sticks as barriers at the top of the steps. People push, sway, and dive through each other to get to the gods. There is no order, no decorum, practically no humor or kindness. There is only the endless press, the swaying and stumbling, the instinctive leap to get ahead of somebody else, to force oneself up on the fourth or fifth step instead of starting at the bottom.

Women, admitted in separate batches, advance their position by tricks or shouting, while men seem to rely more on main force. There are periods of effective police control and periods when control collapses and anarchy reigns, jostling that sometimes pitches someone off the platform to sprawl on the ground below, while the lotus-studded, lantern-decked canopy swings crazily on its bamboo frame as if caught in an earthquake.

3:30 A.M. It is nearly two hours until *arati,* but the audience is pouring in, cramming the huge yard from end to end and lining every inch of the surrounding walls. I take a place close to the front.

Behind me a sea of tightly packed bodies is being subjected to constant pressure by new throngs pushing in. As the stars pale and the event we have come for draws near, roars rise from different parts of the space, but they are not cheers for God. They indicate that some pressure has been exerted that was too much to bear, that has lifted a while mass of bodies and shot it forward like a tidal wave.

Till the last moment my position seems safe. But when the Maharaja marches to the front, a path cut for him by furious police, the whole sea breaks loose and pitches forward, toppling barricades, rolled by its own terrific weight.

We are all one body. No one can hold her ground in that surge any more than a drop can keep its position in the ocean. Throughout *arati,* as the lights blaze and the gongs ring, we are caught in the sea, sometimes on our feet, sometimes nearly on the ground with a blur of bodies over us, sometimes tilted at angles that would be impossible if we weren't at once pushing and supporting each other.

From time to time, over the boiling surface of the crowd, I catch a glimpse of Ram's face. He is still, radiant, and smiling.

LILA

To be vigorously and devotedly involved in the Ramlila for one month is to take an excursion out of ordinary space and time. The *Ramcharitmanas,* along with mainstream devotional Hinduism, teaches that the universe is *lila,* or play, which in Sanskrit as in English means both "drama" and "game." The idea of *lila* is closely akin to that of *maya,* which we may say here refers to the transient and illusory world of forms. I believe that the Ramlila is constructed in such a way as to produce an actual experience of the world as *lila* or *maya.*[7]

The participant not only sees the drama but finds himself acting in it. A vast world is created before and around him. This world is built physically and psychologically performance after performance. The devotee's days are curved around the necessity of being there. Including transportation, attendance often takes seven hours, sometimes more. The tawdry *samsara* of ordinary life pales while the Ramlila world becomes ever more vivid, brilliant, and gripping.

The large space of the Ramlila is extended to a semblance of infinity by the fact that the "play" is set in the "real world." Our stage embraces town, village, field, forest, lake. Our floor is the earth, and our roof is the sky, often awesome during the moments of transition between day and night, in this season of transition between the rains and autumn.

The sense of infinity is enhanced by the impossibility of ever seeing the entire Lila. Though I had privileged status that enabled me to pass through any barrier, there was no way I could see every part of the action in three years' attendance. Crowds, transportation failures, getting lost in the dark, being given the wrong directions, falling back from fatigue or illness, becoming caught up in some interesting conversation or observation, all prevented me from staying with the golden gods every moment. Ordinary spectators may take many years even to hear all the dialogues once.

As there is no clear line between the "play" and the "world," there is also none between actors and audience. I have already indicated the many ways in which the audience "acts." Many of the actors also mingle with the audience. They may be seen stepping into their costumes just before a scene, hiking from place to place with their masks under their arms, watching the performance, or chatting. Similarly, the special Ramlila time mingles with non-Lila time, as every performance is cut by an hour's break while the Maharaja goes to perform *sandhya puja*, or evening worship. At that time the *sadhus* with their *kirtan* become the star performers, the *svarups* are available for a kind of free-form *darshan*, and the Lila fades into the Mela or fair that accompanies it and plays the role of the ordinary world in juxtaposition with the divine Lila world. On the climactic night of Ravan's final defeat (day twenty-five of the Ramlila), the *sandhya* break lasts three hours, culminating when the huge paper effigy of the demon-king is put to the torch. That night, on the far-extending field of Lanka, the interpenetration of cosmos and *samsara*, Lila and Mela, is particularly grand and powerful. The two do not blur or cancel each other out but fade into and out of each other like figure and ground. The gods emerge from the field of the ordinary world; the ordinary world emerges from the field of cosmic forces. (See figures G and H at the Web site http://www.clas.ufl.edu/users/vasu/loh.)

Here is a detailed description of *vijaya dashami*, the "victorious tenth" day of the waxing half of the lunar month of Ashvin, celebrated as the festival of *daśahrā* throughout North India, as I observed it in 1976:

> At the Lila ground, the atmosphere is electric. Things don't move, they sweep. The crowd sweeps around the raised oblong of earth that serves as a stage, the

elephants sweep through the crowd and, startlingly, right up over the stage, so that the two kings (Ram and the Maharaja) momentarily face and balance each other. The Ramayanis sweep into song, their voices swift and exuberant. They sing the ultimate unraveling of a cosmic war, of a god-king's fourteen-year exile, of a city's twenty-five-day spectacle, and a vast population's moving drama. Ram and Lakshman sit on a high throne. There is no dialogue in tonight's drama, and only the briefest action. Ravan removes his mask of ten stylized heads and crowns, along with his twenty wooden arms, and thus denuded, walks down the long platform to Ram, bows, and touches his feet. It is finished. The air vibrates with excitement, happiness, unity.

But the night is far from over. There will be a long break of several hours while the Maharaja performs a long *puja*. The break creates a space in which the world of the Lila, with its huge figures of good and evil, of power and sweetness, of transcendent beings both with and beyond form, is in suspension. For a few hours all is balanced, the monumental struggles neutralized. But still, there is movement. The population of the world, of all the worlds, keeps circulating, many thousands, among lanterns and torches, gods and demons mixing with vendors of peanuts and tea. The *sadhus* sing, "*Jai siyaram*," beating their drums. Monkeys and bears wander among the spectators, and there is no distinction. They are all actors and all spectators, all wearing costumes. It is like Brueghel's great canvas of children playing: no center, just countless people in clusters, in pairs, alone, gathering around points of interest, all separate but all linked. Movement everywhere, but a sense of circularity, circulating around the fairgrounds, the circle of the cosmos, the circle of the four ages, creation, destruction, manifestation, disappearance.

At three cardinal points, forming a triangle that is the locus of "reality" during these hours of suspended narrative action, sit the principal figures.

- Ram and Lakshman sit under a canopy on a gentle rise, brightly lit, surrounded by their attendants, fan wavers, priests, distributors of garlands, receiving with silent but warm dignity the attentions of their worshippers.
- On another high place Sita, the Mother of the Universe, the embodiment of *maya*, the energy of all life and form, sits in a pavilion surrounded by four golden pillars, overhung with leafy trees, visible from every part of the Lila ground. This is the Ashoka Grove, where she has been held captive by Ravan. Now sure of rescue, she relaxes with an attendant, chatting a little, while he sometimes fans her, sometimes massages her feet.
- And on a bare hill is a colossal effigy of Ravan, despoiler of the three worlds, conqueror of the gods, personification of insane arrogance. But that Ravan has just died with the name of Ram on his lips. Now the actor who played

> Ravan for many days has disappeared, and all that remains is this massive paper emblem, inert, devoid of his *maya*, his energy. The evening will climax with a conflagration that will consume even this emblem.
>
> All is balanced. The contending forces of the universe are at peace. But still the countless inhabitants of the world circulate, circulate, circulate.

The elaborate, unlimited, physically and emotionally consuming world that has been created from day one of the Lila dissolves on day thirty-one. It simply disappears. The end can come as a rude shock to a devotee, even though he has known all along that it was bound to happen. To see a vast world take shape, to become part of it, to accept it as real, then to have it cease to exist is to be initiated into the dreamlike evanescence of all our "realities." As Lakshman advises Guha, the tribal chieftain in the forest, "If in a dream the lord of paradise becomes a beggar or a pauper is turned into a king, on waking there is neither loss nor gain. So you should look at this deceiving world."[8]

In addition to the ultimate dissolution with the last performance, there is a dramatic dissolution every night at *arati*. *Arati* is the form of Hindu worship, done in both temples and homes, in which offerings are made and lights are waved before the divine image, often to the accompaniment of songs, bells, and other instruments. The Ramlila ends every night with a spectacular *arati*. The director arranges a tableau that includes those of the five *svarups* who were in that night's Lila, and other important characters. He places special garlands over the garlands the deities already wear and arranges the figures in perfect iconographic positions: bow and arrow just so, lotus in hand, and so forth. Once Hanuman enters the narrative, he stands behind them with his bright red mask, slowly waving a cow-hair whisk. The outstanding devotee-character at that point of the Lila stands before them and waves the tray of burning wicks. The Ramayanis shout their *arati* song. Bells, gongs, drums, and conch shells resound. Meanwhile the people (in maximum numbers at this point) are cheering, straining, taken over by a massive desire to see. The climax is reached when a fireworks specialist lights two brilliant flares. The first is red, and it covers the divine tableau with an intense pink light lasting about thirty seconds. The second glows pink for a moment, then explodes into a shattering white that outlines the gods in a hard dazzle and sends its glare far back over the darkened audience. After another thirty seconds, the white light goes out suddenly; the great tension snaps, and the hours of drama come to a decisive close.

DARSHAN

If you ask people why they come to Ramlila, the great majority will say, "To get God's *darshan*." *Darshan* means "vision." Hindus take *darshan* of a holy person, object, or place, believing that its mere presence, particularly the sight of it, conveys blessings. There is a special term for the *darshan* available at Ramnagar: it is called *sakshat*, or "direct-witness" *darshan*. In some sense, one is looking directly at God. The crowned boy with gleaming decorations on his face is not a symbol. But the full experience of *sakshat darshan* does not occur automatically; it requires the proper attitude and openheartedness on the part of the devotee. This all-important feeling, or *bhavna*, will be discussed below.

Although *sakshat darshan* is available from the moment the crown is placed on Ram's head, everyone feels that *arati* is the time for supreme *darshan*, the greatest chance to get a vision of God. Thousands of people come only for *arati*. Special buses come late in the evening from Varanasi. During the illumination of the gods, spectators sing, pray, recite mantras, or stare rapt with joined palms.

Legends about the origin of the Ramlila indicate that a direct vision of God was what the creators had in mind. According to one story, a disciple of Tulsidas, Megha Bhagat, prayed for a vision of the Lord. Subsequently he saw two boys dressed as hunters but did not take much note of them. Later in a dream he learned that these were indeed Ram and Lakshman. Deeply remorseful because he had failed to recognize them, he was told that if he would stage the Bharat Milap (reunion of the two pairs of brothers after fourteen years' separation) in the Varanasi neighborhood of Nati Imli, he would get his vision. Another version of the story has Tulsidas praying for a vision, again seeing two boys in hunting dress and failing to recognize them, but thinking he had seen a performance of the *Ramayana*. The story of Megha Bhagat has a dramatic ending. He staged the Bharat Milap, and at the moment when the brothers embraced, he collapsed and died.[9] To this day the Bharat Milap at Nati Imli is regarded as remarkably powerful. Even the Maharaja crosses the Ganga to attend—the only time he leaves Ramnagar and misses part of his own Ramlila.

In addition to the nightly *arati* there are a number of moments when the Ramlila action is arrested to produce a strong iconographic tableau. These moments are referred to as *jhanki*—literally, "glimpse." They are accompanied by the same spectacular fireworks as are used for *arati*. Examples are when Ram holds Shiva's bow aloft, about to break it and win Sita as his bride; when Sita raises the marriage garland over his head; and when the brothers embrace at the end of the fourteen-year exile. An especially beautiful *jhanki* occurs on the first day: Vishnu reclining on the serpent Shesha, with Lakshmi massaging his legs and Garuda at his feet, floats out under a black starry sky on a great pool that serves as the Milky Ocean.

These *jhanki*—glimpses of a cosmic, eternal divinity—are like crystallizations of the actions that we see unfolding in space and time. The actions take us a step farther toward the "secret" that the Lila and Tulsidas are presenting.

CHARIT

"Yes, yes, God is in the temple too," replied a woman when I pressed her to explain why the Ramlila *swarups* seemed to offer such a special presence of God, even more powerful than a temple image. "Oho! God is in a stone, a tree, in you, in me, everywhere." She paused to reflect, then went on, "But here it is a walking, talking God."

And a *sadhu*, growing a little impatient with my questions about how five boys from Varanasi could suddenly become God incarnate, boomed: "Form! Form! We believe in the form, the dress! We also know that these are boys, this is someone's son."

The *charit* in *Ramcharitmanas* means "acts." Again the word has the same double meaning in English as in Hindi/Sanskrit: "deeds" and "performances." Tulsidas insists that the best way to know the infinite God is through his finite acts. He even creates an important character to challenge this view and systematically demolishes her position. In the most elaborated of four frames that surround the narrative, Shiva tells Ram's story to Parvati, and Parvati plays the skeptic, saying it is impossible to believe that the transcendent Ram, who is beyond attribute or quality *(nirgun)*, acted out such trivial dramas and expressed such puny human emotions as the avatar Ram did.[10] How could the *nirgun* Lord be prince of Ayodhya, play in Dasaratha's courtyard, go mad over the loss of his wife? Shiva ferociously assails her doubt, insisting on the *sagun* Ram, the actor, and declaring that only a blind fool and a sinner could think of *sagun* and *nirgun* as separate. It is through Ram's acts, his human *lila*, that his great secret can be known. Several times Parvati seems to be convinced, then again raises her doubt. This dialogue goes on in a long prelude and postlude to the actual story of Ram. By the end Parvati's doubts are gone; she is a pure devotee whose greatest delight is to listen to tales of Ram's deeds.

The clearest statement in the Ramlila that the world is a dramatic performance with God as writer, director, star, and audience is put into the mouth of Valmiki, Tulsidas's ancient model in telling the tales of Ram's deeds.[11] Traveling through a forest in the early part of their exile, Ram, Sita, and Lakshman arrive at Valmiki's ashram. The sage begins an eloquent speech on Ram's nature and relationship to his devotees with this address to the Lord:

The world is a show and you are the viewer.
You make Brahma, Vishnu, and Shiva dance.
Even they don't know your secret, so
who else can know you?
They only know you whom you let know you,
and in knowing, they become you.
By your grace, Raghunandan, you become known
to the devotee, sandalwood to his heart.
Your body of consciousness and bliss,
unchangeable—they know who have the right.
Putting on a man's body for the sake of gods and saints,
you talk and act like a natural king.
Ram, when they see and hear your acts,
the foolish are bewildered, the wise feel joy.
All that you say and do is true.
According to one's costume, so should one dance.[12]

We the audience have the same relationship to the Ramlila that God has to the play of the universe: we are watchers of the show. At the same time we are participants in the show; and, in a way that will be discussed later, we are even creators of the show. The roles that we play are a matter of costume, appearance, form. A wise person, one who understands the Lord's ability to play, feels joy on seeing him act out his role as king. Such a person sees the truth in these acts (as the *sadhu* said, "We believe in the form, the dress"). A fool merely feels confused.

On several occasions Ram acts like a human being by showing what seem to be petty emotions. He mourns pathetically when his wife is abducted. He becomes furious when Sugriva, the monkey king, forgets his promise to help. We may be inclined, like Parvati, to complain that either this is no Lord of the Universe or that he is indulging in an absurd charade. But Tulsidas often preempts our complaint by pointing to the incongruity himself:

He of whom the Vedas say, "Not this," and whom
Shiva fails to reach in meditation, ran in pursuit
of a false deer.[13]

In this way he searched and wailed
like a passionate husband suffering the extremity

of separation. Ram, whose every desire
is fulfilled, the summation of happiness,
unborn, indestructible, was acting
like a man.[14]

He whose grace removes all pride
and delusion—could he be angry
even in a dream? These acts
can be understood only by enlightened sages
devoted to the feet of Raghuvir.[15]

Ram behaves the way we humans do not because he is like us, but to get us to realize that we are like him. We are in a dream of conflict, gain, and loss. If we could wake up we would see, as the Lord sees, that it is all a Lila. He is mirroring us (which is, by the way, a time-honored theatrical exercise).

Though the literalness of Lila piety—the rush to touch the feet, to taste the *prasad,* to wear the garland, to commandeer a prop like a lotus or a bamboo arrow, to shout, to hear, and above all to *see* the forms of the gods—may seem naïve to an outside observer, it is indeed one of the great secrets of the Lila's power.

The belief that God is everywhere—the literal-minded belief that God is in you and me or a stone, that God has physical and mental attributes, that he takes on those attributes to make himself accessible to his devotees—is so broadly inculcated and deeply imbibed that it seems to shape the way consciousness is structured. "Symbolic" is too flat a word for this type of consciousness, because it suggests that "there" is a reality and "here" is something else symbolizing it. In this universe, as Ernst Cassirer has said, "by a sudden metamorphosis, everything may be turned into everything."[16] God enters the shape of Ramchandra, Ramchandra enters the body of the boy named Ramakrishna Bandhavkar, the earth enters the form of a cow, past time and eternity enter the twentieth century, Ramnagar's huge Durga pool expands to become the Milky Ocean, last-gap image of the unmanifest cosmos. These transformations, I am imagining, occur naturally in the minds of people who grew up in easy intimacy with the God of personality and paraphernalia, the God who has characteristics like their uncles and cousins and is often as common and unheeded as a household item. Though I learned as a college student to talk of God-immanent and God-transcendent, such transformations are not natural for me. That is why during the Ramlila I kept trying, with fascinated curiosity, to find out how people could believe that cosmic divinity was incarnated in Ramakrishna Bandhavkar for a month, and why they kept smiling at my questions as if I had asked, "Why is sugar sweet?"

BHAVNA

One line in the *Ramcharitmanas* was frequently quoted to me as I asked people to speak of how they saw the five boys who put on the guises of the gods. The line occurs in the arena of the Bow Sacrifice at Janakpur. Many princes have assembled to try to break Shiva's bow and thereby win the hand of Sita. An immense audience watches the spectacle within the story, just as an immense audience is watching the Ramlila at that moment. When Ram and Lakshman enter, everyone is transfixed by their beauty. But not everyone sees them in the same way.

> *Jinha ke rahi bhavna aisi / prabhu murati tinha dekhi taisi //* [17]
>
> According to the feeling within him (or her), each saw the form of the Lord.

To warriors he looks like the embodiment of heroism. To wicked kings he seems terrifying, and to demons he appears as Death itself. Women see him as the erotic sentiment personified; Janak and his queens regard him as their child. The learned see his cosmic form with countless faces, hands, and feet. Yogis see the radiant Absolute, and Ram's devotees see their own beloved personal deity. Thus, the poet reiterates, each one sees the king of Kosala according to his or her feeling.

Similarly, what one sees in the Ramlila depends on one's attitude. A *sadhu* talked about this in a tea-stall discussion:

> Look, this is milk. Do you see anything in the milk? But if you heat it, the cream comes up. It's the same with God. Until we heat it up here [points to chest], we can't know. Just as there is butter mixed in milk, so God is hidden in the world. We must heat this body, we must churn it, to find out. Otherwise we just look and see milk. As you see the world now, you go on seeing it.

The devotee who wishes to have a deep experience in the Ramlila must come with a great emotional openness—particularly with the perfect openness known as love. The *Ramcharitmanas* and the Ramlila based on it teach love, tenderness, selflessness, adoration, all focused on Lord Ram, but tending to become qualities of the devotee's entire character. They teach this love in an endless fugue of examples, variations, refinements, love surpassing love, love filtered through every type of personality, in rapture or in grief. The Lord and his devotees have in common an emotional liquidity that is continually expressing itself in tears.

There is a special elocution in the Ramlila for weeping speeches. As in normal dialogues, the rhythm remains stylized, with small word clusters paced by pauses. But the voice is made to break, to wail, trailing from high pitch to low in a very affecting manner. In the great speeches expressing grief, the actors rarely fail to weep. The audience members also weep. Even this outsider couldn't help weeping, though she didn't take Ram as her personal deity and didn't come with the unalloyed devotion that the text calls for. There is something in the voices, in the collective emotion and the situation, that calls forth a deep and nonsectarian response.

Some actors were particularly effective at delivering their speeches. Others were weak but in important speeches tapped some surprising source of energy. The man who played Brahma was ninety-six years old, could barely walk, and did not speak very clearly. But when he delivered the great supplication to Vishnu on behalf of the gods, his voice suddenly found strength. In an interview, we asked if he felt like Brahma during the speech. He replied,

> The emotion is there—if it wasn't, how could I speak? Definitely the feeling of Brahma is there. When I say the prayer, I pray from my own heart. Afterwards, I move about like this [in ordinary clothes]. As I am, so I behave.[18]

The boys playing the gods are young and tender. Their feelings rise easily to the surface. Even if they are only pretending to weep at the beginning of a speech, they are soon genuinely, sometimes uncontrollably, weeping. Hearing them, one feels an involuntary reaction in one's throat and eyes. It becomes a conditioned response to a certain type of speech, whether delivered by children or by adults; yet the emotion does not seem empty. It seems to well up from an ocean of feeling that is always present under the surface and is merely tapped by this event and this elocution.

Mr. Nair, the Maharaja's personal assistant, a South Indian, commented on this phenomenon:

> At the time of *arati* I feel something. There is a contraction in my throat, tears come to my eyes. I can't explain it. I am a rational man. I don't believe it is really Ram standing there. But I have tremendous respect for the idea of *bhakti*. *Bhakti* is a yoga and the *Ramayana* is a yoga. Perhaps it is contagious: such a great energy is going through the crowd at that moment. In the Tantras it is said that you can

> tell the efficacy of a mantra by whether it affects you in this area [indicates neck and face]. After you practice the mantra for some time, you can't say it without something snapping in your throat and your eyes filling with tears.

An old *sadhu* who seemed to epitomize the faith, devotion, and flowing emotion that the *Ramcharitmanas* recommends used to mutter constantly his own incantation of the divine names—*siyajuram jai ram jai jai ram* (Siyaju is an affectionate form of Sita). I often saw his eyes swimming with tears as he gazed on the *svarups* or ran after them on the road. Once he said to me, "Today I do not feel much joy, because no tear has come yet in this noisy crowd." He also said that if one shed a single tear in listening to the Lord's stories, one's debt could never be repaid.

"If you come with the proper feeling in your heart," said Kedarnath, the man who made the garlands for *arati*, "you will see God. There is no one who comes here regularly who has not experienced some sort of miracle." Asked what sorts of miracles he meant, he replied, "It's some knowledge that enters your heart from the Lord. It's not easy to explain. The Lord causes your mind and heart to be illumined."

A seventy-nine-year-old man who had been coming to Ramlila since he was nine interrupted me as I was trying to question him about the "truth" he experienced. He was breathing fast, his voice trembling:

> Enough, enough, enough. What can I say to you? Yesterday I experienced this: I am sitting in Ramji's court, and today is the Lord's coronation. Today this is also my experience. I am sitting in the Lord's court. In the whole world there is nothing else. There is only the Lord. I have no curiosity, no wish, no desire.

A few minutes later when I tried to ask him about *arati*, he interrupted again:

> At the time of *arati* the Lord himself is present. Whenever and from whatever angle you look, the Lord himself is present. The Lord himself creates this experience, face-to-face, before these very eyes. Whoever wants to experience it, let them experience it.

Similarly, a postman who had been coming for twenty years interrupted me when I tried to find out about differences among the boys who played Ram.

> "Do you feel—," I began.
>
> "I feel beauty," he broke in, "great beauty. There are waves surging in my heart."

"You don't notice any difference?"

"No difference. You shouldn't see difference, you should keep your mind steady."

Then there was the old *sadhu* who said *siyajuram*. He seemed so sincere and pure that I hesitated to intrude on the intimacy of his experience with my inquiries. But he was sweet, kind, and friendly, so I did ask something, as sensitively as I could:

> I have seen you in the Ramlila. You are always in the front. When the Lord moves you move with him, and you stay near him, saying your *japa* [repeated divine names] and keeping your eyes on him. When you look at the Lord at the time of *arati*, what do you feel?

On hearing the question, he withdrew his eyes and began doing his *japa*. Then he fell silent. After a few moments he looked at me again and said,

> It can't be put into words. You try it and see for yourself. You look into those two lotus faces, take *darshan* with a desire for loving attachment *(mamta)*. Then you will know that taste. I can't tell you. *Siyaju ram jai ram jai jai ram, siyaju ram jai ram jai jai ram. . . .*

The much-quoted line about *bhavna* acknowledges that the Ramlila is what you make it. If you come with devotion, you will see God. If you come with cynicism, you will see little boys in threadbare shorts. If you come looking for snacks, you will see refreshment stands. If you come for a spectacle, you will see fireworks. If you come with hostility or fear, that will also color what you see. "According to the feeling within, each one sees the Lord's form": such a statement admits the psychological nature of the Ramlila *darshan*. But it is not, as it might be in a different culture, "merely psychological." It is gloriously, cosmically psychological. Every witness-participant creates the drama in her own mind, and in this drama is at once creator, actor, and viewer. Thus the Ramlila teaches by experience that our realities are mind-made.

One way to explain *maya* or *lila* is to say that form is infinitely transformable. By loving and worshipping form, by experiencing pain when the form changes or disappears, and finally by gaining insight into the Lord's play of appearance and disappearance, the devotee reaches some kind of awakening. But he does not pass beyond the Lord of form, Ram with his dark skin, his bow and arrows, his long arms, his incomparable beauty. He prays to be forever devoted to that form, to be lost in love for those lotus feet. If he ever thinks he has passed beyond it, he will lose not only the beloved form, but the love that brought about and continues to effect his personal transformation.

Yogis talk of supreme dispassion, but the devotees of Ram do not attain or aspire to such dispassion. Rather they attain it with regard to everything except their Lord. Total love for Ram and his *lila* is a condition of their understanding. Believing in a personality rather than in an abstraction, loving a play rather than an idea, they run the risk of suffering when the forms of person and play are withdrawn. But the poignancy of both love and suffering drives them to deeper understanding.

On the thirty-first day of the Ramlila in 1976, a few minutes before the final *arati*, I saw an old man who used to ride in the small boat I took going home from the performances. He was pious and seemed somehow childlike to me; in the boat he sang religious songs that others listened to affectionately. He had two trademarks: a bamboo fan that he always waved, and a cry that he uttered as greeting and comment, as beginning and ending, as if it said everything. The cry was *"O ram ki maya, bhagavan ki maya!"* "Oh, the *maya* of Ram, the *maya* of God!"

Encountering him on the street before the last *arati*, I smiled to hear the familiar words and to see the fan winnowing the air. But there seemed to be something wrong. He was staggering, and his voice was breaking. Then I saw that he was crying. Tears fell down his face as he wailed something that I gradually began to make out: "It's over, God's Lila is over. For a whole year we won't see it. What will we do?"

His legs buckled under him, and a muscular young man helped to hold him up.

"Perhaps he has been drinking," murmured an observer.

"He has not been drinking," said another. "He is absorbed in God."

Spontaneously the young man embraced the old one and lifted him off the ground, shouting the victory cry of the Ramlila: *"Bol raja ramchandra ki jai!"* Others echoed it.

"Someone take my hand and lead me away," said the old man piteously. "It's over, God's Lila is over."

NOTES

I am grateful for the opportunity to publish this revised version of an article that originally appeared in 1983 in a European conference volume. I wish to express my deep appreciation to the American Institute of Indian Studies, which generously supported my Ramlila research (as well as many other endeavors); to Monika Thiel-Horstmann, who organized the original conference in Germany and edited the volume in which the article first appeared; to Richard Schechner, whose enthusiasm and encouragement were entirely responsible for my embarking on this research—originally as his collaborator and junior partner; to Jack Hawley for making this revision and new publication possible; to the late Vibhuti Narain Singh, Maharaja of Banaras, and to the countless individuals—performers, directors, audience members, boatmen, and so on—who shared their lives and enriched mine during the years when these experiences were unfolding.

1. For research on the Ramlila in English in the last few decades, see especially Hein 1972; Hess 1988, 1994; Kapur 1990; Lutgendorf 1989, 1991; Parkhill 1993; Schechner 1985, 1993; Schechner and Hess 1977.

2. When Richard Schechner and I conducted research in the 1970s and 1980s, the Maharaja was Vibhuti Narain Singh—the last maharaja to have been in office before India's independence, thus to have actually served as head of Banaras State. Since his death in 2000, his son has presided over the Ramlila.

3. Lutgendorf 1991, 146–47, 266.

4. Mauni Baba died in the 1980s—an event which, I was told, left the Maharaja depressed for some time.

5. *Ayodhya-kanda, doha* 203, *chaupai* 1, *Shri Ramcharitmanas* (Gorakhpur: Gita Press, 1972), 425. Translations are mine. All citations are from this edition. Henceforth citations will be given in abbreviated form, showing book, *doha,* and *chaupai* numbers. Thus this passage would be cited as 2.203.1.

6. 2.61.2–3, p. 329.

7. For a fuller discussion of *maya* and *lila,* see Hess 1993, 84–90.

8. 2.32.

9. Hein 1972, chap. 5, esp. 105–7.

10. On the frame structure of Tulsidas's *Ramcharitmanas,* see Lutgendorf 1990 and Hess 1993.

11. Valmiki is the poet of the Sanskrit *Ramayana,* dated by scholars to roughly 200 B.C.E.–200 C.E. The sage Valmiki is believed to have lived in Treta Yuga, the same age as the incarnation of Ram—very much earlier than the dates given above. The Sanskrit epic is framed by the story of his inspiration to compose the poem, in which he appears as a character. A new scholarly and literary translation of the Valmiki *Ramayana,* under the general editorship of Robert P. Goldman and published by Princeton University Press, has been appearing volume by volume. Five of the seven books were published between 1990 and 1996.

12. 2.126.1–4, p. 373.

13. 3.26.5, p. 546.

14. 3.29.8, p. 550.

15. 4.17.3, p. 582.

16. Quoted in Rothenberg 1968, 417.

17. 1.240.2, p. 196.

18. In saying, "As I am [i.e., as I am dressed], so I behave," the man who played Brahma unconsciously echoes Tulsidas's "According to one's costume, so should one dance," cited above. Compare also the *sadhu*'s comments on form and dress.

WORKS CITED

Hawley, John Stratton (in association with Shrivatsa Goswami). 1981. *At Play with Krishna: Pilgrimage Dramas from Brindavan*. Princeton: Princeton University Press.

Hein, Norvin. 1972. *The Miracle Plays of Mathurā*. New Haven: Yale University Press.

Hess, Linda. 1983. "Ramlila: The Audience Experience." In *Bhakti in Current Research: 1979–1982*, ed. Monika Thiel-Horstmann. Berlin: Dietrich Riemer Verlag. [earlier version of the present essay]

———. 1988. "The Poet, the People, and the Western Scholar: Influence of a Sacred Drama and Text on Social Values in North India." *Theatre Journal* 40: 236–53.

———. 1993. "Staring at Frames Till They Turn into Loops: An Excursion through Some Worlds of Tulsidas." In *Living Banaras: Hindu Religion in Cultural Context*, ed. C. A. Humes and B. Hertel. Albany: State University of New York Press.

———. 1994. "The Ram Legend as Theatre." In *The Legend of Rama: Artistic Visions*, ed. Vidya Dehejia. Bombay: Marg Publications.

———. 1999. "Rejecting Sita: Indians Respond to the Ideal Man's Cruel Treatment of His Ideal Wife." *Journal of the American Academy of Religion* 67:1: 1–32.

Kapur, Anuradha. 1990. *Actors, Pilgrims, Kings, and Gods: The Ramlila at Ramnagar*. Calcutta: Seagull Books.

Lutgendorf, Philip. 1989. "Ram's Story in Shiva's City: Public Arenas and Private Patronage." In *Culture and Power in Banaras: Community, Performance, and Environment, 1800–1980*, ed. Sandria Freitag. Berkeley: University of California Press.

———. 1990. "The View from the Ghats: Traditional Exegesis of a Hindu Epic." *Journal of Asian Studies* 48: 272–88.

———. 1991. *The Life of a Text: Performing the* Ramcaritmanas *of Tulsidas*. Berkeley: University of California Press.

Parkhill, Thomas. 1993. "What's Taking Place: Neighborhood Ramlilas in Banaras." In *Living Banaras: Hindu Religion in Cultural Context*, ed. C. A. Humes and B. Hertel. Albany: State University of New York Press.

Rothenberg, Jerome. 1968. *Technicians of the Sacred*. Garden City, NY: Doubleday.

Schechner, Richard. 1985. "The Ramlila of Ramnagar." In *Between Anthropology and Theater*. Philadelphia: University of Pennsylvania Press.

———. 1993. "Crossing the Water: Pilgrimage, Movement, and Environmental Scenography of the Ramlila of Ramnagar." In *Living Banaras: Hindu Religion in Cultural Context*, ed. C. A. Humes and B. Hertel. Albany: State University of New York Press.

Schechner, Richard, and Linda Hess. 1977. "The Ramlila of Ramnagar." *The Drama Review* 21: 51–82.

Turner, Victor. 1986. *The Anthropology of Performance*. New York: PAJ Publications.

9 · A Ramayana on Air

"All in the (Raghu) Family," A Video Epic in Cultural Context

PHILIP LUTGENDORF

Rama incarnates in countless ways, and there are tens of millions of *Rāmāyaṇas*.

TULSIDAS, *Rāmcaritmānas 1.33.6*

On January 25, 1987, a new program premiered on Doordarshan, India's government-run television network. Broadcast on Sunday mornings at 9:30 A.M., it represented an experiment for the national network, for it was the first time that the medium of television was to be used to present a serialized adaptation of one of the great cultural and religious epics of India. The chosen work was the *Rāmāyaṇa*—the story first narrated in Sanskrit some two millennia ago by the poet Valmiki and retold numerous times in succeeding centuries by poets in every major regional language, most notably, for North India and for Hindi, in the sixteenth-century epic *Rāmcaritmānas* (The Holy Lake of Ram's Acts) of Tulsidas. The television adaptation, produced and directed by Bombay filmmaker Ramanand Sagar, was itself an epic undertaking. Featuring some three hundred actors, it was originally slated to run for fifty-two episodes of forty-five minutes each but had to be extended three times because of popular demand and eventually grew into a main story in seventy-eight episodes, followed after an interval of several months by a sequel incorporating the events detailed in the seventh book (the *Uttarakāṇḍa*, or epilogue) of the Sanskrit epic. (See figure I at the Web site http://www.clas.ufl.edu/users/vasu/loh.)

Long before the airing of the main story concluded on July 31, 1988, Sagar's *Ra-*

This essay was previously published as "All in the (Raghu) Family: A Video Epic in Cultural Context," in *Media and the Transformation of Religion in South Asia*, ed. Lawrence A. Babb and Susan S. Wadley (Philadelphia: University of Pennsylvania Press, 1995), 217–30.

mayan had become the most popular program ever shown on Indian television, and something more: a phenomenon of such proportions that intellectuals and policy makers struggled to come to terms with its significance. Why and how, observers wondered, had this serial—almost universally dismissed by critics as a technically flawed melodrama—elicited such a staggering response? Did its success point once again to the enduring power of sacred narrative to galvanize the masses, or was it, rather, a cue to the advent of a new force in Indian culture: the mesmerizing power of television? Inevitably the airing of the serial provoked lively debate about such topics as the relationship of folk and elite traditions, the marketing of religion and art, the politics of communalism and of government-controlled mass media, and indeed the message of the *Rāmāyaṇa* story itself.

In seeking to make a modest contribution to this debate, I first present a brief account of the making and airing of the serial and of its public reception, and then consider its relationship to the *Rāmcaritmānas* epic (its principal literary source) and to older and ongoing traditions of performance. The concluding section of this essay examines some critical responses to the serial and the debate it engendered over the impact of television on Indian culture.[1]

SUNDAY MORNINGS WITH RAM

To suggest that the making of a television serial began several millennia ago may appear to risk mimicking studio promotional hype, yet it must be observed that the success of India's most popular serial derives largely from the enduring appeal of the narrative tradition on which it draws. Although the textual and historical problems associated with Valmiki's Sanskrit rendering of the Ram story have fascinated generations of scholars, only recently has significant research focused on the developments that, from the eleventh century onward, contributed to the proliferation of the devotional cult of Ram in northern India and created a religious climate in which its ultimate vernacular vehicle—the epic *Rāmcaritmānas*—could acquire throughout much of the region the status of preeminent text for religious performance.[2] Elsewhere I have traced some of the factors contributing to the adoption of this text by ever wider audiences for both ritual and entertainment purposes—factors that included the patronage of *rājās* and *zamīndārs* in the post-Mughal period and of urban mercantile groups during the latter half of the nineteenth century, as well as the advent of print technology, the rise of literacy among the middle classes, and the ongoing effort to define an orthodox Hindu identity.[3] One result of these trends was the proliferation of increasingly standardized genres of *Mānas (Rām-*

caritmānas) performance: ritualized recitation *(pāṭh)*, oral exposition *(kathā)*, and dramatic enactment *(rāmlīlā)*. All three involve sustained, episodic recitation of the text and use it as a foundation for creative elaboration. As will be shown, the conventions and interpretive strategies of these still-popular genres are reflected in the screenplay of the television serial.

Another background against which the success of the serial must be viewed is the history of motion pictures in India, particularly the film genre "mythological." Drawing on the story traditions of the epics and *purāṇas* and imbued with the emotional piety of regional devotional traditions, mythological films have been part of Indian cinema since the beginning. The pioneer of the Bombay cinema, the Maharashtrian Brahman Dadasaheb Phalke, was inspired by a film on the life of Jesus to create a series of mythologicals beginning with *Rajah Harishchandra* (1912)—the first feature-length film made in India—and including *Lanka Dahan* (The Burning of Lanka, based on an episode from the *Rāmāyana*, 1917) and *Krishna Janma* (The Birth of Krishna, 1919). Although film had been on the Indian scene since 1896 (when the Lumière brothers *cinématographe* was unveiled at Watson's Hotel in Bombay), the actors and themes of early foreign-made films failed to engage the deepest sympathies of the Indian audience. In Phalke's films, however, "the figures of long-told stories took flesh and blood. The impact was overwhelming. When Ram appeared on the screen in 'Lanka Dahan,' and when in 'Krishna Janma' Lord Krishna himself at last appeared, men and women in the audience prostrated themselves before the screen."[4] The devotional behavior of the audience—so striking to a foreign observer—would remain a common response to the screening of religious films and, as we shall see, to the television "Ramayana." Yet the worship of the "flesh and blood" (or celluloid or video) image, far from being a consequence of the "revolutionary" impact of film, was a response with a long indigenous pedigree, rooted in the ritualized but complete identification of actor with deity that is central to Hindu folk performance.

Over the years, a modest number of mythologicals scored as major hits with nationwide audiences. Two of the most notable were versions of the *Rāmāyaṇa:* Vijay Bhatr's *Ram Rajya* (1943; the only film, it is said, that Mahatma Gandhi would consent to see) and Homi Wadia's *Sampoorna Ramayana* (1961). The stronghold of such pictures, however, has not been the Hindi film capital of Bombay, but regional production centers that cater to less urbanized audiences.[5] As was the case in the American film industry, where the 1950s and 1960s saw a flurry of epic religious films, mythologicals have tended to come in clusters, as one successful film generated a series of spin-offs. But while the occasional low-budget effort has produced an unexpected windfall—the best example is *Jai Santoshi Ma* (1975), which, through presenting a new goddess whose time had clearly come, became a runaway hit with women and one of the highest-grossing films of the period—the genre as a whole has seemed riskier than most formulas. Although an audience for such films obviously existed, it was also evident that it was not the regular film-going crowd of young urban males at whom the majority of releases were targeted.

The advent of television did not initially create conditions favorable to the screening of religious narrative. During the 1960s and early 1970s, television sets in India served principally as technological novelties to adorn upper-class sitting rooms, where they provided, for a few hazy hours each night, a droning rendition of the day's news (read in Sanskritized Hindi by a newscaster who always looked directly into the camera—a sort of All-India Radio with a face) and drably edifying cultural programming. The 1970s saw a steady increase in the number of sets and transmission centers, and the advent of color programming, yet the standard audience complaint about Doordarshan remained that it was overwhelmingly dull. The addition of a weekly program of song and dance clips from hit movies (*Chitrahaar*, which immediately became the most popular program on television) and of a Sunday afternoon feature film sparked viewer interest but also confirmed that the appeal of television was largely as an adjunct to the existing film industry, and that the distinctive potential of the small screen had yet to be realized.

In the early 1980s, two related developments transformed Doordarshan: the advent of commercials and the commissioning of serialized dramas from independent studios. Maintaining the national network as a noncommercial preserve had proved a costly proposition and powerful private-sector interests were eager to pay to reach consumers over the airwaves. The decision to accept commercials in turn forced the network to provide more varied and entertaining fare, since sponsors required assurance that audiences would indeed be watching. The new commercials themselves were highly entertaining: financed with high budgets and conceived by advertising directors who kept up with the latest American trends, they burst on the screen in fifteen-minute blocks, sparkling with humor, catchy music, and dazzling special effects, but their glossy look only made the regular programming appear more tired in comparison.

At the same time, Doordarshan began to face competition from videocassette recorders and a burgeoning market in rental movies, which gave viewers the option of switching off the state-controlled channel in favor of taped programs of their choice. The impact of the VCR on Indian culture during the last decade warrants closer examination—it has, for one thing, given Bombay films the truly mass exposure they never enjoyed when confined to cinema halls—but at least one effect was to jolt the officials in Mandi House (Doordarshan's New Delhi headquarters) into the realization that they were in danger of losing their audience, and with it revenues from private sponsorship, unless they were prepared to offer programs that could compete more successfully with the fantasies of the cinema.

The first such effort was Kumar Vasudev's *Ham Log* (Us), a soap opera about a group of families in a middle-class neighborhood. In place of the larger-than-life heroes of the cinema, it introduced a set of believable characters with whom viewers were invited to identify. The runaway success of this fledgling effort prompted the network to commission a whole crop of serials and miniseries, of which the most popular were *Buniyaad* (Foundation, a melodramatic family saga directed by Ramesh Sippy) and *Nukkad* (Street Corner). Though official parlance blessed such efforts with the newly coined Sanskritic genre name *dhārāvāhik* (serialization), the Hinglish word *sīriyal* effortlessly entered popular speech. By any name, serials had come to stay, and during the mid-1980s more than a dozen were airing during any given week. The relative popularity of each was reflected in viewer polls, advertising rates, and the eagerness with which sponsors sought ten-second slots in the blocks of commercials preceding each episode. A new industry was created, employing directors and technicians as well as many stage and cinema actors.

With the rapid proliferation of serials and the liberalization of bureaucratic policies on programming, the subject matter of shows began to display more imagination and diversity. During 1986 two miniseries aired that drew on folklore and mythology: *Vikram aur Vetal* (King Vikram and the Vampire, based on the folktales preserved in the Sanskrit *Kathāsaritasāgara* and in Hindi-Urdu *kissā* texts) and *Krishna Avatar* (Lord Krishna, loosely based on the *Bhāgavata Purāṇa*). Although both were well received by viewers, neither enjoyed enough success to eclipse the popularity of established serials like *Buniyaad*, nor did the religious content of the Krishna series provoke much controversy.

The creator of *Vikram aur Vetal* was Ramanand Sagar (born Ramchand Chopra), a veteran producer-director who, together with his five sons, ran a production company responsible for several hit films, including the high-grossing musical *Arzoo* (Desire) and the espionage thriller *Aankhen* (Eyes)—but never, incidentally, a mythological. Sagar's Natraj Studios fell on lean times in the late 1970s after a string of failures, prompting the director to turn his attention to television. While producing a second miniseries entitled *Dada-didi ki Kahaniyan* (Grandpa and Grandma's Stories), Sagar approached Doordarshan officials with a proposal for an extended serialization of the *Rāmāyaṇa*. By his own account a lifelong devotee of the Tulsi *Mānas,* Sagar claims to have been involved for some twenty-five years in a group that met regularly to recite and discuss the Hindi epic. His proposal was for a detailed treatment in fifty-two episodes, to be based primarily on the Tulsidas version but also drawing on the Sanskrit *Rāmāyaṇa,* the Tamil and Bengali versions of Kamban and Krittibas, and other regional retellings. Initially vetoed by Mandi House, the proposal was revived and resubmitted, but its approval was apparently delayed by concern that the airing of such a serial would arouse communal sentiments.[6] Even when the project was finally given the go-ahead in 1986, it is certain that neither the bureaucrats nor Sagar himself had an inkling of the response it would generate. Significantly, it was assigned a languid time slot at the start of the weekly holiday, when prior network experience indicated few viewers would be watching.

Sagar assembled a cast that combined relatively unknown principals (such as Arun Govil as Ram, Sunil Lahri as Lakshman, and the twenty-year-old Dipika Chikhlia as Sita) with veteran character actors (former wrestler Dara Singh—the serial's monkey-hero Hanuman—had appeared in some two hundred action-adventures). At the secluded hamlet of Umbergaon, on the Gujarat coast some three hours north of Bombay, Sagar laid out "Vrindavan Studios," where the entire crew lived for two weeks each month for the duration of the project.

The serial premiered with a framing narration that situated it in the long tradition of *Rāmāyaṇa* stories in various languages and thus introduced the theme (to be reiterated many times) of the *Rāmāyaṇa* as a symbol of national unity and integration. The story itself opened with a parliament of frightened gods petitioning Vishnu, recumbent on his serpent-couch on the Milky Ocean, to take human form and put a stop to Ravan's depredations; this in turn led to scenes of King Dashrath's fire sacrifice and the birth of Ram and his brothers. Early episodes, while not exactly hurried, moved at a moderate pace through the first of the epic's seven books, showing scenes of Ram and his brothers' childhood, some highly original interpretations of their education in a spartan ashram, and the familiar story of Ram and Lakshman's adventures with the sage Vishvamitra, culminating in the young hero's winning of Sita as his bride.

The rest, as they say, is history. Despite mostly acerbic reviews in the English-language media, condemning the serial as a crude commercialization and decrying its production values and sluggish pace,[7] and a few equally harsh critiques in the Hindi press,[8] the popularity of the serial rose steadily throughout its first six months on the air. In the absence of anything like Nielsen ratings for India, the most telling statistics come from advertising revenues. During its first month, *Ramayan* lagged behind the serials *Bunyaad* and *Khoj*, the weekly Hindi film, and the film-clip revue *Chitrahaar* in the number of advertising spots sold. But it caught up quickly, and the average of fifteen commercials per episode during February jumped to thirty-two by April. In June, *Ramayan* was earning more revenue than any program except *Chitrahaar*, and it passed this competitor the following month. By August, Sagar's program was generating an eighth of the total income of national television. Doordarshan was flooded with requests from some 135 advertisers anxious to pay Rs. 40,000 per ten-second slot to have their products plugged at *Ramayan* screening time, and in September the number of commercials was increased to forty. From that point on, *Ramayan* consistently outgrossed every other program, generating an estimated weekly income of Rs. 2.8–3 million for the network.[9]

What all this translates into in audience numbers is harder to say with accuracy. Conservative estimates of Doordarshan's daily viewership during the period range from 40 million to 60 million, but the response to the *Ramayan* serial was unique. Many sets were mounted in public locations and drew in large numbers of people not normally exposed to television; hence the most popular episodes may have been seen by 80 million to 100 million people—roughly an eighth of India's population. This figure may seem modest by Western standards (the Super Bowl reportedly engages the attention of 40 percent of Americans, while the Academy Awards telecast draws an international audience of some 300 million),[10] but it must be appreciated in terms of the limited number and distribution of television sets in India and the restricted availability of electricity. In fact, it represents an unprecedented regional response to a communicated message.

This response had tangible effects that were repeatedly noted in the press. The spread of "Ramayan Fever" (as *India Today* termed it) generated a flood of newspaper and magazine articles ranging from critical analyses of the serial's content to sensational accounts of its fans' behavior. Throughout most of the serial's run, *Ramayan*-related news appeared with almost daily regularity in local papers. Many reports described the avidity with which successive episodes were awaited and viewed, emphasizing that, for millions of Indians, nothing was allowed to interfere with *Ramayan*-watching. Visible manifestations of the serial's popularity included the cancellation of Sunday morning cinema shows for lack of audiences, the delaying of weddings and funerals to allow participants to view the series, and the eerily quiet look of many cities and towns during screenings—a reporter in Mirzapur observed, "Bazaars, streets, and wholesale markets become so deserted they appear to be under curfew."[11] Other articles reported the decline of traffic on national highways during broadcasts, as truck and bus drivers steered their vehicles to tea shops equipped with television sets, where driver and passengers piled out to watch the episode. On occasion, trains were delayed when passengers refused to leave platform sets until a broadcast was over.[12]

Many articles described the devotional activities that developed around the weekly "auspicious sight" *(darśan)* of epic characters:

> In many homes the watching of *Ramayan* has become a religious ritual, and the television set . . . is garlanded, decorated with sandalwood paste and vermillion, and conch shells are blown. Grandparents admonish youngsters to bathe before the show and housewives put off serving meals so that the family is purified and fasting before *Ramayan*.[13]

Local press reports detailed instances of mass devotion: a Banaras newspaper reported on a sweet shop where a borrowed television was set up each week on a makeshift altar sanctified with cow dung and Ganges water, worshipped with flowers and incense, and watched by a crowd of several hundred neighborhood residents, who then shared in the distribution of 125 kilos of sanctified sweets *(prasād)*, which had been placed before the screen during the broadcast.[14] Such ritualized public viewings were not uncommon: throughout the country, crowds gathered in front of video shops to watch display sets, and some community groups undertook to place sets in public areas. During the final months of the serial, electronics shops reported a dramatic surge in television sales, and all available rental sets were engaged for the crucial Sunday morning slot—sometimes by whole villages that pooled their resources to allow residents to see *Ramayan*. Sporadic incidents of violent protest resulted from power failures during the weekly screening, as when an angry mob in the Banaras suburb of Ramnagar (home of North India's most acclaimed *rāmlīlā* pageant) stormed and set fire to an electrical substation.[15]

The duration of the serial itself became a cause célèbre. Doordarshan initially contracted for fifty-two episodes, but as the story unfolded it became clear both that the audience did not want it to end on schedule and that the pace of the narrative would not allow it to; indeed, by late summer of 1987 it appeared that a termination the following January would leave viewers stranded somewhere in the fifth of the epic's seven books. The slow pace consistently annoyed critics, who complained that Sagar was deliberately drawing out the story to increase his profits, but a public outcry coupled with the financial windfall from advertisers prompted Mandi House to grant two extensions of thirteen episodes each. But as the battle for Lanka raged during June and early July of 1988, concerns were again voiced as to whether the series could end on schedule. At the request of Doordarshan officials, Sagar promised in writing that he would conclude with a special one-hour telecast on July 31.[16] The airing of the final installment was marked by festivities in many parts of the country. Sunday newspapers carried full-page articles on the serial, featuring photos of its stars and headlines like "Farewell to 'Doordarshan Ramayan' ."[17] In Banaras, many neighborhoods were decorated with saffron-colored pennants and festive illuminations, while residents celebrated Ram's enthronement by distributing sweets, sounding bells and conches, and setting off fireworks.[18] In the Maharashtrian city of Nagpur, canopies were erected at principal intersections and color sets installed to allow those without televisions to witness the spectacle.[19] Other municipalities reported homes decorated with earthen oil lamps to welcome Ram's return, prompting one reporter to call it an "early Divali" (similarly, the slaying of Ravan several weeks before had been observed in some areas as an out-of-season *daśahrā* festival).[20]

Yet amid the descriptions of rejoicing, there were intimations of grief and loss as viewers anticipated the first of many Sundays without Ram and Sita. These sentiments found expression in the press a week later, detailing the stages of what one columnist called "the national withdrawal symptom." The front-page headline of *Jansattā* on August 9 announced, "Without *Ramayan* Sunday Mornings Seem Empty." Noting that people throughout the country passed their first *Ramayan*-less Sunday "with difficulty," the paper reported responses to the show's absence by people in various neighborhoods of the nation's capital. These ranged from a betel seller in Shakarpur who observed, "After so many months, I'm finally getting some business on Sunday morning!" to a clothseller in Karolbagh who explained why he had sent his in-shop television set back home by asking, "Why watch television now that *Ramayan* is over?" Anticipating a promised sequel, a woman shopping on Chandni Chowk no doubt summed up the feelings of many devoted viewers: "At least we only have to wait two months. Then Ram will return! Mother Kausalya waited fourteen years for Ram to come back, but I don't know if we can manage for even two months."[21]

THE *KATHĀ* AND THE CAMERA

Clearly, viewer perceptions of the pace and duration of the Sagar *Ramayan* varied greatly. While reviewers in the English-language press complained about the agonizingly slow advance of the narrative—"what with taking practically five episodes to kill Bali and another five to behead Kumbhakarna"[22]—such criticism was less common in Hindi publications, and many viewers protested that the epic was ending too quickly. When asked by *India Today* why he could not fit the events of Valmiki's final book into the original sequence, Sagar himself ingenuously replied, "I had no time. I was given only seventy-eight episodes, fifty-two to begin with. . . . So much had to be omitted."[23]

Perceptible beneath the various responses were varying conceptions of the *Rāmāyaṇa* itself. The English-language critics repeatedly referred to it as a "literary treasure" that Sagar was butchering by dragging it out to enhance his own and the network's profits. Such critics, who often made reference to C. Rajagopalachari's three-hundred-page retelling or R. K. Narayan's even shorter synopsis, could note that films like *Sampoorna Ramayana* had reduced the whole story to three hours, and that the modern ballet *Ramlila,* presented in Delhi each autumn, offered the epic to urbanites and foreign tourists as a four-hour spectacle. For audiences accustomed to such handy condensations, the pace of the serial was irksome indeed. Yet there exist other performance genres in which revered scriptures like the *Mānas* are treated less as bounded texts than as guidelines for imaginative elaboration, and if a storyteller's patrons and audience are willing (as Sagar's were), such performances can be extended almost indefinitely. Indeed, the television version's rambling main narrative, weighing in at just under sixty hours, is far from being the longest popular serialization. The *rāmlīlā* of Ramnagar, which tells roughly the same story, averages three hours per night for thirty-one nights and has been playing to enraptured audiences for a century and a half. And an oral expounder like Ramnarayan Shukla, who proceeds through the epic in daily installments at the Sankat Mochan temple in Bamras, may take more than seven hundred hours (i.e., two years or more) to complete a single "telling"—a feat that makes Sagar's effort seem like a condensation. Since, as I will argue, the *rāmlīlā* and *kathā* traditions have greatly influenced the style and content of the television adaptation, summarizing some of their conventions would be useful here.

In Vaiṣṇava *kathā* (narration or storytelling), a performer, usually called a *kathāvācak* or *vyās,* is invited by an individual patron or community to retell or discourse on a sacred story; a performer who specializes in the Tulsi *Mānas* (the most popular text for *kathā* in North India today) is sometimes called a *Rāmāyaṇī.* Until recently, such storytellers were often hired on a long-term basis to narrate the entire epic in daily installments, usually in the late afternoon when the day's work was done. However, most patrons now favor shorter programs of fixed duration (such as nine, fifteen, or twenty-one days), in which an expounder discourses on only a small section of the text. In both styles of *kathā,* the source text serves merely as the anchor for an improvised verbal meditation that may include almost endless digressions and elaborations, interspersed with relevant quotations from any part of the epic as well as from other revered texts. Tour-de-force performances in which a single line is expounded for days on end are not uncommon and are often cited by devotees as evidence of the talent of a favorite expounder.[24] Another characteristic of such narration is its tendency to "domesticize" epic characters through the retelling of incidents in a highly colloquial style and with details absent from the source text. In addition, events in the story often serve as springboards for homely excursus on matters mystical, philosophical, and even political. Though little studied by academic scholars, *kathā* performance remains a principal form of both religious instruction and popular entertainment in many parts of India.

Rāmlīlā—which occurs mainly at the time of the annual *daśahrā* festival—is similarly extended and episodic, but here the emphasis shifts from hearing to seeing as oral exegesis is replaced by visual and iconographic realization of the narrative. The famous Ramnagar production is often termed a "visible commentary" by its aficionados,[25] who emphasize the opportunity it affords for the experience of divine *darśan*. *Rāmlīlā* is closely related to another Vaiṣṇava performance genre: *jhānkī* (glimpse or tableau), in which consecrated persons or images (usually boys, but sometimes figures of painted clay) are dressed and made up as divine characters and placed in settings intended to evoke mythic scenes. These tableaux are presented for contemplation by audiences, often to the accompaniment of devotional singing.[26]

In the more elaborate *rāmlīlā* cycles, as in other Indian performance genres, great importance is given to facial expression and gesture. Actors are chosen for their physical appearance and trained in all aspects of delivery. The boys in Ramnagar undergo a two-month apprenticeship during which they are taught to identify completely with their epic roles. Such training is thought to facilitate the process whereby the divinity manifests in the body of the actor—an essential element in the theology of Vaiṣṇava performance. And although most *rāmlīlā* plays, like *kathā* performances, are based on the *Mānas,* they too may include episodes not found in the text as well as creative interpretations of its verses. Such elaborations often result in scenes and dialogues much enjoyed by the audience.

Whatever else he may be—movie mogul and shrewd businessman—Ramanand Sagar appears to have a genuine enthusiasm for the *Mānas* and a taste for *kathā*. His reported participation in an ongoing study group must have exposed him to many interpretations of the text, and his interest in the popular expounder Morari Bapu is reflected in his use of excerpts from the latter's performances to introduce several of his marketed cassettes. As the serial unfolded and as he prepared a permanent edition for international release, Sagar became increasingly concerned with his own role as storyteller, frequently appearing in the introductory or concluding portions of each cassette to comment (in typically rambling *kathāvācak* style) on the events being presented.[27] Like Tulsidas, he sought to place himself in a long tradition of *Rāmāyaṇa* narrators, claiming little originality for his screenplay (the credits for each episode cite ten *Rāmāyaṇas* in various languages). Yet Sagar also realized that he was creating a powerful, independent retelling—he remarked to one reporter that "video is like writing Ramayan with a camera"[28]—and in the final, extravagant episode of July 31, he took the ultimate step of placing himself in the narrative, hovering cross-legged on a lotus in the sky above Ayodhya to join assembled deities in singing the praises of the newly crowned Ram. Critics dismissed this as tasteless self-aggrandizement, but viewers apparently took it in stride; wasn't he everywhere being hailed as the "Tulsidas of the video age"?

In both *kathā* and *rāmlīlā*, performers enter a consecrated condition. The oral commentator, no less than the young Brahman actor, purifies himself through dietary and devotional practices and performs rituals before ascending the expounder's dais, where he is garlanded and worshipped as a temporary incarnation of Veda Vyas, the archetypal orator of sacred lore. Sagar was mindful of such conventions, and his widely publicized changes in lifestyle—renouncing alcohol and tobacco and instituting a vegetarian regimen for the film crew—though mocked as hypocritical posing by critics, revealed his concern to accede to his audience's standards for epic performers.

The iconography of the serial combined *rāmlīlā* conventions with the visual vocabulary firmly established through a century of mass-produced religious art. For the consecrated boys of *rāmlīlā*, Sagar substituted adult actors and actresses carefully chosen to reinforce popular conceptions of each character's appearance. In casting his principals, the producer aimed for "exactly that Ram, that Sita, which is in the hearts and minds and perhaps in the souls of millions of people"—and, one might add, on the walls of tea shops and the pages of comic books.[29] That he was extraordinarily successful is attested by numerous posters and calendars featuring garishly colored stills from the serial, or costumed close-ups of Arun Govil with his now-famous enigmatic smile.

The "humanizing" influence of television's close focus imposed its own restrictions on iconography, and certain stock conventions were dispensed with—thus Ram and Bharat did not appear with blue complexions (though Vishnu did in his brief appearances). Yet the depiction was hardly "realistic" in other respects. The costumes and wigs of Ram and Lakshman during their long forest exile, for example, remained immaculate and perfectly arranged (down to a dandified curl at each temple) and their faces clean-shaven, a stylization that bothered critics reared on more naturalistic theater (R. K. Narayan quipped that the brothers "look like Wiltech [razorblade] ads").[30] Hanuman and his legions were depicted according to long-established convention, with muscular but hairless human bodies and only long, padded tails and stylized masking about the mouth and nose to suggest a simian status; their wives were shown as fully human women.[31] Sets and costumes adhered to the garish standard of film mythologicals, which itself reflects poster art and the conventions of the *nauṭankī* tradition and of nineteenth-century Parsi theater. This too provoked criticism—Simran Bhargava in *India Today* quipped that "Raja Janak's palace looks like it's been painted with cheap lurex paint and the clothes look like they've been dug out of some musty trunk in Chandni Chowk's costume rental shops"[32]—yet Sagar made considerable use of outdoor footage, including many impressive sequences of Ram's wanderings through the countryside.

The poor quality of special effects was another fixation of critics, and those accustomed (as some urban Indians now are) to the standards of post-Steven Spielberg Hollywood would indeed find only laughable the pulsating, garishly tinted "divine weapons" and the hovering demons of the television serial, which adhered to a technical standard closer to that of early *Star Trek* or *Dr. Who.* Cost containment was undoubtedly a factor (though some scenes—such as the burning of Lanka—were admirably executed), and Sagar may have shrewdly perceived that the bulk of his audience, accustomed to the modest stagecraft of *nauṭankī* and *rāmlīlā,* would be sufficiently dazzled by cheaper effects. He must also have realized that special effects per se were not crucial to maintaining viewers' interest in the saga, and this leads me to an observation concerning the overall focus of the production. The emphasis in *Ramayan* was squarely on "seeing" its characters. Not "seeing" in the quick-cut, distracted fashion in which modern Western audiences take in their heroes and heroines, but drinking in and entering into visual communion with epic characters.[33]

To most viewers, *Ramayan* was a feast of *darśan,* and its visual aesthetic clearly derived from an indigenous standard. Scenes and dialogues were long (interminable, critics said) and aimed at a definitive portrayal of the emotional state of each character. This was conveyed especially through close-ups (and in moments of intense emotion, repeated zoom shots—a convention favored in Hindi films), so that much of the time the screen was dominated by large heads, either verbalizing or silently miming their responses to events. Every nuance of emotion of every character—each *bhāv* of classical aesthetic theory—was conveyed visually, and in scenes involving many characters (such as the assembly in Chitrakut, when Bharat begs Ram to return to Ayodhya), the camera focused in turn on the face of each principal to record his or her response—grief, surprise, anger, calm—to each new development. Though appallingly overstated by contemporary Western standards, this technique is consonant with the mime or *abhinay* of indigenous genres like Kathakali and Bharat Natyam, in which the audience is expected to focus intently on the performer's facial expressions and gestures. The television screen is particularly suited to this kind of close-up mime, and Sagar exploited its potential to allow his viewers an experience of intense communion with epic characters.

NOTES

All references to the epic are to the popular Gita Press version (Poddar 1938; reprinted in numerous editions). Numbers refer to book *(kāṇḍ)*, stanza (understood as a group of lines ending in a numbered couplet), and individual line within a stanza. When a stanza concludes with more than one couplet, these are indicated with roman letters (e.g., 12a, 12b, etc.). Throughout this chapter, the term *Rāmāyaṇa* is used to refer to the overall tradition of stories about Ram. The title of the Sanskrit epic of Valmiki is similarly transliterated *Rāmāyaṇa*, and the Hindi epic of Tulsidas is generally referred to (as in Hindi sources) as the *Mānas*. Proper nouns from Indic languages are transliterated without diacritics, and certain common romanizations are used—e.g., Doordarshan for *dūrdarśan*.

1. I am grateful to Cynthia Ann Humes, who collected articles on the serial for me (with the help of a newspaper vendor in Mirzapur, Uttar Pradesh) while carrying out research at the Vindhyachal Devi temple in 1987–1988. I am also indebted to Chitranjan Datt of the Landour Language School, who assisted me in translating several articles.
2. Whaling 1980; Bakker 1986; van der Veer 1988.
3. Lutgendorf 1989, 1991.
4. Barnouw and Krishnaswamy 1980, 15.
5. A film often cited as one of the finest and most popular of the genre was the Marathi-language *Sant Tukaram* (1936). In the 1960s and 1970s, the Telugu film industry churned out a steady diet of mythologicals, featuring the star whose portrayal of epic characters in forty-two musicals (he played Ram in six films, Ravan in three others, and in one—through the miracle of the camera—both roles at once) earned him the leadership of a political party—N. T. Rama Rao.
6. Mazumdar 1988, 2.
7. *India Today's* critic carped that "everything seems to be wrong with *Ramayan*. . . . [It] has all the finesse of a high school function" (Bhargava 1987, 70). *The*

Illustrated Weekly (1987, 9) complained that the serial had "destroyed the spirit and the superb literary quality of the original, in its obsession for the megabuck." A critic in *Economic and Political Weekly* termed it "a poorly acted, still more poorly produced, lurid dramatisation of the epic" (Deshpande 1988, 2215).

8. For example, Pachauri 1987; I am grateful to Monika Horstmann for alerting me to this article. While condemning the series as a vulgar commercialization likely to inflame communal violence, Pachauri, like many other Hindi critics, devotes much attention to what he sees as misinterpretations of the *Mānas* text—a line of attack used by few English-language writers (perhaps because they have not read Tulsidas?). This criticism does not seem especially well-informed, however; thus Pachauri mocks the "flower garden" scene of Ram and Sita's first meeting (episode 6), claiming that it shows Ram as "a flirtatious dandy" and is inspired by the love scenes of Bombay films. "Tulsi," he primly asserts, "disposed of Lord Ram's romance in two verses." This is patently untrue: the garden scene in the *Mānas* occupies nearly a hundred lines and, precisely because of its romantic content, has become one of the most beloved passages in the epic.

9. *Illustrated Weekly of India* 1987, 17.

10. Read 1985, 153, 163.

11. *Dainik Jāgaraṇ* 1988c, 7.

12. Reported in "The Ramayan Phenomenon," an article apparently reprinted from an unidentified magazine and included in a promotional brochure distributed by Sagar Enterprises.

13. Melwani 1988, 56.

14. *Dainik Jāgaraṇ* 1988b, 3.

15. *Dainik Jāgaraṇ* 1988a.

16. This decision gave rise to a tumultuous controversy over the deletion of Valmiki's seventh book, the *Uttarakāṇḍa*, which led to strikes, political agitation, High Court cases, and the eventual commissioning of a sequel series of twenty-six episodes that aired during 1989. Fascinating though it was, the controversy is beyond the scope of this essay.

17. *Āj* 1988b, 6.

18. *Dainik Jāgaraṇ* 1988d, 3.

19. *Indian Express* 1988, 5.

20. *Times of India* 1988, 3.

21. *Jansattā* 1988b, 1.

22. Mazumdar 1988, 2.

23. Cited in Jain 1988, 81.

24. The renowned early nineteenth-century expounder, Ramgulam Dvivedi, is said to have once discoursed on a single line from book 1 for twenty-one days. I myself wit-

nessed a seven-evening performance by the Banaras expounder Shrinath Mishra based on one line from book 7 (see Lutgendorf 1989, 1991).

25. See Schechner and Hess 1977.

26. Hein 1972, 17–30.

27. He was not the first director of a religious film to assume this responsibility; cf. Cecil B. DeMille's opening speech, before a golden curtain, at the start of *The Ten Commandments* (1956).

28. Cited in Melwani 1988, 56.

29. Melwani 1988, 56.

30. Cited in De 1988, 5.

31. All such details have a long history and reflect an ongoing controversy over the precise nature of Ram's *vānar* allies, who as incarnations of deities in simian guise both are and are not "monkeys."

32. Bhargava 1987, 70.

33. American movies and television in recent years have favored constant visual stimulation, often at the expense of dialogue and extended character development. The trend is especially striking if one compares films of the 1920s and 1930s with those of the past two decades; in the latter, camera angles constantly shift, scenes often last only seconds, and character is conveyed through a few expressive close-ups and terse exchanges; the style has become such a convention that we may no longer notice it. According to Neil Postman (1985, 86), the average length of time during which a single image remains on the American television screen is only three and a half seconds. The commercial success of MTV in recent years, with its numbing flood of decontextualized images, has further upped the ante on visual stimulation throughout the media.

WORKS CITED

Āj. 1988a. " '*Rāmāyaṇ*' ke daurān parīkṣāẽ na ho" [Exams not to be held during "Ramayan"]. May 26: 4.

———. 1988b. "Alvidā 'Dūrdarśan rāmāyaṇ' " [Farewell to "Doordarshan Ramayan"]. July 31: 6.

Bakker, Hans. 1986. *Ayodhyā*. Groningen: Egbert Forsten.

Barnouw, Erik, and S. Krishnaswamy. 1980. *Indian Film*. New York: Oxford University Press.

Bhargava, Simran. 1987. "Ramayan: Divine Sensation." *India Today*, April 30: 70.

Dainik Jāgaraṇ. 1988a. " 'Rāmāyaṇ' ke mauke par bijlī jāne se upakendra par patharāv, āgjanī" [Stoning and arson at electrical substation due to power failure during "Ramayan"]. March 21: 3.

———. 1988b. "Rāmāyaṇ dekho, mālpuā pāo" [Watch Ramayana and get sweets]. June 6: 3.

———. 1988c. "Dhārāvāhik Rāmāyaṇ: hiy kī pyās bujhai na bujhāye" [The Ramayana serial: The heart's thirst is still unsatisfied]. July 31: 7.

———. 1988d. "Rāmrājyābhiṣek par 21 man dūdh kī khīr bāṇṭī gayī?" [One ton of milk-sweets distributed for Ram's royal consecration]. August 1: 3.

De, Aditi. 1988. "The Man From Malgudi." *Indian Express Magazine,* October 2: 5.

Deshpande, G. P. 1988. "The Riddle of the Sagar Ramayana." *Economic and Political Weekly,* October 22: 2215–16.

Hein, Norvin. 1972. *The Miracle Plays of Mathura.* New Haven: Yale University Press.

Illustrated Weekly of India. 1987. "The Ramayan." November 8–14: 8–17.

Indian Express. 1988. "Fanfare Marks 'Ramayana' End." August 2: 5.

India Today. 1986. Advertisement. March 15: 22.

Jain, Madhu. 1988. "Ramayan: The Second Coming." *India Today,* August 31: 81.

Jansattā. 1988a. "Sāgar ko yakīn thā kī Rāmāyaṇ baṛhegī" [Sagar was confident Ramayan would be extended]. August 1 :7.

———. 1988b. "Binā 'Rāmāyaṇ' ravivār kī subah sūnī-sūnī si" [Without "Ramayan" Sunday mornings seem empty]. August 9: 1.

Lutgendorf, Philip. 1989. "Ram's Story in Shiva's City." In *Culture and Power in Banaras,* ed. Sandria Freitag, 34–61. Berkeley: University of California Press.

———. 1991. *The Life of a Text: Performing the* Rāmcaritmānas *of Tulsidas.* Berkeley: University of California Press.

Mazumdar, Debu. 1988. "Mandi House Had Rejected Ramayana." *Indian Express,* August 1: 2.

Melwani, Lavina. 1988. "Ramanand Sagar's Ramayan Serial Re-Ignites Epic's Values." *India Worldwide,* February: 56–57.

Pachauri, Sudhish. 1987. "Savāl to rāmkathā ke istemāl kā hai" [The real question concerns the use of the Rama story]. *Jansattā,* August 6.

Poddar, Hanuman Prasad, ed. 1938. *Śrī Rāmcaritmānas.* Gorakhpur, U.P.: Gita Press.

Postman, Neil. 1985. *Amusing Ourselves to Death.* New York: Penguin Books.

Read, Michael R. 1985. "Understanding Oscar: The Academy Awards Telecast as International Media Event." In *The Critical Communications Review,* vol. 3, *Popular Culture and Media Events,* ed. Vincent Mosco and Janet Wasko, 153–78. Norwood, NJ: Ablex.

Sagar Enterprises, Inc. 1987(?). "The Ramayan Phenomenon" [reprinted article contained in a promotional brochure].

Schechner, Richard, and Linda Hess. 1977. "The Ramlila of Ramnagar." *The Drama Review* 21 (September): 51–82.

Times of India. 1988. "Early Divali." August 9: 3.

Van der Veer, Peter. 1988. *Gods on Earth*. London: Athlone Press.

Whaling, Frank. 1980. *The Rise of the Religious Significance of Rama*. Delhi: Motilal Banarsidass.

10 · Possession by Durga

The Mother Who Possesses

KATHLEEN M. ERNDL

Although individual Hindu goddesses possess distinctive attributes, their identities also overlap to a considerable extent, and many—if not most—goddesses are, at least in some contexts, considered to be manifestations of the one Great Goddess, Devī. Similarly, goddesses tend to manifest themselves not in a single form but in multiple iconic forms, as well as in such natural phenomena as rocks, plants, rivers, mountains, and flames. This flexibility of identity and multiplication of form are nowhere more evident than in the phenomenon of divine possession.

Divine possession is the most dramatic way to encounter the Goddess experientially, and it also presents the greatest challenge to the Western worldview. It is one thing to read sacred texts about the Goddess or to view her images, to analyze the metaphors of the former or the aesthetic qualities of the latter. It is quite another to meet the Goddess face-to-face. By way of introduction, I will present two brief vignettes that encapsulate some of what I have experienced in my encounter with Goddess possession while doing fieldwork in northwest India and in trying to interpret it in a scholarly context back home.

The first incident took place in the Punjabi town of Mohali, a suburb of Chandigarh, in the winter of 1983. I was sitting on the floor in the home of a lower-middle-

This essay was previously published as "The Mother Who Possesses," in *Devī: Goddesses of India*, ed. John Hawley and Donna Wulff (Berkeley: University of California Press, 1996), 173–83, 192–93.

class family in the company of about fifty festively dressed people—women, men, and children. It was about two in the morning. We were attending a Devī *jagrātā*, an all-night ritual performance in which the Goddess is worshipped with devotional songs and stories of her exploits. The performers, joined by the congregation, were singing a devotional song to the lively beat of a drum. The Goddess was present that night in the form of a flame that had been lit and consecrated, and then surrounded by offerings of fruit and flowers and placed on a platform at the front of the room. She was also present in the form of a sixteen-year-old girl called the "Little Mother," who was seated on another platform, next to the flame. The Goddess had entered her body and was "playing" within her. Her long black hair flew out from her face as though charged with electricity as her head whirled about in rhythmic circles. From time to time, members of the congregation would go up and make offerings to her.

I was tired and, frankly, a little bored, since I had seen all this before—and I found myself wishing that I had chosen to do research on something that took place at a more reasonable hour. Then for some reason I glanced at the woman sitting next to me. She was probably in her mid-fifties, plump, well-dressed, and matronly looking. I had not spoken with her, although earlier we had nodded to each other in greeting. Suddenly, the woman's head began to move from side to side, her eyes glazed over, and she started to shake. Standing up, she began to dance frenetically, her tightly bound hair loosening, then fanning out from her face. I was frozen with fear. The other people were moving away from her and pulling me along with them. Later—I do not remember how much later—she calmed down and sat quietly, but her eyes remained unfocused. I was left wondering whether this could happen to me.

The second event took place in Madison, Wisconsin, in November 1983. Having just returned from India, I had presented a paper at the annual Conference on South Asia on the Devī *jagrātā* as a ritual performance. Although only a small portion of my presentation dealt with the phenomenon of Goddess possession, it was this part that evoked the most comment during the question-and-answer period. Afterward, a senior colleague asked me if I had ever believed that it really was the Goddess possessing those women. I answered impulsively, "Yes." Upon reflection I realized that it was the experience of observing possession, of coming face-to-face with this impressive manifestation of the Goddess's power *(śakti)*, that brought home to me in a very concrete fashion the immediacy with which devotees experience the Goddess's presence. This in turn led me to take seriously the notion of the Goddess as an agent herself, rather than simply a symbol or projection.

Much scholarship on various kinds of spirit possession has assumed (usually tacitly) that the possessing entity is an epiphenomenon, that is, that it does not "really" exist. Anthropologist Manuel Moreno, however, has argued for what he calls a "processual" view of deities, as opposed to a "structural" view. The structural view sees deities as "disembodied symbols" of social realities and human relationships. The processual view, in contrast, accepts deities as effective agents, as personal beings who interact with humans. While acknowledging the value of structural analysis for illuminating aspects of social structure that are not readily apparent through observation, Moreno argues that such an analysis fails to take into consideration the dynamics of the interaction between deities and humans as Hindus themselves understand them.[1] His position is very close to my own: to understand the phenomenon of Goddess possession, one must treat the Goddess herself as an agent who interacts with both the person possessed and the devotees who worship her.

The word *her* at the end of the last sentence is deliberately ambiguous, for the devotees worship both the Goddess and the person who is possessed; both are Mātā. But the question still remains as to whether the Goddess and her human vehicle are completely separate entities, one of which temporarily "overtakes" the other, or whether they are in some sense in a relation of identity with each other, perhaps in a process of exchange or transformation. Here the line between human and divine becomes blurred (so much so that I was tempted to entitle this essay "The Mother Who Is Possessed" rather than "The Mother Who Possesses"). Is it the human vehicle who becomes the sacred female by virtue of the infusion of *śakti?* Or is it the Goddess herself who "inhabits" the human vehicle as her chosen means of manifesting herself to her devotees? Of course, both are true, in much the same way as the "duck-rabbit" drawing is simultaneously both a duck and a rabbit, although only one at a time can be perceived. Also, one must know what to look for in order to see either one. A woman trembles, her eyes glazed, her hair disheveled. Some see a woman expressing her own power. Some see the Goddess herself. Others might see a psychological disorder or an outright fraud. It all depends on one's point of view. Here, my point of view will shift back and forth between that of the Goddess and that of her human vehicles, in keeping with the fluid nature of their complex relationship.

THE SEMANTICS AND DYNAMICS OF GODDESS POSSESSION

My area of study is northwest India, including the territories of Delhi and Chandigarh and the states of Punjab, Haryana, and much of Himachal Pradesh. While certain specifics of terminology and practice may be unique to this region, I believe that similar dynamics of Goddess possession can be found throughout India.[2] In northwest India, the worship of Devī is perhaps the most prevalent manner of religious expression among Hindus. The region boasts a multitude of pilgrimage sites associated with the Goddess, such as Vaishno Devi, Jvala Mukhi, and Chintpurni. Each of these houses a particular goddess who has her own personality, iconography, and cycle of stories, and who is simultaneously considered to be a manifestation of the one all-pervading divine force, *śakti.* When spoken of in general terms, as she often is, the Goddess is commonly called Śerāṇvālī, "Lion Rider" (a nickname of the demon-slaying Durgā) or simply Mātā, "Mother." In her cult esoteric Tantric elements mingle with popular devotional worship *(bhakti)* and folk elements. (See figure J at the Web site http://www.clas.ufl.edu/users/vasu/loh.)

Although this lion-riding mother goddess has mythological and ritual affiliations with the great male deities Viṣṇu and Śiva, it is in her independent form that she is most often worshipped. That is, she is not seen as a consort deity, like Lakṣmī or Pārvatī, whose identity is linked with a male deity. Yet she is not completely different from such goddesses, for on some level all goddesses are one. One way to approach this complex issue is to view the various goddesses associated with Śerāṅvālī as functioning in an independent (as opposed to a consort) mode. It is this mode that most concerns us here, since the Goddess manifestations who typically operate independently—such as Vaiṣṇo Devī, Kālī, Jvālā Mukhī, and Santoṣī Mā—are the ones most likely to possess human vehicles. Although Punjabis and other people in northwest India are familiar with Lakṣmī and Pārvatī and do worship them on occasion, I have never heard them speak of these goddesses as possessing people.

The goddess Śerāṅvālī is both transcendent and immanent, her functions ranging from such cosmic concerns as the creation, preservation, and destruction of the universe to personal concerns—curing diseases, helping people in distress, and so on. She is the embodiment of *śakti,* the dynamic power of the universe. Implicit in the theology of this Goddess is a monism in which matter and spirit are not differentiated but rather form a continuity that is subsumed within *śakti,* the feminine creative principle. Whereas the Śaiva and Vaiṣṇava theologies both recognize *śakti* to be the active (feminine) aspect of the Divine, the complement to the inactive (masculine) aspect, the goddess-focused Śākta theology understands *śakti,* which is identified with the Great Goddess, to be the ultimate reality itself and the totality of all being. The general thrust of Śākta theology is to affirm the reality, power, and life force that pervades the material world. Matter itself, while always changing, is sacred and is not different from spirit. The Goddess is the totality of all existence; accordingly, as a reflection of the way things really are, she takes on both gentle *(saumya)* forms such as Vaiṣṇo Devī and fierce *(raudra)* forms such as Kālī. Creation and destruction, life and death, are two sides of the same reality. The Goddess encompasses both. Furthermore, the Goddess is not just a transcendent ideal but also an immanent presence in the lives of her devotees.

The Goddess is worshipped in various contexts and in various of her manifestations—at pilgrimage sites, in ritual performances, and at household shrines in forms such as stone, flame, and icon. The most dramatic way in which devotees experience the Goddess, though, is through her possession of human—and usually female—vehicles. This type of possession is not regarded as an affliction but rather as a sign of grace, as the Goddess's chosen method of granting a sacred vision *(darśan)* to her devotees. While the concern of this essay is specifically divine possession within the Goddess cult, it is worth pointing out that many other kinds of spirit possession are prevalent in South Asia, such as unwanted possession by malevolent or mischievous spirits, ghosts, or ancestors *(bhūt-pret)*. Susan Wadley, writing about Uttar Pradesh, John Stanley, writing about Maharashtra, and Gananath Obeyesekere, writing about Sri Lanka, all refer to differences between afflicting or evil spirits and invited or divine spirits.[3] Similarly, in northwest India possession by an evil spirit must be exorcised by force or appeasement, but possession by a benevolent deity such as Śerāṅvālī is usually encouraged and cultivated, even if not initially sought. Possession by an evil spirit is seen as an affliction or punishment; possession by the Goddess is seen as a gift, a sign of grace—a positive, albeit awesome and often troublesome, appearance. But what exactly is possession? To describe this cross-cultural phenomenon, the following definition provides a good starting place: "any complete but temporary domination of a person's body, and the blotting out of that person's consciousness, by a distinct alien power of known or unknown origin."[4] Yet the word *possession* is inadequate except as a very rough gloss of what is actually a complex set of related phenomena. In Hindi and Punjabi certain phrases are used in the context of the Goddess cult to describe these phenomena, although the terminology naturally varies throughout India.

Two of the most common expressions are "wind form" *(pavan rūp)* and "playing" (Hindi, *khelnā;* Punjabi, *kheḍnā*). When a woman is possessed, the Goddess is said to take on a "wind form," enter her, and "play" within her. Her hair, no matter how tightly bound, is said to come undone and fly freely in response to the force of the wind *(pavan)*. The state of possession is characterized by glazed eyes, a change in voice, and the whirling around of the head, with hair flying loose. Under normal circumstances, a respectable woman's hair is tied up and braided, not allowed to hang loose. In a discussion of hair symbolism among Hindu and Sikh Punjabis, Paul Hershman mentions that, among the contexts in which the expression *val khūle* (loose hair) is used, we find "a woman possessed who in a trance whirls her head with her hair flying free."[5] In this instance, the Goddess is said to have taken on *pavan rūp*, "wind form."

Yet there are also times when the Goddess assumes her "wind form" without entering a human vehicle. In that sense, it is invisible yet perceptible. "Wind" is a subtle form that occupies an intermediate position between the unmanifest Goddess and a concrete manifestation. It is a form characterized by motion and breath that the Goddess takes on to move from one place to another or to display her power, but without becoming fully visible. For example, in several versions of the story of Queen Tārā, the charter myth for the all-night songfest *(jagrātā)* honoring the Goddess, the word *pavan* describes such a form: when King Harīcand's wakefulness prevents Tārā from attending the sweepers' *jagrātā*, Tārā prays to the Goddess, whereupon a cool breeze *(pavan, havā)* arises and puts the king to sleep. Likewise, a holy man who serves at a Durgā temple once told me that he had been called there by the Mother, who had come to him in the form of "wind." Whenever he forgets to do some work, she again comes into his mind as "wind" to remind him. When this happens, he said, she enters his mind through the breath in his mouth, and he then sees her in his mind. This is not possession in the usual sense of the term.

Similarly, the expression "playing" is used variously. It can, for instance, refer to the wild and "playful" head and body movements of the person who is possessed. The Goddess is said to be "playing" in that person, as in the expression "The Goddess plays in X," although sometimes the human vehicle is the agent, as in "X started playing." A slightly different but related use of "play" occurs in devotional songs that turn on the image of young girls *(kanyā, kañjak)*, representative of the Goddess in her virgin aspect, playing in the temple courtyard.[6] These songs represent the sweet and lovable aspect of the divine play, evoking *vātsalya bhāva* (parental love)—one of the principal modes of religious devotion *(bhakti)*—much as in the cult of the child Krishna. These expressions are tied in with general notions of divine play in the Hindu tradition.[7] Stories connected with the Goddess variously describe her actions as play *(khel)*, drama or sport *(līlā)*, and art or fabrication *(kalā)*. These terms are used more or less interchangeably to suggest the Goddess's exuberant, but seemingly (to humans) purposeless creativity. The word *possession* can thus provide only a rough and partial semantic equivalent for what is a fluid, multifaceted set of concepts.

The person possessed is called the *savārī*, "vehicle" (as in "she is the vehicle of Kālī"); *savārī* here designates the woman whom the Goddess, having assumed a particular form, rides on or inhabits and through whom she speaks. *Savārī* also used to describe the Goddess herself: she is *savārī rūp*, "[one who has a] vehicle form," again referring to her action of "riding" or "mounting" a possessed person.

In reading about South Asia, one often gets the impression that possession, along with related ecstatic behavior, belongs to the "little tradition" and is thus largely confined to the lower castes and the poor and uneducated in rural areas. However, in my experience, the phenomenon of possession in the cult of Śerāṅvālī is widespread throughout the population. I have witnessed Goddess possession in both village and urban settings, among low and high castes (including Brahmins), the poor and the rich, the uneducated and the educated, Sikhs as well as Hindus. As far as gender is concerned, possession by the Goddess, though occurring in both sexes, is more frequent among women, while possession by a male deity such as Bābā Bālak Nāth is more common among men. At the same time, possession experiences vary considerably in their intensity, duration, and frequency. The degree of recognition, respect, and encouragement given to possession vehicles by other members of society is similarly quite variable.

Unplanned, uncontrolled possession occasionally occurs in a nonritual context. Although I have not directly observed this type of possession, I have heard reports of young girls "playing" for hours on end without warning. Such descriptions typically form part of the hagiographies of women who later achieved some control and regularity over their possession and have come to understand it in terms of the theology and religious practice of devotion to Devī. At the time of the initial possession, however, neither the vehicle nor others may have recognized (or accepted) that the possessing deity was the Goddess. Family members and others often suspect sorcery, insanity, or possession by a malevolent spirit, since these all exhibit similar symptoms.

Unplanned, uncontrolled possession may occur in devotees who participate in ritual activities such as a *jagrātā*, devotional singing, or pilgrimage. While the music is playing and the drums beating, someone may spontaneously start to shake, roll the head, or dance, as I described in the opening vignette of this essay. No one seems unduly surprised or disturbed when this happens, and in many cases it remains an isolated event in the person's life. However, such spontaneous possession experiences do sometimes occur repeatedly, developing into a periodic pattern that becomes a planned part of the person's devotional and spiritual practice. I came across an example of this development while interviewing a man of the Kāyasth caste from Chandigarh who was on a group pilgrimage to the major Devī temples. In a discussion of his long-standing devotion to the Goddess and the miracles she had performed for him, he volunteered the information that he had recently started to "play," describing his experience as follows.

> I do *pūjā* twice a day. When I go to a *jagrātā,* I get the experience of possession. I see Devī seated on a lion, and my head starts whirling around. This has been happening for five or six months now. . . . I get a feeling of wind *(pavan)* overwhelming me like a whirlwind and see the image of Devī. I am not afraid of this experience. I sit in front of a flame every day and concentrate. The wind comes when I am listening to a beautiful song. At first my wife worried that I would renounce the world, but now she and the children realize what it is.[8]

This informant's description of a vision *(darśan)* of the Goddess accompanied by the sensation of wind is typical of possession experience. The vision of the Goddess and the statements she makes while inhabiting her vehicle are the major signs that distinguish possession by Devī from possession by other deities or spirits.

In a performance situation such as a *jagrātā,* possession is often found to be planned, even orchestrated, plus which there seems to be a progression from an initial spontaneous incident to more controlled and periodic possessions. A woman may start to become possessed on a specific day of the week, such as Tuesday or Friday, or on the eighth day of the bright fortnight of the lunar month—days traditionally associated with Goddess worship. When news of this spreads outside her family, people may come on these days to sing devotional songs, offer her gifts, and ask for her help as an oracle or healer. The woman may start to hold ritual functions in her home on a regular basis; she may be invited to participate in these events at others' homes. She may build a small shrine or temple and/or start making pilgrimages with her devotees to Devī temples. In this way, a small cult begins to form.

During the spring and fall Navarātras and the ten-day festival during the month of Sāvan (July–August), pilgrimage places such as Jvala Mukhi, Chintpurni, and Naina Devi are besieged by these women (called Mātās, "mothers") and their entourages. They come from villages and towns all over the greater Punjab, bearing red flags and other offerings. They bring drums, cymbals, and musical instruments—nowadays even a cassette tape player—and set up "stage" in the temple courtyard. After lighting incense and a lamp, they start drumming and singing, and the Mātā begins to "play." People in her entourage and other pilgrims at the temple approach the Mātā to worship, make a small cash offering, and then ask for a prophecy or favor.

At any given time during the festival season, and occasionally at other times, one can see several of these performances going on at once amidst the other temple activities: *pūjā* (ritual offerings), *āratī* (waving of the flame), ecstatic dancing and singing, the ritual shaving of childrens' heads, and the worship of virgin girls. Pilgrims eat and distribute *prasād* (consecrated food), priests recite the *Devī Māhātmya*, and people shout the ubiquitous cry of joy, *Jay mātā dī* ("Victory to the Mother").

The goddess Śerāṅvālī is like the great gods Viṣṇu and Śiva in her power, purity, and universality. At the same time, she shares characteristics such as accessibility, immanence, and intimacy with the lesser deities and saints. While the great male gods of the Hindu pantheon do not generally possess their devotees, the more minor divinities do. When I asked informants why the Goddess possesses people, whereas Viṣṇu and Śiva do not, they were usually unable to provide a reason. One informant, however, the secretary of the newly built Bābā Bālak Nāth temple in Chandigarh, gave this explanation:

> Bābā Bālak Nāth and Devī can both enter a man or a woman. Just as there are different branches of the government, so do different gods have different functions. Full avatars [incarnations of the Divine] do not enter people. Viṣṇu and so forth do not. But Mā is *śakti;* she is everywhere. Therefore, she does not fall into the category of avatar.[9]

The monistic identification of spirit and matter found in Śākta theology may help explain why possession by the Goddess occurs far more frequently than possession by such supreme male deities as Viṣṇu and Śiva. As we have noted, male deities do possess human devotees, but these tend to be lower-level functionaries such as Bābā Bālak Nāth or Guggā Pīr, with the occasional exception. The cults of Narasiṃha in Himachal Pradesh and Venkaṭeśvara in Andhra Pradesh—both incarnations of Viṣṇu—involve divine possession, but these are atypical.

The general understanding of possession is that the Goddess plays in people and speaks through them as a means of helping her devotees and revealing her *śakti*. She may also wish to castigate those who have committed some evil or issue a demand that she expects her devotees to fulfill. It is not unusual for new temples to be built or old images to be "rediscovered" as the result of a command from the Goddess speaking through a possessed medium. A small temple in a village that is now part of the city of Chandigarh, for example, was built in the late nineteenth century after a young girl became possessed by the Goddess and told the villagers that only by building a temple could they eradicate a severe epidemic. Similarly, Nainā Devī temple was built on a hillside outside Kalka in 1950 on the orders of the Goddess, who entered a small girl and commanded those listening to dig up an ancient image of Nainā Devī that lay buried and forgotten there.

There are various explanations as to why some people get possessed and not others. Some say that it is solely due to the divine play of the Goddess. Others say that it is the fruit of karma or because of a *saṃskāra* (mental impression or predisposition) from a past life. Others say that it is the reward for faith and devotion to Devī. Sometimes it runs in a family; the *śakti* is passed from generation to generation. Or it can be the result of a spiritual discipline *(sādhanā)* in which one attempts to bring on possession as a means of identifying with the Goddess.[10] Purity is also cited as a requirement for a suitable vehicle; she should not eat meat, drink liquor, or be unchaste. That is why young girls who have not yet reached the age of puberty and unmarried women are thought to be especially suitable vehicles for the Goddess.[11]

Charges of chicanery, commercialism, and exploitation are not uncommon in connection with possession, even among those who consider themselves devotees of Śerāṅvālī. An informant who grew up in a village near Jullunder told me that, in his childhood, during the yearly pilgrimage to Chintpurni, fights would break out between rival parties over whether or not a possession was legitimate. He summed it up as follows.

> When one camp undertakes a pilgrimage out of reverence, and the other for commercial purposes, there is a clash. When a group holds a *jagrātā* with commercial intent and a girl becomes possessed *(devī khelnā)*, it is often a fake. Some groups have several women who regularly stage these possessions. My father had a friend with a red turban who used tests for distinguishing real possession from fake. He would take an iron rod and prod the woman with it. An even more foolproof method is to put a lighted incense stick under the person's nose. If the possession is real, she will not flinch. There was a group who used to come to Chintpurni every year from about 1950 to 1955 who would stage possession. They would do this every night. We did not mind it if they did it on their own, but they used to do it in public when other *jagrātās* were going on. Then fights would break out. Our group would not let them have a session inside the temple, because they were using it as a regular business. They would also have *jagrātās* at their home and made quite a bit of money out of this.[12]

People will also ask the possessed person questions in order to test her clairvoyance—a mental rather than physical test. They might, for example, ask how much money is in someone's pocket. A certain amount of skepticism thus exists as to the validity of possession, at least in individual cases.

The same informant, however, recalled a case of what he considered to be a valid, spontaneous possession. During a *jagrātā* to which four different singing parties had been invited, a young woman started to "play." She had always been a devotee of Devī but had recently been married into a family that ate meat and drank liquor. During her possession, she was tested by a leader from one of the singing groups, who put lighted incense under her nose and struck her with a metal bar. She did not flinch. She spoke as Devī and ordered all people who were drunk to leave the *jagrātā*. After this, the young woman was so drained that she had to remain in bed for two months. As for her in-laws, they were so shaken by the experience that they became vegetarians and teetotalers.[13]

Hinduism does not draw a clear dividing line between divine and human; gods can become humans, and humans can become gods. There are numerous forms of worship of deified humans, such as ancestors, heroes, gurus, *satīs*, yogis, *siddhs*, and *nāths*. Similarly, certain women who are regularly possessed are worshipped as Mātās or living goddesses, as manifestations of Śerāṅvālī. Such a woman is said to embody the *śakti* of the Goddess during her possession—that is, to become a human icon. But the sanctity of the possession experience also carries over into her normal life, and she gradually becomes a religious specialist and the object of worship.

Is it the Mother who possesses, or is it the Mother who is possessed? To answer exclusively one way or another would presuppose a dualistic mind-set that is foreign to Hindu ways of thinking about the Goddess and *śakti*. *Śakti* is not an object or an entity; it is an all-pervasive force. It can be present in greater or lesser degrees; it can move around and become manifest in various forms. Indeed, it is this very fluidity of identity among the myriad forms of the Goddess and between divine and human beings that is so essential to understanding the phenomenon of Goddess possession.

NOTES

Material for this essay is taken from my book *Victory to the Mother: The Hindu Goddess of Northwest India in Myth, Ritual, and Symbol* (New York: Oxford University Press, 1993) and from more recent research I have conducted on village women healers in the Punjab and Himachal Pradesh, India. Fieldwork was funded by Fulbright-Hays research fellowships in 1982–1983 and 1991.

1. Manuel Moreno, "God's Forceful Call: Possession as a Divine Strategy," in *Gods of Flesh, Gods of Stone: The Embodiment of Divinity in India*, ed. Norman Cutler, Joanne Waghorne, and Vasudha Narayanan (Chambersburg, PA: Anima Books, 1985), 103–20. For a recent study that makes excellent use of this approach in a context outside India, see Karen McCarthy Brown, *Mama Lola: A Vodou Priestess in Brooklyn* (Berkeley: University of California Press, 1991).

2. See also, for example, Margaret Trawick Egnor, "The Changed Mother, or What the Smallpox Goddess Did When There Was No More Smallpox," in *Contributions to Asian Studies*, vol. 18, *South Asian. Systems of Healing*, ed. E. Valentine Daniel and Judy F. Pugh (Leiden: E. J. Brill, 1984), 24–45, in which I describe the possession of a woman in Madras by the goddess Mariamman. See Sarah Caldwell, "Bhagavati: Ball of Fire," in *Devī: Goddesses of India*, ed. John S. Hawley and Donna M. Wulff (Berkeley: University of California Press, 1996), 195–226.

3. See Susan Wadley, "The Spirit 'Rides' or the Spirit 'Comes': Possession in a North Indian Village," in *The Realm of the Extra-Human: Agents and Audiences*, ed. Agehananda Bharati (The Hague: Mouton, 1976), 233–52; John M. Stanley, "Gods, Ghosts, and Possession," in *The Experience of Hinduism*, ed. Eleanor Zelliot and Maxine Berntsen (Albany: State University of New York Press, 1968), 26–59, esp. 26; and Gananath Obeyesekere, "Psychocultural Exegesis of a Case of Spirit Possession in Sri Lanka," in *Case Studies in Spirit Possession*, ed. Vincent Crapanzano and Vivian Garrison (New York: Wiley, 1977), 235–94, esp. 290.

4. Ann Grodzins Gold, "Spirit Possession Perceived and Performed in Rural Rajasthan," *Contributions to Indian Sociology*, n.s. 32, no. 1 (1988): 3511. Peter J. Claus distinguishes between spirit possession and spirit mediumship, defining the former as "an unexpected intrusion of the supernatural into the lives of humans" and the latter as "the legitimate, expected possession of a specialist by a spirit or deity, usually for the purpose of soliciting the aid of the supernatural for human problems" ("Spirit Possession and Spirit Mediumship from the Perspective of Tulu Oral Traditions," *Culture, Medicine, and Psychiatry* 3, no. 1 [1979]: 29). Although his point is well taken, I prefer not to make such a hard-and-fast distinction, as there is often considerable overlap, as well as transition, from one to the other.

5. Paul Hershman, "Hair, Sex, and Dirt," *Man*, n.s. 9, no. 2 (1974): 277.

6. An example of this kind of song is "Dātī de darbār kanjankāṅ kheḍdiyā," written by Camanlāl Jośī and sung by Narendra Cancal (Polydor Records no. 2392 894). The words are printed in the pamphlet *Mātā dīyāṇ bheṭāṅ, ghar ghar vic mahimā terī* (Delhi: Aśokā Prakāśan, n.d.), 7–10.

7. For a full-length study of the concept of play in Hinduism, see David Kinsley, *The Divine Player: A Study of Kṛṣṇa Līlā* (Delhi: Motilal Banarsidass, 1979).

8. Interview, Cāmuṇḍā Devī temple, June 9, 1983.

9. Interview, Bābā Bālak Nāth temple, May 13, 1983.

10. This seems to be the case in the ceremony described by Ruth S. Freed and Stanley A. Freed, "Two Mother-Goddess Ceremonies of Delhi State in the Great and Little Traditions," *Southwestern Journal of Anthropology* 18, no. 3 (1962): 346–77. I am also personally familiar with the case of a male astrologer in a Kangra village who, as a result of performing an arduous religious regimen, acquired the magical power *(siddhi)* of being able to act as a medium and transmit the words of the goddess Dakṣiṇakālī. He

was in such demand for this skill that his activities as a medium eventually displaced his astrology business.

11. The same idea is operative in the Kumārī cults of Nepal, in which specially chosen young girls occupy a ritual position as a goddess until their first menstruation. See Michael Allen, *The Cult of Kumari: Virgin Worship in Nepal* (Kathmandu: Tribhuvan University, 1975).

12. Interview, New Delhi, February 14, 1983. Similar cases of conflict have been recorded from the late nineteenth century, during the heyday of the ārya Samāj reform movement. See Kenneth W. Jones, *Arya Dharm: Hindu Consciousness in Nineteenth-Century Punjab* (Berkeley: University of California Press, 1976), 190.

13. Interview, New Delhi, January 12, 1983.

PART V · GURUS

11 · Anandamayi Ma

God Came as a Woman

LISA LASSELL HALLSTROM

I begin by posing a provocative question: How would our lives be different if we had been raised with the conviction, the surety, that God exists as our Divine Mother, all-loving and all-powerful?

Over the past two decades, this question has been posed by many Western feminist theologians who assume that a move away from patriarchal images of God as father and king toward powerful yet compassionate female religious images would empower women and help create a more balanced and humane society. It has provoked a passionate interest in and nostalgia for real and imagined ancient goddess cultures, such as those proposed to have flourished in the fertile valleys of the Old Europe of prehistory.

Yet we need not look to the past to stimulate the reimagining of God as Mother or to examine the impact on women and men of worshipping the Divine Feminine. India has one of the oldest, continuous traditions of goddess worship in the world, and even today the Goddess is worshipped by devout Hindus in both her multiplicity and her unity. Although most Hindus devote some part of their devotional life to the worship of Devi in some form, those who relate to the Absolute primarily as feminine principle are called Shaktas, or those who are of the *shakti*, or the dynamic, creative power of the universe.

This essay is published for the first time here.

Shaktism, then, is the worship of the primordial power underlying the universe personified as a female deity who is considered to be the Supreme Being. Although worship of the Goddess has its roots in India in pre-Vedic times, the Shakta path developed as a formal sectarian option between the sixth and the tenth centuries and was legitimated by two Sanskrit texts, the Devi Mahatmya and the Devi Bhagavata. While the Devi Mahatmya emphasized the dreadful aspect of the Goddess; the Devi Bhagavata, written in the eleventh or twelfth century, emphasized her supremely compassionate side.

The Devi Bhagavata, mimicking one of the most beloved Hindu devotional texts, the Bhagavad Gita, articulates four important principles of the Shakta path: the heart of the path is devotion to Devi, the Great Mother, for its own sake; the Great Mother possesses both an individual, divine form and exists eternally as formless consciousness or Brahman; the divine as Devi exists in the world of form, animating and pervading all that we see and do; and finally, the Goddess, Devi, can manifest herself in various incarnations, in the same way as the god Vishnu took form as Lord Krishna and Lord Ram, for the sake of her devotees.

It is this last doctrine that brings us to a second and even more provocative question: How would our lives be different is we had actually spent our lives, from childhood through adulthood, with a person whom we believed was that all-loving and all-powerful God the Mother?

The doctrine of *avatara*, or divine incarnation, was formally introduced around the turn of the Common Era in the Hindu epic, the Mahabharata, but was developed more fully in the Bhagavad Gita. According to the Hindu tradition, there are two progressions along the continuum between human and divine. The first is the ascending progression from human being to perfected being (for example, a *siddha* or *sadguru*) in which matter is considered to have been spiritualized by the will and spiritual practices of a human being. The second is a descending progression from God into perfect being, or *avatara*, in which spirit is considered to have become material by the will of God. An *avatara* is described in the following way, referring usually to Lord Krishna or Lord Ram: he is born free, without *karma*, completely liberated from the bonds of the ego; he takes human form in response to his own will in order to be accessible to those who long to seek refuge in him; he has full recall of his former births and is aware from birth of his divine origin; and, finally, his devotees need only recognize his divine nature to be saved.[1]

In the past several hundred years, the doctrine of *avatara* began to be reinterpreted and applied to many male historical figures. Perhaps the first was Krishna Chaitanya, a sixteenth-century ecstatic worshipper of Lord Krishna, who was proclaimed a full incarnation of Krishna. Since then, it has become more common for disciples of a master to claim that he is an *avatara*. The nineteenth-century Bengali master, Sri Ramakrishna Paramahamsa, was declared an *avatara* when he was in his twenties and went on to attract thousands of devotees, among them Swami Vivekananda, who established the worldwide Ramakrishna Mission. In all cases, the *avatara* is considered to have been fully conscious of his divinity at every moment, so that everything he does is seen as simply playacting, or *lila*.

For the last four centuries Hindus have referred to certain male historical figures as *avataras*. The subject of this essay, however, is a female religious figure of this century who has been and still is worshipped by hundreds of thousands of devotees as an incarnation of the divine.

Anandamayi Ma was born as Nirmala Sundari to a poor Brahmin family in Bengal in 1896. She was married at the age of twelve but lived with her husband until his death in 1938 not as his "wife," as Hindu *dharma* (sacred law or duty) would define it, but as his guru. As her sacred biographies recount, early in their marriage Nirmala withdrew more and more from everyday activities and spent a large part of her day in states of spiritual ecstasy. She began to attract devotees who saw her as an extraordinary spiritual being. Her husband, while bewildered at first, soon became convinced that his wife was a manifestation of the Goddess. He received spiritual initiation from her and spent the rest of his life following her spiritual instruction, mediating between her and her growing number of devotees and caring for her physical well-being, as she seemed completely disinterested in her body. (See figure K at the Web site http://www.clas.ufl.edu/users/vasu/loh.)

In 1926 Ma—or "Mother," as Nirmala had come to be called—completely stopped feeding herself and for the rest of her life was fed by the hands of her close devotees. That same year Ma completely abandoned her *dharma* as a Hindu wife and began her endless travels around India, accompanied by her husband and attracting devotees wherever she went. Thousands came to receive her blessings and bathe in her ecstatic spiritual state. Many reported that one glance from Ma awakened in them a spiritual energy so powerful as to redirect their entire life.

After her husband's death, Anandamayi Ma continued to grow in stature and influence. Referring to Ma in his book, *Autobiography of a Yogi*, Paramahamsa Yogananda reports, "Never before had I met such an exalted woman saint." Many heads of state, intellectuals, and prominent businesspeople considered Ma their guru and, in some cases, their deity. In the last decade of her life, Anandamayi Ma's devotees numbered in the hundreds of thousands; and ashrams, schools, and hospitals were established in her name all over India. By the time of her death in 1982, this illiterate woman, who called herself simply "this body," had become the spiritual guide and focus of reverence for people all over India.

Anandamayi Ma's teachings can be reduced to one statement, "God alone exists." The Divine Absolute veils him-/herself in order to enjoy the divine play of life in the world of form, the world of duality in which everything is impermanent and illusory. The person who has forgotten that he or she is God suffers as things change and eventually turns within to find that which is permanent, the Self of All. Ma recommended that people begin the process of turning within at whichever point they find themselves, and she prescribed different practices depending on an individual's inclination and capacity. Yet always the message was one of restraint of the senses, one-pointedness on the Divine, and repetition of one's chosen name of God. Ma was tireless in stating her conviction that anyone can know God, indeed can become God, if only he or she possesses the desire.

On August 28, 1982, in the foothills of the Himalayas, a funeral procession made its way between the Indian towns of Dehradun and Kankhal. It took longer than usual to make the twenty-seven-mile trip because the procession had to stop every few minutes to allow crowds of mourners to have their last *darshan,* their last glimpse, of the one whom they simply called Ma, or Mother.

By the time the body of eighty-six-year-old Anandamayi Ma, or the Bliss-Filled Mother, had reached its final destination at her ashram in Kankhal on the banks of the Ganga, an unending stream of people had begun to gather to pay their respects. *India Today* reported, "One could see them coming as far as the eye could see. They came in cars, rickshaws and on foot. Many were in a state of dazed shock." While some kept up the twenty-four-hour chanting of the divine name, mourners continued, hour after hour, to *pranam,* or bow, in front of Ma's body, many weeping profusely. Among them was Indira Gandhi, who had flown in by helicopter and who considered Ma her spiritual mother. On that day Mrs. Gandhi left the following message of condolence at the ashram:

> Anandamayi Ma was the living embodiment of devotion and love. Just with a glimpse of Her, countless problems are solved. She considered humanity Her true religion. Her spiritually powerful personality was a source of great guidance for all human beings. I offer my homage to Her!

On Sunday, August 29, Anandamayi Ma was buried as a realized being according to strict scriptural injunctions presided over by some of India's most renowned Brahmin priests. Her shrine has become a place of worship and pilgrimage renowned for its spiritual power. Her twenty-eight ashrams, a charitable hospital, schools, and dispensaries continue to be administered by the nonprofit society established in her name. Yet while nearly every Hindu in India knows of Anandamayi Ma as a *mahatma*, or great soul, a saint, those who consider themselves to be her devotees, her disciples, who number in the hundreds of thousands, worship her as an *avatara*, as God who came in the form of a woman for the sake of her devotees. It was my good fortune to spend 1990–1991 traveling throughout India interviewing close devotees of Ma, in particular the women among them who described enjoying a rare privilege—that of intimately caring for the body of God as Mother.

I did not come to India in the summer of 1990 prepared to do research on someone considered a female incarnation of God. I had my own agenda, which was to study a woman saint who might serve as a powerful model for her women devotees, offering them an inspiring alternative to the sometimes oppressive paradigm of the devoted Hindu wife. The book that came out of this research, *Mother of Bliss: Anandamayi Ma (1896–1982)*, reflects a dramatic change of focus, which was foreshadowed by the following incident.

In September 1990, full of anticipation and excitement, I was traveling on a train from Banaras to Allahabad. Things were beginning to come together. I was about to meet and interview the most prominent biographer of Anandamayi Ma, Bithika Mukerji, professor emeritus at Banaras Hindu University, with whom I had been corresponding for several years. From the train station in Allahabad, I took a horse-drawn wagon to the grand Victorian house that is Bithika's family home. We were greeted very graciously by Bithika-ji, who is a strikingly handsome, brilliant, yet serene woman, and told that dinner was almost ready.

I was quite nervous to be sitting down to a meal with the person whom I expected would be central to my research in India. As the first course was being cleared, Bithika-ji, wasting no time, asked me to tell her about my work. I said, "Well, I am very excited to be doing this study on Ma. You know, I have been interested in women saints for a long time." A look of alarm, and even horror, came over Bithika's face. "My dear Lisa," Bithika said emphatically, "Ma was neither a woman nor a saint!" She added, "Once I was invited to give a talk on Ma at a conference on women saints. I refused! They obviously did not have an understanding of who Ma was!" I was speechless.

Indeed, this interaction has been central to my research. Although I had considered myself particularly respectful of the Hindu tradition, here I was being called upon to deconstruct and transcend the categories of "woman" and "saint" and to entertain new and less familiar categories.

In the course of my interviews, I asked twenty-six of Ma's closest devotees, "Who is Ma?" Not surprisingly, the answers were as diverse as the devotees themselves. Narendranath Bose said, "You see, for everybody, Ma was a very different person because she responded to individual vibrations. You will have to draw your own conclusions." But the most common reply to the question was, "Ma was God." Nearly all devotees were interviewed in English, and although some went on to give equivalent Sanskrit terms such as Parabrahman or Devi, the first word that came to them to describe Ma was God.

One celibate female renunciant, or *brahmacharini*, Malini, spoke poignantly about knowing Ma since birth, having been born into a devotee family:

> When I was in school (I was about seven or eight years old), the Christian nuns over there, they said that God never comes on earth. And so, I was very upset. I said, "No, I have spoken to God!" And they said, "You can't speak to God. There is no such thing. God never comes to earth. Only Jesus Christ can, and no one else!" They said unless you believe in Jesus Christ, you can never reach God. So I was very perturbed. All these things I was told. And when I came back home, I cried and cried. So my mother asked, "What is the matter?" So I told her. "They have been telling me that unless I become a Christian, I won't reach God. And I told them, 'No, I have met God. I have talked to Her. I have seen Her. For on our holidays, we go to God!' How can they say those thmgs?" So my mother said, "Don't worry, they won't understand this. But, yes, your God talks to you."

When I asked Malini, "Did your family have a chosen deity?" she replied, "No, we believe in Krishna and Ram and things like that, but as children we were taught that Ma was everything. For us Ma was Krishna, Ma was Ram, Ma was Shiva, Ma was everything. To us the name of God was Ma."

Sita Gupta, a housewife, reiterated this theme when she said, "My children and grandchildren know of no other God except Mother. You say Ram or Krishna or Shiva or Devi, they think Ma. They don't know these others, just Ma."

Naren Bose, a sophisticated young Calcutta businessman, trained at Boston University and Harvard, who also grew up in a family devoted to Ma, put it this way: "For me, Ma is God. I have no deep knowledge of the Hindu scriptures or any scriptures. So my conviction in any one established religion is not there. All my convictions are what I have seen through Ma. All my belief is only Ma. And God for me is Ma. Ma is my life. Very simple. Everything."

For some devotees, recognition of Ma's divinity took time. Uma Chatterji said, "After I met Ma, I could not immediately associate Ma with God. But after some time, it became Ma and God, the duality. It took years to identify Ma with God as One. And it took place because of fantastic experiences and dramatic situations. But for Ma there is no beginning and end to the story. It is all her *lila*."

One such fantastic experience that obviously became a part of the family's perception of Ma was reported by Gita Bose:

> My grandfather was a doctor from the medical school in Calcutta. There were only ten of them at that time sitting around Ma. All of a sudden grandfather started feeling drowsy, and he thought, Why am I feeling like that? I just got up from an afternoon sleep. His eyes just closed all of a sudden. And then he opened them forcibly, and he saw there was no Ma. And in the place of Ma, there was one of the ten *avataras* of Devi. The form he saw was Chinnamasta. You know, the body was here, and the head she is holding in her hand. He saw that form, and the nine other people, they each saw a different form. And another devotee was a judge. He saw all ten forms. And after that the drowsiness went away. And everybody asked each other, "What have you seen? I don't know what to think!" And the judge said, "I saw all ten forms." And they ran to him and said, "You are so lucky!" My grandfather told me this when I was little.

Regardless of whether devotees thought of God as an incarnation of Devi, of Krishna, or of the formless Brahman, she was to each of them the means and the goal of spiritual life.

How were Anandamayi Ma's female devotees affected by God coming in the form of a woman? In most of my interviews with Ma's women devotees, after they had told me that Ma was not a woman, not a saint or guru, but was God incarnate, I asked them why God had chosen to come into this world as a woman. They had no problem answering. They all agreed: "Ma came for the ladies." It became clear, however, that they did not mean that Ma came to show women how to be. Rather they were saying that God's taking female form as Ma enabled women in particular to be physically close to the divine.

Rupa Vishvanathan, a householder devotee, said, "There are so many rascals masquerading in the garb of a renunciant, taking advantage of women. It is utterly safe to be with Mother. You are always closer to Mother than to Father. You can confide; it's very intimate." Sita, another householder devotee said, "God takes the form of sometimes Father, sometimes Mother. Some are more comfortable with Mother. I am. We can touch her, massage her legs. Ma used to lie down, and one person would be massaging her arms, and one person her legs, and we would all be talking and laughing. You see, intimacy like that you cannot get except with the Mother.

So soft, just like a newborn baby, so soft to massage, so smooth. The ladies understood her better and felt closer to her than the men."

Indeed, several male devotees bemoaned the distance they had to keep from Ma. Swami Premananda, who met Ma as a twenty-five-year-old graduate student, said, "When I came to stay with Ma, I could not accept that it was not possible to be near the body of Mother. Her being a lady and I being a man, there were certain limitations. I would follow her everywhere, and I would cry when she scolded me. She was once being fed by someone, and I said, 'I also want to feed you.' And her hair—she had very long black hair, and I just wanted to comb that. It took me a long time to accept."

Thus the primary way in which Anandamayi Ma's being a woman particularly benefited and inspired women was in granting women intimate access to her divine presence. Their privileged position close to Ma offered them a rare opportunity to have a personal relationship with God as Ma, caring for and being cared for by her.

The second way in which Ma's being a woman benefited women was that as a result of their intimacy with her, Ma was better able to advocate for women's spiritual equality with men. Ma kept close track of "the girls," as the celibate women who lived around Ma were called, encouraging them in their spiritual practice and holding them to the highest standards. The fact that the families of these young women were willing to allow them not to marry, but rather to stay with Ma as her caretakers and her closest disciples, is credit to the power Ma held in Bengali society. In exchange, they could take pride in the fact that their daughter was "under Ma's spiritual wing."

Swami Gitananda, one of "Ma's girls," said, "We who wanted to be closely related to Ma were treated differently. Ma would scold us for the smallest infractions. Later Ma would say, 'Now I scold you with all of my heart. I do not hide anything.' We thought we were special. With us Ma felt every little behavior had to be as fragrant and fruitful as a rose in full bloom. You see, Ma wanted us to blossom into perfection." Furthermore, Ma established a Sanskrit school for girls in Banaras, offering a spiritual education for girls that had been unavailable since early Vedic times, an education that prepared them to choose the life of a *brahmacharini* if they wished. Ma also arranged for the sacred thread of Brahmin initiation, formerly given only to males, to be given to several of her close women devotees. Finally, Ma empowered several of "the girls" to plan, fund-raise for, and build a *yajnashala*, to house the sacrificial fire of Vedic ritual at her ashram in Kankhal. All of these things were manifestations of Ma's advocacy for women's spiritual equality.

The third way in which Ma's birth in a female body might have particularly benefited women was that different women could identify with different stages of Ma's life and be inspired. The *lila* of Ma's life included both a short period of time where she played the role of a young housewife and a much longer time when she played the role of a renunciant. Clearly Ma's life as a housewife provided radical challenges to the ideal of the Hindu wife described in the sacred law-books and epics—her marriage to Bholanath was never consummated, and rather than serve him as her god she, in fact, became his guru, orchestrating his spiritual life until his death in 1938. Yet Ma's message to most householder devotees was "Do as I say, not as I do." For example, although she instituted the chanting of *kirtans,* or devotional songs, for women, she made sure that happened at a time that did not interfere with women's household duties. She seemed to recommend a kind of piety for married women that Caroline Walker Bynum calls (reconsidering Weber) an "innerworldly asceticism," a piety that unites action and contemplation in such a way as to provide continuity in women's lives as they become more spiritualized.[2] At the core, however, was the idea that most women should pursue their *dharma* as wives who serve their husbands as their Lord. We can conclude, then, that, while Ma was an advocate of women's spiritual equality, in many ways she reinforced the classical ideal for women that her life contradicts.

Yet when I asked Ma's women devotees whether or not Ma was a model for them of how to live their lives, I was met with a look of disorientation that took me to the heart of the paradox of Ma's gender. It brought me back to the response that Bithika Mukerji had given me when I told her that I was interested in Ma as a woman saint. It became clear to me that within the Hindu tradition, Ultimate Reality is conceived of as beyond form and beyond gender, and as such, Ma could not be seen as a woman at all. While the difference in the Hindu tradition between male and female among ordinary people is highly marked, it seems that in the realm of extraordinary people, as in the realm of the divine, there is almost a third gender. Male and female holy people are more like each other than they are like other men and women. In fact, the goal of the spiritual path is a kind of transcendence of gender, a shedding of the limitations of one's sexual identity, an identity that simply reflects the limited, dualistic world. That which is aspired to, Ultimate Reality, on the other hand, is often conceived of as formless, genderless consciousness. Anandamayi Ma herself said, "You are the Self of All, you are He. He is neither masculine nor feminine. Therefore here, too, there is no question of man or woman. In all men and women is He alone. The Self in everybody is genderless."[3]

Taking into account the Hindu understanding of the gender of God, as well as its emphasis on disidentification with the body, it is not difficult to understand why

Ma's women devotees fail to identify with Ma as a woman. If they have listened to Ma well, they have come to believe that they, too, are neither woman nor man but are, instead, the Self of All.

There is a second important but related factor that seems to inhibit Anandamayi Ma's potential to serve as a model for women, and that is the very fact of her being considered a deity, albeit a deity in female form. When I asked Malini if Ma was her role model, she replied, "No, you see, to model yourself on Ma was very, very difficult because Ma was the embodiment of perfection." I pushed her a little further, saying, "But you had somebody to look up to?" Her answer reflects what most of Ma's devotees see as the unbridgeable gulf between the human and the divine: "*Really* look up to! Way, way up!" While we might have expected that Ma's women devotees would have imitated Ma's life in both minor and major ways, from wearing their hair loose and displaying ecstatic spiritual states to casting aside all worldly goals to pursue Self-realization, we find that most women felt, as Malini did, that what Ma did was not applicable to them. Those who chose the renunciant life did not report that they chose it because Ma lived such a life. Rather, they cited other reasons: because Ma suggested it, because Ma's spiritualizing presence inspired them to renounce the world, or because they simply wanted to be close to Ma's side.

It seems that once devotees accepted Ma as embodied God, no matter how many times she told them that they, too, were God, it was difficult for them to believe her because they naturally assumed that she was more God than they were. They persisted in seeing her as "way, way up" and out of reach. Yet Ma's devotees would say, "The fact that I cannot identify with Ma is not important. Ma is my Mother, my God incarnate, and therefore my association with her will carry me to rest with her eternally. I need only to sit in the lap of Mother to have it all, both worldly and spiritual fulfillment." Indeed, this reminds us of one of the central doctrines of the *avatara:* a devotee need only recognize a person of divine origin to be saved.

In January 1991, nearly nine years after Anandamayi Ma's passing, I sat near the banks of the Ganga at the feet of Swami Samatananda, the head of Ma's Calcutta ashram. With a twinkle in his eye, Swamiji was explaining the "Motherly approach" to me:

> The first thing is this. The ultimate force, the Absolute, whichever name you may call it, has got two main aspects: one is the dynamic aspect, which we call Shakti, the other is the static or formless aspect, or Shiva. We prefer to approach from the

dynamic aspect, from the *shakti* of the Mother because that is where we are. The Motherly approach is easy because you can experience this *shakti;* you can see that everywhere in the world there is change. When you approach the Mother, she will reveal to you the eternal, unchanging fabric upon which this world is woven. But what is the goal of human life? The goal is to be in the safest place to sit and enjoy the whole world. What is the safest place in the whole world? A child knows that the lap of the Mother is the best place in the world. So sitting in the lap of the Ma you can enjoy the whole world, because Ma will protect you from every evil thing. So this is the Motherly approach.

Swamiji went on:

In our ashram there are many practices. Most people meditate on a picture of Ma. Lisa, you would not believe the experiences people have had of Ma. She is still here! But no matter what the practices, the goal is Ma. By meditating on Ma we can reach whatever we could ever want. If we catch hold of Ma's hand, then Ma will lead us to whatever is needed for us. So we do not create a beautiful idea like "I'll become this and that." We think only, I will meditate on Ma and I will love Ma and she will show me. She took form for us. Ma told us, "You called for me, you prayed for me, you got this body. As long as you want this body, it will stay. If you don't want this body, it will vanish." God comes to this world because God loves us. We are the children of God. We are the children of Mother. So Mother will come down upon this earth one hundred times. Where her children are playing she can not leave this earth. So she comes—the Ultimate Shakti.

NOTES

1. See Daniel Bassuk, *Incarnation in Hinduism and Christianity: The Myth of the God Man* (Atlantic Highlands, NJ: Humanities Press, 1987) for a complete discussion of *avatara.*

2. Caroline Walker Bynum, *Fragmentation and Redemption: Essays on Gender and the Human Body in Medieval Religion* (New York: Zone, 1991), 70.

3. Satsang Tape no. 20, Vrindaban, November 1967, pp. 9–10.

12 · Radhasoami

The Healing Offer

SUDHIR KAKAR

I attended my first Satsang immediately after my arrival in Beas on a cold December morning. The Satsang was to be held in the large open space behind the Satsang Ghar, the imposing congregation hall built during the early part of this century that dominates the township and the plains around it. With its hundred-foot-high ceiling, marble floors inlaid with mosaic designs, and profusion of arches, columns, and towers, the Satsang Ghar is a medley of architectural styles. In fact, at first glance, before the aesthetic eye can become clouded over by the film of faith, the Satsang Ghar looks like a Punjabi petty official's fantasy of a building that combines both Victorian imperial grandeur and Mughal oriental splendor. On this particular day, the *bhandara* of Babaji, the congregation was especially large, numbering well over fifty thousand. Swaddled in rough woolen blankets and huddling close together for warmth against the chilly wind blowing down from the distant Shivalik hills, barely visible through their shroud of steel-gray haze, the crowd was impressive in its silent orderliness. The noise, the bustle, and the confusion that are an inherent quality of a large Punjabi or, for that matter, any Indian gathering were remarkable by their absence.

As I made my way through the patiently squatting men—the women were sit-

This essay was previously published as "The Healing Offer," in *Shamans, Mystics, and Doctors: A Psychological Inquiry into India and Its Healing Traditions* (Chicago: University of Chicago Press, 1982), 128–40.

ting on the other side—my strongest impression was of a pervasive friendliness, bubbling over into welcoming smiles and the low-murmured cultic greeting of "Radhasoami!" Most of the men and women in the congregation belonged to the Sikh peasantry—the men tall and bearded, with fierce faces yet gentle eyes, and the women stately in their traditional knee-length shirts and floppy trousers that narrowed sharply at the ankles. There were others too: hill people from Kangra and Jammu, petty traders and small housekeepers from dusty towns of the Punjab and from as far away as (I discovered later) Mehsana in Gujarat and Bhopal in Madhya Pradesh. Right up at the front, in a separate enclosure just below the fifteen-foot-high dais from where Maharajji would address the congregation, sat the "elite" Satsangis. Among these fifty-odd European and American Satsangis—many of them reclining comfortably on cunningly designed chairs without legs that give a person an appearance of squatting cross-legged without his actually doing so—there was a sprinkling of industrialists, former diplomats, retired high government officials, and an ex-prince of an obscure Indian state with a retinue of daughters, daughters-in-law and a brood of solemn-eyed children.

While we waited for Maharajji, we sang. The mellifluous voice of a *panthi*—the chanter of Sikh scriptures—drifted out of the loudspeakers strung out on the grounds as he sang of man's spiritual longing for the *Satguru*. The crowd joined in the refrain at the end of each familiar and well-loved verse, fifty thousand voices merging into one deep-throated chant that was scarcely a song any longer but more an emotion, a yearning broken into patterns of sound. To anyone sitting within the vast belly of the crowd, a choir of fifty thousand feels like an elemental sound of nature—the rumbling of a volcano full of melody and meaning or, perhaps, like the sound of high wind and torrential rain that has been shaped into a musical pattern. Here I am deliberately emphasizing my subjective experience of the Satsang, on this day as on the following days, and the fantasies that bubble up to the fore of consciousness as one sits esconced in the warmth and closeness of thousands of bodies. At first there is a sense of unease as the body, the container of our individuality and the demarcator of our spatial boundaries, is sharply wrenched away from its habitual mode of experiencing others. For as we grow up, the touch of others, once so deliberately courted and responded to with delight, increasingly becomes ambivalent. Coming from a loved one, touch is deliriously welcomed; with strangers, on the other hand, there is an involuntary shrinking of the body, their touch taking on the menacing air of invasion by the Other. But once the fear of touch disappears in the fierce press of other bodies, and the individual lets himself become a part of the crowd's density, the original apprehension is gradually transformed into an expansiveness that stretches to include the others. Distances and differences—of status, age, and sex—disappear in an exhilarating feeling (temporary to be sure) that individual boundaries can indeed be transcended and were perhaps illusory in the first place. Of course, touch is only one of the sensual stimuli that hammers at the gate of individual identity. Other excitations, channeled through vision, hearing, and smell, are also very much involved. In addition, as Phyllis Greenacre has suggested, there are other, more subliminal exchanges of body heat, muscle tension, and body rhythms taking place in a crowd. In short, the crowd's assault on the sense of individual identity appears to be well nigh irresistible; its invitation to a psychological regression—in which the image of one's body becomes fluid and increasingly blurred, controls over emotions and impulses are weakened, critical faculties and rational thought processes are abandoned—is extended in a way that is both forceful and seductive.

It was in such a mild state of "altered consciousness," pervaded with a feeling of oneness and affection for every member of the crowd, that I waited for Maharajji to appear. There is little doubt that I (along with the rest of the crowd) was in a heightened state of receptivity for whatever might come next.

The chanting stopped, and there were minutes of hushed silence as Maharajji's chauffeured Fiat came into view, driven slowly down the empty road and stopping behind the high podium from which he would hold the *satsang*. All eyes were now raised up to the dais. The canopy above it fluttered lightly in the breeze that rippled through its bright-blue canvas. And then Maharajji appeared at the top of the steps behind the dais. A majestic figure with a long white beard and a neatly tied white turban covering his head, he was dressed in a cream-colored *kurta*, well-cut *churidars*, and a sleeveless tan woolen jacket, with a beige *pashmina* shawl wrapped round his shoulders. Tall and well built, Maharaj Charan Singh is a stately figure, and I remember the fleeting thought that this is what God's younger brother must look like (see figure 8). With a brisk tread belying his sixty-three years, Maharajji stepped up to the low divan at the front, bowed, and touched his forehead to the seat in a gesture of reverence to his predecessors. He then mounted the divan and sat down cross-legged, adjusting the shawl around his broad shoulders as he pulled the microphone in front of the divan closer. The silence continued, broken occasionally by a cough, while Maharajji sat there impassively, slowly turning his head from one side to the other in a wide sweep, surveying his flock from under bushy white eyebrows and through slightly hooded eyes while his right hand moved up and down rhythmically, stroking and smoothing down errant hair that had escaped from the luxuriant growth of his beard.

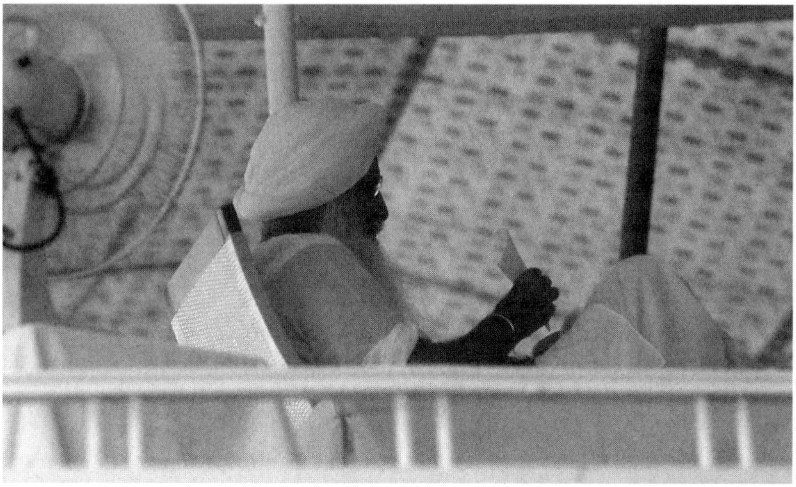

FIGURE 8
Seated on a platform raised high above a giant canopied area at Beas, Maharaj Charan Singh reads mail from followers worldwide while devotees assemble below to take his *darshan*. Photo by John Hawley.

The people around me were transfixed, overwhelmed by the presence of the *Satguru* who to a *satsangi* is God made flesh, divine made human. This was *darshan*, "viewing," in its most intense form. There were tears of emotion running down the cheek of the middle-aged man sitting next to me, merging with drops of saliva dribbling out of the corner of his mouth, and I had the distinct feeling that my neighbors were visually feasting on Maharajji's face. Meanwhile, there was movement on the stage as a frail old Sikh appeared and sat on one side, where a second microphone had been strategically placed. Untying the knots of a bundle wrapped in a red muslin, he took out a thick tome—the Adi Granth—and peered nearsightedly at the pages, which he riffled through rapidly till he came to the page he was looking for. Replacing the open book on the book rack in front and crossing his arms across his chest, the old *panthi* settled back, slowly rocking on his haunches as he too waited for the *darshan* to end.

Maharajji cleared his throat, a rasping sound instantaneously amplified into a thunderous rumble by the loudspeakers, and as if he were only awaiting this signal, the *panthi* started singing a poem by Guru Amar Das from the Adi Granth. His voice was indescribably appealing, full of wise tranquillity and spirited longing at the same time, both old and childlike at once, melodious and yet somehow also conveying that it was unmindful of such criteria as timbre and melody. He sang a short verse before Maharajji began to elaborate on the verse in clear and idiomatic Punjabi. His voice was soft and low, the tone intimate, the diction full of assurance and easy authority.

"Look where we will," he began, "we find nothing but pain and suffering in this world. The more we try to find peace and happiness in the shapes and forms of this world, the deeper is our misery. By their very nature, the things we seek are transient. Consequently, the pleasure derived from them is invariably short-lived."

The devaluation of the objective world contained in Maharajji's opening sentences, his emphasis on the misery of the world and his perfunctory dismissal of its splendors, are of course in the mainstream of Indian spiritual tradition, the prism through which Indians have traditionally viewed the outer world. It is, however, deeply reassuring for a sufferer to be told that his suffering does not connote any individual failure or deficiency on his part, something of which almost every patient is unconsciously convinced. On the contrary, Maharajji ennobles individual suffering by characterizing it as a part of the eternal "nature of things"—part of a scrutable divine plan. For someone in pain, it is even more comforting to be told that everyone else too is a sufferer, actual or potential. This *democratization* of suffering was made more concrete as Maharajji proceeded to give homely illustrations that were obviously resonant with the situation of the members of his audience and addressed the concerns of their daily life. "Marriage is a happy and festive event in our life, but if our partner turns out to be quarrelsome, overbearing, and unaccommodating, the resulting tension and strife turn the whole household into a veritable hell. Some are dogged by illness, others by the curse of unemployment. Some are denied the privilege of parenthood, and they yearn for a child day and night. Others have children who cause them endless misery and worry. Some are worried because they cannot secure a loan, others because they cannot repay one. We daily witness the sorry spectacle of beggars and destitutes clamoring for alms by the roadside. We have only to visit a hospital to hear the doleful cries of patients writhing in agony, or a jail to listen to the tales of woe and distress of the unfortunate inmates. If this is the fate of man in this world, the position of the lower species can better be imagined than described. One shudders to think of their lot. Man is considered the 'top of the creation' and made in the image of his Maker. Yet no one, even in this coveted form, can claim to be happy and contented. By far the largest number of people look for happiness and peace in amassing wealth. They toil day and night and sacrifice many a principle in this ignoble pursuit. But soon they are disillusioned to find that riches and happiness are not synonymous. Stark misery stares them in the face when the pile starts shrinking, for money soon begins to slide into the doctor's pocket for treatment of all kinds of ailments, or into the lawyer's purse when they get involved in prolonged and expensive litigation.

"Then, again, some seek pleasure in wine and whiskey and in eating the flesh of animals, fish, and fowl. These things may give them pleasure of the palate; they may appear to be rich and savory, but quite often they also land them in hospitals and nursing homes, sometimes even in prison cells, entailing hard labor."

Maharajji then went on to the riddle of why peace and happiness are so elusive and why pain and pleasure are so intermingled in every life. Taking the question of personal misery onto the existential plane, he proceeded to give the traditional Indian answer to the cause of suffering, namely, the workings of karma.

"Sages and seers have called this world the 'field of karma,' for here we have to reap what we have sown. Crops of pleasure and pain, joy and sorrow, grow strictly according to the seeds of good and bad karma. If we sow seeds of pepper, we shall harvest pepper. If we plant mangoes, we are entitled to enjoy the taste of mangoes. It's the load of karma that is keeping us in this prison house of 'eighty-four' [a reference to the traditional Indian notion of there being 8,400,000 species in creation—"wombs" through which one must be successively reborn to attain *moksha*]. Look at our present state. After every death, the messengers of Death lead us before Dharma Rai, the Divine Accountant, who takes into account our unfulfilled desires and wishes and accordingly decides where and when we have to be born again. We are not yet rid of the shackles of one body when the sheath of the next one is already there to confine us. Like branded habitual criminals, we are fettered and shifted, as it were, from one cell of the prison house to another. Neither through good deeds nor through bad ones can one obtain release from this prison of lives. If bad deeds are iron fetters, then good deeds are fetters made of gold. After exhausting their fruits, we are back to misery, sorrow, and pain. Our situation is indeed like that of a man clinging to the branch of a tree whose roots are being gnawed by rats while a deadly cobra waits for the man to fall on the ground. In this predicament two drops of honey [of sensual pleasure] fall on his tongue, and he becomes oblivious to everything as he savors their sweetness."

The *panthi* sang:

All treasure is within thy home.
There is naught without.
Thou shalt attain it through Guru's grace
When thy inner door is opened.

Maharajji continued,

"If we long for permanent peace and happiness and freedom from the laws of karma, we must seek the Lord within. Our soul is of the essence of the Lord. 'Just as oil is in sesame seeds,' says Kabir, 'and fire is in flint, so does he reside in your body, the Lord whom you seek day and night.' Jesus Christ also pronounces in the Bible, 'The kingdom of God is within you.' As Christ says, our body is the 'temple of the living God,' for it is within our body alone that he can be realized and experienced.

"One can see for oneself how ignorant we are when we look for the Lord in man-made shrines instead of the temple made by God himself to reside in. The saints advise us, therefore, that if we want to realize God, we must look for him within ourselves and nowhere else. Naturally the question now arises that if God is within our own body, which is the true temple of God, why do we not see him? What is the obstacle, and how can it be removed? The obvious reply is that it is our desires and wishes, our love and attachment for the world and its objects, that generate the love and attachment in us. Naturally, it is our own mind. Whatever karma the mind impels us to do, the consequences have to be suffered by the soul also, for the mind and soul are knotted together. We know that water in the clouds is pure, but when it falls on the ground as rain, it gathers all kinds of impurities. The condition of our soul is no way different from that of rainwater. It is of the same essence as God himself, but having become subservient to the mind, it has gathered dirt and dross and lost its purity. As long as the soul does not free itself from the clutches of the mind, it cannot know its source.

"All genuine seekers realize the importance of controlling and subduing the mind. To that end they try diverse methods and techniques. Some resort to austerities and repetition of holy names, some indulge in charitable acts, others leave their hearths and homes and seek the seclusion of mountains and forests. There are still others who make endless rounds of temples, mosques, churches, gurdwaras, and devote themselves to the study of scriptures and sacred books and listen to learned discourses. All these functions are solely directed to one end, namely, to control the mind. The truth, however, is that the cravings and desires of the mind have only been suppressed for a while; they have not disappeared, nor have they been conquered. The more we suppress a thing, the more it rebounds and reacts."

Maharajji then went on to say that the only way of detaching the mind was to attach it to something higher—to the God within. This could be done by seeking the company of like-minded believers in the experience of Satsang such as the one we were all engaged in; by devotion to the guru who is a conduit to the divine and especially by the spiritual practices of *surat shabd yoga,* through which the "divine nectar within can be tasted, the divine melody resounding within can be heard and the divine light shining within can be seen."

The direct quotations of passages from Maharajji's long discourse—a discourse that he has delivered hundreds of times before with minor variations—are intended to convey its flavor as much as its content, if not more. I certainly realize that without giving due attention to the nonverbal signals contained in the movement of his hands, the play of his body, the changes in the pitch of his voice, flavor can only be imperfectly conveyed, even by a verbatim reproduction of his imagery and metaphors. I have also omitted here some of the parables Maharajji is so fond of using—parables obviously suggesting to members of his audience that each one of them is like a child in an amusement park who is happy only as long as he is holding onto his father's hand; or that he is like a child absorbed in play but only as long as he does not remember his parents.

The intellectual contents of Maharajji's discourse are familiar because they are common to many mystical traditions. To list some of these repetitive elements: there is the derogation of the perceived real world and an emphasis on its painful, withholding nature; there is the suggestion of mystical withdrawal as a solution to the individual's psychic needs and life problems; there is the offer of a system of psychological and physiological practices by which a person can deliberately and voluntarily seek detachment from the everyday, external world and replace it with a heightened awareness of inner reality; and, finally, there is a shared conviction that this inner world possesses a much greater reality than the outer one.

Emotionally, to an Indian, the familiarity of the message, repeated often enough since the beginning of childhood, constitutes its greatest strength and attraction. Once again the men and women were transported to the time when, their small hands clutched in those of older family members, they had sat up late into the night, in the midst of a group of neighbors and kinsmen, sleepily listening to wandering *religiosi* expound the mysteries of life. It was familiar from the many after-death ceremonies where they had listened to the priest and the family elders talk of the laws of karma, the cycles of birth, life, and death, and the *mukti* that was every being's goal. Maharajji's talk was then a murmur from the past—both individual and collective—that had suddenly become audible. I too must confess to a curious mixture of elation and unease as I listened to him. The source of the elation was difficult to pinpoint then, though now I would describe it, somewhat fancifully to be sure, as a stirring of the blood to the call of the Indian Passion, the overflow of a feeling of oneness with one's (idealized) community and its traditions. He had touched an atavistic chord in me of which I would have perhaps preferred to remain unaware.

The unease is much easier to define. It sprang from what I can only call an outrage to "liberal, humanist sentiments." These too are part of my inheritance, as they are of all those, in every country around the globe, who are heirs to a still-emerging modern world. I was neither bothered by nor am I referring here to what appears as an element of medieval feudalism in the relationship of the *Satguru* with the members of his cult. Maharajji, of course, means "great king," and the meaning of *gaddi*, which indicates what he sits on—and has succeeded to—is "throne." The lithograph of Soamiji, the founder of the cult, that hangs in many public places and in the homes of devout initiates shows him clad in expensive-looking silks and brocades, richly bejeweled and benecklaced, and quite indistinguishable from the coppery daguerreotypes of Indian princes and "nabobs" that occasionally used to adorn the pages of turn-of-the-century British periodicals. Nor am I too much troubled by the fact that in the Satsang (as in most Indian mystical cults) favored treatment is given to the wealthy and powerful and that these marks of favor are rationalized by the gurus as being deserved by the disciples on account of their past good karma. I have also little quarrel with the very comfortable, if not opulent lifestyle of Maharajji and other mystics. The proverbial problems of the rich man trying to negotiate the eye of the needle are more a part of the Christian than the Hindu heritage; the link between ascetism and poverty on the one hand and spirituality and transcendence on the other has been denied by Indian saints more often than it has been affirmed.

My unease had more to do with the repeated assertion of Maharajji (and of his predecessors) that a "seeker" should not only endure but cheerfully and actively *accept* the iron law of karma. Saints, he says, perhaps rightly, are not social reformers who have come to change the world—although even here too one may doubt the validity of such a clear-cut demarcation between inner and outer changes, individual and social transformations, saints and revolutionaries. To recommend, however, a joyous acceptance of the existing social order—with its economic, social, and sexual inequities—as the prerequisite for a state of mind that leads to highest mystical truths, to advise women to conform cheerfully to the meek subservient roles laid out for them by a repressive patriarchy, does go against the grain of modern identity, even if Maharajji considers such acquiescence to be absolutely essential for progress on the mystical path. (A cynic, pointing to the fact that Maharajji himself is a rich landowner who is allied by kinship and marriage ties to some of the wealthiest families in northern India, might observe the curious coincidence that the will of God and the "eternal law of nature" seem to be identical to the economic and political interest of a feudal elite and the convenience of a patriarchal order. This, however, would be doing Maharajji an injustice, since his position on the law of karma and its individual and social consequences is not idiosyncratic but is shared by a vast majority of his compatriots and lies unexceptionably within the mainstream of Indian religiosity.)

After the *satsang*, I took a leisurely walk through the Dera township. People streamed past me in groups—small contingents of *satsangis* from different villages, large families with women and children placed protectively in the middle while the men walked at the periphery, guarding them like sheepdogs. Many of them were on their way to the huge tents erected near the Satsang Ghar; each of which could accommodate up to a thousand people in its cavernous insides. Others strolled through the freshly swept streets, the clawlike marks made by the twig brooms still visible in the earth, their festive mood proving to be more than a match for the whipping cold wind. The afterglow of the Satsang was still reflected on their friendly faces and in their smiles, which seemed to affirm joyously each other's existence and value. I remember that my own greetings of "Radhasoami!" in response to those directed at me by total strangers were without a trace of the earlier self-consciousness and embarrassment I had felt at being (in a sense) an imposter among true believers. For a short while, I was prepared to believe that social relations need not necessarily be organized according to either of the two fundamental categories that sociologists since Ferdinand Tönnies have prescribed. The *satsangis* were neither a *community,* with the community's uncritical acceptance of roles and relationships, where the individual tends to merge into others, nor did they constitute a *society,* with its rational-contractual bonds and its calculating coolness, where the individual is at a distance from others with whom he is also in competition. The sect members seemed to be living, however temporarily, in a third kind of association, which Eugen Schmalenbach has called "communion" and which only a few social scientists have explored as being either desirable or possible. Here a more or less freely chosen, nonbinding brotherhood dominates; the individual is enhanced (unlike in a community), and yet the emotional bonds go deep (unlike in a society). I could therefore understand how the Radhasoami Satsang (and perhaps most mystical sects) can become a haven for so many Indians who are in flight from the oppressiveness of an all-embracing community, as well as for those Westerners who are moving in the other direction, namely, away from the cold isolation and competitiveness of an individualistic society.

In the meantime, Maharajji had returned to his house, its approaches guarded by volunteers who politely but firmly turned back the more curious and intrepid of his disciples. Behind the high walls surrounding his mansion, Maharajji reclined on a wicker chair in his rose garden, attending to his correspondence and affairs of the trust that manages the *satsang*'s far-flung activities with exemplary efficiency. A dozen of his intimate disciples—the specially special ones—sat around him at a respectful distance. They watched Maharajji work, savoring the great privilege of his nearness, grateful for being allowed to participate, however vicariously, in his activities. Maharajji's every movement—whether the opening of a letter, the adjustment of his reading glasses, or a gentle burp as he meditatively stroked his beard—seemed to be greeted by silent hosannas. They followed him, again at a respectful distance, to the guesthouse where Maharajji was to give a special *darshan* to seventy-odd mostly foreign members of the cult. The *darshan* itself did not take too much time. Maharajji approached them with folded hands raised in greeting and sat down on a sofa placed in the middle of the guesthouse lawn, with rows of chairs arranged in a semicircle around it. Without any preliminaries, he looked steadily for a couple of minutes at one section of his small audience, then regally turned his face and stared unblinkingly at another section—a virtuoso use of look and silence. The transformation of the disciples' faces as their eyes looked into his was remarkable. The eyes glazed over as they drank in his visage. Visibly, their brows smoothened out, their jaw muscles slackened, and a beatific expression slowly spread on the faces. The whole transformation was startingly similar to the nursing infant when he takes the breast into his mouth and the milk begins to spread its soothing warmth, generating those good feelings that gradually obliterate all the earlier unease, the tension, and the plain anxiousness. The *darshan* ended around noon. Keeping a few paces behind him, all of us followed Maharajji to the venue of his next engagement, the blessing of the food at the *langar*—the community kitchen. "Kitchen," of course, is a euphemism for a sprawling complex of large rooms and open spaces where eighty thousand meals were being prepared for lunch and where hundreds of volunteer cooks and helpers—men and women—were carrying out their assigned tasks with a military precision. Thick *masur dal* steamed and gurgled in a row of burnished copper vats, each one the height of a man; the cloying sweet smell of jaggery-flavored rice wafted out of oval cauldrons; flat, pancake-shaped breads—the *rotis*—were being taken out of clay ovens dug deep into the earth, and then stacked up in mounds. As we approached the *langar,* we could already hear the women, busy kneading and rolling the dough for the *rotis,* singing:

> *Charan kamal tere dho dho peeyan*
> *Deen Dayal Satguru mere*
>
> I wash your lotus feet and drink the water,
> O my compassionate and merciful *Satguru.*

The scene as Maharajji briskly walked around the "kitchen" with his hands raised in benediction is one of my most striking memories of Beas. Squatting on their heels, their hands clasped together in supplication, their glittering black eyes shining with the light of purest pleasure, and their broad smiles expressing a child's unreserved delight, the women sang louder as Maharajji passed close to them, while their heads and the upper halves of their bodies seemed to strain toward him in unbearable longing. In contrast, the men quietly raised their faces toward Maharajji in a look of dumb devotion that was also full of awe—if not fear. In fact, whenever the *Satguru* came upon a man working alone, the man would immediately squat down on his heels and visibly cringe, as if prepared to receive a capricious blow. The Punjabi daughter's early experience of her father, I reminded myself from clinical experience, is indeed very different from that of the Punjabi son. The mutual adoration and idealization characteristic of the former relationship is missing in the latter.

PART VI · CASTE

13 · A Dalit Poet-Saint

Ravidas

JOHN STRATTON HAWLEY,
with MARK JUERGENSMEYER

Oh well-born of Benares, I too am born well known:
My labor is with leather. But my heart can boast
the Lord.

RAVIDAS, *Adi Granth* 38

Benares, Hinduism's oldest city and a citadel of the Brahmin caste, fits along the left bank of the Ganges as if it were an elaborately embroidered sleeve. A long and complicated city, like the religious tradition it symbolizes, it opens at its southern extremity onto the spacious grounds of Banaras Hindu University, and for most people it stops there. But just beyond the high wall that surrounds the university, at its back gate, there is one more settlement, a dusty little enclave called Sri Govardhanpur. It is the last collection of houses before the country begins, and there is a reason that it has grown up where it has. This is a village inhabited almost entirely by Untouchables, outcastes. Even in a secular India committed by its constitution to the abolition of untouchability, their pariah identity still has its geographical symbol. (See figure L at the website http://www.clas.ufl.edu/users/vasu/loh.)

The people of Sri Govardhanpur have no intention of accepting their lot as if it were decreed by fate or religion. Since 1967 they have devoted many of their efforts toward the completion of a large temple that is designed to put Sri Govardhanpur on the religious map of Benares. They hope that their four-story edifice will rival temples in other sectors of the city and become a familiar part of the pilgrims' circuit—or if not that, at least serve as a magnet for low-caste people who are not always welcome in the city's other temples. The project by no means belongs to the

This essay was previously published as "Ravidas," in J. S. Hawley and Mark Juergensmeyer, *Songs of the Saints of India* (Delhi: Oxford University Press, 2004), 9–23, 175–78.

people of Sri Govardhanpur alone. Much of the organization came from a "mission" headquartered in New Delhi that was dedicated to advancing the Untouchables' cause, and regular financial support has been provided by urbanites of Untouchable background who live in the distant but prosperous province of Punjab or lead even more comfortable lives in England and America. Clearly, even people who have managed to escape the worst strictures of caste care about erasing the shame of untouchability. In fact, many eschew the word: they are Dalits, "the oppressed."[1]

The new edifice in Sri Govardhanpur is not just another Hindu temple. In fact, there is some debate about whether it should be called Hindu at all, for it is dedicated to the remembrance of a saint whose person, perspective, and teachings place him in a sense outside the Hindu pale. His name is Ravidas; he was a man of Benares; and though he lived in the fifteenth or sixteenth century, he still qualifies today as the great Untouchable saint of North India. If one means by Hinduism the religious system whose central rituals are entrusted to Brahmins, whose central institutions require a set of reciprocal but unequal social relationships, and whose guiding ideas set forth what life should be within this hierarchically variegated world and how it may rightly be transcended, then Ravidas was not really a Hindu. As he saw it, there was nothing fundamental about the institutions of caste. His position in society helped him see the point, for he was a leatherworker, a *camar,* a shoemaker, someone whose work brought him into daily contact with the hides of dead animals. Strict Hindus either shun the touch of such skins altogether, believing them to be polluting, or contact them only with the lowest portion of their bodies, the bottom of their feet. And that, by extension, is what the *camar* is in relation to almost all of Hindu society.

But Ravidas was special; he was a poet and singer, and the hymns he sang evidently had such a ring of truth that even Brahmins came to hear them. His poet's charisma must have been equally powerful, for he says that the Brahmins actually bowed before him, in a total inversion of religious and social protocol (*AG* 38).[2] Yet he never forgot his own condition. In praising God he habitually contrasted the divine presence to his own: God, he said, was finer than he, as silk was to a worm, and more fragrant than he, as sandalwood was to the stinking castor oil plant (*AG* 9).

Ravidas's clear perception of his lowly condition made him poignantly aware that it did not belong just to him, but to every shoemaker and scavenger of this world. These, he felt, included not only his caste fellows but everyone who exists inside a body. No living being is spared the degradations of the flesh, and whoever prefers to think otherwise is dwelling in a world of make-believe (*AG* 9, 27). Ravidas thought it ridiculous that caste Hindus could set such store by rituals demanding the use of pure substances, when in truth there is nothing on earth that is not polluted. "Can I offer milk?" he asked in one poem, referring to the substance Hindus regard as purest of them all, since it emerges straight from the holy cow. His answer was that even it had been polluted by prior use: "The calf has dirtied it in sucking its mother's teat" (*AG* 13).[3] Nothing is spared the taint of the flesh, so he railed against anyone who treated another person as trash (*AG* 28, 31). Even kings, he said, dream that they are beggars; only the absence of love in one's life makes one truly an Untouchable (*AG* 14, 35).

The wonder is that God is precisely the sort of being who cares for those who are troubled and lowly. As Ravidas puts it, he "rescues even tanners of hides" (*AG* 19). In relation to God, every person is untouchable; yet because God is who he is, every person is touched.

AN OUTCASTE IN THE FAMILY OF SAINTS

Such a message appeals on every front to the hardworking, socially oppressed people of Sri Govardhanpur; that Ravidas was a Benarsi makes him even more naturally their patron. But he does not belong to Untouchables alone. Ravidas is one of the *bhakti* family, and as such he is venerated by Hindus of all backgrounds and stations. The sharing in God that *bhakti* implies creates networks of human beings that cut across the divisions society erects—even those that it dignifies with religious significance. In many of its expressions *bhakti* has called into question that version of Hinduism that ties itself intimately to the caste system. Hence even upper-caste Hindus who regard themselves as its beneficiaries take care to include in the hagiographical pantheon at least one representative of caste groups normally considered too low to qualify as "twice-born"—ritually pure—members of society. When the *camars* of Sri Govardhanpur began building their temple to Ravidas, then, there was an aspect of Hindu religion to which they could appeal. On a *bhakti* construction of what Hindu religion is about, a temple to Ravidas had a genuine claim to being included in the religious universe of Benares.

Ravidas himself indicates the *bhakti* family in which he felt he belonged by naming in his poetry several of his predecessors in the faith. One of the names he gives is that of Namdev, a fourteenth-century saint of western India who was a tailor and a member of the relatively low caste associated with that profession (*AG* 11.4, 33.5). Another was Trilocan, also from the west (*AG* 33.5). A third—whose name he mentions more frequently than any other—was Kabir, the crusty fifteenth-century iconoclast who, like Ravidas, lived in Benares (*AG* 11.3, 33.5, 39.6). Kabir too came from the lower echelons of society. He was a weaver and belonged to a caste, the *julahas*, many of whose members had found their place in Hindu society sufficiently distasteful that they had turned to Islam. In mentioning these three as recipients of divine grace along with himself, Ravidas underscored his sense of solidarity with a tradition of *bhakti* that flowed with particular animation in the lower ranks of society.

This, however, is only Ravidas's immediate *bhakti* family, the one that he constructs for himself in several of the poems that have a good claim to being regarded as authentically his. These compositions are included in the *Adi Granth*, the *bhakti* anthology that serves as scripture to the Sikh community and features poems of the Sikh gurus. Its precursor, the *Kartarpur Granth*, was compiled in 1604 C.E. and contains the oldest substantial collection of poetry attributed to Ravidas: forty full-length poems *(pads)* and an epigrammatic couplet. All of them survive in the *Adi Granth* itself.

But many more poems than these are generally thought to have been sung by Ravidas,[4] and many more connections between him and other *bhakti* figures are accepted by tradition. One of these traditional links is with Nanak—a connection that Sikhs see as almost a tenet of faith, since they understand Nanak, whom they regard as their founding guru, to have been inspired by the other poets anthologized in the *Adi Granth*. It is commonly accepted that Nanak and Ravidas were contemporaries who met at a place in Benares that is now called, fittingly, Guru Bagh ("The Gurus' Garden"), but the estimation of who learned more from whom depends upon whether one is primarily a follower of Nanak or of Ravidas.[5]

Another saint mentioned in Ravidas's company is Mirabai, the woman poet of Rajasthan, who is said in a modern text called the *Ravidas Ramayana* to have traveled all the way to Benares to obtain initiation from Ravidas.[6] Another is Gorakhnath, a renowned yogi who is usually thought to have lived several centuries earlier.[7] Still another is Ramanand, the Brahmin who is said to have played a critical role in the expansion of *bhakti* Hinduism by transferring it from its original home in South India to Benares, where he came to live. To judge by the account of Priyadas, the influential commentator who in 1712 fleshed out the skeleton provided by Nabhadas's somewhat earlier anthology of *bhakti* saints (the *Bhaktamal*, ca. 1600), Ramanand managed to gather around himself a more dynamic circle of devotees than North India has seen before or since. As indicated in a list given by Nabhadas himself, both Kabir and Ravidas were included in their number.[8]

These and many other traditions about Ravidas's place in the community of *bhakti* saints abound. Unfortunately, they cannot all be taken at face value. There is some indication, for example, that Ramanand lived a full century before Ravidas, which makes it hard for any but the most committed (who are willing to grant Ravidas a life span of 150 years or so) to think that the two could have met. Nor is there anything in the oldest collection of Ravidas's poetry to point to Ramanand. With the Mirabai story too there are problems. It appears that the tale concerning her was grafted onto Priyadas's similar but earlier account of a Jhali-lineage Rajput queen who, like Mira, came to Ravidas from the city of Cittor to be initiated by him as his spiritual child. In time the Jhali queen was forgotten as the fame of Mira, the queen's musical counterpart, grew.[9] But the debatable accuracy of these stories matters less than the spirit that gave them rise. What is important is that for many centuries after Ravidas, and right down to the present day, there has been a persistent desire to connect the cobbler-poet with a larger network of *bhakti* heroes. Ravidas's low-caste followers are not the only ones to have felt this urge; other writers, including Brahmins, have done the same.[10]

The reason is that the *bhakti* tradition by nature runs in families—this is a piety of shared experience, of singing and enthusiastic communication—and each clan, to be inclusive, needs to have at least one representative from the Untouchable castes. In South India, where the *bhakti* movement can be traced back much farther than in the north, this meant that Tiruppan, an Untouchable, and Tirumankai, a member of the thief caste, were set alongside Brahmins and high-status Vellalas in building the family of Alvars—devotees to Vishnu who lived from the sixth to the ninth century. In the west of India one found Cokhamela, the Untouchable who on occasion transported carrion, and Namdev, the lowly tailor, in the company of such higher-caste divines as Jnandev and Eknath. And in North India, Kabir and especially Ravidas filled out the family of saints by providing it with poor cousins from the lower end of the social spectrum. The message proclaimed by this tradition of family associations is that the love of God transcends the givens of the social order, bringing together people who otherwise could not have met and creating an alternate, more truly religious society capable of complementing and challenging the one established by caste. It was often the saints situated on the lower rungs of the social ladder who envisioned this other society most clearly.

Some of the most vivid episodes in the traditional life stories of Ravidas take up this point. They reconstitute society according to a *bhakti* definition by showing that Ravidas belongs at its religious apex, that is, in the company of Brahmins. In all of these tales, those who are Brahmins by blood are the last to see the point.

The story of Queen Jhali (Priyadas talks as if this was her proper name) is a good example. Priyadas says that she traveled to Benares with some of her court Brahmins, who were then scandalized at her choice of gurus. They went to the king of Benares for justice, expecting a sympathetic ear, but the wise ruler, who had already had some experience with Brahmins jealous of Ravidas, submitted the matter to even higher arbitration. He brought both the Brahmins and Ravidas into the presence of the royal icon and announced that he would value the claim of whoever could show that the Lord inclined in his direction. The Brahmins chanted the correct Vedic verses, but these seemed to have no effect. When Ravidas began to sing, however, intoning a verse in which he asked God to reveal himself as the one whose nature is to rescue the fallen *(patit pavan)*, the image responded by jumping directly into the poet's lap.[11]

Queen Jhali insisted on taking Ravidas to her home in Rajasthan for a time, and the disgruntled Brahmins could do no more by way of protest. Yet nothing could persuade them to share a meal with the Untouchable saint. When the queen prepared a great feast to honor her newfound teacher, these religious aristocrats declined to eat from the same vessels that he did. Jhali bowed to their compunctions by giving them the ingredients separately, so that they could cook their own meal, and Ravidas issued no protest. When they all sat down, however— Ravidas on his side of the hall and the Brahmins on theirs—and the Brahmins raised the food to their mouths, they discovered to their horror that between each of them a Ravidas had miraculously materialized. Evidently he belonged in their row after all. They fled in consternation and challenged him on his right to be there, but when they did so he peeled back the skin from his chest and revealed a golden sacred thread that lay within, clear evidence of his inner brahminhood.[12] (See figure M at the Web site http://www.clas.ufl.edu/users/vasu/loh.)

The *camars* of Sri Govardhanpur love to tell this story, along with others testifying to Ravidas's spiritual superiority. Another favorite is the tale of how the Ganges herself, a Hindu goddess with intimate ties to a wide range of brahminical rituals, acknowledged Ravidas's claim. When the Brahmins of Benares challenged Ravidas's right to preach as he did, the two sides agreed to let the river goddess decide the case: if each threw something into the water, which would she support on her surface? The Brahmins tossed in a piece of wood, but it sank like a stone. Yet when Ravidas threw a stone into the river, it floated.[13]

The people of Sri Govardhanpur find such stories about spiritual brahminhood congenial enough, but they are understandably reluctant to accept any hint that Ravidas was physically a Brahmin or even that he desired to be adopted into the spiritual care of Brahmins. The story that Ravidas sought initiation at the hands of Ramanand, a Brahmin, is an old one—it is told by Priyadas—but the Untouchables of

Sri Govardhanpur deny it. Pursuing the new historical connections first suggested by B. R. Ghera, a retired civil servant living in Delhi who was the intellectual spearhead of the Ravidas mission in Sri Govardhanpur, they insist that Ravidas's teacher was instead a certain Saradanand, about whom little has hitherto been heard.[14]

They are even more vehement in contesting the validity of another story told by Priyadas. They refuse to accept that Ravidas was a Brahmin in the life that preceded his incarnation as a *camar.* That they should find such a story offensive is no surprise, since it suggests that no leatherworker can become a saint unaided, but several details reported by Priyadas are particularly heinous. His explanation of why Ravidas was born a *camar* is that in the saint's former life as a pupil of Ramanand he compromised his teacher's Brahmin purity by offering him food donated by a merchant who had been tainted by business dealings with *camars.* According to the story, Ramanand could tell instantly that the food was contaminated by its distant association with Untouchables. Equally offensive is Priyadas's depiction of what happened when this Brahmin pupil died and was reborn into a family of leatherworkers. He says that as a baby Ravidas refused to receive milk from his own *camar* mother. Only when Ramanand heard of the newborn's distress and came to adopt him would the child take sustenance.[15]

No one can deny that such stories are *ex post facto* attempts to brahminize Ravidas, and it is hard not to feel exactly the way the people of Sri Govardhanpur do about the light that they cast on *camars.* Still, the desire of Brahmins to claim Ravidas's charisma as their own is worthy of note. What galls the inhabitants of Sri Govardhanpur and other low-caste communities, however, is that this ecumenical spirit is almost never extended from the realm of *bhakti* hagiography into the real world. The people of Sri Govardhanpur had to appeal to the city government for more than a decade before the road that passes by the new temple was grudgingly paved. They know, too, that many of the Brahmins of Benares scoff at the procession that passes through the city each year on the day they celebrate Ravidas's birth. And they have often had to endure humiliations such as those suffered by a group of Benares Ravidasis who traveled the long road to Rajasthan to visit the temple of Mirabai in her natal village of Merta, only to be denied entrance once they arrived.

BHAKTI AND SOCIAL PROTEST

The question that lingers here is whether the message of *bhakti* is a message of social protest. Is the equality it celebrates fundamentally a social reality—and therefore something revolutionary in its Indian context—or is it only spiritual, in which case it can coexist with brahminical Hinduism even if it does not endorse it?

On the one hand it seems clear that a poet like Ravidas raises crucial questions about the social order. His perception of Brahmins and others who set store by standard Hindu texts and rituals is scarcely complimentary, and he has contempt for all who denigrate people belonging to other sectors of society than their own (*AG* 31). He insists that

> A family that has a true follower of the Lord
> Is neither high caste nor low caste, lordly or poor. (*AG* 29)

The number of times he refers to his own caste position suggests that he was always mindful of it.[16] On the other hand, he does not propose any religious legislation that would change the current social order. To the contrary, it often seems that he values his own lowly position as a vantage point from which the truth about everyone comes more clearly into view. His *bhakti* vision seems to be not so much that God desires to reform society as that he transcends it utterly, and that in the light of the experience of sharing in God, all social distinctions lose their importance. At the end of the poem most recently quoted he speaks of how the person of faith may "flower above the world of his birth" as lotuses float upon the water (*AG* 29). And he often dwells on the miracle that God has come to him as an implicit sign of how remarkable it is that the holy should touch any human life (*AG* 9, 30, 33).

Ravidas's *bhakti,* then, is an answer to caste Hinduism, but not explicitly a call for its reform. Even though he speaks of a kingdom "where none are third or second—all are one" and where the residents "do this or that, they walk where they wish," still he admits that it is his "distant home," and he issues no direct call for realizing it here on earth (*AG* 3).

Indeed, when he speaks of earth his emphasis is quite different. He characterizes life in this world as an inevitably difficult journey and asks God for help along the way (*AG* 4). Death stands waiting at the end of the road, he knows (*AG* 4, 26), and when it strikes, even one's closest relatives scurry to keep their distance (*AG* 27). As for the body, it is a fiction of air and water, nothing more than a hollow clay puppet (*AG* 19, 12). About all there is to do in such circumstances—as bewildering to human beings as the wider world is to a frog in a well—is cry for help (*AG* 5). Fortunately, remarkably, there is a friend who answers that lonely call, someone who is at times confusingly, disconcertingly near, someone to whom people are tied by what Ravidas calls on several occasions "the bonds of love" (*AG* 10, 15, 18). That friend, of course, is God.

THE RAVIDAS LEGACY

The *bhakti* of Ravidas, then, is a gritty, personal faith, so it is fitting that the response of Untouchables to it and to him has a number of facets—social, liturgical, conceptual, and, of course, personal. The first of these responses is indeed the demand for social reform, and at various points over the past several decades it has been couched in frankly political terms. One of the organizations involved in building the Ravidas temple in Sri Govardhanpur was called the All India Adi Dharm Mission, a body established in 1957. Working from a heritage that extends back into the early years of the twentieth century, it has at its core the idea that the lowest echelons of modern Indian society are the survivors of a noble race who inhabited the subcontinent long before the Aryan Hindus arrived from Central Asia. They were a people who "worshiped truthfulness, justice, simplicity and who were benevolent and helped one another at the time of difficulty." This was India's *adi dharm*, its "original religion" or "original moral order," something that was substantially destroyed by the Aryan incursion, but that God saw fit to revive by raising up sages and gurus such as Nanak, Kabir, and preeminently Ravidas.[17]

Over the course of its episodic but now relatively long history, the Adi Dharm (or, as it is sometimes called, Ad Dharm) movement has attempted to mobilize the lower castes of North India, particularly in the Punjab, to achieve greater social justice.[18] Even the establishment of the Ravidas temple in Sri Govardhanpur serves a potentially political purpose. The current plan to extend the educational activities of the temple by founding a Ravidas college in Sri Govardhanpur is aimed at preparing lower-caste people for jobs in a literate society and enlarging the pool of candidates available to fill positions in government service that are reserved for members of the lower castes.[19]

When Ravidas's name is sounded in religious circles, then, the social message associated with him is never inaudible—even if, to judge from the compositions anthologized in the *Adi Granth*, the saint himself was not entirely preoccupied with the matter. But this is only one facet of the modern response to Ravidas. Another is more specifically cultic and ceremonial: at Sri Govardhanpur and a number of Ravidas *deras* (sacred compounds) in the Punjab, he serves as the actual focus of the community's worship.

Considering the liturgical importance of Ravidas, it is surprising that for years none of the verses most likely to have come from the mouth of the master himself played a role in the worship services that take place at Sri Govardhanpur. When the old liturgist sat down in front of the large, handwritten book from which he chanted, the turgid verse he intoned had almost no relation to the vivid compositions collected in the *Adi Granth*. Though each of the poems he recited bore Ravidas's oral signature, as is customary in the *pad* genre he employed,[20] these dutiful compositions seem to be about Ravidas, rather than by him. Each of them praises the greatness of one's guru and underscores the importance of preserving one's fealty to the master. The following, the second in the book, is typical:

Project the guru's image in your mind,
  hold it ever steady in your thought.
Purity, charity, making yourself a name—
  these only bolster your pride,
But to utter the name of the guru in your heart
  will make you unshakably wise. . . .

And so forth, ending with the phrase, "so says Ravidas."[21] The language of this poem is flatter and more plodding than what one meets in the *Adi Granth*. Its simplicity has the advantage of making the verse easily intelligible to its hearers, but because its style is so different from those likely to be authentic, the chances are that the poem is not very old. Though it purports to be the verbiage of Ravidas himself, it has a flaccid, contemporary ring and could scarcely have been produced before the nineteenth century. Even that seems improbably early.

To understand this poetry, one must know who created the book in which it is inscribed. It was B. R. Ghera, the retired civil servant who was so critically involved in launching Ravidas on his most recent career. His intention, like several Adi Dharmis before him, was to draw together the poems of Ravidas into a collection that would rival the anthology of poems that Sikhs take as their scripture, the *Adi Granth*. To do so, he made frequent trips between 1963 and 1967 to a teacher named Harnam who lived in a *dera* in Moradabad District, not far east of Delhi. Ghera reported that Harnam, who himself came from a lower-caste background, was exclusively a follower of Ravidas, so his collection of Ravidas poems was to be trusted as authentic. Ghera intended to use it as the basis for a series of volumes he would entitle the *Guru Ravidas Granth*. The title has a familiar ring. Ghera's idea was that when this *Granth* emerged before the public eye, it would be received as comparable in size and depth to its Sikh namesake.[22]

These efforts were not entirely successful. In the 1980s the modest audience that assembled morning and evening heard only a small selection of these didactic verses from a manuscript version of Ghera's work, and since then the scriptural initiative has passed firmly into the hands of Ghera's parent organization, the *dera* of Sant Sarvan Das located in the Punjab. There was a dispute in which issues of property ownership, institutional authority, and scriptural correctness were at stake. It was said that Ghera's version of the temple's founding events substituted his own agency for that of Sant Sarvan Das, and that he had obscured the words of the true Ravidas and put his own in their place. The whole thing landed in the courts, and they ruled against Ghera.[23] In the end a very different version of Ravidas emerged in the songs sung daily at Sri Govardhanpur. Nowadays the liturgist chants the whole of a little red book in which are printed the forty-one compositions that appear in the *Adi Granth*, simultaneously connecting Ravidas with the Sikh context and liberating him from it. In preaching from the text he aligns Ravidas with God and the inner soul, and the service concludes with a recitation of the guru lineage going back to Sant Sarvan Das. Copies of the little red book, published by Sant Sarvan Das's organization, are available to the public at the spacious Ravidas Park that has opened on the banks of the Ganges not far away.

The consolidation of the community's identity behind the figure of Ravidas proceeds apace. He has become their guru—the founder of their faith and the source of their inspiration—as Nanak is for Sikhs. But he has also become the sort of guru that would be familiar in many Hindu communities. Whereas Sikhs proscribe the use of any image in their places of worship *(gurdvaras)*, preferring to meet Nanak and his successors entirely through their words, the Ravidasis of Sri Govardhanpur can establish visual contact with the master, as Hindus typically do. A multicolored, life-size image of the great saint is installed at the center of the altar area, and there is another upstairs in the pilgrims' dormitory. As songs praising the guru's greatness are sung, he receives the community's adoration in person.

A third way in which the sixteenth-century *camar* saint matters in the lives of his latter-day caste fellows goes beyond social reform and religious cult. Through Ravidas, Untouchables are able to map out their relation to other aspects of Indian society in a manner that is clearer and more satisfying to them than the conceptual grids through which others are apt to see them.

One expression of this process of conceptual clarification is an enormous construction effort long under way on the opposite side of Benares from Sri Govardhanpur. There, on a bluff overlooking the Ganges, one of the most important Untouchable political figures of recent memory, Deputy Prime Minister Jagjivan Ram, began building a temple to Ravidas as the last great project of his career. Work proceeds at a slow but regular pace, and the edifice is splendid indeed. Covered entirely with marble on the inside, it contains a vast sanctuary, a huge kitchen, and quarters for ascetics and visiting scholars. It will also house a museum in which will be deposited not only memorabilia relating to Ravidas but those documenting the life of Jagjivan Ram as well. In the circular appealing for funds, in fact, these two share the spotlight: a picture of Jagjivan Ram is on one side of the page, and a picture of Ravidas is on the other.[24]

Jagjivan Ram's temple says many things. First and foremost, of course, it says that Ravidas belongs on the highlands along the Ganges as much as any other Hindu god or saint. Fortunately Jagjivan Ram's political connections enabled him to acquire from the government the land necessary to make such a statement. Second, the temple says something about Ravidas's place among the other *bhakti* saints of North India: it puts him right in the center. Near the temple's entrance a picture of Ravidas was for many years flanked by others depicting Kabir and Surdas, and in the sanctuary one finds not only a central altar dedicated to Ravidas but an ancillary shrine to Mirabai. Third, the structure states the relation between the veneration of Ravidas and India's major religious communities. Spires on each of the corners symbolize Sikhism, Buddhism, Christianity, and Islam, and in their midst one glimpses the great spire to Ravidas. The message is that what Ravidas represents stands at the center of all the great religions and illumines them equally. Hinduism is notably occluded.

Finally there is a political message. The person long charged with day-to-day operations at the temple, Ram Lakhan, a former member of Parliament and minister in Indira Gandhi's government, declared it to be "the people's temple," with the implication that the people provide the basis upon which all other structures rest. To speak this way is to cast Ravidas in the role of vox populi and to suggest not too subliminally that the Congress Party, in which both Jagjivan Ram and Ram Lakhan served, is the organization best able to unite adherents of all communities.[25] But nowadays there is stiff competition for lower-caste votes from parties whose social base is actually there.

The people of Sri Govardhanpur and their many pilgrim visitors do certainly visit this new monument, but they are well aware that it was Jagjivan Ram's establishment connections that made its construction possible. Some quip that it is less a temple to their saint than to the political figure who posed as his devotee. And they have their own way of charting the territory that ties them, through Ravidas, to the wider world. The contents of their own Ravidas edifice may be less imposing than what is being assembled across town, but they serve essentially the same function.

First of all, there is a life-size statue of the bespectacled Sant Sarvan Das, the Punjabi religious leader whose Ravidas following contributed the financial means that made the temple possible and whose far-off *dera* welcomes pilgrims from Sri Govardhanpur into what seems a pan-Indian community.[26] Through the years, the pictures that line the walls of the sanctuary have served a similar purpose. For instance, there used to be a map of India recording in careful detail the journeys that Ravidas took around the subcontinent. It showed how he traveled from Kashmir in the north to the Deccan in the south and spanned the distance between Puri and Dvaraka, two great hubs of pilgrimage on the east and west coasts—a total journey of 5,946 kilometers, as the legend announces. This map had the effect of placing Ravidas in the great tradition of philosophers and theologians who circled the land to establish the paramount legitimacy of their views.

Other illustrations do the same thing in other ways. One painting, for instance, depicts the moment in which Ravidas initiated Mirabai. It relates him to the figure who is probably the most popular member of the North Indian *bhakti* family, but who stands at the head of no formalized cult or community of her own. This makes it less dangerous than it otherwise might be for these lower-caste people to assert their guru's primacy over her, and thereby suggest that he is the ultimate cause of her celebrity. Another picture once showed the master's own lineage, situating him as the central figure in a genealogy of revelation that extends from the present era of world history all the way back to the beginning of time.[27]

Of course, the people of Sri Govardhanpur are aware that other people see things other ways, and they themselves have not always accepted everything these pictures imply. No problem. They understand that history has a tendency to be forged after the fact by communities that wish to shape it. After all, how many stories of Ravidas himself have been suppressed or twisted by upper-caste groups eager to rewrite history so that it serves their own interest? Furthermore, they take it as given that things seem different from different perspectives, and that people emphasize what matters most to them. In this perception they are not alone. This feature of Hindu thinking seemed so pervasive to the pioneering Indologist Max Müller that he felt he had to coin new words to describe it. He spoke of "kathenotheism" and "henotheism," both referring to the Hindu tendency to worship gods one at a time yet regard each as ultimate for the period during which that god is at the forefront of the believer's attention.[28] Similarly, when it comes to saints and society, Hindus find it natural that people should draw toward their own point of focus all that concerns them, as the Untouchables of North India have consolidated much of the general *bhakti* heritage around Ravidas.

The henotheistic habit of mind makes it possible for people like those who live in Sri Govardhanpur to assign themselves a convincingly important position in the broad sweep of Indian society and religion. If others do not orient themselves by the same map, it does not greatly matter. For these Benarsis the figure of Ravidas, a gift from the past, serves as a major point of reference, and for that reason he is very much alive in the present, shaping the world half a millennium after his death.

POEMS OF RAVIDAS

Translated with Mark Juergensmeyer

I've never known how to tan or sew,
 though people come to me for shoes.
I haven't the needle to make the holes
 or even the tool to cut the thread.
Others stitch and knot, and tie themselves in knots
 while I, who do not knot, break free.
I keep saying Ram and Ram, says Ravidas,
 and Death keeps his business to himself.[29] (*AG* 20)

A family that has a true follower of the Lord
Is neither high caste nor low caste, lordly or poor.
 The world will know it by its fragrance.
Priests or merchants, laborers or warriors,
 half-breeds, outcastes, and those who tend cremation fires—
  their hearts are all the same.
He who becomes pure through love of the Lord
 exalts himself and his family as well.
Thanks be to his village, thanks to his home,
 thanks to that pure family, each and every one.
For he's drunk with the essence of the liquid of life
 and he pours away all the poisons.

No one equals someone so pure and devoted—
  not priests, nor heroes, nor parasolled kings.
As the lotus leaf floats above the water, Ravidas says,
  so he flowers above the world of his birth.[30] (*AG* 29)

The house is large, its kitchen vast,
  but after only a moment's passed, it's vacant.
This body is like a scaffold made of grass:
  the flames will consume it and render it dust.
Even your family—your brothers and friends—
  clamor to have you removed at dawn.
The lady of the house, who once clung to your chest,
  shouts "Ghost! Ghost!" now and runs away.
The world, says Ravidas, loots and plunders all—
  except me, for I have slipped away
    by saying the name of God. (*AG* 27)

The day it comes, it goes;
  whatever you do, nothing stays firm.
The group goes, and I go;
  the going is long, and death is overhead.
What! Are you sleeping? Wake up, fool,
  wake to the world you took to be true.
The one who gave you life daily feeds you, clothes you.
  Inside every body, he runs the store.
So keep to your prayers, abandon "me" and "mine."
  Now's the time to nurture the name that's in the heart.
Life has slipped away. No one's left on the road,
  and in each direction the evening dark has come.
Madman, says Ravidas, here's the cause of it all—
  it's only a house of tricks. Ignore the world. (*AG* 26)

The regal realm with the sorrowless name:
  they call it Queen City, a place with no pain,
No taxes or cares, none owns property there,
  no wrongdoing, worry, terror, or torture.
Oh my brother, I've come to take it as my own,

my distant home, where everything is right.
That imperial kingdom is rich and secure,
where none are third or second—all are one.
Its food and drink are famous, and those who live there
dwell in satisfaction and in wealth.
They do this or that, they walk where they wish,
they stroll through fabled palaces unchallenged.
Oh, says Ravidas, a tanner now set free,
those who walk beside me are my friends.[31] (*AG* 3)

NOTES

1. I mean no disrespect by retaining the term Untouchable here. I do so only because Ravidās refuses so pointedly to avoid it. The literature on Śrī Govardhanpur is principally confined to Julie Womack, "Ravidas and the Chamars of Banaras," an essay written for the Junior Year Abroad Program of the University of Wisconsin in Benares, 1983. Also relevant are B. R. Gherā, *Śrī Guru Ravidās jī kā Samkṣipt Itihās* (n.p.: All India Adi Dharm Mission, n.d.); Mark Juergensmeyer, *Religion as Social Vision: The Movement against Untouchability in 20th-century Punjab* (Berkeley: University of California Press, 1982), 260–62; and R. S. Khare, *The Untouchable as Himself: Ideology, Identity, and Pragmatism among the Lucknow Chamars* (Cambridge: Cambridge University Press, 1984), 40–50, 94–104.

2. This and most other citations of poems of Ravidās are drawn from the series recorded in the Sikh scripture, called *Ādi Granth [AG]* or *Gurū Granth Sāhib.* They have been sequentially numbered by Padam Gurcaran Simh, *Sant Ravidās: Vicārak aur Kavi* (Jullundur: Nav-Cintan Prakāśan, 1977), 191–204.

3. Ravidās was not the first poet to voice this sentiment. For an earlier example from South India, see A. K. Ramanujan, *Speaking of Śiva* (Baltimore: Penguin, 1973), 90.

4. Printed collections of poetry attributed to Ravidās are given a systematic listing in Darshan Singh, *A Study of Bhakta Ravadāsa* (Patiala: Punjabi University, 1981), 3–4. To this list should be added the edition compiled by Candrikāprasād Jijñāsu, *Sant Pravar Raidās Sāhab,* rev. ed. (Lucknow: Bahujan Kalyāṇ Prakāśan, 1969 [1959]), and, notably, the two-hundred-odd poems assembled in B. P. Śarmā, *Sant Guru Ravidās-Vāṇī* (Delhi: Sūrya Prakāśan, 1978), 66–142. The most ample English translation is that of K. N. Upadhyaya, *Guru Ravidas: Life and Teachings* (Beas, Punjab: Radha Soami Satsang Beas, 1981), 76–210.

5. The version reported at Śrī Govardhanpur is that Nānak came to Guru Bāgh in quest of the meaning of spirituality. Ravidās satisfied him with a sermon on the subject, in consequence of which Nānak took initiation from Ravidās before departing (Kāfi Dās, interview, Varanasi, August 20, 1985).

6. The standard version of this text is that of Bakhsīdās, edited by Rājā Rām Miśra

(Mathura: Śyām Kāfi Press, 1970); the Mīrābāī section occurs on pp. 67–81. An entirely revised and even more recent version is to be found in Girjāśaṃkar Miśra, *Raidās Rāmāyaṇa* (Mathura: Bhagavatī Prakāśan, 1981), 92–98.

7. Bakhsīdās, *Ravidās Rāmāyaṇa,* 81–82; Miśra, *Raidās Rāmāyaṇa,* 98–102.

8. Nābhādās, *Śrī Bhaktamāl,* with the *Bhaktirasabodhinī* commentary of Priyādās (Lucknow: Tejkumār Press, 1969), 282, 471–72, 480–81. There is a second major source of early hagiographical writing about Ravidās, Kabīr, and a number of other *nirguṇa* saints: the *paricayīs* (accounts) of Anantdās, which purport to have been written near the end of the sixteenth century and therefore to have been approximately contemporary with the core text of the *Bhaktamāl*—Nābhādās's own verse. Anantdās's *paricayīs* are considerably less well-known than the *Bhaktamāl* and have not been published until very recently, so I will focus on the *Bhaktamāl* here. Valuable work on Anantdās has been done by Trilokī Nārāyaṇ Dīkṣit, *Paricayī Sāhitya* (Lucknow: Lucknow University, 1957), Lalitā Prasād Dūbe, *Hindī Bhakta-Vārtā Sāhitya* (Dehra Dun: Sāhitya Sadan, 1968), and David N. Lorenzen in collaboration with Jagdish Kumar and Uma Thukral, *Kabir Legends and Ananda-Das's Kabir Parachai* (Albany: State University of New York Press, 1991). Readers of English have access to Anantdās's *paracaī* on Ravidās through the translation provided by Winand M. Callewaert in *The Hagiographies of Anantadās: The Bhakti Poets of North India* (Richmond, Surrey: Curzon Press, 2000), 303–35.

9. Priyādās's account is found in Nābhādās, *Bhaktamāl,* 477–78. In recent times, perhaps because of renewed awareness of the *Bhaktamāl,* there have been different attempts to clarify the relation between the two queens of Cittor. One oral tradition, alive at the temple of Mīrābāī in Brindavan, specifies that Jhālī was Mīrā's mother-in-law and states, following Priyādās, that it was she, not Mīrā, who took initiation from Ravidās. The conclusion drawn in Brindavan is that Mīrā herself was not Ravidās's pupil and that the popular legend to that effect is a case of mistaken identity (Pradyumna Pratāp Siṃh, interview, Brindavan, August 30, 1985). On the other side are those who are committed to retaining the tradition that Mīrā accepted Ravidās as her guru. The author of the *Ravidās Rāmāyaṇa,* for example, retains both stories but recounts that of Mīrā first and at greater length, relegating Jhālī's encounter with the master to the end of the book and giving the queen's name not as Jhālī but as Yogavatī (Bakhsīdās, *Ravidās Rāmāyaṇa,* 111, 117–19; cf. Miśra, *Raidās Rāmāyaṇa,* 114–16).

10. An influential example is V. Raghavan, *The Great Integrators: The Saint-Singers of India* (New Delhi: Publications Division, Government of India, 1966), 52–54. This book is based on a series of lectures broadcast over All India Radio, December 11–14, 1964.

11. Priyādās in Nābhādās, *Bhaktamāl,* 477–78. His account is extremely condensed at points; it is reported here as interpreted by Sītārāmśaraṇ Bhagavānprasād Rūpkalā.

12. Priyādās in Nābhādās, *Bhaktamāl,* 478. It is possible that the model for this story was provided by an incident included in relatively recent tellings of the *Rāmāyaṇa,* in which Hanumān's unparalleled devotion to Rām, Sītā, and Lakṣmaṇ is proved by his

tearing open his chest to reveal their images ensconced within. See K. C. Aryan and Subhashini Aryan, *Hanuman in Art and Mythology* (Delhi: Rekha Prakashan, n.d.), 78, pls. 31, 111, 112.

13. Dhannū Rām et al., interview, Śrī Govardhanpur, August 13, 1985. Versions of this story appear in Bakhsīdās, *Ravidās Rāmāyaṇa,* 51–52, and Miśra, *Raidās Rāmāyaṇa,* 57–60; and the temple to Ravidās now being built in memory of Jagjīvan Rām at Rājghāt in Benares (see further text discussion) is said to mark the spot where this miracle occurred.

14. Gherā, *Saṃkṣipt Itihās,* 1. Gherā reports (p. 3) that it was not Ravidās who sought instruction from Rāmānand, in fact, but precisely the other way around. In other Ravidās communities it is not disputed that Rāmānand was Ravidās's teacher, but it may be pointed out that Ravidās substantially changed the nature of what he was taught. This view has been expressed by Mahadeo Prashad Kureel (interview, Lucknow, November 28, 1986).

15. See Priyādās's commentary in Nābhādās, *Bhaktamāl,* 471–72.

16. In "signing" his poems, he refers to himself in *AG* 3, 4, 5, 9, and 19 as "Ravidās the leatherworker" *(ravidās camār, ravidās camārā)* and as "Ravidās the slave" *(ravidās dās, ravidās . . . dāsā).* Or he may speak of his low birth directly, as in *AG* 2, 30, 38, and 39.

17. B. R. Gherā, *All India Ādi Dharm Mission* (New Delhi: All India Ādi Dharm Mission, n.d.), 5–6.

18. Juergensmeyer, *Religion as Social Vision,* 33–155.

19. B. R. Gherā, personal communication, December 9, 1983. Cf. Juergensmeyer, *Religion as Social Vision,* 254.

20. Some traditions also attribute *dohās*—couplets—to Ravidās, but only one of these is found in *the Ādi Granth.*

21. Poem no. 2 in the *Guru Ravidās Granth* (handwritten in Devanagari on the basis of a published original in Gurmukhi) as transcribed for Virendra Singh. I am grateful to Virendra Singh for permission to make use of this copy.

22. B. R. Gherā, personal communication, December 9, 1983. Another anthology of Ravidās's poems in current use is that of Candrikāprasād Jijñāsu, *Sant Pravar Raidās Sāhab.* It contains 102 *pads* (poems) and 18 *sākhīs* (couplets).

23. Prakāś Māhī, Bījendra Kumār Pradhān, and Sant Aughad Nāth Kavi, interviews, Śrī Govardhanpur, November 11, 2003.

24. Jagjīvan Rām, "Appeal: Nirmāṇādhīn Guru Ravidās Mandir, Kāśī" [1985].

25. Rām Lakhan, interview, Varanasi, August 19, 1985.

26. On Sarvan Dās and his *derā* at Ballan, see Juergensmeyer, *Religion as Social Vision,* 84–85, 260–61, 264, and the sixth unnumbered plate.

27. Other figures included in that genealogy are Lonī Devī, the goddess of "the original inhabitants" *(ādivāsīs)* of India, whose power is in effect from the beginning of time; Śaṃbuk, belonging to the third world age *(tretā yug)*, counting back from present time; Sudarśan, belonging to the second *(dvāpar yug)*; and Dhanā and Cetā in our own era, the *kali yug.*

28. F. Max Müller, *Lectures on the Origin and Growth of Religion* (London: Longmans, Green, 1882), 277.

29. In Ravidās's usage, the term Rām refers not to Rāmacandra, the hero of the *Rāmāyaṇa* and the seventh avatar of Vishnu, but to God in general. In part because it rhymes with the Hindi word for "name" *(nām)*, Rām is a name of God especially worthy of human contemplation. The phrase *rām nām* is also used in *AG* 27 below.

30. In the phrase "Priests or merchants, laborers or warriors" Ravidās lists the four classical divisions *(varṇa)* of Indian society. But even beneath the lowest of these, the laborers, are others: "half-breeds" *(caṇḍār)*, "outcastes" *(malech)*, and "those who tend the cremation fires" *(ḍom)*. These are all Untouchables.

31. The phrase "Queen City, a place with no pain" translates the Hindi *begam purā*. *Purā* means plainly "city," but *begam* has two possible meanings. The easiest way to construe it is as the Urdu word meaning "a lady of nobility"—whence the translation "queen"—since Indian cities with a Muslim past often have names such as this. The alternative, however, is to hear it as a compound of *be*, "without," and *gam*, "pain." The translation attempts to preserve the ambiguity. This poem is notable for the extent of its Urdu vocabulary, but that should occasion no surprise. If Ravidās has a poem that borders on being genuinely political, it is this, and the overriding political institutions of his time were Muslim. The friend or friends mentioned in the last line may be any companion in Queen City or that special companion, God.

14 · A Brahmin Woman

Revenge Herself

LALITAMBIKA ANTARJANAM

Lalitambika Antarjanam was born in 1909 in the Kottarakara district of southern Kerala of literary parents who both wrote poetry. She herself had little formal education. In 1927 she was married to Narayanan Nambudiri. She was an active participant in the Indian National Congress and was later associated with the Kerala Marxist Party. All through her life she was a political activist and social reformer. Her published works consist of nine collections of short stories, six collections of poems, two books for children, and a novel, *Agnisakshi* (1980), which won the Kerala Sahitya Akademi Award for the best literary work of the year. She died in 1987.

Lalitambika's short story "Revenge Herself," published in the Malayalam journal *Mathrubhumi* in 1938 and here translated by Vasanti Sankaranarayanan, is based on an actual event. Nambudiri Brahman women (belonging to the caste represented by the story's protagonist, Tatri) were also known as Antarjanam—literally meaning "the secluded ones," on account of being more or less confined to the inner courtyard and verandah. The Nambudiris—unlike the Nayars and some other castes of Kerala, which were matrilineal—maintained a patrilineal form of family organization. A Nambudiri woman had no control or rights over her own sexuality; a Nayar woman—within certain limits, mainly of caste—did. A Nayar woman

This essay was previously published as "Revenge Herself," in *The Inner Courtyard: Stories by Indian Women*, ed. Lakshmi Holmstrom, trans. Vasanti Sankaranarayanan (London: Virago, 1991), 3–13.

could have relationships with visiting husbands that could be begun and ended without formality. But a different ideal was required of a Nambudiri woman, as an Antarjanam.

In "Revenge Herself," Lalitambika describes the lifestyle of Tatri, a young Nambudiri woman in the late nineteenth century. She made ritual garlands out of *karuka*, or herbal grass, every day; sang songs in praise of Siva and Parvati to accompany the ritual folk dances of the Tiruvadira Festival (dedicated to Madana, god of erotic love); and recited the story of Seelavati, who ordered the sun not to rise so that she might save her dying husband. Tatri, like other Nambudiri women, was brought up to believe that her husband would be her *pratyaksha deivam*, visible god; her *pati devata*, husband god. A good woman was a *pati vrata*, her husband's devotee. Lalitambika's novel *Agnisakshi* also refers to Parasurama, one of the ten incarnations of the Lord Vishnu, who according to legend threw his axe into the sea and raised a piece of land that later came to be known as Kerala.

REVENGE HERSELF

Midnight. I sat alone in my study. Sleep beckoned me with compassion, caressing my work-weary body and soul. But if I should put away my writing materials, there would be no returning until the next day—to the same hour, the same weariness. Silence all around, broken only by the occasional chatter of the married mice in the attic, or the snoring of the sleeping children in the next room. From the solitary lamp on the table a pale light was cast, somehow terrifying against the dense darkness outside. Somewhere owls hooted in warning. I am a coward by nature, let me admit it. I was more so that night, in those eerie surroundings.

I shut the window and bolted it, adjusted the wicks of the oil lamp, checked on the children to see if they were awake, came back and sat in my usual place. I had to write. But what should I write about? Where to begin? The problem overwhelmed me. It is not easy to write a story, particularly for a woman in my position. I want to write out of my convictions, but I fear to hazard my name, my status. When my stories mirror the reality of society, I am open to the criticism of all kinds of people. When they abuse me, how should I retaliate? I dare not even approach the question of religious customs. And yet in spite of all these scruples, whom will I displease this time? Which literary movement will I offend?

I threw my pen down in disgust, leaned back in the chair and shut my eyes. Many possible characters seemed to walk by: seen, unseen, alive, dead, women and men;

suffering souls, voiceless, but with thunder and lightning in their hearts. Were they commanding me to record their lives? I was frightened, but exhilarated too.

Suddenly I heard the sound of approaching footsteps. What was this? I shivered and sat up. Had I forgotten to close the door and bolt it? I hadn't heard the sound of the door being opened. It was midnight, the time when spirits walk. And though I am not naturally superstitious, I was afraid, I felt faint, my eyes closed. The footsteps seemed to come nearer and nearer, yet I could not move.

Minutes ticked by. Five minutes? An hour? I don't know. After some time I heard a woman's voice nearby, speaking to me softly but firmly: "Are you asleep? Or are you just scared?"

I did not stir. Or rather, I did not have the courage to stir. The voice continued in a slightly sarcastic tone: "You claim to be a writer, and yet you are afraid. I thought that experienced writers were accustomed to observing horror and tragedy without so much as batting an eyelid."

My curiosity to see this person who knew this much about me overcame my fear. I opened my eyes. Before me, as though from a dream, stood a woman, neither young nor old; ageless. Her expression seemed a mixture of sorrow, bitterness, hatred, and despair. Her eyes seemed to burn with the intensity of revenge. I thought she was a figure from the pages of recent history—known but forgotten.

She continued authoritatively, yet with some kindness too. "Mine is not a social visit. I thought you were in a dilemma, floundering without a theme for a story. I can offer you an excellent one: shelved and rotting, waiting to be written. With your permission—if you are not afraid . . . "

By this time I had pulled myself together somewhat.

"Yes," I said, "I am scared. Of this night. Of all that is happening now. Who are you? How did you manage to come here? Weren't the doors closed?"

"Who am I?" She laughed aloud. "So you would like to know who I am. You want to know whether I am human being or devil, ghost or evil spirit. You have courage."

Her laughter had the sound of a wild river that had burst its dam. Wave upon wave of that unearthly laughter filled the room, echoing, reverberating. By this time I was prepared.

"I admit I am a coward. But tell me who you are. Without knowing that how can I proceed? As human beings we need to know—even about the remotest stars—their names and station."

"As human beings? I would rather you didn't call me one," she cut in angrily. "Once upon a time, I was proud to carry that name, and I struggled hard not to dishonor it. Now I no longer wish to be known as a human being, particularly a woman. One lesson I have learnt, and perhaps I have taught it too: the human condition is one of cruel betrayal and suffering."

"Perhaps," I agreed. "But isn't suffering and pain the special gift granted to humankind—the golden chain that links human and divine?"

She dismissed the notion summarily.

"Suffering, a golden chain? What absolute nonsense! Just tell me one thing. As a means of bondage, is gold any different from iron? At least one knows where one is with iron. Gold hides behind its seductive facade. Iswara! That, after all, is the difference between devil and man too."

By now, her face, charged with hatred, had taken on an inhuman aspect, though I could not quite understand how the change had come about. Sorrow, hatred, pride, and revenge seemed to flit across it, making it extraordinarily vivid, strangely attractive. I wondered what it was that she had endured in her past life.

"Are you waiting to hear my story?" she asked after a pause. "Well, it is my intention to tell you. It is an old story, of true events that happened half a century ago. At that time it turned history on its head. You weren't even born then. Neither were these new-fangled social reformist organizationswith their tall claims nor their leaders around then. Few characters from my story are alive now. But the echoes of those events have not quite died. . . . Did you ever hear of Tatri of—?"

I shivered. So this was she. Whose name our mothers had prohibited us from speaking. A name which to us had become obscene. I was speechless.

She saw my hesitation. Sadly she said, "O yes, which Nambudiri woman hasn't heard of Tatri, 'fallen object,' 'tainted goods'? Though none of you will so much as admit to that knowledge. But child, can you now try and understand why that hated one gave up her life?"

"To begin with, she was as innocent as any one of you. She too once made *karuka* garlands. She too prayed like you, raptly clasping her black string. She fasted on all auspicious days. She was innocent, she had neither looked upon a man nor spoken with him. Grandmothers used to uphold Tatri as a model of propriety to all the young girls who come of age.

"But you know that all those rituals are, after all, charades. You know that by the time we are seventeen or eighteen we are shrewd enough to control our most secret thoughts. On moonlit nights we sit in the inner verandah reciting prayers, our sighs suppressed. We sing 'Parvati Swayamvaram' and 'Mangala Atira' and dance, the catch in our voices unheard. And all the time we wait, with bated breath, for the men's voices in the outer verandah. We offer austere leaves of *kuvalam* in strict prayer, while our hearts are filled with the sensuous fragrance of mango blooms. And so we wait . . . days, months, even years. . . . At last one day our mothers come with henna and silver ring. And our hands are given into the hands of a man—old or young, invalid or lecher. That is our destiny. That is our entire life.

"Mine was a lucky fate, or so people said in those days. He was in his prime, it was his first marriage, he had sufficient means. So I began my marriage with no worries. I soon found he was a man with aggressive sexual needs. I learnt in time to meet those demands, to please him in his taste for sex with the same attention and care that I gave to his taste for food. After all, one's husband is considered the *pratyaksha deivam,* the "seen" God. And it was to please that God that I learnt the art of the prostitute. If it were not for that, dear sister, I too—like so many women of our community—would have remained a mere wife, a neglected and ignored wife. Perhaps, too, none of the wretched consequences would have followed. On the other hand, it might be that in learning to serve him I unleashed my own instinctual being. I don't know. But I swear to you that at that time he alone was at the center of my life.

"So it was that when he started drifting away from me, I was desolate. Often he didn't come home at night. I used to think, at first, that he was at a festival or a private feast. Perhaps he was at the *variyam* or was needed at the palace. I would cry and sulk on the rare occasions when I saw him. There was no one else to share my grief.

"He laughed in response to my heartbroken complaints. A man, he said, is as free as a bird. His life should be one of enjoyment. Surely a man cannot be expected to waste away his entire youth married to one woman, and that a Nambudiri wife.

"Sometimes I was filled with anger and bitterness. Sometimes I even wished to put an end to my life. I often cursed my lot as a Nambudiri woman, thinking, if only I belonged to any other caste of Kerala, one which would have given me the right to reply, to match his male arrogance with my freedom.

"But no. Each month, upon the recurrence of his birth star, I bathed and prayed that he should have a long life, making offerings of tumba flower garlands and *nevillakku* lit with ghee. When I came of age I had prayed to be granted a good husband; now I prayed that I should be granted my husband's love.

"The steward of our estate was a kind man who made sure I had plenty to eat. But what about one's inner hunger, that other greed? Once kindled it is not easily quenched. It flows like molten lava, like fire through the very lifeblood. He, my husband, knew this too. But he was a man and I a woman. A woman born in a cursed society.

"I too would have suffered in silence like all those other Nambudiri women except for what happened unexpectedly. One night he came home with a new wife. They were to sleep that night in the very bedroom I had shared with him. I could bring myself to serve food to this woman, but to be actually asked to prepare their nuptial bed! Yes, I had chanted the 'Seelavati charitram' again and again. . . . But an Antarjanam is a human being too. . . . I cursed her aloud. In my grief and outrage, I called her a whore. In that instant I saw him turn into a devil. He flung my words back at me: 'I know perfectly well she is a whore—I love her for what she is. If you could be like her, I might like you better.'

"I could bear the physical violence, but those words were a far worse assault. I was numb with the horror of it. A *pati vrata,* a woman of honor to be as much as told by her husband, "If you want me to love you, be a prostitute!" For a blinding moment, I was overcome by a furious thirst for revenge. Somehow I held myself together. But I knew I had had enough. I could not stay in that place a moment longer.

"I did not speak to him again. I withdrew into myself. Desolate and grief-stricken, yearning for consolation, I returned to my own home. There followed days without love, uneventful days. There were no rays of light in the tunnel. All Nambudiri houses are dark prisons, after all. Is one any better than another? My father had died, but his five wives were still alive. My brother was looking for a bride to replace his fourth wife who was now dead. My two widowed sisters were there too. The third one, driven insane because of the ill-treatment she had received from her husband, wandered about aimlessly. Two younger sisters, now grown up, were unmarried—a burden to the house and a grief to my mother. When I joined this lot, it was exactly like jumping from the frying pan into the fire. Living in such a bleak, claustrophobic world, who could be blamed for seeking some comfort? I was young, healthy, egoistic. I thought I was more beautiful than any of my husband's mistresses. In those days, when I combed my hair, freshened my face, and glanced covertly through the windows, all I wanted was a glimpse of the outside world. I had an innocent desire to be seen and admired. There were some who caught those glances and smiled at me. I smiled in return. And that was all. Those aristocratic Nambudiris who were attracted to me knew well enough the consequences I would suffer for even this. As for themselves, they would have been ready for any kind of liaison, provided it was discreet.

"Meaningful glances. Hushed whispers. Gossip and scandal. The inmates of the inner rooms turned out to be fifth columnists. My mother never lost an opportunity to curse me: 'You sinner, born to be the ruin of your family's reputation. I wish I had never carried you in my womb.'

"And one day my sister-in-law was peremptory with her order: 'Don't step into the kitchen.'

"I still cannot understand why I was punished so. I hadn't so much as touched a man other than my husband. I hadn't the boldness to nurture such a desire. There had been a few glances through the window. A few men had been attracted. Was that my fault? But the world was never concerned with reason or logic. The innuendos continued till they numbed my heart. Terror at the thought of dishonor threw me off balance, pushed me to the verge of the very abyss I dreaded. I was long past suffering. In all directions there was only darkness. It was as though through whirling coils of dark smoke my enemies waited, ready to strike, like snakes. To survive that final struggle I had to be a snake too. At last I gave way to those long quiescent storms of anger and revenge.

"If I should tell you what I decided to do, you would be appalled. But please remember, my sister, that it was done for you too, and for all Nambudiri women. As a matter of pride. As a show of strength. I enjoyed the humiliation of those men, for there never was any value attached to our own tears. Yet, after all, in the end I gained nothing, for even you women hated me, dreaded me more than the devil. Years have passed, but even to you of a modern time Tatri is no more than a fallen woman."

As she spoke, her eyes filled with tears, and overcome with grief she laid her head upon the table. I watched her in silence, wondering what sort of future a woman such as she could have expected. If her life had been shattered and strewn around the wilderness like pieces of a broken bottle then was it her fault or that of society's? There could have been only two alternatives for her: madness or prostitution. Both tragic.

After a moment she sat up, her eyes dry once more and aflame with intensity. "No, child," she said, "I shall not cry again. That was a momentary weakness." She resumed her story. "Nothing could shock me any more—neither the waves breaking the bounds of the sea, nor even the skies falling down. Life and death had all become the same. Yes, I made my decision. I thought that since I had chosen my destiny, it should also be an act of revenge on behalf of my mothers and sisters. If I should be victimized, it should not be on false grounds. If I should be made an outcast, it should not be for being innocent. Women, too, I thought, can willingly choose the path of debasement. And if I should choose to fall, I would bring down with me several cruel men who were the means of that fall. I would see to it that in the clear light of justice many more men than I should deserve excommunication.

"On a certain night a new courtesan appeared on the festival grounds and temple precincts. She was beautiful and witty. Her modesty attracted men even more than her beauty. Princes, courtiers, and Nambudiris, all sought her company. At first she kept them all at arm's length, saying she was a married woman with a husband who was still alive. She withheld a crucial detail about herself, however—the community to which she belonged. They brushed aside her pleas to be left alone. They argued that in Kerala, the land of Parasurama, a woman was allowed as many husbands as she chose. The only women who were outside this rule were the Nambudiris. The rest, they said, were free to enjoy their pleasure. Oh, these men who seem so honorable, so saintly! Men who expect unquestioning faithfulness from their own wives, but who are quite willing to ruin another's!

"So many men were attracted to me. So different from the ostracism of the inner rooms. I melted, I was moved. I could not have enough of their adulation.

"The new courtesan grew famous. Those who came to her went away happy. From each of them, in return for their pleasure, she received—or took—gifts and mementos. And so, gradually and deliberately, she gained possession of the honor of many men who claimed to be pillars of our society.

"There was one man who was yet to come. There was one man for whom she waited and watched. She knew he would not fail to come, once he had heard of this true pleasure seeker. We had not seen each other for five years. But I recognized him the moment I met him at my usual rendezvous near the temple. He, however, did not know me. How could he see in this proud and famous woman his old Antarjanam?

"I shall not forget that night. For that night I had debased myself; for that night I had lived and waited. From the moment he had last spoken, this idea had rankled, then seeded and grown in my mind. If a woman should go to the lengths of becoming a prostitute in order to please her husband, can she be called a *pati vrata?* For if that were so, I too was one; a veritable 'Seelavati.' Through my corruption I could please him, and yes, he was pleased.

"Just before he left me, he said, 'In all my life, I have never met a woman so beautiful and so clever. I wish I could live with you always.'

"At the very moment that he slipped the ring—once again—on my finger, I asked him, 'Are you sure you have never before met one like me?'

"Holding his sacred thread with both hands, he said, 'No, I swear by my Brahmasvam. No. I have never before met a woman of your wit and intelligence.'

"I smiled with triumph. I raised my voice very slightly and said, 'That's false. Think of your wife. Was she any worse than I?'

"In the hesitant light of that pale dawn he looked at me once again. A strangled cry escaped him. 'O my God, my Lord Vadakkunatha, it is Tatri. Tatri.' And he fled from my sight, disappearing immediately.

"That's all I need to tell you. You know very well all that happened afterwards. As an Antarjanam I was brought to trial for defilement, and under threat of losing caste. It was a trial that shook the whole of Kerala. As it got under way, they were all terrified—yes, princes and Nambudiris too—that their names would be spoken by the prostitute. Then some went into hiding. Others frantically made offerings to the gods. Each hoped desperately she had forgotten him.

"I had more than names, I had proofs; a golden ring with a name engraved upon it, a golden girdle, a gold-bordered *veshti.* And so, sixty-five men, priests among them, were brought to trial. I could have been the means of excommunicating sixty thousand men, not merely sixty-five. Any woman who was beautiful enough and clever enough could have done the same, such were the decadent landlords and Nambudiris of those days. I could have insisted on continuing the inquiry. But no. In the end, for all the submerged rage of all Nambudiri women, only sixty-five men were brought to trial. Those sixty-five were indicted. That was my revenge. Was it my revenge alone?

"And now, tell me, sister. Which one do you think was worse, the man who led a woman into prostitution for his own satisfaction, or the woman who willed herself into prostitution to counter him? Which one should you hate? Which one should you shun?"

I had not uttered a word throughout her strange account, and now I was dumbstruck. She misunderstood my silence and spoke in a voice full of disappointment and despair: "Why did I come here? I made a mistake. Why did I try to speak to a slave of a woman who has no self-respect or honor? Oh no, you will never change."

I was not offended by what she said. At last I began to speak: "My poor wronged sister, I don't blame you. I do sympathize with you. I understand that you were speaking for many—for the weak against the strong, for women calling out for justice, for all human beings whose emotions and instincts have been stamped upon. What you did was not just an act of personal revenge, it was a protest born out of grief and despair.

"But then, think of this, too. Was it not impulsive and headstrong to take up such a responsibility on your own? Individual effort cannot yield lasting results; sometimes it can be positively dangerous. Just think of that. That storm that you raised—what good did it possibly do to society as a whole? In the end, men used it as an excuse to victimize us even more: the memory of that event was a means of humiliating us, forcing us to hang our heads in shame. Remember too that you hardly brought any consolation to the families and womenfolk of the excommunicated men."

By this time, I too was stirred, my voice shook as I spoke. "You must excuse me. But I have to say that for most of us, what you choose to describe as the sacrifice of Tatri was nothing more and nothing less than the trial of a prostitute. True, it created a storm, but it did not point to a clear direction for us. The end cannot justify the means, sister. Of course, I applaud your courage and your pride, but I have to denounce the path you took.

"But, all the same, we as Nambudiris can never forget Tatri. From your world of darkness and silence you hurled a random firecracker as a warning and a challenge. Nevertheless it ignited a torch for us in our generation, and there will be greater fires in times to come. Your revenge will be forgiven because of those radiant future fires."

I held out my hands to her in love and compassion. But the face of the female form had paled, its eyes were lifeless, it vanished away into the morning fog, wailing. "I must not let my shadow fall upon you. For you I am, and always will be, a sinner, a fallen woman, a devil." The cock crowed. I woke up from that strange dream.

PART VII · DIASPORA

15 · Hinduism in Pittsburgh

Creating the South Indian "Hindu" Experience in the United States

VASUDHA NARAYANAN

Do not reside in a town where there is no temple.

AUVAIYAR, *Tamil woman poet, ca. second century* C.E.

In southern India, where the landscape is studded with temple towers and where deities are said to have manifested themselves spontaneously, it was hard to live in a town where there was no temple. When the early Saiva Brahmins crossed the seas to Cambodia and Indonesia in the fifth and sixth centuries C.E., they carried on their temple-building activity. It may never be known whether these early emigrants ever considered leaving the land that Manu, the lawgiver, describes as "where the black antelope naturally roams." Manu urges members of the higher classes to dwell in the land that extends as far as the eastern and western oceans, for this is the land of the Aryas, the land that is "fit for the performance of sacrifice" (Manu Smrti 2: 22–24).

Manu notwithstanding, the process of emigration has continued for several centuries. In this essay I will examine how some Hindu emigrants in the last quarter of the twentieth century transformed a land where there are no obvious *svayam-vyakta* (self-announced) deities (and where one is hard pressed to see the black antelope) into a sacred place where the lord graciously abides. The essay's focus will be the Srivaisnava temple at Penn Hills (near Pittsburgh) and its development as a religious and cultural center of a large South Indian Hindu urban professional immigrant population. I will investigate how this temple seeks to replicate the rituals

This essay was previously published as "Creating the South Indian 'Hindu' Experience in the United States," in *The Sacred Thread: Modern Transmission of Hindu Traditions in India and Abroad*, ed. Raymond Brady Williams (Chambersburg, PA: Anima Publications, 1992), 147–76.

and atmosphere of other Srivaisnava temples in general and the Sri Venkateswara temple in Tiru Venkatam (Tirupati), India, in particular; and more important, in what ways it is different from its parent. Specifically, I will discuss how the Hindus near the Penn Hills temple adjust the sacred calendar to coincide more closely with long weekends in the United States, but also affirm almost in mythic terms the sacredness of the land where the lord dwells. I will also consider how dreams and visions sometimes precipitate the building of a temple or discovery of a Hindu deity in America; and finally I will discuss a few specific methods of self-interpretation that some Hindus have adopted in order to explain their tradition(s) to themselves and their children.

My discussion is based on information obtained from several sources: years of observation and participation in Srivaisnava temples in India and the United States; interviews with priests *(bhattars)* at Penn Hills and in India; study of pamphlets and bulletins from the Penn Hills temple over the last fifteen years; and participation in the larger South Indian/Tamil/Srivaisnava community in northern Florida, where two temples are to be constructed near Orlando and Tampa.

While a few places of worship had been built in the New York area, the first really ambitious South Indian temple that sought to reproduce the traditional architecture and recapture the flavor of a Vaisnava *divya desa* (sacred place) was the Sri Venkateswara temple built in Penn Hills, Pennsylvania, in 1976. Right from the beginning, the community took pride in this "authentic" temple, as noted frequently in its bulletins and pamphlets:

> Construction of an authentic Temple in Pittsburgh dedicated to Sri Venkateswara commenced on June 30, 1976 with the assistance of Tirumala Tirupathi Devasthanam.
>
> Visitors from all over the U.S., Canada, and India have expressed their gratification at being able to pray in an authentic temple constructed on the North American soil."[1]

This temple has been successful in attracting large numbers of devotees from all over the eastern seaboard; until similar temples were built in other parts of the country, it attracted pilgrims from all over the United States and Canada. It is still seen as the trend-setting South Indian temple in its celebration of expensive, time-consuming, and intricate rituals; many younger temples want to be like the one in Penn Hills when they grow up. The temple's success story is overwhelming; in an annual report, the chairman of the temple's board of trustees reported that "as an established religious organization . . . the temple has extended modest interest-free loans to temples that are in embryonic stages."[2]

The Penn Hills temple enshrines a manifestation of Vishnu in which he is called Venkateswara, or lord *(isvara)* of the hill known as Venkata in South India. Venkateswara temples now exist in Penn Hills, Pennsylvania; Malibu, California; Aurora, Illinois; and Atlanta, Georgia. The word "Venkata" is said to mean "[that] which can burn sins."[3] The American temple was built with the help, backing, and blessing of one of the most popular, richest, and oldest temples in India. The Indian "sponsor" was the Venkateswara temple in Tiru Venkatam, better known as Tirumala or Tirupati. The Penn Hills temple bulletin specifically says that "Tirumala Tirupathi Devasthanam . . . of India will be the main consulting institution on religious matters."[4] The deities were carved in India under the supervision of this temple, and officials from Tiru Venkatam attend the major rituals that the Penn Hills temple undertakes.

While the temple at Tiru Venkatam has always been well known and has enjoyed royal patronage in the last thousand years, it is only in the last hundred years that it has attracted exceedingly large numbers of pilgrims and revenues. The popularity of the temple is said to have increased phenomenally after the *maha santi samproksanam* in 1958. Cars, diamonds, and approximately twenty kilograms of gold (from various pieces of jewelry dropped in the *hundi*) are collected every month. The temple is located on 10.75 square miles of Tirumala Hills and until 1965, when the government took them over, owned more than six hundred villages. Thus the temple was in a unique position to offer help in tangible forms to the new shrine in Penn Hills.[5]

The temple at Penn Hills (like the one in India) can be called Hindu in that it is sectarian; it is a Srivaisnava temple. The Srivaisnava community became important about the tenth century C.E. In fact, the first occurrence of the term "Srivaisnava" itself, as far as I have been able to trace it, occurs in an inscription in the Tiru Venkatam temple in India, in the year 966. The community recognizes the validity of both Sanskrit and vernacular (Tamil) scripture and the philosophical vision of the Vedantic teacher Ramanuja. Since the eleventh century, the community has instituted in all their temples the recitation of specific Sanskrit texts and the Tamil works of the *alvars,* poet-saints who lived between the seventh and ninth centuries C.E. Although the Tiru Venkatam temple has attracted devotees from all over India and has been a center of national pilgrimage, it has not compromised the particular, sectarian, Srivaisnava nature of its rituals, conducted according to the *vaikhanasa* scripture, nor the recitation of both Sanskrit and Tamil scripture.

The temple at Penn Hills carries with it some of the clout and prestige associated with the Indian temple on which it is modeled. The history of the Penn Hills temple can be traced back to January 14, 1972, when (in connection with the Festival of Pongal/Makara Sankaranti celebrated by Tamil- and Telugu-speaking people), a few residents of the area established a shrine in the basement of a shop; here they kept pictures of various deities. Later that summer, a "granite statue" of Ganesha was sent by Mr. R. Balakrishna Naidu of Coimbatore to the Pittsburgh-area devotees.[6] Since Ganesha is the god worshipped before the commencement of any ritual or auspicious act, a temple pamphlet explains that he was received by devotees as "a good omen to invoke blessings to a larger project."

In 1972, with the assistance of the Hindu Temple Society of New York, negotiations were begun with the Tirumala-Tirupati board in India. The commissioner of endowments as well as a traditional sculptor from India visited America, drew the architectural plans, and selected a site that reminded them of the "hilly terrain" in India where the original Sri Venkateswara temple is located (see figure 9). The site was purchased on June 30, 1976, and construction began. Fifteen sculptors and one architect trained in traditional forms of temple construction arrived to make sure that the temple was built according to the very precise instructions in the sacred texts. Local American builders laid the foundation and also constructed a community activity area. It is important to note that community outreach was emphasized right from the beginning—a feature conspicuous by its absence in many Srivaisnava temples in India. On June 8, 1977, the major consecration *(mahakumbhabhisekam)* of the whole temple took place. Further construction and improvements are ongoing as money continues to pour in from devotees all over the country.

RECAPTURING THE TIRU VENKATAM EXPERIENCE

In both the daily and the seasonal routines of prayers and services, the Penn Hills temple tries to remain faithful to the parent temple at Tiru Venkatam. The morning wake-up prayer *(suprabhatam)*, the offering of food to the lord, the daily round of worship *(arcana)*, and the recitation of particular *alvar* verses during the day are all followed correctly; however, unlike the Indian temple, here community participation is seen primarily on the weekends. And so, the ritual bathing of the lord, which normally takes place on Fridays in Venkateswara temples in India (at Tiru Venkatam and at Fanaswali, Bombay), is done on Sunday mornings in Penn Hills, and a large group recitation of the suprabhatam is also done on weekends at the Penn Hills tem-

FIGURE 9
Sri Venkateswara Temple, Penn Hills, Pittsburgh, showing the hilly surroundings and adjacent freeway. Photo by John Hawley.

ple, as well as at a much later time in the morning than in India. (Considering that the morning suprabhatam is recited sometime around 3:00 A.M., or earlier, in India, it is easy to understand why the Penn Hills temple has scheduled it to a more reasonable time, like 9:00 A.M. on weekends). These may seem like minor differences from the parent temple, but in a ritual schedule where timing is important such adjustments to local devotee needs often seem unacceptable to orthoprax priests.

Despite the desire to remain faithful to the code and sequence of rituals, there are some compromises and innovations. While the Penn Hills temple chooses to celebrate a few seasonal festivals, it tries as far as is astrologically possible to plan big events around the holidays of the American secular calendar. Thus the bulletin in 1988 announced:

> Maha Brahmotsavam was celebrated during the 4th of July weekend. Labor Day weekend celebration will be climaxed by a "Pushpa Pallakhi," a float decorated with flowers and lights. Other religious and cultural events planned for the Labor Day weekend are listed.[7]

The same bulletin also stated that restoration of the main tower *(rajagopuram)* was completed in time for the Fourth of July weekend. In 1989, the "Temple News

Briefs" reported the following: "Thanksgiving Weekend (1987)—All deities were decorated with silver kavachas. A special Poolangi Seva was performed to Lord Venkateswara."[8] In 1990 the inauguration of the special hall for weddings with the ritual celebration of the wedding of Venkateswara and the goddess Padmavathi was held during the Thanksgiving break, and in 1991 a special Satyanarayana Puja was held in conjunction with the Memorial Day weekend. Thus the sacred-time orientation of the temple is made to coincide, as far as the ritual almanac will allow it, with the secular calendar of the country in which it is located. While the reasons for this time orientation are obvious—unlike in India, the festivals at Penn Hills are organized by people working in other places, and long weekends are a time when many families do long-distance traveling—it is also important to note the coordination with the American secular calendar. The Penn Hills temple is not the first to acknowledge secular holidays; some temples in India have organized special New Year's Day *darshans*, and the Tiru Venkatam temple generally records the greatest monetary collections in the hundi on January 1.[9]

In 1986 the Penn Hills temple issued a cassette of popular devotional songs *(bhajans)*. In it, the Pittsburgh area devotees praise Lord Venkateswara thus:

America vasa jaya govinda
Penn Hills nilaya radhe govinda
sri guru jaya guru, vithala govinda

Victory to Govinda who lives in America—
Govinda who, with Radha, lives in Penn Hills.
Victory to the teacher,
Victory to Vithala,
Victory to Govinda.

Glorifying the lord as abiding in a particular place is similar to the devotees' personal consecration of the deity in a temple and within themselves. While all temples undergo formal ceremonies of vivification with pitchers of sanctified waters, the devotees' songs give life to the deity in the temple and in the heart. Srivaisnava devotees celebrate the lord's accessibility more than his supremacy; and to make himself accessible, he is said to abide in a local shrine, close to the devotee. In Srivaisnava theology, the lord's supremacy is seen in his containing, including, and yet transcending the entire universe, and by having it as his body; while his accessibility is seen in his incarnating himself on earth *(avatara)* as an area, easy to approach and ready to be worshipped. Here, he is wholly, fully god—not a symbol, not an image, nor a conduit to the supreme, but wholly, completely there. Thus he is totally present in Tiru Venkatam, India, and this is important; but even more important, this lord is now perceived as abiding in a local shrine at Penn Hills. The devotees in Pittsburgh, like the alvars who celebrated it, see the lord as being physically close to them, sanctifying the land they live in. Just as the earlier poet Auvanyar wanted it, they now live in a town with a temple, a temple on a hill, just as it is in Tiru Venkatam. Tiru Venkatam is hailed in literature as a piece of heaven on earth,[10] and the temple at Penn Hills, a piece of Tiru Venkatam in America.

The concept of sacred land is not just abstract for the devotees of the American temple. They see the terrain where the lord dwells in Penn Hills as being physically very similar to the Tiru Venkatam hills. One of the earliest brochures of the community says:

> It is a beautiful wooded area located on a hill and offers a panoramic view of the surroundings. According to numerous visitors, the hill with lofty trees is reminiscent of Tirumala. A small stream flows along the path leading to the temple site.[11]

The Tiru Venkatam temple in India is reached after crossing seven hills; and the words "seven hills" are associated only with that particular temple. The Penn Hills temple calls its official bulletin *Saptagin Vani*, "The Voice of the Seven Hills." While the American temple is not located on seven hills, it is constructed on one verdant hill, and this similarity is close enough for the devotee.

In fact, it is not just Penn Hills, but the greater Pittsburgh area that seems to be geographically similar to the sacred land of India. The excitement of the Penn Hills temple *bhakta*, drawing upon puranic lore and recalling the importance of Prayag (the sacred place in India where the rivers Ganga, Yamuna, and the underground Sarasvati meet), and also the deity Sangamesvara ("the lord of the meeting rivers") in Karnataka, is seen in this statement issued in 1986:

> Pittsburgh, endowed with hills and a multitude of trees as well as the confluence of the three rivers, namely, the Allegheny, the Monongahela, and the subterranean river (brought up via the 60-foot-high fountain at downtown) to form the Ohio river is indeed a perfect choice for building the first and most authentic temple to house Lord Venkateswara. The evergrowing crowds that have been coming to the city with the thriveni Sangama of the three rivers to worship at the Temple with the three vimanas reassure our belief that the venerable Gods chose this place and the emerald green hillock to reside in.[12]

It is interesting to note that the concept of "sacred land" is not recognized only by the Penn Hills devotee. Republicans from the Hindu community near the Fort Worth-Dallas area understand the notion of "karma bhumi," the land where actions bear fruit, in a far more general manner than Manu and his compatriots intended. The following passage from a document produced by a small group of Hindu Republicans who took an active interest in the 1984 elections reinforces the importance many Hindus give to the sacredness of land. V. S. Naipaul brought the passage to the attention of his readers while reporting on the Republican convention at Dallas.

> Indians immigrated to the USA to pursue their "DREAM" to achieve fully their potentials in this land of "Opportunities." They came in pursuit of their dreams, visions, happiness and to achieve excellence. . . . During the last few years most of the people have changed from "Green card holder" status to that of "U.S. CITIZENS," thus enabling themselves to be full participants in socioeconomic and political processes. They have chosen, by their free will, the USA as the "KARMABHUMI"—the land of Karma or action.

Naipaul's commentary on it is equally fascinating:

> Texas as the theater of karma . . . what would Trammel Crow [Naipaul describes this gentleman as the "real-estate king" of Texas] have made of that! But it was, really, no more than a Hindu version of . . . fundamentalism, and in this Hindu version certain things could be seen fresh. To embrace one's economic opportunity and good fortune was more than a political act; it was also an act of religion.[13]

Texas and America interpreted as the *karmabhumi*—the place where actions could produce merit or demerit—is a new idea in the topography of Hinduism. According to Manu and other lawmakers, the land of the Aryas and the land where the black antelope freely roams was the only land that could be called karmabhumi. Some Hindus in the United States—at least the Republicans near Fort Worth-Dallas—interpret these references as signifying the land of spacious skies where the deer and the antelope play.

THE ARTICULATION OF A FAITH

SYMBOLS AND THEIR INTERPRETATION

Srivaisnava theology emphasizes the reality and tangibility of a temple, the deities enshrined in it, and the importance of serving the lord in the temple. However, many Hindus in this country, if one had to generalize, are wary of being known as "idolators"; early Western missionary terminology still rings in their ears.[14] Perusal of the publications of the Malibu and Penn Hills temples reveals that the topic of "idolatory" is of great concern to writers, and many seem to be responding to nineteenth-century criticisms by writing *apologias* based on neo-Advaita-Vedanta. One writer from California (a C. A. P. Iyer), after quoting Dr. S. Radhakrishnan, the Sankaracharya of Kanchipuram, and Dr. Benjamin Rowland, says, "When a devotee worships an idol in a temple, the worship is paid to what the image stands for in philosophical interpretation. The worship is never paid to the idol per se."[15] The "Visitor's Guide," a pamphlet issued by the Penn Hills temple in 1979, emphatically explains, presumably to an American visitor, "Where the Hindu worships the idols in the shrines, he is aware that it is to God that he really offers his worship. It is wrong, therefore, to characterize Hinduism as an idolatrous religion. The idols are symbols of the invisible spirit." These sentiments are repeated by a *brahmacarini* of the Chinmaya mission who wrote frequently for the Penn Hills bulletin; she states unequivocally that "the ritual of worshipping God represented by an idol or *symbol* is replete with significance" and later adds, "The elaborate rituals of Tiru Aradhana are prescribed for propitiating the Lord *symbolized* in an idol" (italics added).[16] Words like "represent" and "symbol" give the impression that what people are worshipping is only pointed to or signified by the "idol." These sentiments are at variance with traditional Srivaisnava *acaryas,* who held that the deity in the temple is totally, completely God; the *arca* (literally, "that which is worshipped") has a nonmaterial form composed of a nonearthly substance called *suddha sattva,* and this incarnation in the temple is as real as the incarnations of Rama or Krishna.[17] Nevertheless, several issues of the *Saptagiri Vani* contain articles that emphasize the importance of this allegorical or "symbolic" interpretation and insist that not to do so would make us think of Hinduism as "absurd." One article states:

> If one has to appreciate the real essence of Hinduism, one must learn to appreciate this science of symbolism. In absence of such an understanding the whole periphery of Hinduism will appear funny, unintelligent, and absurd. In the process of knowing this science of symbolism one discovers the deeper meaning of the real Hindu tradition which apparently appears to be superficial.

The article then gives the "symbolic meaning" of various rituals (when one burns camphor, the priest burns "all your past notions, beliefs, conclusions etc. . . . the act of burning camphor stands for *Guru Upadesha*"; the breaking of a coconut symbolizes the breaking of the ego, or *ahamkara,* and so on).[18] It is my impression that many Hindus in this country accept the "symbolic" meaning as their heritage, and this generic neo-Advaita package seems to be entirely acceptable to them. This is particularly significant when the meaning given to any particular concept or ritual is strikingly at variance with the orthodox Tirumala-Tirupati (Srivaisnava) viewpoint. For instance, in Srivaisnava theology, Garuda, a bird, and Sesa, a divine serpent, are the two eternal servants of the lord, ready to serve him every second. Sesa, the serpent, is the paradigmatic devotee and servant of Vishnu. In the mythology of the Tiru Venkatam temple, the hills on which the lord stands are said to be an embodiment of Sesa; the hills are called "Sesachala" or "Sesadri." There is a tradition that out of respect for Sesa, some acaryas would not walk on the hills (that would be disrespectful) but would ascend them by crawling on their knees.

Given the importance of Sesa, the following passage from a pamphlet issued by the temple in 1986, which portrays Garuda, Gaja (an elephant), and Sesa as the animal instincts of a human being, is rather odd. The passage appears in the context of a description of various *vahanas* (palanquin-vehicles) for the lord (the Penn Hills temple acquired three *vahanas* in 1986). After describing the vehicles, the author of the article goes on to explain:

> The disciplining of one's undesirable qualities is symbolized in a subtle manner by the taming and conquering of an animal (instinct) and the servitude of the animal to the Master. Thus GARUDA (symbol of soaring AMBITION and DESIRES), GAJA (symbol of EGO that is usually found in the wealthy and powerful when the mind is not disciplined and virtues are lacking) and SESHA (symbol of ANGER and WRATH) each is enslaved and taken in a triumphant procession of the conquering Hero, symbol of VIRTUES, the Lord by assembled devotees. Total cost of each Vahana is $24,000.[19]

This symbolic mode of interpretation certainly seems to owe more to some Western modes of analyses than to traditional Hindu exegesis. Ganesha, Siva *linga*, Tiru *aradhana*, Maha Sivaratri, the Temple, and the details of an *arcana* (worship ritual) are all interpreted as symbols.[20]

Many Hindus in India have been exposed to neo-Vedantic interpretations of their religion and have some acquaintance with the publications of the Ramakrishna and Chinmaya missions. The preponderance of symbolic interpretations in the Penn Hills temple's publications can be understood against this background. It should be noted that the authors of the articles seem not to be Srivaisnavas. Some issues of the bulletin (vol. 15 [November 1990] and vol. 16 [February 1991]) have added this disclaimer: "The views expressed in the articles published are those of the writers and do not necessarily reflect those of the S. V. Temple management." The *Saptagiri Vani*, despite listing the Srivaisnava festivals and almanac, and despite being a voice of a temple with predominantly Srivaisnava rituals, is not necessarily a Srivaisnava bulletin; two issues have stated that it is "the intention of [the] S. V. Temple management to provide through its publications, articles and other items that represent our rich cultural and religious traditions." In pursuit of this goal, articles have appeared on such topics as rituals like Jirnoddharanam or Ashtothra Satha Kalasa Abhiseka (with details of the celebrations according to the *samhitas*), Carnatic music, "origins of dance," and children's word games.

The influence of these articles in the temple bulletins should not be underestimated. In India, newspapers and regular television programming provide glimpses of varied rituals and synopses of religious discourses, but in the United States articles in temple bulletins are often the only regular "religious education" temple members get. The articles' publication in the bulletins also makes them seem authoritative. Thus there may be an entire generation of young Hindus growing up in this country who have been educated on the myths recounted by Amar Chitra Katha, India's best-known "classic comic" series, where again one story line is presented and is ratified as "true," unlike the oral tradition, which may present alternative versions of a story and symbolic meanings of temples, deities, and rituals. The effects of this controlled diet will have to be judged in future years.

SYNCRETISM

The Penn Hills temple has included many small rituals in its repertoire, even though they are not traditional in Srivaisnava temples. The most important is worship of Satyanarayana, especially on full-moon days. While Satyanarayana is a form of Vishnu, the worship of Satyanarayana is probably quite late in origin and is not part of traditional Srivaisnava lore. This *puja*, usually a domestic one in India, is popular in the Marathi-, Kannada-, and Telugu-speaking regions and in some communities in North India and in Tamilnadu. In India, the ritual is sometimes performed by family members, and sometimes by a priest who is brought in for the occasion. Because there are very few priests to go around in this country, the *Satyanarayana* puja, which has traditionally not been part of Srivaisnava rituals, is conducted in the Penn Hills temple. The *Varalaksmi Vratham*, another largely domestic and non-Srivaisnava rite (though addressed to Lakshmi), is also conducted in the temple, by Smartha women.

In this connection, it should be noted that there is a blurring of lines between domestic, community, and temple rituals in Hinduism as practiced in the United States. Domestic rituals, such as the prenatal rites, are conducted in the temple; family festivals like Deepavali are conducted by the whole community, which gathers in a school gym, a church auditorium, or, if there is one nearby, a temple. The celebration of rituals and festivals in suburban America seems to be similar in many ways to their celebration in village India, where both domestic and temple rituals become community-based celebrations. There are very few really private domestic functions in villages. Such functions are invariably community-based celebrations, where one or two families are responsible for food and hospitality. Similarly, even temple rituals in small Indian villages, especially where the temples have no fixed endowment, become the responsibility of a few "sponsoring" families and again are community-based.

The Penn Hills temple, unlike other Venkateswara temples in this country, but more like other Srivaisnava temples, does not have other non-Vaisnava deities (except for Ganesha). The Penn Hills temple obviously is syncretic to a limited extent; it strikes a balance between the needs of its devotees and what is permissible by the written and practiced codes adopted by the Tiru Venkatam temple. Thus while syncretism extends as far as some Telugu and Kannada practices, the temple has not actively sought to fulfill the needs of Hindus from many other regions. It appears from the cultural programs sponsored by the Penn Hills temple (Bharata natyam, Kuchipudi dances, and Carnatic music, with lavish celebration of the Thyagaraja *utsavam*) and the language classes it offers (Tamil, Teluga, and Kannada) that many of its devotees—like those of the Tiru Venkatam temple in India—are from the states of Tamilnadu, Andhra Pradesh, and Kamataka. Just a few miles from Sri Venkateswara temple is another beautiful place of worship, known simply as the Hindu-Jain temple. The architecture, deities, and rituals here are principally "north-Indian," and the two temples serve the Pan-Indian Hindu community in tandem.[21]

SELF-INQUIRY AND SELF-PERCEPTION

The Penn Hills temple sponsors several workshops and lectures based on connections between psychology and the Hindu tradition. The "Living In Freedom—an Enquiry," or LIFE, workshop lasted four days and was conducted by Swami Sukhadodhananda from Bangalore. According to the temple bulletin, "the workshop demonstrated how the Vedantic principles of self-enquiry can be used to resolve the day-to-day problems faced by individuals." Material for the workshop "was drawn from the Bhagavath Geetha, the Upanishads, the Bible, the Koran, Tibetan Buddhism and Zen." Participants in the workshop examined "inhibitions that usually cloud the thinking process" and saw how special techniques like meditation, yoga, music, and dancing pave "the way for unfolding the path to self-examination." The event was billed as "a supreme stress management program spiritual workshop."[22] Similar language is seen in the interpretation of a *vratam*, a votive act usually observed by women, which is described as "human resource management."[23] This form of self-inquiry is also seen in the youth camps that the temple has sponsored since 1981; in 1985, the camp theme was "positive thinking and living." The Chinmaya Mission West has sent volunteers to run the camp; Swami Sukhabodhananda, who ran the LIFE workshop, was sometimes in charge of the camp, and at other times, people from Bharatiya Vidya Bhavan have been responsible for camp activities. An emphasis on "self-help" has also been evident in lectures sponsored by the temple. Lecture titles have included the following: "Bhagavad Gita helps to reduce stress," "Molding modern children with ancient Indian culture," and "Value systems for positive thinking."[24]

It is never easy to perceive oneself clearly and to articulate one's faith and tradition to oneself, one's children, and the community. It is especially difficult if one has had no formal training or education in the field. Many Hindus in this country face such a predicament. Growing up in India and being immersed in the Hindu religious experience does not make one a specialist in it. Yet Hindus in the United States are forced to articulate over and over again what it means to be a Hindu and an Indian to their friends and children and often feel ill-equipped to do so (see figure 10). Frequently, all a person remembers about a festival in India is the food that was prepared for it; he or she was never called upon to explain Deepavali or Sankaranti, to say nothing of Hinduism. In India, most people probably never thought much about yoga, city dwellers had nothing more than a nodding acquaintance with the sacred cow, and certainly meditation was considered to be the province of specially chosen holy people. To conclude, I will try to give some sense of how Hindus perceive themselves and how they portray their religion. In a sense, it is like Alice looking through the "looking glass," since I, a Hindu, am looking at Hindus looking at themselves, or like Arjuna at the Viswarupa scene, looking at himself looking at himself.

I have already identified three major areas of emphasis at the Penn Hills temple—a symbolic or psychological explanation of religious phenomena, a syncretic approach to deities and rituals, and exploration of connections between religion, "self-help," and stress management. I see these focal points as part of a larger picture. Many educated Hindus, here and in India, hold particular views about themselves, which I would characterize as the "mythic structures" of the young urban profes-

FIGURE 10
An Indian American boy from the Philadelphia area brings members of his Boy Scout troop to visit the Pittsburgh temple, 2003. Photo by John Hawley.

sional Hindu. These perceptions about their own religion are extremely important to this group and condition their view of themselves and other religions. I will identify and discuss a few of the main perceptions that I have noted over the years as part of the Hindu community in this country. Some are reinforced by temple bulletins. I do not present these positions or attitudes as correct or incorrect. I merely wish to point out that they have become so common that they comprise a "generic Hindu" outlook that is unique to the late twentieth century.

1. *Hinduism is not a religion; it is a philosophy, a way of life.* This statement is often followed by the statement that "Hinduism is the oldest religion in the world." The two assertions are probably the most common pronouncements of Hindus in this country. I have heard from various friends who teach religion in the United States that second-generation Hindu students often repeat these sentiments. The "Visitor's Guide" to the Penn Hills temple itself states that "Hinduism might be better described as religious culture rather than a religion."

2. *Hinduism is a tolerant religion.* The statement in the "Visitor's Guide" to the Penn Hills temple that the most significant feature of Hinduism is its belief in religious tolerance is typical. The Vedas proclaim, "As the different streams having their sources in different places mingle their water in the sea, so the different paths which men take through different tendencies, various though they appear, all lead to the same one God." Statements like "Truth is one, Paths are many" are voiced even as India experiences separatist violence repeatedly.
3. *The supreme being is seen as a trinity.* Many educated Hindus seem to consider the "trinity" as the most important feature of the "godhead." Statements such as the following are heard frequently: "The Godhead has three main functions: Creator (Brahma), Preserver (Vishnu), and Destroyer (Siva)." Yet Brahma has no more than a walk-on part, and an extremely important deity—the Goddess—is left out of this picture. While the notion of the trinity is found in Hindu scripture and, above all, in Hindu iconography, it is given more importance in nineteenth- and twentieth-century thinking than it warrants. Statements about the trinity such as that above lead the uninitiated Western audience to believe that Brahma the Creator is very important and that Siva the Destroyer could not be very good. Such statements about the trinity mislead more than they inform, and obscure more about the Hindu tradition than they clarify.
4. *All rituals have an inner meaning that has to do with promoting good health and a safe environment.* In other words, science and Hinduism are fully compatible. I have already discussed at length the "inner meanings" of rituals; what I did not touch on is the compatibility between science and religion, the perceived value of yoga and meditation and their impact on the human brain and body. Many discussion groups in this country focus on the merits of these activities or other religious rituals, which are seen as leading to better human health or creating a safer environment. The "antiseptic" properties of turmeric or cow dung are promoted, for example.

The Penn Hills temple and other temples in the United States provide examples of both continuity and innovation in Hindu traditions. The temple at Penn Hills has given participating communities (a) a local place of worship, where icons of the lord have been formally consecrated and formal prayers can be offered by priests on behalf of individuals; (b) a place to conduct sacraments; (c) a place to send offerings of devotion either in gratitude or as a petition for particular favors, and to receive a token of the lord's grace *(prasada)* in return; (d) an institution for educating the younger generation born in the United States, through weekly language and religion classes, frequent lectures, sponsorship of classical music and dances (which have a broad religious base in India), summer camps, and an "outreach" bulletin that is mailed to anyone who wants it. New temples are rising up all over the American landscape.

Two new temples have been planned in central Florida, and funds are being raised for the construction of shrines in Tampa and Orlando. The community hall for the Orlando temple will be built before the shrine. The community hall is a place where different groups can meet and where language, music, and dance classes can be held. It will give Hindus in the Orlando area a place to feel their strength and assert their identity in the midst of a larger society in which many feel marginalized culturally and linguistically. Organizing groups have not yet made a decision on which deity is to be enshrined and how worship will take place; it is in this context that there is greatest fragmentation among the Hindu traditions. Devotees of Vishnu, Siva, the Goddess, or Ganesha and those who worship Vishnu as Rama or Krishna want the temple to be dedicated primarily to their particular deity; others who believe themselves to be "noncontroversial" and "liberal" advocate a nondenominational, almost antiseptic, room of meditation, with an abstract sacred syllable as focal point and no deity enshrined. Animated discussions arise from these suggestions. A member present at the deliberations remarked wryly, "It is a pity that a temple that was meant to unite our Hindu community here becomes the focal point of division." The key word is "community"; because of the many communities and many traditions, a consensus is almost impossible. Stands are taken on sectarian, caste, and regional lines, and the debates continue.

The Penn Hills temple, meanwhile, continues its leadership as one of the "premier" Hindu institutions in the United States. While sacred time is gently manipulated to coincide with secular time—or to at least make the word "holiday" mean literally that—Hindus, sometimes inadvertently, sometimes quite self-consciously, affirm the importance of sacred land in a very traditional way. In interpreting their religion and trying to make it more relevant and meaningful, some Hindus have favored the view that all religious phenomena are to be understood as symbols of an inner, hidden truth; and occasionally these symbolic interpretations have more in common with Western dream analysis and popular psychology than they have with traditional Hindu exegesis. As Hindus in the United States and in India build temples and try to explain their religion to their children and the community at large, several dominant motifs have emerged in their self-understanding. With enough repetition, these ideas may bc ratified.

NOTES

This essay was originally written in 1983, updated in 1991, and published in 1992. The temple it describes was one of only a few major Hindu temples existing in the United States at that time. Since then hundreds of American Hindu temples have been built—perhaps the largest number to be erected in any country outside of India after the burst of construction that occurred in Southeast Asia almost a thousand years ago.

1. *Sri Venkateswara Temple* (1977): 2–3. This pamphlet was published sometime after April 14, 1977, when the sculptors arrived from India, and just before the *mahākumbhābiṣeka* ceremonies on June 8. The pamphlet contains photographs of the early stages of temple construction.

2. "Annual Progress Report," *Saptagiri Vani* 15 (November 1990): 2.

3. Along with this familiar derivation, a lesser-known etymology is also given by Sri K. V. Santhanagopalachari in his discourse entitled "Shri Shreenivasa Kalyanam." He says that *veṃ* is sometimes interpreted as "the ambrosia that gives salvation," and *kaṭa* is *aiśvarya*, "earthly good fortune." Thus *veṅkaṭa* suggests that the hill gives earthly and otherworldly auspiciousness.

4. *Saptagiri Vani* 6, no. 3 (Third quarter, 1981): 14.

5. The Tirupati Devasthanam at Tiru Venkatam has also helped the temple at Aurora, Illinois (outside Chicago). It loaned the Aurora temple one million rupees (Rs. 10 lakhs) in 1985, which was used for the making of the deities and transportation. In 1987 it gave another million rupees to be used toward the salaries of the traditional Indian sculptors.

6. The pamphlet issued by Sri Venkateswara temple during the dedication ceremonies on October 22, 1978, mentioned the "granite statue." It is interesting to note in this context that one of the principal points made by the thirteenth-century Srivaisnava theologian Pillai Lokacarya is that one should not think of the material with which the lord's form is composed. I have discussed this in "Arcāvatāra: On Earth as He is in Heaven," in *Gods of Flesh, Gods of Stone,* ed. J. P. Waghorne and N. Cutler (Chambersburg, PA: Anima, 1985). However, it may be argued that prior to the consecration, it is permissible to talk of Ganesha as a "granite statue."

7. *Saptagiri Vani* 13, nos. 2 and 3 (Second quarter and third quarter, 1988): 2–3.

8. *Saptagiri Vani* 13, no. 4 (Fourth quarter 1987 and first quarter 1988): 3. On p. 2 we learn that a special "kalasa" puja was performed for the Labor Day weekend.

9. On January 1, 1990, alone, the income of the Tiru Venkatam temple was reported to be Rs. 3,155,000 ("The Gold Haul," *The Week,* March 25, 1990, p. 19).

10. An interesting passage in Kamban's Tamil Ramayana makes this point very well. The monkeys who are ready to embark on a journey to search for Sita are exhorted not to go to Tiru Venkatam, or anywhere near it. The reason, we are told, is that Tiru Venkatam grants *mokṣa* (liberation) immediately; the monkeys may get liberation and stay there, and therefore not continue to search for Sita!

11. Pamphlet (ca. May 1977): 2. This pamphlet was issued just prior to the *mahākumbhābhiṣeka* on June 8, 1977.

12. *Kavachas for the Deities* (1986) This pamphlet was issued toward the end of 1986.

13. *The New York Review of Books*, October 25, 1984, p. 5.

14. On this issue, see Joanne Waghorne's introduction to *Gods of Flesh, Gods of Stone.*

15. Hindu Temple Society of Southern California, Sanctification of the Rajagopuram, Lord Venkateswara Temple, Oct. 1987, Los Angeles.

16. Brahmacharini Pavitra, "Worship of the Lord and Its Significance—'Tiru Aradhana' ," *Saptagiri Vani* 7, no. 1 (May 1982): 2–3.

17. For a more complete discussion, see my article "Arcavatara: On Earth as He Is in Heaven," in *Gods of Flesh, Gods of Stone.*

18. *Saptagiri Vani* 15, no. 2 (November 1990): 16–17.

19. *Kavachas for the Deities* (1986).

20. See, for example, Swami Sukhabodhananda, "Symbolism in Hindu Culture," *Saptagiri Vani* 15, no. 2 (1990); Brahmacharini Pavitra, "Significance of Maha Sivaratri," *Saptagiri Vani* 10, no. 1 (Third quarter 1985); Swami Chinmayananda, "Shri Ganapati-Vinayaka," *Saptagiri Vani* 6, no. 2 (1981); 8, no. 2 (August–September 1983); and 10, no. 3 (Third quarter 1985); A. Parthasarathy, "Brahma," *Saptagiri Vani* 10, no. 4 (Fourth quarter 1985); Swami Chinmayananda, "Deepavali Festival," *Saptagiri Vani* 12, no. 3 (Third quarter 1987); Brahmacharini Pavitra, "Temple and Its Significance," *Saptagiri Vani* 13, no. 4 (Fourth quarter 1987).

21. There is close cooperation between the Education Committee of the Penn Hills temple and the Hindu-Jain Temple, and the two distribute achievement awards to graduating high school students.

22. "Temple News Briefs," *Saptagiri Vani* 15 (February 1990): 4, 15.

23. Bri. Pavitraji, "Varamahalakshmi Vratam," *Saptagiri Vani* 10, no. 2 (Second quarter 1985): 7.

24. *Saptagiri Vani* 10, no. 4 (Fourth quarter, 1985): 3.

16 · A Diasporic Hindu Creed

Some Basic Features of Hinduism

SITANSU S. CHAKRAVARTI

GOD: THE ONE IN MANY

Hinduism is a monotheistic religion in which God is believed to manifest Himself or Herself in several forms.[1] One is supposed to worship the form that one finds most appealing without being disrespectful to other forms of worship. The religion has evolved over thousands of years with a spirit of tolerance toward different ways of spiritual fulfillment.[2] This explains why Hinduism does not lend itself to conversion to or from other religions, for it holds that religions are alternate ways of worshipping the same divine principle and thus should not claim monopoly of spiritual wisdom. Hinduism believes in a continuity, on a graded scale, of religious practices, in conformity with the pace of the aspirant's spiritual progress. It does not hold any point on the scale as having an absolute position in isolation, nor are all the practices suitable to the needs of everyone, given the variations in personal temperaments and constitutions. Hindu rituals have embedded layers of meaning, from gross to refined, viewed according to the participant's station in spiritual life.

This essay was previously published as "Some Basic Features of Hinduism," in *Hinduism: A Way of Life* (Delhi: Motilal Banarsidass, 1991), 23–28.

SANATANA DHARMA

In India, Hinduism is called Sanatana Dharma, which means literally "the eternal religion." There are two reasons why it is so called. First, unlike other religions, it has no propounder, and consequently its beginnings cannot be traced to a specific date in antiquity. Second, with all its subdivisions, it can be said to incorporate the spirit of the world's diverse religions,[3] and thus can be equated with the eternal *Religion* itself. The Sanskrit word *dharma* refers to both man's nature and his religion. Thus, according to the Hindu, religion is a means toward establishing a person's real nature, which is the fulfillment of the divinity in man—an inner harmony with the world to which he belongs. The principle of harmony itself is his God. The way to the realization of this harmony, of the one in many, varies according to the seeker's psychological makeup and is determined to a large extent by the beliefs of the society in which he has been brought up. As Sri Ramakrishna, a Hindu mystic of the nineteenth century, would say, "As many are the views, so many are the ways."

THE "PERSONALIZED RELIGION"

Victor Frankl, a guru of modern psychiatry, refers to the "profoundly personalized religion" that Hinduism is.[4] "Hinduism," observes the psychologist Gordon Allport, "recognizes that the temperament, needs and capacities of the initiate himself in large part determine his approach to religious verities," reiterating what has already been pointed out. "Although other religions provide personal counsel for the initiate at the threshold of maturity," Allport continues, "probably none goes to such lengths in making a close analysis of the youthful personality. . . . In this practice we have a rare instance of an institutional religion recognizing the ultimate individuality of the religious sentiment."[5]

KARMA

Like Judaism, Christianity, and Islam, Hinduism believes that life does not end with death. Hindus hold that everyone has a chance of being born again to undo the mistakes committed in past lives. The form of the future life is determined by the actions performed in previous lives.

CASTE SYSTEM

The majority of Hindus follow the caste system, broadly a fourfold classification of people based originally on four types of human nature: Brahmin (spiritual-introvert, i.e., *sattvik*), Kshatriya (spiritual-extrovert, i.e., *sattvik/rajasik*), Vaishya (extrovert, guided by the constraint of inertia, i.e., *rajasik/tamasik*), and Shudra (guided by the principle of inertia, i.e., *tamasik*). Different duties in life have been assigned to each group depending on the nature of the people who constitute it, which, to a large extent, is determined by their family environment. Teaching and priestly duties fall to the Brahmin, protection of country and maintenance of justice to the Kshatriya, agriculture and commerce to the Vaishya, and the duty of assisting others to the Shudra. We have to keep in mind that this division uses *dharma*—religion and righteousness—as its frame of reference; it recognizes variations in human beings and must be viewed in the setting of the universe that includes them. From the perspective of *dharma*, the worth of any work is measured in terms of the spiritual progress it occasions in the agent. It is, however, possible for an individual to transcend the hierarchy of social duties and become a renunciant, that is, a *sannyasi* or *sannyasini* in his or her personal spiritual quest, irrespective of birth or background, but only if one is ready for such a step. In the Hindu tradition a true renunciant has always been a guiding force for the whole society. People from all walks of life still flock in reverence to the feet of these holy people for guidance, which psychological counseling in the world of today only feebly approximates.

Untouchability has unfortunately been practiced by the Hindus for a long time. A concern for hygiene and cleanliness at a time when germicidals were nonexistent likely explains the establishment of this institution. It has been argued that the institution is not a part of Hinduism, because it goes against the spirit of universal love encouraged in the scriptures. Mahatma Gandhi tried hard to eradicate the custom, giving the name Harijans, literally "people of God," to the so-called Untouchables. The custom is very much on the wane with the rise of public consciousness and the adoption of various legislative measures. It will take some time, however, before it is completely eradicated.

In spite of indications to the contrary in the *Mahabharata*, the caste system has long been understood as hereditary and typically serves as the basis for the choice of one's partner for marriage.

THE FIVE MANIFESTATIONS OF THE ONE

Hinduism has developed over centuries of dialectical discussion and has come to encompass a broad spectrum of spirituality, ranging from theism, with its belief in a personal God, to atheism. Most Hindus worship the divine in five personal manifestations *(panchopasana)*: (1) the sun, (2) Shiva (the static principle), (3) Shakti (the dynamic principle), (4) Vishnu (Krishna and Rama are His two important incarnations), and (5) Ganesha (the dispeller of obstacles and bestower of fulfillment). All Hindu deities reduce to these five and their associates, who in their turn are but one and the same. It is possible for a Hindu to believe in (a) a personal God with manifestations in forms worthy of worship, (b) a personal God without such manifestations, or (c) an impersonal principle. The idea, again, is to awaken divinity within oneself according to one's inclinations and capabilities, in the pursuit of spirituality. To rule fanatic parochialism out, Hinduism has the mandatory practice of paying obeisance to all five forms before engaging in special worship of any one of them, highlighting the fact that divinity is one, though approaches to it may vary.

ICONS

Although their use is not a must, icons are accepted in Hinduism. An icon serves an important purpose in man's search for the infinite in and through the finite. The rare individual who can establish a relation with divinity directly does not need any icons. However, the less-advantaged majority, and those who have a fascination for encountering the Supreme in forms, worship it in images on the understanding that the infinite, which is without limits, can express itself in all kinds of ways.

The images of Gods and Goddesses have deep spiritual meanings. Even the concrete images, on analysis, turn out to be abstract symbols for the one divine principle. The black color of Krishna and Kali means that they are not physical beings but are beyond the perception of ordinary mortals because of their transcendental nature. The flute of Krishna stands for the inner beauty, harmony, and rhythm of the universe, and the enchanting call of the divine to be heard at the spiritual level. The Ganges on the head of Shiva represents the constant flow of divine bliss. Shiva's trident *(trishul)* stands for the state of equilibrium that characterizes the primordial elements—*sattva*, *rajas*, and *tamas*. The crescent moon signifies the gradual awakening of divine consciousness.

DIVINE INCARNATIONS

According to Hinduism, divinity incarnates itself, whenever the need arises, to save humanity in distress. God is not only omnipotent but is also the lover and the subject of love, who always responds to the inner call of the devotee. He has planned creation through an ongoing process of evolution, a concept Hindus have been aware of since ancient times.

LOVE OF ALL LIFE: NONVIOLENCE

Hindus believe that divinity is present in all forms of life—human or otherwise. In an endeavor to relate to the world outside in a meaningful and harmonious way, Hindus approach all life in the same way, with love and without violence. No exception is made for animals. In fact, Hinduism's emphasis on nonviolence is so strong that many Hindus do not eat meat. Mahatma Gandhi, the father of modern India, strove to establish the Kingdom of God *(ram rajya)* through his nonviolent application of Hinduism, following the dictates of the *Gita,* the spiritual backbone of the religion. He was one of a succession of leaders who have contributed, since ancient times, to the ongoing process by means of which Hinduism has cleansed itself of accumulated impurities of doctrine and ritual.

CONTRIBUTIONS TO THE WORLD

Scholars believe that the law of *karma* (present suffering or happiness is due to past actions), with its concomitant theory of the transmigration of the soul, was passed on to Buddhism and Jainism from Hinduism in ancient times. Yoga and meditation may be Hinduism's two greatest contributions to the modern world . These techniques for attainment of mental peace have been adopted by people of many different faiths without their having to abandon their own creeds. Today, Hinduism has an important role to play in promoting mutual understanding among the people of the world based on the acceptance of differences. The well-known theologian Ninian Smart describes the essence and expectations of this ancient religion in his analysis of the future shape of world religions:

> Hinduism itself then appears as the unifying force in world religion because of its all-embracingness. It contains, essentially, all faiths, and all forms of religious experience within it. It has evolved over the centuries a mode of life where different aspects of religion can live together in harmony. And with the Indian emphasis on non-violence it holds out a real hope of giving an ethical basis to inter-religious peace.[6]

NOTES

1. Cf. Rig-veda 1.164.46, which stated about 4,000 years ago that "Truth" is one, though the wise name it differently.

2. Cf. A. L. Basham, *The Wonder That Was India*, 3d ed. (New York: Taplinger Publishing, 1968), 312, 347.

3. Cf. Ninian Smart, *The Religious Experience of Mankind*, 3d ed. (New York: Scribner, 1984), 580.

4. Viktor Frankl, *The Will to Meaning* (New York: World Publishing, 1969), 154.

5. Gordon Allport, *The Individual and His Religion* (New York: Macmillan, 1950), 11.

6. Smart, *Religious Experience of Mankind*, 580.

PART VIII · IDENTITY

17 · Militant Hinduism

Ayodhya and the Momentum of Hindu Nationalism

JOHN STRATTON HAWLEY

The galvanizing event in the recent history of religion in India was the destruction of the so-called Babri Mosque in Ayodhya, a sleepy pilgrimage town on the Gangetic Plain southeast of Delhi. There, on December 6, 1992, Hindu militants pulled down a Mughal mosque stone by stone as two hundred thousand people watched and cheered. They were clearing the ground for a massive temple to Rama on the site they believe to be this god's birthplace—a site, therefore, where no mosque ever belonged.

The dispute about Rama's birthplace is a long and intricate one. Many Hindus would date it to the construction of the mosque itself, by a lieutenant of the Mughal emperor Babar in 1528. Why but for the fact that Ayodhya was a major Hindu place of pilgrimage, they say, would this little town have warranted such a grand Muslim edifice? Activists typically go on to claim that a Hindu temple on that exact site was destroyed to make way for the mosque. This claim, plausible enough when one considers the history of other sacred places in India and around the world, has nonetheless been hotly disputed on the basis of the evidence at Ayodhya itself. Academics have weighed in on both sides of the debate.

Turmoils at Ayodhya have had a way of coinciding with major political shifts.

This essay was previously published as "Ayodhya and the Momentum of Hindu Nationalism," based on a version that appeared in *SIPA News*, Columbia University School of International and Public Affairs, Spring 1993, 17–21.

Confrontations between groups of Hindus and Muslims shortly preceded the British takeover of that part of India in 1856 and again followed the great anti-British revolt of 1857. About a century later, in 1949, soon after the British had "quit India" and the subcontinent had suffered a bloody partition into the sister states India and Pakistan, an image of Rama suddenly appeared inside the precincts of the mosque. Heralded as a miracle by some and as a hoax by others, this event led to a long moratorium in which the mosque/temple was closed to worship, by court order. When judges opened the doors again in 1986, the struggle intensified, this time primarily under the pressure of a massive campaign waged by the Vishwa Hindu Parishad (VHP, or World Hindu Council), a group with close ties to the major instrument of Hindu nationalism in India today, the Bharatiya Janata Party (BJP).

The BJP depicted itself to voters across India and to expatriates around the world as the one force capable of rescuing India from the long-ruling Congress Party's policies of socialism, unbalanced secularism, slavish submission to the demands of minorities, and general corruption. The BJP portrayed itself as the superior party on two fronts. First, it was clean and efficient—a claim that enjoyed somewhat greater credence before the BJP actually acceded to rule in several states. Second, it was a party with a central agenda, and an agenda about a center. That center was Hinduness *(hindutva)*, a concept it borrowed from Hindu groups who had been active since the early decades of this century. The BJP filled out the concept by giving it a physical focus: it held up Ayodhya as the symbolic center of Hindu life. Ayodhya was depicted as the ideal city, the city where the god Rama had watched over his golden-age kingdom *(ram rajya)*. As the divine exemplar of sovereignty, Rama himself was to be India's ruler again, with the BJP (and implicitly sister groups such as the VHP) as his chief instruments of power.

The problem as the BJP saw it was that Ayodhya, once a truly sacred center, had been defiled. Its most massive building was now a mosque, a structure representative of a polity and religion that the BJP and VHP depicted as belonging to an invader—politically Mughal, religiously Muslim. The mosque must go if India was to recover the sacred core of its identity. A new temple marking Rama's birthplace would supplant it. Several times in the 1980s and early 1990s the VHP and BJP mobilized the paraphernalia of pilgrimage to create that sense of center. In a VHP "temple-chariot journey" *(rath yatra)* that raced through much of India in 1985, trucks replaced the traditional wooden temple carts as conveyances for images of Rama and his consort Sita, who were shown behind bars. Their jailers were the twin forces of antireligious secularity and undue Muslim power over India, and the gods were to be freed in Ayodhya at the end of their sojourn. Their "liberation" *(mukti)* would be represented by the (re)construction of the Temple of Rama's Birthplace. In 1989, another set of performances followed, in which bricks were consecrated in local communities all over the subcontinent and abroad, then sent to Ayodhya for inclusion in inaugural ceremonies for the new temple—another great ingathering calculated to sharpen the city's profile as sacred center. The next year the BJP's leader, L. K. Advani, performed a 10,000-mile "temple-chariot journey" himself, again with Ayodhya as the destination.

Toward the end of 1990, drama yielded to confrontation as the BJP and its allies sent the first "troops" to attack the mosque itself. Tens of thousands of activists massed, and six of them were killed by police in the fray. Instantly, they became martyrs. From then onward clouds gathered thickly as electoral struggles intensified—there were major BJP victories at the polls in 1991—and at the end of 1992 another major thrust against the mosque was organized. This time hundreds of thousands of militants flooded into Ayodhya, camping in regional groups and often in settings prepared with near-military precision. December 6 was the day announced for attack ("liberation"), and a flurry of last-minute measures involving the provincial and central governments and the judiciary ultimately did nothing to deflect it. To many people's surprise—and horror—the government failed to intervene in any decisive way. In five hours' time the mosque came down, its three great domes crashing into a dusty sea of rubble.

Where is all that rubble? On a visit to Ayodhya only a month afterward (January 1993), I could see almost none. True, there was a vast mesa of crushed stones that would soon become a thoroughfare connecting the main highway directly to Rama's birthplace and eerily avoiding the rest of the town. Ayodhya had been an amiable warren of temples, tombs, and ashrams constructed over the years to express the pieties of many generations of Hindus, Jains, and even Muslims—often with the help of governments captained by Muslims. Now these truckloads of stone had been brought in to bypass all that and lead in a no-nonsense way to the new "tourist park" surrounding the mosque/birthplace that the BJP-controlled state government had vowed to create. Here one saw in graphic terms what someone hoped would be a sleek new Hinduism that could circumvent, cut through, repackage, and obscure the old.

The stones that built that road were new stones. Like most of the BJP and VHP activists themselves, they had been imported into Ayodhya from beyond the city limits, and they bore no physical relation to either the long-lost original temple (if ever it stood there) or the mosque that is said to have supplanted it. These were the stones of Hindu modernity.

A very different kind of stone stood at the site of the erstwhile mosque itself. This bit of rubble was claimed to be truly indigenous and had been raised to the status of an altar. Still there today, it is a segment of a pillar that is said to have emerged from the walls of the Babri Mosque during its destruction. The claim is that the mosque's builders cannibalized it from an earlier temple that stood on the site until Muslims destroyed it. Despite vigorous denials in important scholarly circles, this and related matters were still being debated two years later, so intensely that the argument disrupted the proceedings of the world archaeological conference held in Delhi in December 1994. There is no way to prove the cannibalization theory from the pillar itself. In the Pala style, with no distinguishing iconography, it could as well have come from a Jain temple as from a Hindu one. That is significant, for there was a time when the Jain presence in Ayodhya was more impressive than the Hindu, although you'd never know it from the rhetoric of Hindu revivalism today.

So much for "Hindu" rubble. But where is the *Muslim* rubble? Where is the rest of the mosque? Some say the vast Hindu crowd took it away piece by piece, as souvenirs and objects of veneration. This sounds plausible. The cause of Rama would have transvalued these infidel stones into holy relics, and pilgrims are notorious for dispersing such *sacra*. Yet many of the blocks that made the mosque were reputedly enormous. Where did they go?

One answer was offered by a judge whom I met in Ayodhya in early 1993. Recently retired from the Lucknow branch of the provincial High Court, he had come with a high police officer to worship in one of Ayodhya's many temples. He explained that the disappearance of the great stones was—well—inexplicable. Referring to the monkey god who is Rama's greatest devotee and the very image of strength and speed, he said, "It was all Hanuman's miracle. For a huge mosque like that to come down in a few hours—with tridents and pickaxes! And now no trace! What can it be but Hanuman's miracle?"

Perhaps we should not be surprised to find a well-educated, English-speaking judge invoking the miraculous. We have already alluded to the Lucknow court's role in the Ayodhya controversy, and a full account would make for a pained and convoluted story. It would be understandable if the judge hoped, in some corner of his consciousness, that this record might helpfully be set straight by the intervening hand of God.

Nor should we be surprised to find a high-ranking police officer at prayer beside him. In that part of India, the force has been overwhelmingly Hindu by design since shortly after independence, and by everyone's account it played a major part in allowing the mosque to be destroyed. Although the commanding officer tried to protect the mosque, others apparently gave the demonstrators an hour to demolish it, then extended the deadline when the task proved more formidable than had first been imagined. Several retired police officers, along with a group of civil engineers, were involved in the demolition itself. They organized the younger volunteers, showing them, for example, how to dismantle the mosque's protective railing and use the segments as battering rams.

How could they not be involved? From their point of view, they weren't creating rubble; they were clearing, consolidating, building! There was a definite sense throughout Hindu Ayodhya that such workers were part of something to be proud of—something large and unitary for a change, the wave of a coherent future, something clean and right. Something sanctified by the blood of martyrs, too. Many pages in the ubiquitous little souvenir books about Ayodhya are taken up with gory photographs of the six young men who died when police were ordered to repulse the 1990 assault on the mosque. Oddly, the precedent for such books of martyrs comes from the Sikhs, as does the term invariably used to designate Hindu activist volunteers, *kar sevak*. Even more striking, the word used to name the martyrs themselves, *shahid*, comes from Islam. (See figure N at the Web site http://www.clas.ufl.edu/users/vasu/loh.)

In the West there is a deep-seated belief that the rubble of Ayodhya and places like it is caused by pulling the pillars out from under the temple of modern secularism. This is a new version of the colonial view "If we go, they'll kill each other." (That prophecy fulfilled itself all too easily in the months following independence in 1947.) Hindus in Ayodhya see it the other way around. The mosque was a symbol of desecrating foreign rule, a long colonial past. It was also tied up with the self-proclaimedly secular Congress Party government that inherited the British mantle in New Delhi and helped preserve its hold on power by projecting itself as the protector of Muslims in exchange for their support on election day.

So the confrontation at Ayodhya was not just Hindus versus Muslims, but Hindus versus secularists as well. As one man put it, using an English word in a Hindi sentence, it was the "unqualifieds" standing up against the English-educated "qualifieds" who get all the good jobs, especially in government. Self-made men like himself (he owned his own taxi) were pulling down the massive rubble of a bureaucratized, colonial past. A vivid wall painting showed Prime Minister Narasimha Rao sweating bullets and crying, in Hindi, "Save my government!" My government—not just "my" of the Congress Party, but of all those complacent, self-interested "qualifieds."

Marx is surely turning over in his grave to find that religion provides the language of anticolonial struggle in much of the world today. Some opiate! But as the temple of postcolonial secularism is attacked, so also are real temples—or, in this case, mosques and tombs. On the outskirts of Ayodhya stands the tomb of a Muslim saint that has served as a focus of worship for centuries. On December 6, 1992, after the Babri Mosque came down, one part of the great visiting mob set upon this tomb too, destroying the saint's grave and dislodging many bricks from the walls (see figure 11). "Most of the people who worship here are Hindus," reported an immaculate, soft-spoken local Muslim leader whom I encountered there. "We have always lived together in peace. Whatever happened downtown, we never thought it would come here. Yet. . . . "

Here is rubble of another kind—neither the rubble of the imperialist incursion that the Babri Mosque represented to many Hindus nor the simple product of age-old Hindu-Muslim rivalries, as secularists sometimes like to think. This is rubble created by a newly streamlined brand of Hinduism. One can perhaps sympathize with the desire to remove a mosque built by a religious culture aggressive enough to raze many Hindu temples, possibly including one that stood on the site of the Babri Mosque itself, as alleged. But here the crowds were erasing from memory a symbol of the fact that Hindus and Muslims have so often prayed together. This unruly mix is one of the glories of India, giving the lie to all those airtight textbook chapters on Hinduism, then Islam. Such a tradition is more than tolerance: it's life together, unbrokered by secularism or any other mediating ideology.

Ayodhya is being reshaped by a new kind of Hinduism: a syndicated, textbook Hinduism that offers a new sense of political agency to many in the majority who have so far felt left out. As this new Hinduism takes hold, the tomb of Sisle Hazrat Islam and all it stands for is in danger. So is the intricate network of arrangements symbolized in the ashrams and temples of the old Ayodhya, as a great road is bulldozed from the edge of town to the as-yet unbuilt Temple of Rama's Birthplace.

And what about the rubble, the huge stones that once were the great building-blocks of Babar's Mosque and are now, in their absence, the stuff of miracles? Where did they go? There are some good-sized rocks lying near the place where the mosque once stood, but nothing to rival what visitors would see if they visited the great Mughal mosques that have so altered the landscape of great Hindu cities such as Mathura and Benares.

The answer, as it turns out, is quite simple. The mosque was not actually constructed of such stones. It predated the fine mosques of Mathura and Benares and

FIGURE 11
"Most of the people who worship here are Hindus": Muslim leader surveying the wreckage of the tomb of Sisle Hazrat Islam, Ayodhya, January 2003. Photo by John Hawley.

used a more modest medium: large bricks of the Jaunpuri style. So the miracle of the stones, as proclaimed by the justice from Lucknow, was a miracle in his mind.

And its major predecessor is little different. For years Hindu enthusiasts have spoken as if the image of the child Rama that was discovered in the Babri Mosque on the morning of December 23, 1949, got there as a result of divine intervention in the affairs of this world. After all, some of the most important images in Hindu temples throughout India are said to be *svayambhu*—self-manifested. For the child Rama of Ayodhya, that may still be so in a symbolic sense, but we now know that it is not true in a literal one. Recently, after decades of public silence, an ascetic living in Ayodhya has confessed that he and several comrades were responsible for placing the image inside the mosque during that night in 1949. The man says it was easier to let people surmise that this was a miracle than to explain the facts, because if they had done so, they would have been prosecuted. They saw their mission as above the courts, whose actions would only have confused matters. In their eyes, that mosque *was* a temple, since the place on which it was built was Rama's birthplace. It deserved to be restored to its intrinsic glory—and to its proper owner, Rama.

The crowds who filled the streets of Ayodhya in late 1992 said similar things in the graffiti art with which they covered the walls. "It isn't a question of justice," one placard said. "It's a question that goes beyond the boundaries of the courts. The issue of Lord Rama's birthplace is not a subject for the courts!" The reason for this, as another poster made clear, is that in the minds of at least some Hindus there is a court above the courts, a true state that defines what statecraft really is. In this poster the young Rama appears as an archer ready to put his arrow to its bow. The caption reads, "The love of Rama is the strength of the state."

Since 1993, for a variety of reasons, the rhetoric of the BJP has slowly shifted away from the idiom of religious triumphalism. Many Indians have breathed a sigh of relief. Yet the ability of the Congress Party to shepherd the country through a period of fundamental redefinition is still in doubt, and the economic and ideological power of Islamic states not far away continues to rankle an Indian (and, still more, a Hindu) sense of dignity. Then too, the issue of what will be constructed on the site of "Rama's birthplace" remains unsettled.

In such circumstances it is hard to predict the future of religious nationalism in India, but with the BJP regularly garnering about a third of the vote in elections throughout North India, and with the Congress weakened in the south, it does not seem that it will go away. The Temple of Rama's Birthplace is still invisible to the eyes of most who travel to Ayodhya, except as a canopy spread across the area where the sacred pillar and the image of child Rama are displayed for pilgrims' veneration. Yet thanks partially to Ramanand Sagar's *Ramayan*, the long-running television series about Rama's life that was seen at least in part by most of the Indian populace, the image of Rama's eternal palace in an ideal Ayodhya is shared in a way it has never quite been before.

Many who soaked in the TV "Ramayana"—Muslims among them—cringe at the idea of trying to play it out against the landscape of Indian politics today. But for some, Ayodhya and places like it are the natural theater where "Hindu sentiments," purportedly wounded for centuries, can be healed. How large a group is this, and can they succeed in persuading others to join their cause in a sustained way? Only time will tell.

18 · Tolerant Hinduism

Shared Ritual Spaces—Hindus and Muslims at the Shrine of Shahul Hamid

VASUDHA NARAYANAN

In contrast to what is commonly perceived as Hindu-Muslim conflict in the Indian Subcontinent, the sharing of a metaphoric world and the mutual adaptation of religious vocabulary and ritual among Hindus and Muslims may be found in the Tamil-speaking region of South India. A striking example of this mutual adaptation can be found at the *dargah* (shrine) of Shahul Hamid (ca. 1513–1579) in the city of Nagore.

Nagore is on the eastern coast of South India, and the dargah is right on the Bay of Bengal. This is where Shahul Hamid lived in the later part of his life, and where he is buried. Shahul Hamid was apparently a thirteenth-generation descendant of Muhiyudin Abd al-Qadir (Katiru) al-Jilani, a renowned Sufi saint. When just a child, he was visited by the prophet Kiliru (Khazir) and blessed by him. Kiliru spit into Shahul Hamid's mouth, thus transmitting divine grace (a common motif in Tamil Islamic poetry). Shahul Hamid did not get married but is said to have spiritually fathered a son. (This son, Yusuf, and a daughter-in-law are also buried at Nagore.) At the age of 44, after extensive travels all over the Middle East, Shahul Hamid reached the city of Nagore. He was received with honor by Achutappa Nayakar, the Hindu ruler of Thanjavur, who is said to have donated two hundred acres of land to his entourage. Later, another Hindu ruler—Raja Pratap Singh

This essay was previously published as "Shared Ritual Spaces: Hindus and Muslims at the Shrine of Shabul Hamid in South India," *Religious Studies News*, February 1998, 15, 30, 41.

(1739–1763)—paid for the dargah's fifth minaret (the tallest of the five), after he was blessed with a son through the grace of Shahul Hamid. Yet another Hindu king, Tulasi, is said to have bestowed fifteen villages on the dargah.

When one visits the Nagore shrine today, one is struck by the number of Hindus offering worship to the saint (see figure 12). According to the managing trustee of the dargah, about 60 percent of the premises has been built by Hindus, and about 50 to 75 percent of pilgrims on any given day are Hindu.

Some patterns of worship at the shrine parallel Hindu worship in temples. Hindus as well as Muslims come here, for example, to shave the head of a child for a first tonsure. While this is also a Muslim custom, most of the Hindu participants in the ritual are not aware of the Islamic precedent. Hindus and Muslims also buy tin- or silver-plated facsimiles of body parts, houses, sailboats, motorcycles, and the like to offer to the saint, just as they would make an offering to a deity in a Hindu temple. The image of a particular body part is offered when one requests a cure in that part of the body. Similarly, tiny models or etchings of houses or motorcycles are offered when devotees petition to procure the real thing. When a cure is effected or when one obtains what one wants, a return pilgrimage is made to offer a thanksgiving donation.

There are other symbols of worship that suggest the Hindu cultural context (see figure 13). Shahul Hamid's footprint is preserved in the dargah. Veneration of footprints or the feet of a guru is typical of many Hindu traditions, but not as common in an Islamic context. Generally in Tamil Islamic literature, the motif of spitting into a disciple's mouth is seen as a spiritual and "biological" conductor of right lineage, functioning like the feet and their imprint in Hindu circles. What we find in the case of Shahul Hamid is the image of saliva in literature and the foot in ritual, bringing together two cultural markers of veneration.

While the trappings of worship sometimes reflect the Hindu cultural context, the architecture does not. It may not be possible to speak of "Hindu" or "Muslim" architecture in northern India, but in the south the architecture of a mosque is clearly different from that of a temple. The dargah of Shahul Hamid is more Muslim minaret and dome than Hindu tower and pillar.

The central part of the dargah is the tomb of Shahul Hamid. It is set like a Hindu inner shrine *(garbha grha)*, which one approaches through seven thresholds. Four of these doorways are made of silver, and three of gold. To the left (as one faces the tomb) are two other shrines—those of Shahul Hamid's son Yusuf and daughter-in-law Ceytu Cultan (Sayid Sultan) Bibi. The doors to the tombs (called *samadhi*, using a Sanskrit word) are usually closed; they are open only very early in the morn-

FIGURE 12
Muslim descendants of Shahul Hamid say prayers for Hindu clientele, Nagore, Tamil Nadu. Photo by Vasudha Narayanan.

ing and late in the evening. Hindu and Muslim men and women mingle freely and go up to the doorways to offer their prayers. The dargah, therefore, becomes a negotiated space for Hindus, Muslims, men, and women to come together and worship a common source of power, a power that is called *barkath* or *shakti* by followers.

Behind the shrines is a well. According to one of the hereditary trustees of the dargah, the waters of this well and the waters of *zam zam* (the spring at Mecca) have the same source. Beyond the well is a large "tank"—similar to the temple tanks found all over South India. Pilgrims wash their feet or take a dip in the water before going in to worship. The waters serve as markers for the two emphases of this dargah—the connection with the Middle East and the connection with the local Tamil Hindu culture. The activities near the dargah tank are similar to those that take place near any Hindu temple of Tamilnadu; and yet the waters of the well nearby are considered to be miraculously connected to the *zam zam*, near Mecca. The figure of Shahul Hamid has the same dual connection; while he is uniquely part of the Tamil landscape, he is inextricably linked with al-Jilani and parts of the Middle East.

While terms like "Hindu" and "Muslim" are often used today to compartmentalize people and to articulate politically rigid categories, a nuanced understanding

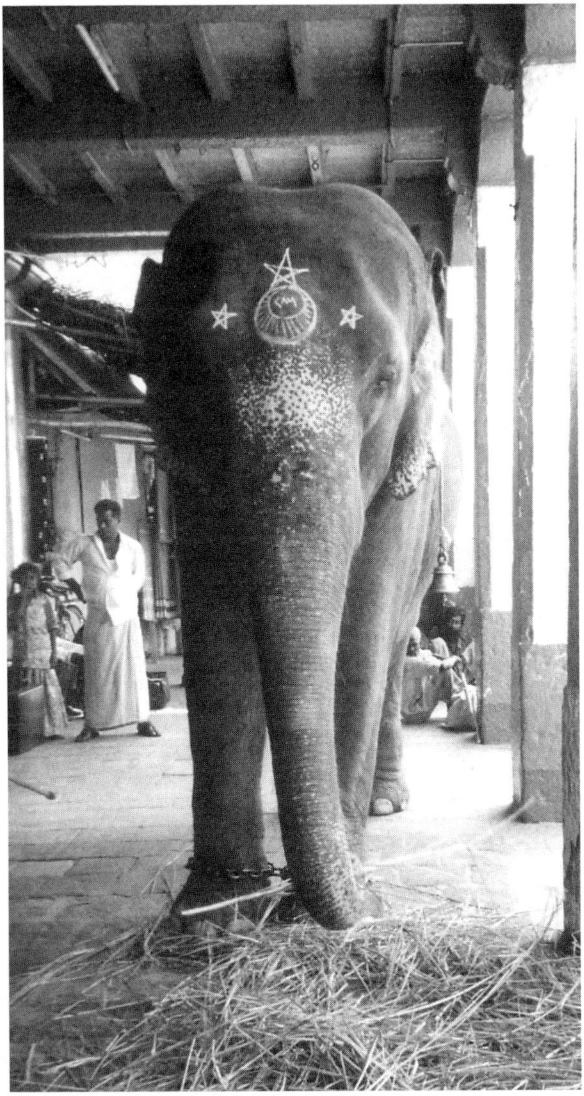

FIGURE 13
Fatimah, the shrine elephant—after the fashion of Hindu temple elephants, but with Islamic insignia—Nagore, Tamil Nadu. Photo by Vasudha Narayanan.

of the relationship between Hinduism and Islam must take into account the political, social, and intellectual contexts of the two traditions. There are, of course, some strict caste and community boundaries within the many Hindu traditions (marking, in particular, issues of diet and marriage), but there are also many permeable boundaries between the Hindu communities and Islam. A visit to the dargah of Shahul Hamid in Nagore reminds us of this permeability and helps us to understand just how frequently religious "boundary crossings" can and do happen in India.

19 · Hinduism for Hindus

Taking Back Hindu Studies

SHRINIVAS TILAK

> The master's tools will never dismantle
> the master's house.
>
> AUDRE LORDE

This essay is a response to writings by Rajiv Malhotra on RISA-L scholarship and Hinduism that appeared on the Web site sulekha.com.[1] I have written it in my capacity as a Hindu living in the diaspora and as a member (albeit marginalized!) of RISA-L. The essay is addressed to the readers and members of sulekha.com as well as those Indians and other scholars, researchers, and sympathizers of Hinduism who work with, alongside, and for disciplines that may come under the rubric of Hindu studies as part of the larger discipline of Indology. More particularly, it seeks to initiate a dialogue with the growing number of Hindus in the diaspora whose professional field of research is not Hinduism or Hindu studies but who nevertheless have received training in the Western academic setting and are familiar with disciplinary methodologies of the humanities and social sciences.

The impetus for this essay is the growing dissatisfaction on the part of Hindus in the diaspora with the way Hindu deities such as Ganesha or Hindu religious leaders like Shri Ramakrishna have been depicted by North American scholars of Hinduism. This dissatisfaction has been voiced and reiterated in a number of articles and comments on articles on the Web site sulekha.com. Hindu community activists like Ms. Mona Vijaykar have voiced their concern at gatherings such as the DANAM (Dharma Association of North America) conference in Atlanta, Georgia, which

This essay was previously published as "Taking Back Hindu Studies," www.sulekha.com, January 6, 2004.

some RISA-L members also attended. Others, like Devendra Potnis, a graduate student at Louisiana State University, have successfully generated petitions protesting misrepresentation of Hindu deities like Ganesha, which were signed by thousands.

CREDO, QUIA OCCIDENTALE

Professor Albrecht Welzer is one of the few Western academics to acknowledge that scholars of Europe and North America have frequently been guilty of misinterpreting many key Hindu concepts.[2] By way of illustration, he discusses the prevailing notion of *varna* in Indology and in academic literature dealing with India in general. Traditionally, *varna* means "sounds of speech or language." In the nineteenth century, however, scholars like H. H. Wilson wrongly identified *varna* with "a letter of the alphabet." This misrepresentation was continued in the works of T. Benfey, H. T. Colebrooke, Franz Bopp, and others. Though grammatically *varna* is derived from the social term denoting "class" (as attested in Panini 2:1.69, 5:2.132, 6:3.85), it nevertheless acquired the now commonly accepted (though incorrect) meaning of "color."[3] Following Western scholars, most modern Indic scholars (including K. V. Abhyankar, Balakrishna Ghosh, and Ganganath Jha) rendered *varna* as "letter in the Sanskrit alphabet," rather than as "sound."

Welzer raises the question, Why did Indic scholars acquiesce to and even imitate such mistakes committed by European Indologists, in spite of the fact that they could and should know better? The answer, according to Welzer, lies in part in India's colonization. He alludes to the answer in the Latin expression that forms part of the title of his contribution to the volume *Studies in Mimamsa: "Credo, Quia Occidentale,"* which points to the widespread overestimation of Western culture and the blind belief that anything of Western or European origin must be superior to the corresponding element of Indic culture.[4] The resulting "inferiority complex" has had a shattering and traumatic effect upon Indic scholarship and academic output. Unfortunately, this trend continues even in postindependent India and among Indians living in the diaspora today.

EXTANT SCHOLARSHIP ON HINDUISM IN NORTH AMERICA

Research was one dominant category and way in which the underlying code of imperialism and colonialism was both regulated and realized. It was regulated through the formal rules of individual scholarly disciplines and scientific paradigms, and through the institutions and funding agencies (including the state) that supported and sustained them. Exegetical imperialism was similarly instituted in manifold ways of representation and in ideological constructions of Hinduism as the "Other" in scholarly and popular works, which helped select and recontextualize those constructions in such things as the media, official histories, and school curricula. Ashis Nandy argues that the structures of colonialism contained precise codes and rules by which colonial encounters occurred and dissent was managed.[5] Recent controversies involving scholars like Jeff Kripal and Paul Courtright and diasporic Hindus suggest that such encounters continue even today without much change in the form and institutional mechanism set during the heyday of colonialism. Many Hindus in the diaspora feel that exegetical imperialism and colonialism continue to frame Hindu studies: whether in India or in the diaspora.[6] As a discursive field of knowledge, Indology is one such idea and spirit with many forms of realization designed to subjugate the Indic/Hindu Other. Writing, theory, and history are key sites in which Western research in Indology and Hinduism has evolved. The modern academy claims theory as thoroughly Western and thus constructs the rules by which the Hindu world has been theorized.

A Western or modern education prevents many Hindu scholars from writing or speaking from a "real" and authentic Hindu or Indic position and perspective. Those who do dare to speak from a traditional Hindu perspective are criticized for not making sense. Alternatively, their arguments are "suitably translated" or reduced to some "nativist" discourse by Western (and many Westernized Hindu) academics. More often, their ideas are dismissed as naive, contradictory, and illogical. This positions today's Hindus in North America in a difficult space both in relation to the general Indic populations and within the Western academy. For each Hindu scholar who does succeed in the academy, there remains a whole array of unresolved issues about the ways North American Hindus in general relate inside and outside of Hindu studies, inside and outside the academy, and between all those different spaces and worlds.

TAKING BACK INDIA'S HISTORY

Historiography is a modernist project that developed in concert with imperial beliefs about the Other. The discipline of history developed from two interconnected ideas: (1) there is a universal history with fundamental characteristics and values that all human subjects and societies share; (2) universal history is one large chronology or grand narrative. History is about developments over time; it charts the progress of human endeavor through time. The actual time events take place also makes them "real" and "factual." To start the chronology, a "beginning" or time of "discovery" has to be established.

Possession of a chronology allows one to go backwards and explain how and why things happened in the past. Societies are believed to move forward through time in stages, developing much as an infant grows into a fully developed adult being. As societies develop, they become less primitive, more civilized, more rational, and their social structures become more complex and bureaucratic. History is similarly deemed to be about human moral development, moving in stages through the fulfillment of basic needs, the development of emotions and the intellect, and culminating in morality. Just as the individual moves through these stages, so do societies. The story of history therefore can be told in a coherent narrative.[7]

A skilled historian can assemble all the facts in an ordered way so that they reveal to the reader the truth, or at least a good idea of what really happened in the past. History as a discipline is held to be innocent, since the "facts" speak for themselves. A good historian simply marshals the facts and weaves them into a coherent, concise, and cogent narrative. Once all the known facts are assembled, they tell their own story, without any need of a theoretical explanation or interpretation by the historian. History therefore is a pure discipline, unsullied by ideology, interests, or agenda. All history has a definite beginning; and there are clear criteria for determining when history begins: literacy, rationality, scientific spirit, social and political formations, and so on.[8]

In the context of Indology, the upshot of the above view and understanding of history is the argument that only a historian trained in historiography can write a "true" and accurate history of Hinduism and Hindu culture and society. The disciplines of history and anthropology, accordingly, were implicated from the beginning in the construction of totalizing master discourses to control the Indian as the Other and to deny the Indian's view of what happened and what the significance of historical "facts" may be to the colonized.[9] "If history is written by the victor," argues Janet Abu-Lughod, "then it must, almost by definition, 'deform' the history of the others."[10]

Research using Western paradigms assumes that Western ideas about the most fundamental things are the only ideas possible to hold, certainly the only rational ideas, and the only ideas that can make sense of the world, of reality, of social life, and of human beings. This line of thinking has been carried over into Hindu studies and conveys a sense of innate superiority and a desire to overwhelm research in Hinduism spiritually, intellectually, socially, and politically.

Research imbued with this "attitude" or "spirit" assumes ownership of the Hindu and Indic world. It has established systems and forms of governance that have embedded that attitude in institutional practices. These practices determine what counts as legitimate research and who counts as a legitimate researcher. In this enterprise, the objects of research do not have a voice and do not contribute to research, science, or knowledge. An object (in this instance, Hinduism or Hindus) has no life force or spirit of its own, no humanity; "it" cannot, therefore, make any active contribution. For all practical purposes, the "benevolent" impulse of modern Indology to represent Hindus and Hinduism effectively appropriates their voice, reducing them to the category of the subaltern.

True, this perspective was not deliberately insensitive. Perhaps the rules of practice did not allow such a thought to enter the scene (this comes across in one of Paul Courtright's messages posted on the RISA-L list). It nevertheless reaffirmed the West's view of itself as the center of legitimate knowledge, the arbiter of what counts as knowledge and the source of all "civilized" knowledge. Such knowledge is generally praised as "universal" knowledge, available to all and not really "owned" by anyone until non-Western scholars make claims to it.

History is suitably revised whenever claims like the above are contested, so that the story of civilization continues to remain the story of the West. For this purpose, the Mediterranean world, the ancient Near East, and ancient Greek culture are conveniently appropriated as part of the story of the Western civilization, Western philosophy, and Western knowledge. More recently, this practice has also been extended to such elements of Indic civilization and culture as yoga. Rajiv Malhotra's "U Turn" thesis has convincingly demonstrated and documented its increasing prevalence.[11]

The nexus of cultural ways of knowing, scientific discoveries, economic impulses, and imperial power enabled the West to make ideological claims to having a superior civilization. The idea of the "West" became a reality when it was represented to the people of Africa, Asia, and Oceania through colonialism. Colonial education was used to create new indigenous elites to colonize indigenous disciplines of knowledge.

CONTESTING WESTERN RESEARCH AND METHODOLOGIES

Under colonialism, Indians had to become reconciled to Western-inspired studies and a Western history of India. While a few struggled against the received version of India and Hinduism, most Indians complied with the dominant, Western view of Hinduism and its history. Hindus allowed the history of their religion to be told to them and, in the process, became alienated from it. They became outsiders as they heard and read a contrived version of their religion and its history. The system of education that the British introduced into India was directly implicated in this process of alienation from Hinduism.

The creation and legitimization of a genuine discipline of Hindu studies, therefore, represents a special battlefield. Hindu intellectuals and scholars must bear a major responsibility in this battle in a number of ways, in the manner suggested by Franz Fanon, who has left us a revolutionary manifesto of decolonization and the founding analysis of the effects of colonialism upon colonized peoples and their cultures. Following Fanon, one may identify three levels through which the westernized, diasporic Hindu intellectuals will have to make their journey back over the line.

In the initial phase, such intellectuals and academics tend to be keen to prove to their Western peers that they have been thoroughly assimilated into the Western culture of knowledge. While most remain content to settle for the status quo and spend all their academic life submerged in this milieu, a small minority of them begin to enter a second phase, in which they become restless and dissatisfied with their assimilation. Now they have a desire to recognize and find their academic and cultural roots and to recover the fast-receding connection with their own past. In the third phase, these intellectuals begin to realign themselves with their own history, culture, and tradition and actively seek to awaken their brethren by producing "revolutionary" literature that is reinterpreted anew.[12]

The growing interest at present in doing away with the misrepresentation of Hinduism in the diaspora may be understood in this light. The challenge for many Hindu intellectuals and scholars is how to position themselves strategically as intellectuals (1) within the academy, (2) within India, and (3) within the Western world, where many of them actually work. Following Gayatri Chakravorty Spivak, one may argue that the major problem for Hindu scholars remains the problem of being taken seriously:

> For me, the question "Who should speak?" is less crucial than "Who will listen?" "I will speak for myself as a Third World person" is an important position for political mobilization today. But the real demand is that, when I speak from that position, I should be listened to seriously; not with that kind of benevolent imperialism.[13]

TAKING BACK HINDU HISTORY AND HINDU STUDIES

Coming to know India's past must become part of the critical pedagogy of decolonizing Hindu studies. This must be accomplished by creating an alternative history of Hinduism, which in turn would generate alternative pathways to knowledge about Hinduism. Is the history of Hinduism in its modernist and Western construction relevant and useful to Hindus today? For most Hindus, the answer would seem to be self-evident, because they assume that when the truth comes out, a true account of Hinduism will be given. *Wrong.* How then to write a new history of Hinduism and India? Particularly when Aimé Césaire observed (in his *Discourse on Colonialism*) that the only history is white? How can the Hindu find his or her voice? Can the Hindu subaltern speak?

I think a beginning must be made by raising and debating issues that have to do with taking back Hindu history and studies. Toward that objective, it is possible to extrapolate from the urgent claims that Gayatri Chakravorty Spivak makes in "Can the Subaltern Speak?" via the critical theory of Theodor Adorno.[14] Following Spivak's lead, Hindus in the diaspora and academics and students of Hinduism in India must begin by asking, Who does research in Hinduism? Who funds, defines, and owns such research? Whose interests does it serve? Who benefits from it? Who designs the research framework, the questionnaire, and frames the scope of this research? Who carries it through and writes it up? How are its results disseminated?

HINDU AWAKENING IN THE DIASPORA

Taking back Hindu studies will require Hindus to revisit site by site the history of Hinduism that was constructed under colonial and Western eyes. This in turn will require developing a theory and approach for engaging with, understanding, and then acting upon the received history of Hinduism. Rewriting the history of Hinduism, reclaiming Hindu studies, and giving testimony to the distortion of India's past will have to be the basic strategies of decolonizing Hindu studies.

It is unlikely that such an endeavor will be readily accepted and acknowledged on the international scene. But we must persist in this enterprise. Decolonization need not mean the rejection of all theory or research or Western knowledge. Rather, it should focus on concerns and worldviews about Hinduism as Hindus understand it, and then frame Hinduism within the broader theory and research from the perspective of India and Indic culture in general.

DECODING THE ARCHIVE OF THE WEST

Michel Foucault uses the metaphor of an archive to convey how the West draws upon a vast history of itself and multiple traditions of knowledge, which incorporate cultural views of reality, and of space and time. Particular knowledges, philosophies, and definitions of human nature form what Foucault has referred to as the West's cultural archive. This archive is a veritable storehouse of histories, artifacts, ideas, texts, and images, which are classified, preserved, and represented. Foucault suggests that this archive reveals rules of practice that the West and Western scholars themselves need not subscribe to, inasmuch as they operate within rules and conventions that are thoroughly internalized and therefore are taken for granted.[15] Western scholars use this archive to retrieve, enunciate, and represent knowledge of and from the Other.[16]

To take back Hindu studies, it will be necessary for Hindu researchers to decode the West's archive and its rules of practice, because theories about research are underpinned by (1) a cultural system of classification and representation, (2) views about human nature and human morality and virtue, (3) conceptions of space and time, and (4) conceptions of race and gender. Hindu scholars will need to learn how ideas about these things are formulated in the West in order to determine what counts for real in the eyes of the West and Western researchers. It is only after being confronted by alternative or competing conceptions of other societies or cultures that the reality of the West-sponsored knowledge will become reified and may then come across as something not necessarily "better" or reflecting "higher orders" of thinking, and so on.

The Hindu and Vedic conceptions of spiritual relationships to the triple cosmos, to the social and material universe, to the landscape, and to stones, rocks, insects, and other things (seen and unseen) have generally been difficult for Western systems of knowledge to deal with or accept. Yet they offer at least a partial indication of alternative or different worldviews and ways of coming to know and of being. Hindu concepts of yoga and spirituality, which Christianity and Western scholars of Hinduism first attempted to destroy, then to appropriate, and finally to claim, are therefore critical sites of resistance for Hindu scholars. The values, attitudes, concepts, and language embedded in beliefs about spirituality provide, in many ways, the clearest contrast between the Hindu and Western worlds. To date, Hindu spirituality is one of the crucial aspects that the West could not decipher or understand and therefore could not control.

ETHICAL RESEARCH PROTOCOLS

The huge credibility problem the Western research community faces today with respect to Hinduism must be addressed from within a Hindu agenda. It must be affirmed that the first beneficiaries of knowledge of Hinduism must be the direct indigenous descendants of that knowledge. Hinduism-centered research must be about bringing to the center and fore privileging indigenous values, attitudes, and practices rather than disguising them with Westernized labels.

Research on Hinduism in the West is organized primarily around the interests of like-minded scholars and Indologists. The development of particular research topics and research groups tends to occur organically within the boundaries of what is known as a "research culture" embedded in the values of academic life. Much research on Hinduism is carried out in closely formed and protected cliques that share methodologies of mutual interest. Thus one often reads in the messages posted on RISA-L requests for leads or references concerning a Hinduism-related topic of research "my" student has chosen.

EMIC AND ETIC OF RESEARCH ON HINDUISM

Many of the issues that may arise while doing research on Hinduism are addressed in the literature about the emic and etic dimensions of research. Most Western research methodologies assume that the researcher is an outsider who nevertheless should be able to observe without being implicated in the scene. This view originates in positivism and relies on notions of objectivity and neutrality. But a Hindu researcher must problematize the emic, or insider, model differently because the critical issue with emic research is the constant need for reflexivity. At a general level, emic researchers must devise ways to think and to critically assess their thought processes and their relationships to research subjects, cultures, and societies. They must guard against the uncritical collection of their data and its analysis. True, the same caution applies to etic research, but the major difference is that, as an insider, the Hindu researcher will have to live with the consequences of his or her research on a day-to-day basis as a member of the culture or society that provides the subject of research.

For this reason, as an emic researcher, a Hindu scholar will need to build clear, research-based support systems and relationships with his or her community. He or she will have to devise much clearer "lines of relating" specific to the project and "at arm's length" from the regular lines of family and community networks. Spelling out the limitations of a project—the issues or things that are not addressed—will also be important. The emic researcher must also devise a suitable model for closure and must possess the courage to say no and stand up to peer pressure from insiders. Insider research has to be as ethical and respectful, as reflexive and critical, as outsider, or etic, research. It also needs to be modest and humble, because the researcher is likely to have various roles and relationships in his or her community that may be at odds with the demands of research in an etic setting.[17]

RESEARCHED [HINDUS] MUST BECOME RESEARCHERS

A major challenge for Hindu researchers is to retrieve sufficient space to convince the various fragmented but powerful research communities (Western and Hindu/Indian in the diaspora or in India) of the need for greater Hindu involvement in research on Hinduism. Yet another challenge is to develop approaches toward research that take into account, without being limited by, the legacies of previous Western-dominated research and the parameters of both previous and current approaches. Finally, Hindu researchers must devise a framework for structuring assumptions, values, concepts, orientations, and priorities for such research. When Hindus become the researchers and are no longer mere research subjects or the researched, the activity and direction of research on Hinduism will be transformed. Questions will then be framed differently, priorities ranked differently, problems defined differently.

Hindus must begin by questioning the most fundamental belief behind Western research on Hinduism: Do all researchers have an inherent right to the knowledge and truth of Hinduism? Research in itself is a very powerful intervention, even if carried out at a distance, because it has traditionally benefited the researcher, the knowledge base of the researching community and the sponsoring agency. Researchers acquire privileged information, which is usually interpreted within an overt theoretical framework. But it can also be interpreted within a covert ideological framework. The researcher has the power to distort, to make invisible, to overlook, to exaggerate, and to draw conclusions based not on factual data, but on assumptions, hidden value judgments, and, often, outright misunderstandings. The researcher has the potential to extend knowledge or to perpetuate bias and ignorance.[18]

INDIGENIZING RESEARCH ON HINDUISM

Can a non-Hindu researcher carry out research on Hinduism? The answer must be a qualified yes: yes, but not on his or her own. He or she would need to devise a way to suitably position him- or herself as a non-Hindu researcher. Research on Hinduism should involve "mentorship" of responsible Hindu/Indic scholars, who in turn must satisfy the rigor of research. Such research must be supervised by a Hindu/Indic researcher, not by a researcher who happens to be an Indologist. Indigenizing research on Hinduism means drawing upon the body of knowledge and corresponding code of values that have evolved over the millennia through the input of indigenous Hindu commentators and scholars.

Hindu indigenism is grounded in an alternative worldview and a value system that locate individuals in sets of relationships with the environment and levels of beings and existence. Reframing research on Hinduism is about assuming greater control over the ways in which issues and problems pertaining to Hinduism are discussed and handled. The reframing of an issue is about making decisions; about its parameters; about what is in the foreground, what is in the background; and what complexities exist within that frame. It means resisting being boxed in and labeled according to alien categories that may not fit.

PARADIGMS OF THEORY AND RESEARCH ON HINDUISM

The question will inevitably arise, whether Hindu-directed research on Hinduism is or can be its own paradigm. It would be unproductive to engage in a debate over this right now because it might set up comparisons with Western research on Hinduism. Suffice it to say that, given its incipient phase, Hindu-directed research on Hinduism will remain in the near future both less than and more than a paradigm. A start may be made by undertaking research based on articles compiled in *India through Hindu Categories,* edited by McKim Marriott (1990).

Creation of new parameters and methodologies for undertaking research on

Hinduism should also be informed by modern critical theory, in particular by the notions of critique, resistance, struggle, and emancipation. Research on Hinduism can be situated advantageously within the framework of reinterpretation of critical theory advanced by the "Subaltern Studies Group" led by Ranajit Guha and others in India.[19] Thus intrinsic to the proposed research on Hinduism will be analysis of existing power structures and inequalities surrounding current research on Hinduism, which is dominated by Western (and Westernized Indian) scholars.

Research on Hinduism can draw upon critical theory for the purpose of exposing underlying assumptions that serve to conceal the power relations that exist within the institutions of learning about Hinduism in the West and the ways in which dominant groups construct concepts of "common sense" and "facts" to provide ad hoc justification for the maintenance of inequalities in research. This type of research on Hinduism will likely remain a fledgling approach operating within the relatively small community of Hindu/Indic researchers, which in turn exists within a minority culture that continues to be represented within antagonistic colonial discourses.

TAKING BACK HINDU STUDIES: THE PRACTICAL DIMENSION

The project of taking back Hindu studies in the diaspora will necessarily have a practical dimension because Hindu-directed research on Hinduism must simultaneously be a joint social project weaving in and out of Indic and Vedic cultural beliefs and values as well as Western ways of knowing and lifestyle patterns. Research on Hinduism will be involved with sites and terrains that are also sites of contestation and struggle, since Western researchers have also claimed each of these sites as "their" turf.

Research on Hinduism must be based on the assumption that research that involves Indians and Hindus as individuals and as communities must make a positive difference for those who are researched. This does not mean an immediate or direct benefit. The point is that research has to be defined and designed with some ideas about likely short-term or longer-term benefits. Obvious as this may seem, it must be remembered that historically Indians and Hindus have not seen the positive benefits of research on their culture, society, or religions.

Research on Hinduism must incorporate processes such as networking and community consultations to assist in bringing into focus the research topics that are significant to Hindus in India and in the diaspora. In practice, all such elements of research will have to be negotiated with individual communities. This means researchers will have to share their "control" of research and seek to maximize the participation and interest of Indians in general and Hindus in particular. To stimulate research on Hinduism, it will be necessary to induct young Hindu researchers and students into projects in which they will be employed as trainees. Support systems and mentoring processes must be instituted to bring these young people into close contact with senior Hindu researchers and to prepare them for work inside their own communities and within their own value systems and cultural practices.

STAGING *SATYAGRAHA* TO TAKE BACK HINDU STUDIES

Leaders of the Hindu community in North America disagree with the claims of many RISA-L members and faculty teaching Hinduism-related courses in North American teaching institutions that there is no misrepresentation of Hindu values, norms, or practices in Hinduism courses taught by the members of RISA-L. Developing nonviolent strategies based on the Gandhian principles of *satyagraha*, as proposed by Rajiv Malhotra, can therefore be introduced as a practical aspect of "taking back" Hindu studies. According to Gandhi, *satyagraha* is the ideal way to resolve conflicts, which usually involve a clash between both persons and principles. Behind every struggle lies another clash, a deeper one: a confrontation between two views that are each to some measure true. Every conflict, to Gandhi, was on some level a fight between differing angles of vision illuminating the same truth.

In trying to find a suitable solution to a given conflict, the initial temptation or response is to remove the adversary by force and settle the argument quickly. But while it may remove the person, forced victory leaves the underlying conflict between principles intact and simmering. It may erupt again as soon as the adversary has recouped his or her losses and mustered enough new strength. Common sense and pragmatism may recommend accommodation and compromise with the adversary, thereby allowing each side to win a little. This solution is often described as a "win-win" situation. For Gandhi, however, this stance overlooks the truth that each side loses a little as well.[20]

The modern democratic spirit suggests the use of arbitration and law to determine and judge which side is right. This solution, however, may sacrifice the truth (or rather, the element or share of truth) in the losing side's position. Thus, according to Gandhi, *satyagraha* would be a better way to fight injustice than any one or more of the methods suggested above because it consciously avoids the pitfalls in them and instead seeks a new position, which is more inclusive than the old ones, and moves into it.

Ideally, therefore, the practical steps that diasporic Hindus need to take in their struggle to remove misconceptions about Hinduism should be based on the Gandhian principles of *satyagraha* articulating (1) negotiations over the differences with the adversary and attempts to resolve them, and (2) mobilization and proper training of supporters and volunteers to lead the struggle if negotiations fail.

Ideally, negotiations would follow this sequence: recognize the truthful and untruthful elements on each side; put the truthful elements from each side together; form a new side and adopt it while struggling with your opponent; continue revising and refining the new position as the negotiations or fight continues; end the struggle only when both sides agree to occupy the same side.

Satyagraha would involve creation of small groups of dedicated Hindu scholars to study and document instances of misrepresentation of Hindu values, practices, norms, and so on. Other groups would be needed to coordinate such activities as letter writing, petiton writing and signing, and establishing dialogue with teaching faculties at the university level.

The real adversary in this struggle is likely to be apathy, both on the part of Hindus in the diaspora and the average North American. Such apathy will have to be shattered through a dramatic demonstration of concern. This can be accomplished by creating and opening several fronts simultaneously: making an appeal to the general public in North America through newspaper and magazine articles, producing leaflets advertising forthcoming courses on Hinduism at colleges and universities across North America to attract the attention of the average North American, organizing rallies, and opening alternative centers for teaching courses on Hinduism.

Experienced Hindu academics will have to be recruited to act as consultants to guide diasporic Hindus in writing and circulating petitions or leading protests against the misrepresentation of Hinduism. An annual inventory of outlines of courses on Hinduism should be made, and Hindu scholars invited to evaluate the courses and offer suggestions for improving the teaching of Hinduism. Hindu scholars and community leaders should engage in an ongoing dialogue with book publishers in India and abroad. The latter may be invited to send manuscripts on Hinduism that they have received to a committee of Hindu academics and scholars for fair evaluation and assessment to avoid the perpetuation of glaring misrepresentations or falsehoods concerning Hinduism.

According to the ideals of Gandhian *satyagraha*, if the measures described above fail, then a noncooperation movement, including boycotts, strikes, peaceful disruptions, blockades, and sit-ins, should be launched. If this fails to produce a settlement (i.e., a fair and accurate representation of Hinduism and Hindus), then creation of a parallel entity to replace the opponent's facilities would be necessary. In the North American context, this would mean setting up independent Hindu schools and universities on the model of the Catholic schools and universities that have existed for centuries.

NOTES

1. The epigraph by Audre Lorde is quoted in Smith 1999: 19. RISA-L is the listserv of the Religion in South Asia section of the American Academy of Religion.

2. The section heading is a pun on the famous *credo, quia absurdum* (see Welzer 1994: 241 n. 80).

3. Welzer 1994: 229–30.

4. Ibid., 232–34.

5. Nandy 1983: 2–3.

6. Read, for instance, messages posted on such Yahoo! newsgroups as Indian Civilization to realize the depth of Hindu discontent with academics teaching Hinduism in North America. This seething discontent is matched by the smugness of scholars who have contributed to the massive (over 600-page) anthology edited by Joseph Elder et al. (1998) lauding achievements in Indology at universities in the United States.

7. For an insightful analysis of this topic see Young 1990: esp. 119–40 (chap. 7, "Disorienting Orientalism").

8. Smith 1999: 30–31.

9. According to Ashis Nandy (1983: 17), the colonial ideology postulated a clear disjunction between India's past and its present. The civilized India was in the bygone past; now it was dead and "museumized." The present India was India only to the extent that it was a senile, decrepit version of its once youthful, creative self.

10. Cited in Smith 1999: 67.

11. Smith 1999: 62–63. [Malhotra's "U Turn" theory alleges that it is common for Westerners to learn Indian ideas and practices such as yoga, then bring them back in disguise—in a Christianized or otherwise Westernized form—without acknowledging their Indian inspiration, or even demonizing the Indic source. See Rajiv Malhotra, "The Case for Indic Traditions in the Academy," posted at http://www.infinityfoundation.com, accessed February 14, 2006. For a visual representation, see www.swaveda.com/journal.php?jid=4&j=Evam&art=63. Eds.]

12. Fanon 1966: 178–85.

13. Chakravorty Spivak 1990: 59–60.

14. One cautionary note: Chakravorty Spivak can be unnecessarily dense and obtuse when approached for the first time. Morton 2003 is a good stepping stone and guide to her thought. He also provides a comprehensive bibliography of her works updated to 2003 (including her famous 1985 essay "Can the Subaltern Speak? Speculations on Widow-Sacrifice"). The origins of the theory of inner colonization, the main plank of the "Frankfurt School" of critical theory, is to be found in the statement of Marx that "it is not the consciousness of men that determines their being, on the contrary, their social being that determines their consciousness" (cited in Hanks 2002: 1).

15. Cf. Foucault 1972: 12, 126–31.

16. Smith 1999: 44.

17. Ibid., 137–39.

18. Ibid., 176.

19. See the eleven volumes published to date by the Subaltern Studies Group. See also Hanks 2002.

20. I owe this discussion of Gandhian *satyagraha* to Mark Juergensmeyer (2002).

WORKS CITED

Chakravorty Spivak, Gayatri. 1990. *The Post-Colonial Critic: Interviews, Strategies, Dialogues.* Edited by S. Harasym. New York: Routledge.

Elder, Joseph, et al., eds. 1998. *India's Worlds and U.S. Scholars.* New Delhi: Manohar and American Institute of Indian Studies.

Fanon, Franz. 1966. *The Wretched of the Earth.* Translated from the French by Constance Farrington. New York: Grove Press.

Foucault, Michel. 1972. *The Archaeology of Knowledge.* Translated from the French by A. M. Sheridan Smith. New York: Pantheon Books.

Guha, Ranajit, et al., eds. 1982–2000. *Subaltern Studies: Writings on South Asian History and Society.* Delhi: Oxford University Press.

Hanks, Craig J. 2002. *Refiguring Critical Theory: Jurgen Habermas and the Possibilities of Political Change.* Lanham: University Press of America.

Juergensmeyer, Mark. 2002. *Gandhi's Way: A Handbook of Conflict Resolution.* Berkeley: University of California Press.

Marriott, McKim, ed. 1990. *India through Hindu Categories.* New Delhi: Sage Publications.

Morton, Stephen. 2003. *Gayatri Chakravorty Spivak.* London: Routledge.

Nandy, Ashis. 1983. *The Intimate Enemy: Loss and Recovery of Self under Colonialism.* Delhi: Oxford University Press.

Smith, Linda Tuhiwai. 1999. *Decolonizing Methodologies: Research and Indigenous Peoples.* Dunedin: University of Otago Press.

Welzer, Albrecht. 1994. "*Credo, Quia Occidentale:* A Note on Sanskrit *varna* and Its Misinterpretation in Literature on Mimamsa and Vyakarana." In *Studies in Mimamsa: Dr. Mandan Mishra Felicitation Volume,* edited by R. C. Dwivedi. Delhi: Motilal Banarasidass.

Young, Robert. 1990. *White Mythologies: Writing History and the West.* London: Routledge.

20 · Hinduism with Others

Interlogue

LAURIE L. PATTON
and CHAKRAVARTHI RAM-PRASAD,
with KALA ACHARYA

This essay is presented as a prolegomenon to building constructive and collegial relationships between Hindu and non-Hindu both inside and outside the academy. Our work was born out of a set of conversations and experiences among the three of us that we believe to be far more extensive and everyday than is usual in the present intellectual climate, where there is suspicion on one side and resentment on the other. This essay is an attempt to put the Gandhian principles of *satyagraha*—which were articulated at one scholarly meeting in 2002 and are now sadly at risk of being mired in unproductive exchange—into philosophical practice within the academy.[1] We believe that the cumulative effect of everyday acts of understanding and cooperation between Hindu and non-Hindu is extremely powerful and can help shape our world. Such acts, rather than the recalcitrant memories of bitter exchange, deserve our focus and exploration.

INTERLOGUE: A NEW WORD FOR AN OLD CONCEPT

We begin with some questions, based on our everyday experience, that break down the categories that currently dominate the language of the debate about the representation of Hinduism. We start with these queries because we are interested in the

This essay is published for the first time here.

concrete reality of people in all their particular and variegated difference, not merely as essentialized beings called "Hindu" or "non-Hindu." While we acknowledge that people refer to themselves in broad ways, we believe that there is no simple dichotomy to be resolved, no brute binarism to be negotiated. To mark this conviction that the engagement of people with diverse identities is both normal and complex, we refer to this engagement as an "interlogue." The term "interlogue" is a new way to translate *samvada,* a term usually translated as "colloquy or dialogue." In all of its complexity in the Sanskrit tradition, *samvada* conveys the idea of a transformation through conversation. In the *samvadas* of early and classical India, there might be two or more speakers, but the participants were many—witnesses, audiences, praisers, and detractors. And all acknowledged the social transformation that takes place in the *samvada.*[2]

So, too, the term "interlogue" implies an interaction that is far more meaningful than a mere verbal exchange. We wish to show not a dialogue between two essentialized entities that we call "Hindu" and "non-Hindu," but an "*inter*-logue" between people in various, multiple, complex, and changing historical circumstances. Moreover, the exchange itself is an actual *ex*-change, or "change outwards" to a new form of relationship.

QUERIES

First, we query the binary opposition of Hindu/non-Hindu. There are endless practical examples that make such binarism meaningless and unnecessarily oppositional. Spouses and children participate in many kinds of relationships across traditions; marriages, in-law relationships, spiritual bonds between gurus and disciples, and student-teacher relationships are among the many lifelong and transformative relationships that move happily and unremarkably across the apparent Hindu/non-Hindu divide. Moreover, at a more "official" religious level, caste and sect groupings (Dalits, tribals, ISKCON) have reworked the sense of being Hindu to the point of asserting a new form of Hinduism (ISKCON, Munda) or of not counting themselves Hindu at all (certain forms of Dalit societies). In addition, there are many Western academics with committed Hindu lifestyles—they are Hindu doctrinally, practically, but most of all, intellectually. The diversity of ways in which one can be Hindu or non-Hindu raises questions about the drawing of any dividing lines.

Similarly, we question whether it is right to divide people into two opposing camps when they express feelings of reservation, hurt, or self-justification. And is such division sustainable? Once the temptation to treat people as interchangeable members of an oppositional group is overcome, we believe that a step will be taken toward a more nuanced and context-sensitive treatment of views and opinions in place of generic attacks. In addition, if we treat people as interchangeable members of an oppositional group, we tend to attribute to the entire group the same motivations (imperialism, nationalism, etc.). In our view, the complex and lifelong relationships outlined above would preclude such attributions; in the context of such relationships, motivations are always complex and rarely reducible to one binary or another.

Second, we query the present state of the discussion about "representing the other." We find it an obligation to wonder, constantly, who represents whom, and how. We have found that everyday acts of representation tend to involve not the two overarching categories "Hindu" and "non-Hindu" but a rich set of alternatives. A nonessentialized view of "the other" would recognize complexities in such labels as "imperialist" and "subaltern." To take two salient examples: we would be suspicious of a Hindu software professional in the United States being classified as a "subaltern"; and we would be equally suspicious of classifying as "fundamentalist" an Indian Hindu who simply articulates some sort of offense at an intended or unintended slight to his or her tradition. Neither label works in any meaningful global way.

The most troubling issue in recent debates is the historically and otherwise problematic representation of a monolithic Hinduism. This is largely a Western fiction. However, Western culture and academic practice have also been represented in these debates, and with equal amounts of distortion, misunderstanding, and bias, both Western and Indian. We recognize that certain distortions have greater power than others, but we also acknowledge that institutional, financial, social, and academic contexts often determine the impact of such distortions. This view explains our emphasis on the specific. Western representations may indeed have an asymmetrical relationship with Hindu representations in general, but we notice that in each case power relations determine the asymmetry, not religion or ethnicity. So, once again, it is clear that brute binarisms are misleading. We would suggest, rather, that each situation be considered on the basis of who wields what sort of power.

Special difficulties arise in the Indian diaspora. It is surprisingly hard for diasporic Hindus to shake off a sense of epistemic marginality, even when they are economically and perhaps also socially well-settled. The self-representation of many Hindus in the West conveys a sense of unease that contrasts with their economic well-being. There are Hindus who express their sense of self in terms of powerlessness, marginality, or exploitation—terms that often seem singularly unsuited to their material conditions. This can be morally problematic if it implies an equivalence between themselves and those in truly marginal positions in society in India.

Yet to draw attention to the contradiction in diasporic Hindus' self-representation is not to deny that there is a genuine historical-structural problem of knowledge and power. Our world of culturally plural interpretive strategies and sensibilities is so far from being truly de-centered that we must recognize the need to find ways to acknowledge epistemic marginality. This sense of marginality may arise, in part, from the experience of lacking terms, concepts, performances, and meanings that are organically derived from the tradition in which one imagines oneself at home. This is not to say that the academy is invariably insensitive to such needs on the part of a diasporic group; rather, we are simply suggesting that all sides should recognize that there are diverse subalternities.

By engaging in this sort of recognition, we create a continuing process of moral inventory about our own intellectual practices. This is a kind of *samkalpa*, an inventory of intention, as discussed in the Yoga Sutras and other early Indian texts concerning meditation and enlightenment. The word *samkalpa* carries with it both the connotation of "conceptions" formed in the mind or heart and that of "intentions" or "expectations." What are our intentions in beginning any endeavor, whether it be the *jnana marga* of Hindu knowledge, or some larger knowledge of Hinduism in a global context, and how can we assess their relative purity? We might think of purity here as the acknowledgment of bias, of potential *doshas* (faults) to be overcome in the process of inquiry. The discovery and naming of bias does not, in and of itself, give us the intellectual or moral high ground, as it itself may sow the seeds of new bias. Yet we suggest that such a process of inventory might help to minimize the kind of unproductive oppositional thinking that plagues us at present.

Let us expand our thinking here. In representing the other, the challenge is to not let our presuppositions determine our argument. This is easier said than done, but in multicultural contexts, as in the university, there are practices that, if followed scrupulously, provide us with at least an intellectual procedure for limiting prejudice. In his work *We Scholars,*[3] David Damrosch argues that in a multicultural university it is best to follow the Talmudic intellectual discipline of beginning by laying out all the options—itself a Herculean task but one that is essential to perform before even thinking about choosing or prioritizing one's final arguments. Damrosch is not familiar with Sanskritic forms of argumentation, but the intellectual practice he recommends is quite similar to the procedures followed in many traditional commentaries. For example, the fourth-century B.C.E. Vedic commentator

Shaunaka begins by laying out all the early grammatical opinions about whether actions come before names, or names before actions, before he comes to his own *siddha,* or successful conclusion, on the subject.[4] In fact, this is the standard procedure in classical Indian philosophy. Generally, the tradition treats with greatest respect those who make the most forceful case for their various opponents before presenting their own argument. There is enlightened self-interest in this move: the more powerful your interlocutor, the more persuasive your position! But it is bought at the price of giving up the easier option of knocking down a straw man. Despite the absence of a modern bibliographic apparatus, we can use these texts to trace views back to their sources, because they are usually scrupulous in quoting verbatim from others.

Ancient Indian philosophers, despite their use of polemic against opponents *(purvapaksha),* are also patient and detailed in laying out their views. Even the destructive dialectic of the Advaitin Sri Harsha, which seeks openly to refute a variety of positions, nevertheless is faithful in the construction of the opponent's argument. Seldom is it possible to criticize Sri Harsha on the grounds that he misrepresents his opponent; the best comeback is to find flaws in his arguments or to develop better theories that escape his objections. We see this in the way his major opponents, thinkers of the Nyaya school, responded to him by patiently reworking their ideas to take note of his critique, rather than mindlessly rejecting his probing questions.[5] Challenge and response are both salutary models for interlogue.

If we are to represent anyone other than our individual selves—and very little research is autobiographical in content (even if so in tone, perspective, and mood)—then our simple slogan would have to be "Let the other speak." This is actually an astonishingly difficult thing to do. Most of us are guilty of not paying attention to uncomfortable voices, which we exclude by appealing to deeply held if vague notions of standards—of fairness or sympathy or rigor or something else—that the other is deemed as failing to meet. So, in the process of representing "the other," we want to know whether we have patiently taken up all the views on offer, and engaged with them before we proceed to our own ideas. This patience is part of *samkalpa*—or intention—which we view as the process of moral inventory that precedes action.

Third, we query how we are experienced by the other—whether we are doing enough to be aware of our own location in intellectual and cultural space. Part of this process is the well-established but often neglected practice of examining hermeneutic prejudice. Another, more elusive part is attempting to understand how each of us is seen by the other. This might seem a thankless task when we are confronted with hateful words and hostile attitudes; but many cases of hurt result from insufficient recognition of how others are intimidated by our (real or perceived) power. Impatience with the other's emotional and intellectual uncertainties does nothing to promote mutual understanding in a plural world, and the last of our queries focuses on the realities of that plural world.

Fourth, we query the claim of any single ideology, including liberalism, to be the sole and incontestable ideology of interpretation. Rather, we are committed to exploring the tensions between liberalism and pluralism. The dominant academic/critical ideology of Hindus and non-Hindus alike is liberalism, which is not pluralistic but emphasizes certain values, in particular the concept of "free" inquiry and speech, without constraints on the individual. Exclusive liberalism is committed to the rejection of values and symbols that do not conform to its own; indeed, it asks for their defeat.[6] The exclusively liberal study of Hinduism typically wishes to subject values such as the psychological reality of existential faith-commitments, religious symbolism, and emotional identity to the unrestricted scrutiny of putatively uncommitted disciplinary analysis. As we know, this ideology has led to conflict between scholars and adherents.

To put it another way, the study of Hinduism is forced to partake in the perennial paradox of liberalism. It must insist on tolerance and inclusion of others' religious voices even as it argues with those religious voices that are not tolerant. Wendy Steiner describes this paradox as follows:

> In a state controlled by fundamentalist ideas a liberal cannot speak, but in a state controlled by liberal ideas a fundamentalist cannot act. The ideas of a fundamentalist are exclusionary and performative, i.e., valid only when turned into actions; an article of faith is not a mere topic of discussion to the believer. Thus, the liberal, in insisting on tolerance, is insisting on not only his idea but his practice. In the considerable commentary about the Rushdie affair in America, the absolute value of tolerance or free speech emerges as a point of dogmatic blindness for some and a logical embarrassment for others. Leon Wieseltier states without irony, "Let us be dogmatic about tolerance," but for Norman Mailer the issue is not so easy: "We believe in freedom of expression as an absolute. How dangerous to use the word absolute." [7]

The scholar of Hinduism insists, and has traditionally insisted, that everyone must practice tolerance even as his or her analytic categories of study imply judgment. Liberalism is often confronted with an antipluralistic inner reflex when it attempts to control and contain challenges to its views. And the practical implication of this paradox for everyday life is that the demands of a pluralism committed to the liberal idea of free speech are high.

The key question is whether a pluralist framework of some sort will deliver sufficient intellectual satisfaction to both scholars and adherents. Pluralism seeks to guarantee even conflicting values. Its framework must therefore rest on metavalues that are derived from neither the liberalism of scholars nor the beliefs of adherents but nevertheless accommodate both. These metavalues, articulated in principles of engagement between those with conflicting or at least asymptotic approaches to Hinduism, should guarantee these approaches and yet not exclude the other.

The final section of this essay seeks to present some such principles of pluralist interlogue. But before moving on to that, we have a final query: Is tolerance enough? Tolerance is a liberal value par excellence; scholars in recent controversies have been baffled and enraged by the refusal of adherents to "tolerate" interpretations that the latter deem incompatible with Hinduism. Tolerance is valid as a value only when it has already been granted that every individual has a right to hold and express any view that he or she wants; hence the standard debates over hate speech and so on. Clearly, many Hindu adherents (like Muslims, Christians, and others, in America and elsewhere) find that presupposition impossible to assimilate into their worldview. Yet we (the authors), at least, find no appeal in intolerance. We cannot grant the right to verbally abuse, to threaten physically, or to issue death threats, even religiously sanctioned ones. So we ask for modes of engagement that practice tolerance, but whose appeal comes from pluralism.

In genuine pluralism, one acknowledges symmetrical commitments to allow oneself to be constrained by the sensitivities of the other: thus the adherent is constrained by the scholar's deep commitment to rigorous inquiry, while the scholar is constrained by the adherent's equally deep commitment to cultural and religious sensibilities. Persons who are able to count themselves members of both communities simultaneously will of course be able to move freely across these boundaries, but they too must be mindful of the need in their work and life to acknowledge and respect plurality. Pluralism, then, should not be seen by scholars as a weak-kneed surrender of academic responsibility, for its insistence on mutuality does not sacrifice intellectual integrity. For adherents, similarly, pluralism should not be seen as an abrogation of faith or religious loyalty.

We have found in everyday exchanges between Hindus and non-Hindus that certain forms of committed, long-term coexistence, as exemplified in the relationships enumerated above, are especially conducive to this highly demanding kind of pluralistic discourse. In teacher-student, brother-brother, guru-disciple, in-law to in-law, and other such relationships, there are important reasons for keeping the interlogue going even amid the demands of this kind of pluralism. One of the authors of this essay has committed herself to just such a Hindu-Christian interlogue, lasting a lifetime for all members concerned. In that context, experience shows that elation, shame, anger, disagreement, and synthetic thinking abound.[8] This is only one of many everyday examples that teach us how there can be a productive frame to the discourse other than, and transcending, the frame of "Hindu/non-Hindu." By exploring and accepting such frames, we widen the scope for modes of speech that might otherwise remain unintelligible or seem injurious.

PRINCIPLES

In purely intellectual terms, the demanding plural and liberal discourse between Hindu and non-Hindu must acknowledge two things: (1) a nonrelativistic frame or common reality, and (2) the possibility of a profoundly irreducible difference of opinion. We find principles in Indian tradition that might allow for both in such an interlogue and might indicate what can be done in the case of irreconcilable differences between participants. Here are the principles as we see them.[9]

First, Indic tradition teaches that multiple interpretations can be held simultaneously. This is the metavalue of multiplicity. As early as the fifth century B.C.E. the thinker and lexicographer Yaska argued that there were multiple schools of Vedic interpretation. Many of these schools debated at length about the sacrifice that was then at the heart of Hindu life. One can imagine that the debaters in Yaska's time felt as passionately about modes of sacrifice as we do about contemporary interpretations of Hindu gods. Yaska noted the *niruktan, yajnikan,* and *itihasikan* (etymological, ritual, and historical/legendary) schools of interpretation. Each of these coexisted with the others; each of them seemed reductive to the others; and Yaska himself, while acknowledging and valuing these facts, nonetheless waded in and engaged in the debates. So, too, we today do well to acknowledge our own disagreements with interpretations of Hindu gods and with practices that seem offensive, disrespectful, or dishonest. Yet at the same time we should affirm that even in debate we join together in learning from texts and ceremonies that surround ideas and practices we all hold in reverence. In other words, we must stay committed to reading pluralistically together. That is what Yaska himself teaches us. Shaunaka's *Brihaddevata* 1.16 states, *vaividhyam evam suktanam iha vidyad yathatatham,* "One should know the variety of hymns as they arise and as appropriate." Thus even the Vedic tradition argues the case for seeing pluralistic knowledge—in this case the plurality of hymns—as essential knowledge.

Second, Indic tradition teaches that works should always be read in their entire context. This is the metavalue of contextuality. The Mimamsa interpreter Jaimini said something like this in the third *akhyana* of his Jaimini Sutras. Four out of six principles he enunciated for applying mantra to distinct situations involve looking at the context. One of them particularly stresses context: *asamyuktam prakarnat, iti kartavya arthivat [mantra],* "If a mantra is not correlated to something else, it becomes correlated by context" (*Jaimini Mimamsa Sutra* 3.3.11). Jaimini teaches that if we are to understand Vedic instruction properly, we must look at nearby sentences, nearby paragraphs, as well as what might be assumed by the readership and authorship of a given text.

Jaimini's principles suggest a group of practices that we should all adopt in acts of literary interpretation. As we read together pluralistically, following the first principle, we must see any given statement in relation to the utterances that surround it. What do neighboring sentences tell us about the overall meaning of a given statement? Are other interpretations offered by the same author, to which we should be paying attention? If so, then these must bear on assessment of the work at hand. If a non-Hindu is speaking, are there clear signals to the reader that certain interpretations are not views that Hindus themselves might hold? Do we find similar signals when a Hindu of one persuasion is speaking to another? In our own acts of constructing meaning on the basis of the signals we are sent, are we doing our best to be fair—to consider not just a single statement but its intent and the context in which it is set? In Jaimini's terms, are we paying attention to the surrounding sentences? Finally, we must ask ourselves whether claims are made about the relative truth of any given interpretation. If so, is the author honest about that truth?

There is an important further consideration. Jaimini extends the idea of contextual reading beyond the domain of the text itself. He teaches us to look at the human context, to consider who the participants are in any particular debate. He argues that a person's name, role in the community, and prior record of good deeds have a great deal to tell us about how we must receive what they say. We ought to follow Jaimini in doing each other the honor of taking the whole person into account when we read together pluralistically.

Third, the Indic tradition teaches the principle of *upaya,* or learning in stages. This is the metavalue of incrementalism. *Upaya* is heavily stressed in the Buddhist tradition, but it also provides a clear pedagogical modus operandi in the ancient Indian educational system as a whole. Similarly, when we construct curricula of our own, we should pay attention to sequence. We may well begin with basic texts and move upward from there. When we introduce a theoretical perspective, particularly a controversial one, we should make sure that students understand it is not the only interpretive option, perhaps not even the best. Even far up the educational ladder, at the graduate level, we do well not to teach any single approach as if it alone embodied the truth. We should follow Yaska in our teaching of any controversial theory, asking students to read many different interpretations—both Indian and Western—at once.

Fourth, Indic tradition teaches how to choose battles. This is the metavalue of building commonality. Krishna was constantly thinking about the nature of his alliances in the Mahabharata, trying to determine which battle was larger, more important; which most advanced the cause of *dharma*. Certainly, in his dialogue with Yudhishthira about whether going to battle is appropriate (5.71.30–35), Krishna still strives for the larger cause of peace, even as he fears that the signs for war are mounting. Perhaps, in this spirit, it would be best for all engaged in interlogue to determine which battles are the most important in a university context. The most important battle of all may concern the study of Hinduism at the university level. There is no guarantee anywhere in America or Europe that Hindu studies will remain a permanent part of university curricula. Budget cuts always threaten. Many scholars have devoted their lives to changing that fact, making Hinduism an integral part of the curriculum. This work involves persuading people every day that Hinduism and its teachings are of enduring value—historically, philosophically, socially, and from a broadly human point of view. Hinduism deserves a place in the Western cultural world. It is important to remember that all scholars of Hinduism—writers, teachers, chairs, and deans—participate every day in the effort to support the study of Hinduism. There is no guarantee that this effort will ultimately succeed; hence scholars and teachers need the help of members of Hindu communities wherever they reside. We shouldn't underestimate the work involved in integrating Hindu studies into university curricula. Many Americans and Europeans simply don't care about the field, and others are actively opposed to its inclusion in the university curriculum.

Krishna understood that it is far more important for us to recognize the larger battle and fight it together than to waste our energies arguing with each other. In an angry scolding to Duryodhana, who attempted to capture him before the epic war, Krishna showed the futility of these kinds of acts against *dharma* by displaying his true and terrifying form to the Kauravas (5.128–30). By doing so, he was pointing to—or literally manifesting—the larger issues at stake. We, too, must constantly be mindful of larger forms of struggle. The larger issue for us is that, without attention to the greater concerns of survival per se, the study of Hinduism could simply lose its place in the university curriculum and be ignored or disrespected in the culture at large. The struggle to prevent this from happening is more important than any particular interpretation of a point within the field.

Together, we need to turn our full energies toward this cultural project. We won't all contribute to the cause in the same way, and that is fitting. Coexistence requires acknowledging our different as well as our similar interests. This is key to conflict mediation. In the Mahabharata, Yudhishthira characterizes various *dharmas* as the *param dharmam*—the "highest duty." Following his lead, we might coin a Sanskrit slogan of our own: *sarvadharme yuddhate, tat satyam param*. To translate: "One must struggle with the *dharma* of everyone"—our global *dharma*, one might say. "This is the highest truth."

Fifth and finally, Indic tradition teaches that the life of the mind is constantly concerned with self-correction and growth. This is the metavalue of reflexivity. The *kavya* poet Ashvaghosha inspires us in a similar way in his *Buddhacarita*. He writes that the great works of the ancient *rishis*, or sages, were carried out and approved by their sons, who were also *rishis*. They honored their fathers' work as crucial, and then tried to adapt it to the roles and concerns of their own times (1.46–51). The growth of the great commentary traditions of the *darshanas* illustrates this process splendidly, as respect is offered to forebears in the process of remembering their words, and freedom is possible in the process of reading and interpreting them. We too need to embrace such a self-corrective intellectual tradition.

Presenting wood to those who acted as one's teachers was a common, everyday act in ancient India. It was also an act that acknowledged that one's partner in an interlogue had superior knowledge—even if that relationship was temporary. Perhaps we might conceive of our global interlogue *(samvada)* in this way—as the everyday act of presenting wood to those who might be our superiors, even if only temporarily. In pursuing our global *samvada* and in embracing the act of presenting wood to all of our teachers, both permanent and temporary, we suggest that we continually consider the five queries we have raised, and enact in as many ways as we can conceive the five metavalues taught in Indic tradition. The life of Hinduism has depended upon such exchanges for millennia, at least since Yaska and probably before. We would do well to preserve the vitality of these exchanges into the next millennium as well.

NOTES

1. See C. Ram-Prasad, "Non-Violence and the Other," *Angelaki* 8.3 (December 2003): 3–22, which draws on Gandhi and Jain philosophy, the latter a key influence on Hindu thought. For an interlogue kind of reading, which expands on views exchanged over a decade of conversation between Hindus and Christians, see Kala Acharya, Lalita Namjoshi, and Giuseppe Zanghi, eds., *Bhakti, Pathway to God: The Way of Love, Union with God, and Universal Brotherhood in Hinduism and Christianity* (New Delhi: Somaiya Publications, 2003).

2. See Laurie L. Patton, "Samvada: A Literary Resource for Conflict Negotiation in Classical India," in *Evam: Forum on Indian Representations* (Delhi: Samvad India, 2003), 177–90.

3. David Damrosch, *We Scholars: The Changing Culture of the University* (Cambridge, MA: Harvard University Press, 1995).

4. *Brihaddevata* 1.19–27.

5. Phyllis Granoff, *Philosophy and Argument in Late Vedanta* (Dordrecht: Reidel, 1978); Stephen H. Phillips, *Classical Indian Metaphysics: Refutations of Realism and the Emergence of "New Logic"* (La Salle, IL: Open Court, 1996).

6. J. Kekes, *The Morality of Pluralism* (Princeton: Princeton University Press, 1993).

7. Wendy Steiner, *The Scandal of Pleasure* (Chicago: University of Chicago Press, 1995), 123.

8. Kala Acharya, personal communication, March 2004.

9. Many of these principles were articulated at the first DANAM meeting, at the 2003 conference of the American Academy of Religion in Atlanta, and were first published in *Contemporary Issues in Constructive Dharma, Proceedings of the First DANAM Conference*, ed. Rita Sherma and Adarsh Deepak (Westminster, MD: Heritage Books, 2003).

CONTRIBUTORS

KALA ACHARYA holds a doctorate in Sanskrit from the University of Mumbai and is director of the K. J. Somaiya Bharatiya Sanskriti Peetham, Mumbai, a research and teaching institute focused on the development and preservation of Sanskrit language and literature and the fostering of interreligious and intercultural dialogue. She is the author of *The Puranic Concept of Dana* (1993) and *Buddhanusmriti* (2002), and editor, with Lalita Namjoshi, of *A Dialogue: Hindu-Christian Cosmology and Religion* (1999), as well as many other works on the Indian *bhakti* movement and Hindu-Christian relations.

LALITAMBIKA ANTARJANAM (1909–1987), a well-known author and poet, was born into a progressive family within the conservative Nambudiri (Kerala Brahmin) community. Antarjanam ("woman in the inner courtyard") is a traditional suffix added to the first names of Nambudiri women. A number of Lalitambika's works of fiction deal with the struggles of Nambudiri women against gender oppression; several are set in the context of the Indian freedom movement. Lalitambika is especially remembered for her collections of short stories, including *Aayira Thiri* (A Thousand Wicks). Her novel *Agni Sakshi* (Witness by Fire) received India's highest literary honor, the Sahitya Akademi Award, in 1977 and was also made into a popular movie.

OM LATA BAHADUR is the author of two best-selling books on Hinduism: *The Gods of the Hindus* (2001) and *A Book of Hindu Festivals and Ceremonies* (1994). The latter, from which the essay in this volume has been excerpted, has been reprinted ten times to date since it was first published.

AGEHANANDA BHARATI (1923–1991) was born in Vienna as Leopold Fischer. His early interest in Hinduism led ultimately to his being initiated into the Dasanami Sannyasi monastic order, whereupon he received the name Agehananda Bharati. After many years as a renunciant and teacher in India, Bharati took up residence in the United States as a professor of cultural anthropology at Syracuse University. He is the author of numerous books and articles, including an autobiography, *The Ochre Robe* (1962), and *The Tantric Tradition* (1970).

MARGARET H. CASE, who holds a doctorate in the history of India from the University of Chicago, was for many years Asian Studies editor at Princeton University Press. Since retiring in 1992, she has made several extended visits to Vrindaban. She has been volume editor of numerous books on South Asian subjects, and in 2000 published *Seeing Krishna*, which expands on the context for the essay included in this volume.

SITANSU S. CHAKRAVARTI, who comes from a family of well-known Sanskritists, holds a doctorate in philosophy from Syracuse University with a concentration in philosophy of language. He has served as visiting professor of philosophy at the University of Rajasthan, in Jaipur, and at Visva-Bharati, in Santiniketan. Chakravarti has published in the *Notre Dame Journal of Formal Logic* and the *Journal of Indian Philosophy* and has contributed an essay on the spirituality of Tagore to the Crossroads World Spirituality Series. He is the author of *Hinduism: A Way of Life* (1991) and *Modality, Reference, and Sense: An Essay in the Philosophy of Language* (2001) and is currently working on a book entitled *Ethics in the Mahabharata: A Philosophical Inquiry*. In all his writings Chakravarti combines the philosophical perspectives of East and West. He has represented Hinduism at several forums in Canada, where he lives with his family.

DIANA L. ECK is professor of comparative religion and Indian studies at Harvard University and president of the American Academy of Religion for 2005–2006. She is also the founding director of the Pluralism Project, which seeks to document the growth of less-well-known religious communities in the United States, including Hindus. Her books on India include *Darsan: Seeing the Divine in India* (1981), *Banaras, City of Light* (1982), and a *Festschrift* for Charlotte Vaudeville entitled *Devotion Divine* (1991), which she coedited with Françoise Mallison. Eck's award-winning book *Encountering God* (1994) is a comparative study of Hinduism and Christianity. Her research on Hindus living in the United States can be seen in *On Common Ground*, a CD-ROM she has edited with the Pluralism Project (rev. ed., 2000), and in her most recent book, *A New Religious America* (2001).

KATHLEEN M. ERNDL is associate professor of religion at the Florida State University. She received her doctorate in the religions of South Asia from the University of

Wisconsin-Madison. She is the author of *Victory to the Mother: The Hindu Goddess of Northwest India in Myth, Ritual, and Symbol* (1993) and coeditor of *Is the Goddess a Feminist? The Politics of South Asian Goddesses* (2000). She has written numerous essays on goddess traditions and women in South Asian religions and is currently at work on a book entitled *Playing with the Mother: Women, Goddess Possession, and Power in Kangra Hinduism*. Her other research interests include gender and religious hybridity in India and the United States. She is the recipient of grants from the John Simon Guggenheim Foundation, the National Endowment for the Humanities, the Fulbright-Hayes program, and the American Institute of Indian Studies.

SHRIVATSA GOSWAMI is a member of an eminent family of spiritual leaders and scholars at the Sri Radharamana Mandir, Vrindaban, India. He is director of the Sri Caitanya Prema Sansthana, a research institution devoted to Vaishnava studies and the culture of the Braj region, whose Vraja Nathadvara Prakalpa project is sponsored by the Indira Gandhi National Center for the Arts. Acharya Goswami is the author of a number of scholarly articles and books including, most recently, *Celebrating Krishna* (2004), and he is the editor of the volume on Caitanya that will appear in the *Encyclopaedia of Indian Philosophy.* He has been a visiting scholar at Harvard University (1977–1978) and the University of Heidelberg (2004), and delivered the Hibbert Lecture at Oxford University in 2000.

LISA LASSELL HALLSTROM has pursued the study of the Hindu and Buddhist traditions through doctoral work at Harvard University as well as through personal practice. She has taught religion and Asian studies at Bard, Mt. Holyoke, and Smith colleges and at the University of New Mexico. She is the author of *Mother of Bliss: Anandamayi Ma (1896–1982)* (1999). She is currently teaching courses and workshops on Hindu and Buddhist spirituality while working on a book on women whose spiritual practice is focused on the goddesses Kuan Yin and Green Tara. As a professional singer, she leads *kirtan*, or devotional chanting, in the Boston area.

JOHN STRATTON HAWLEY is Ann Whitney Olin Professor of Religion at Barnard College, Columbia University, and the author or editor of some fifteen books. Most concern India, but others—most recently *Holy Tears: Weeping in the Religious Imagination* (2005), coedited with Kimberley Patton—are comparative in nature. His recent publications on Hindu India include a second revised edition of *Songs of the Saints of India* (2004), with Mark Juergensmeyer, and *Three Bhakti Voices: Mirabai, Surdas, and Kabir in Their Time and Ours* (2005). Hawley's major work, a translation and analysis of the earliest poetry attributed to Surdas, is forthcoming as *Sur's Ocean*, a title it shares with the critical edition on which it is based, by Kenneth E. Bryant. He has been a John Simon Guggenheim Fellow.

LINDA HESS has worked on Hindi *bhakti* poetry since 1970 and has studied it through text, performance, and reception. She has published a number of articles on the Ramlila and Tulsi Ramayana based on four years of fieldwork in the annual thirty-day Ramlila of Ramnagar, Varanasi. Her main work has focused on Kabir and includes *The Bijak of Kabir,* a book of translations (co-translated with Shukdeo Singh) and interpretive essays (2002 [1983]). Since 2002 she has been studying Kabir oral traditions in North India, folk and classical music, oral texts, performance, and social contexts. She has taught in the Department of Religious Studies, Stanford University, since 1996.

STEPHEN P. HUYLER is an art historian, cultural anthropologist, photographer, and author. He has spent a large part of the last thirty-two years traveling in Indian villages documenting craftsmanship and traditional and contemporary cultures. He has worked extensively on the sacred arts of the Hindu tradition. He has also curated many museum exhibitions devoted to informing the public about the cultures and peoples of India, including Puja: Expressions of Hindu Devotion at the Smithsonian's Arthur M. Sackler Gallery (1996–2000) and Meeting God: Elements of Hindu Devotion at the American Museum of Natural History in New York (2001–2002). He is the author of several books, including *Village India* (1985), *Gifts of Earth: Terracottas and Clay Sculptures of India* (1996), *Painted Prayers: Women's Art in Village India* (1994), and *Meeting God: Elements of Hindu Devotion* (1999).

DORANNE JACOBSON is an anthropologist, writer, photographer, and lecturer whose work has taken her to more than seventy countries. She is director of International Images, an educational consulting and photographic resource firm in Springfield, Illinois. She received her doctorate in anthropology from Columbia University, where she is a seminar associate at the Southern Asian Institute. She has conducted extensive research in India on gender roles and social change and has also worked in the American Southwest and Latin America. She is the author of five books and over fifty articles and is also a widely published photographer whose work has appeared in hundreds of publications and exhibits. Her photographic volume *India: Land of Dreams and Fantasy* won a Writer of the Year award and was cited in an Asia Society publication as one of the six "Most Useful Books" on India. A frequent lecturer on South Asian society and culture, she has led many study tours to South and Southeast Asia.

SUDHIR KAKAR is a psychoanalyst and writer. He has served as professor of organizational behavior at the Indian Institute of Management, Ahmedabad, and head of the Department of Humanities and Social Sciences at the Indian Institute of Technology, Delhi, and has been professor at research universities on several continents, including Harvard, Chicago, McGill, Melbourne, Hawaii, and Vienna. His fourteen books of nonfiction include *The Inner World; Shamans, Mystics, and Doctors; The Analyst and the Mys-*

tic; Culture and Psyche; and *The Colors of Violence.* Among his four works of fiction are *The Ascetic of Desire* and *Ecstasy.* He has also published a new translation of the *Kamasutra* (with Wendy Doniger) for Oxford World's Classics and the novel *Mira and the Mahatma.* His books have been translated into eighteen languages around the world.

PHILIP LUTGENDORF has taught in the University of Iowa's Department of Asian Languages and Literature since 1985, where he offers Hindi language classes as well as courses on written and oral narrative traditions of South Asia, including Indian film. His *Life of a Text* (1991), on the performance of the epic Ramayana, won the A. K. Coomaraswamy Prize of the Association for Asian Studies. He received a Guggenheim Fellowship in 2002–2003 for the book project that has resulted in *Hanuman's Tale: The Messages of a Divine Monkey* (forthcoming). His research interests include epic performance traditions, folklore, and mass media. He regularly teaches courses on Hindi cinema and runs a Web site devoted to this subject (www.uiowa.edu/~incinema)

MCKIM MARRIOTT is one of the world's best-known anthropologists of South Asia. He received his doctorate from the University of Chicago and went on to become professor of anthropology and of social sciences at the same institution, retiring in 1998. He has researched villagers and urbanites of India and professionals of both South Asia and Japan. He is the author and editor of several books and articles, including the well-known *Village India: Studies in the Little Community* (1955) and *India through Hindu Categories* (1990). His influence on his many students is legendary.

VASUDHA NARAYANAN is Distinguished Professor of Religion at the University of Florida and a past president of the American Academy of Religion (2001–2002). She was educated at the Universities of Madras and Bombay in India, and at Harvard University. She is the author or editor of six books, including *Hinduism* (2004), and more than ninety articles and encyclopedia entries. Her research has been supported by grants and fellowships from several organizations including the American Council of Learned Societies, the National Endowment for the Humanities, the John Simon Guggenheim Foundation, and the Social Science Research Council. She is currently working on Hindu temples and Vaishnava traditions in Cambodia.

LAURIE L. PATTON is Winship Distinguished Research Professor of Religion and Chairperson at Emory University. She received her doctorate from the University of Chicago. For several years during the last two decades she has made her Indian home in Pune, Maharashtra. Her scholarly interests include the interpretation of early Indian ritual and narrative, comparative mythology, literary theory in the study of religion, and women and Hinduism in contemporary India. In addition to many articles in these fields, she is the author or editor of seven books, including *Myth as Argument: The Brhadde-*

vata as Canonical Commentary (1996), *Myth and Method* (with Wendy Doniger) (1996), and *Jewels of Authority: Women and Text in the Hindu Tradition* (2002). Her translation of the Bhagavad Gita is forthcoming from the Penguin Press Classics Series. She was a Fulbright scholar in India in 2004, completing research for her forthcoming book, *Grandmother Language: Women and Sanskrit in Maharashtra and Beyond.*

CHAKRAVARTHI RAM-PRASAD studied history, politics, and sociology in India before completing a doctorate in philosophy at Oxford. He taught at the National University of Singapore and was a research fellow at Trinity College, Oxford, and Clare Hall, Cambridge. He is now senior lecturer in Indian religions at Lancaster University. His publications include *Knowledge and Liberation in Classical Indian Thought* (2001), *Advaita Epistemology and Metaphysics* (2002), *Eastern Philosophy* (2005), and *The Consequences of Knowledge* (2005). He is currently completing a book on religion and politics and continuing research on consciousness in the classical Indian traditions on a John Templeton Foundation grant.

SHRINIVAS TILAK is an independent research scholar who holds a doctorate in the history of religions from McGill University. He is author of *Religion and Aging in the Indian Tradition* (1989), *The Myth of Sarvodaya: A Study of Vinoba's Concept* (1984), and *Understanding Karma in Light of Paul Ricoeur's Anthropology and Hermeneutics* (2006). His research interests include cultural gerontology, hermeneutics, and Indology.

INDEX

Alternate spellings of certain frequently used Indic words can be found in "A Note on Transliteration." Page references in italics refer to illustrations.

Text	10/13 Galliard
Display	Galliard
Compositor	Binghamton Valley Composition, LLC
Indexer	Roberta Engleman
Printer and binder	Maple-Vail Manufacturing Group